Strategies for eCommerce Success

Bijan Fazlollahi, Ph.D.
Georgia State University, USA

IRM Press
Publisher of innovative scholarly and professional
information technology titles in the cyberage

Hershey • London • Melbourne • Singapore • Beijing

Acquisitions Editor:	Mehdi Khosrow-Pour
Managing Editor:	Jan Travers
Assistant Managing Editor:	Amanda Appicello
Copy Editor:	Amanda Appicello
Cover Design:	Tedi Wingard
Printed at:	Integrated Book Technology

Published in the United States of America by
    IRM Press
    1331 E. Chocolate Avenue
    Hershey PA 17033-1117, USA
    Tel: 717-533-8845
    Fax: 717-533-8661
    E-mail: cust@idea-group.com
    Web site: http://www.irm-press.com

and in the United Kingdom by
    IRM Press
    3 Henrietta Street
    Covent Garden
    London WC2E 8LU
    Tel: 44 20 7240 0856
    Fax: 44 20 7379 3313
    Web site: http://www.eurospan.co.uk

Library of Congress Cataloging-in-Publication Data

Fazlollahi, Bijan, 1939-
   Strategies for ecommerce success / Bijan Fazlollahi.
     p. cm.
  Includes bibliographical references and index.
   ISBN 1-931777-08-7 (paper)
    1. Electronic commerce. I. Title.

HF5548.32 .F39 2002
658.8'4--dc21   2001059430

eISBN: 1-931777-29-2

British Cataloguing in Publication Data
A Cataloguing in Publication record for this book is available from the British Library.

Other New Releases from IRM Press

- **Effective Healthcare Information Systems,** Adi Armoni (Ed.)
  ISBN: 1-931777-01-2 / eISBN: 1-931777-20-9 / approx. 340 pages / US$59.95 / © 2002
- **Human Computer Interaction Developments and Management,** Tonya Barrier (Ed.)
  ISBN: 1-931777-13-6 / eISBN: 1-931777-35-7 / approx. 336 pages / US$59.95 / © 2002
- **Data Warehousing and Web Engineering,** Shirley Becker (Ed.)
  ISBN: 1-931777-02-0 / eISBN: 1-931777-21-7 / approx. 334 pages / US$59.95 / © 2002
- **Information Technology Education in the New Millennium,** Mohammad Dadashzadeh,
  Al Saber and Sherry Saber (Eds.) /
  ISBN: 1-931777-05-5 / eISBN: 1-931777-24-1 / approx. 308 pages / US$59.95 / © 2002
- **Information Technology Management in Developing Countries,** Mohammad Dadashzadeh
  (Ed.) / ISBN: 1-931-777-03-9 / eISBN: 1-931777-23-3 / approx. 348 pages / US$59.95 / © 2002
- **Collaborative Information Technologies,** Mehdi Khosrow-Pour (Ed.)
  ISBN: 1-931777-14-4 / eISBN: 1-931777-25-X / approx. 308 pages / US$59.95 / © 2002
- **Web-Based Instructional Learning,** Mehdi Khosrow-Pour (Ed.)
  ISBN: 1-931777-04-7 / eISBN: 1-931777-22-5 / approx. 322 pages / US$59.95 / © 2002
- **Modern Organizations in Virtual Communities,** Jerzy Kisielnicki (Ed.)
  ISBN: 1-931777-16-0 / eISBN: 1-931777-36-5 / approx. 316 pages / US$59.95 / © 2002
- **Enterprise Resource Planning Solutions and Management,** Fiona Fui-Hoon Nah (Ed.)
  ISBN: 1-931777-06-3 / eISBN: 1-931777-26-8 / approx. 308 pages / US$59.95 / © 2002
- **Interactive Multimedia Systems,** Syed M. Rahman (Ed.)
  ISBN: 1-931777-07-1 / eISBN: 1-931777-28-4 / approx. 314 pages / US$59.95 / © 2002
- **Ethical Issues of Information Systems,** Ali Salehnia (Ed.)
  ISBN: 1-931777-15-2 / eISBN: 1-931777-27-6 / approx. 314 pages / US$59.95 / © 2002
- **Intelligent Support Systems: Knowledge Management,** Vijay Sugumaran (Ed.)
  ISBN: 1-931777-00-4 / eISBN: 1-931777-19-5 / approx. 318 pages / US$59.95 / © 2002
- **Human Factors in Information Systems,** Edward Szewczak and Coral Snodgrass (Eds.)
  ISBN: 1-931777-10-1 / eISBN: 1-931777-31-4 / approx. 342 pages / US$59.95 / © 2002
- **Global Perspective of Information Technology Management,** Felix B. Tan (Ed.)
  ISBN: 1-931777-11-4 / eISBN: 1-931777-32-2 / approx. 334 pages / US$59.95 / © 2002
- **Successful Software Reengineering,** Sal Valenti (Ed.)
  ISBN: 1-931777-12-8 / eISBN: 1-931777-33-0 / approx. 330 pages / US$59.95 / © 2002
- **Information Systems Evaluation Management,** Wim van Grembergen (Ed.)
  ISBN: 1-931777-18-7 / eISBN: 1-931777-37-3 / approx. 336 pages / US$59.95 / © 2002
- **Optimal Information Modeling Techniques,** Kees van Slooten (Ed.)
  ISBN: 1-931777-09-8 / eISBN: 1-931777-30-6 / approx. 306 pages / US$59.95 / © 2002
- **Knowledge Mapping and Management,** Don White (Ed.)
  ISBN: 1-931777-17-9 / eISBN: 1-931777-34-9 / approx. 340 pages / US$59.95 / © 2002

Excellent additions to your institution's library!
Recommend these titles to your Librarian!

To receive a copy of the IRM Press catalog, please contact
(toll free) 1/800-345-4332, fax 1/717-533-8661,
or visit the IRM Press Online Bookstore at: [http://www.irm-press.com]!

Note: All IRM Press books are also available as ebooks on netlibrary.com as well as
other ebook sources. Contact Ms. Carrie Stull at [cstull@idea-group.com] to receive
a complete list of sources where you can obtain ebook information or
IRM Press titles.

Strategies for eCommerce Success

Table of Contents

Foreword

The Internet technology has created an opportunity to increase the productivity of traditional businesses as well as to start new highly productive businesses based on novel business models. The labels, old economy and Internet economy, point to the significant difference in productivity. The Internet economy revenue is growing twice as fast as Internet economy employment. However, both types of economies are expected to converge as traditional businesses rapidly adopt the Internet technology.

In entering the e-business world, a firm strategically positions itself to conduct its activities differently from its competitors. E-business is about the radical redesign of traditional value chains and the construction of new ones. E-business makes demand driven production possible where customer orders serve as signals for production. By integrating all members of the supply chain, the end demand can be immediately communicated to all supply chain members. The computer manufacturer Dell is an outstanding example. Also, major automotive manufacturers have launched initiatives to build vehicles to meet individual customers' specifications and deliver them in one to two weeks.

Internet enabled traditional and the newly created dot-com businesses engage in e-commerce. E-commerce is defined as the use of technology mediated exchanges by business for the purposes of selling goods and services over the Internet. E-Commerce is growing fast. The sales of global e-commerce grew from millions in 1997 to billions in 1998 and to hundreds of billion in 2000 and are expected to reach into trillions. E-commerce is categorized into Business-to-Business (B2B), Business-to-Consumer (B2C), and Consumer-to-Business (C2B). The majority of sales is in B2B and is projected to grow from 43 billions (1998) to 1.3 trillion (2003). During the same period B2C is expected to grow from 7.8 billions to 108 billions.

B2C is growing much slower than B2B and is only 0.5% of the e-commerce business. It is predicted that on-line purchases will increase from $20B in 1999 to $50B in 2002. U.S. online sales for the month of August 2001 were running at 4 billion dollars per month with 15 million households shopping online. There is about 25% year-on-year increase in the volume of sales. Contributors to slower growth include high Internet access costs, lack of PC at home, lack of customer trust, concern about privacy and security, lack of government regulations. Surveys show that over 70% of consumers do not trust the companies to preserve their privacy. Several studies have explored the antecedent factors of consumer trust in the context of on-line shopping (reputation and size), most dot-com ventures do not have either. Also, consumers give up after a few attempt and look for alternative sites. Furthermore, breaking old habits is difficult. Most consumers prefer to shop in a real store, taking their purchases home with them. Some products such as books and CDs are more suitable merchandise for EC than groceries that may need inspection. Using EC for digital goods has significant advantage because goods are also delivered through Internet. There are additional market impediments for global e-commerce. Difficulties in fulfillment may be the reason why 70% of U.S. Companies selling on-line do not accept international orders.

Customers need more than just the product. They demand superior shopping experience spanning the entire process from articulating to fulfillment of their needs. Fulfillment impacts customer satisfaction 10 times more than selling. Fulfillment problems include lost orders, incomplete or inaccurate product availability information, and late shipments. Customers expect not only on-time delivery but also instant access to their order histories, shipping information and up-to-the-second product availability information. Many of these functions require deep integration between front-end on-line ordering systems and back-end supply chain and logistic applications. Both FedEx and UPS offer systems that can integrate delivery status and other information from the shippers directly into the e-commerce systems. They can also provide on-line capability for customers to initiate return of packages on the web and link them to drop-off locations. They also provide the customer with the ability to track returns and check account information. Ironically, consumer concerns on late delivery has increased and concerns over the security of credit cards and personal information has decreased from 1999 levels.

B2C is uniquely customer centric. Heterogeneity of user profile has become a major problem facing online shopping service providers. One universal service is not likely to satisfy all public users whose cognitive and demographic profiles differ substantially. Consumers exhibit different behavior and express varied concerns that firms must take into account. For example, 1/4 browse on-line and buy from brick and mortar stores, 1/5 buy from merchants they know, and 1/5 are interested in saving time and maximizing convenience. Firms such as American Express have learned to compile customer information from a range of sources and build a comprehensive view of the customers. They have developed capabilities to anticipate and meet customer needs in real time by delivering customized services superior to their competitors, leading to higher revenues and customer retention.

Electronic commerce is at an early stage of development and vaguely understood. There are few established rules on how to organize and implement e-commerce. The majority of EC business models are innovative and unproven. The source of e-commerce knowledge is generally unreliable. The knowledge often comes from venture capitalists, investment bankers, and technically oriented entrepreneurs. They do not have a good track record of building e-business organizations that endure the test of time. Compared to the US, European dot-coms have had a lower rate of failure. This may indicate a higher level of scrutiny in Europe before money was made available to dot-com businesses. The question is what are the appropriate methods for acquiring e-business systems. Current e-business projects are required to be completed in "Internet Time". System development techniques must reflect responsiveness and flexibility in meeting changing requirements. The current trend is for highly customizable packaged software for data warehousing and enterprise resource planning (ERP) and On-line outsourcing of Applications to Application Service Providers. Firms may need to develop new investment models that include measures of market expansion, revenue per customer, and customer satisfaction metrics.

Implementing e-commerce projects in "Internet time" is an enormous challenge. E-commerce is the use of information technology in business. The novel organization strategies, CRM, personalization and mass customization needs to be incorporated into the business models. Use of information technology by an organization usually requires major restructuring of the organization. The scale of change may be enormous depending on the organization and nature of the opportunity. CISCO Systems is a success story and an example of a restructured organization that is reportedly transacting over 90 percent of its dealings with the distributors over the Internet.

The web site is where the consumer and the firm conduct their business and must become the focus of attention. The web site must have the functionalities that enable the firm to acquire, sell and retain customers. E-commerce sites are eminently easier to leave than physical store as the customer has less time invested than shopping in a physical store. Customer support was claimed as the main reason for the demise of many dot-coms. Consumers are frequently disappointed at how little depth exists beneath the user interface for providing customer support. Improved scales to measure all the dimensions of perceived quality of web sites must be developed.

E-commerce is developing along several fronts. One trend is towards providing same day fulfillment. E-commerce companies are forming alliances with local affiliates. Customers are enabled to pick-up and return their purchases in locations close to their favorite shopping areas. Personalization is another area of common concern for future development of e-commerce. An objective of personalization is to enable the firm to know their customers and interact with them one-on-one to provide each customer with a unique website experience. Personalization allows businesses to customize their marketing mix. For example, instead of competition on the bases of price alone, it would be possible to treat each customer differently as a frequent buyer enjoying perks and special treatments. Each customer may also be targeted with useful advertisements that inform his/her needs, and given credit for viewing the advertisements. Targeted customer may also get discounts for introducing friends who buy from the same site. Furthermore, targeted customers may be provided with customized products that fit their individual needs and served in locations that are attractive to them.

Internet offers the medium for the adoption of technologies that can enhance e-commerce further. For example, the cyber space is the natural habitat for intelligent agents. Intelligent agent technology offers a very powerful and suitable mean to integrate the Internet in a synergistic way. Intelligent agents can be personalized for each individual to perform tasks 24 hrs a day. The tasks may range from simple stimulus-response to complex deliberative decisions. For example, intelligent agents can provide support for making purchasing decisions for customers as well as for companies. These agents are goal-driven, capable of planning, and reasoning under uncertainty with imprecise and incomplete information, and learning. The software core of the intelligent agent may incorporate fuzzy logic and other soft-computing techniques. Intelligent agents can provide assistance and inform all phases the purchase decision from information gathering to generation of alternatives to making a choice. Mobile agents are a special type of intelligent agent that can find information for such activities as brokering, negotiation and payment. Mobile agents can roam wide area networks, interact with foreign hosts, perform tasks on behalf of their users and subsequently return to the original computer after achieving the goals. Mobile intelligent agents raise concerns in such areas as security, export controls, legal jurisdiction, taxation and international issues that need to be addressed.

In the long-run, the Internet economy and the old economy will converge giving rise to more innovative and productive businesses capable of competing in the global arena. Organizations will learn how to build and successfully deploy quality e-commerce systems. New technologies will enable more powerful systems that support new business models. In particular, in spite of all the challenges, e-commerce systems based on intelligent agent technology is inevitable. Intelligent agents will be part of the information architecture of next generation of e-commerce software and websites will be powered to serve the customer as well as the firm.

Bijan Fazlollahi
October 2, 2001

Preface

Electronic commerce and its various applications from online auctions to business-to-business buying is revolutionizing organizations in the 21st century. Consumers worry about security, and businesses continually need to improve online services and add value-added services to stay competitive. Businesses of all size, from the Fortune 500 to small businesses, are all getting into the business of electronic commerce. The following book is a compilation of essays about the most recent and relevant aspects of e-commerce. The authors of the following chapters discuss the most current theories for business thinking about e-commerce and practical suggestions for improving existing e-commerce initiatives. The research is the most up-to-date and is useful for academicians who are teaching and studying the trends within the electronic commerce industry. As electronic commerce throughout the world reaches into the billions and even trillions of dollar industry, the research contained in this volume will prove to be invaluable to business persons, researchers, teachers and students alike.

Chapter 1 entitled, "Cyber Shopping and Privacy" by Jatinder N.D. Gupta and Sushil K. Sharma of Ball State University (USA) focuses on privacy issues that arise in cyber shopping. The authors address the fundamental questions of how an online shopper can keep information about his/her Internet browsing habits safe and how to insure safe buying. The authors specifically review the recent publications on privacy that have appeared in various journals.

Chapter 2 entitled, "Structural Influences on Global E-Commerce Activity" by M. Lynne Markus of City University of Hong Kong (Hong Kong) and Christina Soh of Nanyang Technological University (Singapore) argues that global information management researchers should not lose sight of structural conditions related to business-to-business and business-to-consumer e-commerce activity. The authors discuss the implications of structural conditions, namely physical, social and economic arrangements, that shape e-commerce. The authors argue that these conditions vary from location to location and are not necessarily based upon natural culture.

Chapter 3 entitled, "Social Issues in Electronic Commerce: Implications for Policy Makers" by Anastasia Papazafeiropoulou and Athanasia Pouloudi of Brunel University (United Kingdom) examines how social concerns such as trust and digital democracy pertain to all levels of Internet and electronic commerce policy. The authors discuss different scenarios that influence the construction of an effective and socially responsible strategy for electronic commerce.

Chapter 4 entitled, "Identifying Motivations for the Use of Commercial Web Sites" by Thomas Stafford of Texas Women's University and Marla Royne Stafford of the University of North Texas (USA) applies the perspective of uses and gratifications to better understand the factors motivating commercial Web site use and identifies a new media use gratification unique to the Internet called socialization. The research reports the results of a two-part study that begins with the identification of 179 motivations for Web usage and ultimately reduces those to five primary factors. The authors discuss these factors and their implications.

Chapter 5 entitled, "Signalling Intentions and Obliging Behavior Online: An Application of Semiotic and Legal Modeling in E-Commerce" by James Backhouse of the London School of Economics and Edward K. Cheng of Harvard Law School explores the semiotic and legal aspects of online contracts. The paper creates a model of the contract creation process and applies it to electronic commerce in intangible goods. Since electronic commerce extends beyond any jurisdiction, the need for high level abstraction and model comparison is bound to increase. This paper addresses those needs.

Chapter 6 entitled, "Customer Loyalty and Electronic Banking: A Conceptual Framework" by Daniel Tomiuk and Alain Pinsonneault of McGill University (Canada) presents a conceptual framework that helps to understand and assess the impacts of information technology on customer loyalty in retail banking. The authors define customer loyalty and identify its antecedents. They conclude that because it reduces the amount of face-to-face interactions customers have with bank personnel, online banking is likely to lead to lower levels of loyalty of communally-oriented customers and to higher levels of loyalty for exchange-oriented customers.

Chapter 7 entitled, "Electronic Commerce and Strategic Change Within Organizations: Lessons from Two Cases" by Robert Galliers of the London School of Economics and Sue Newell of the University of London (United Kingdom) reviews and contrasts the experiences of two major companies in attempting significant change projects incorporating information and communication technologies. The chapter points out that although much attention is currently focused on e-commerce industry transformation and inter-organizational relations, e-commerce can also impact complex internal relations and communication.

Chapter 8 entitled, "Trust in Internet Shopping: Instrument Development and Validation Through Classical and Modern Approaches" by Christy M. K. Cheung and Matthew K. O. Lee of the City University of Hong Kong (China) proposes a theoretical model for investigating the nature of trust in the specific context of Internet shopping. The instrument discussed represents a rigorously developed and validated instrument for the measurement of various important trust related constructs.

Chapter 9 entitled, "Electronic Broker Impacts on the Value of Postponement in a Global Supply Chain" by William Robinson of Georgia State University and Greg Elofsen of Fordham University (USA) investigates whether adding a market-making electronic broker to a supply chain increases the value of postponement. The authors test the relation by comparing the results of agent-based simulations that vary between early and late differentiation strategies and the use of an electronic broker.

Chapter 10 entitled, "Internal Audit of Internet-Based Electronic Commerce Transactions: A TQM Approach" by Haider H. Madani of King Fahd University of Petroleum and Minerals (Saudi Arabia), addresses the nature of electronic commerce transactions and the control considerations associated with them. The thesis of the chapter is that the Internet-based electronic commerce transactions introduce an unfamiliar set of risks to the business setting, which can be minimized through a Total Quality Management (TQM) framework that enhances the internal audit effectiveness and efficiency. This framework is based on five principles: activity analysis, control analysis, evaluation analysis, risk assessment and continuous improvement. This approach provides appropriate monitoring of business practices and internal controls to ensure audit effectiveness and efficiency.

In Chapter 11, entitled, "Electronic Commerce Acceptance: A Study Comparing the United States and the United Kingdom," Donna McCloskey from Widener University (USA) and David Whiteley from Manchester Metropolitan University (UK) address the issues of what consumers buy, what factors motivate them to buy via the Internet and what keeps them from shopping more. The chapter reports the results of a survey carried out in both the United States and the United Kingdom that was aimed at discovering what people bought online, why they did or did not use Internet e-commerce, any differences in activity between the USA and the UK and what might persuade people to take part in online shopping in the future.

Chapter 12 entitled, "Intelligent Software Agents in Electronic Commerce: A Socio-Technical Perspective" by Mahesh Raisinghani of the University of Dallas (USA), Chris Klassen of The Software Construction Company (USA) and Lawrence Schkade of the University of Texas at Arlington (USA) investigates software agents as possessing goal-directed and possessing abilities such as autonomy, collaborative behavior, and inferential capability. These agents can take different forms, and can initiate and make decisions without human intervention and have the capability to infer appropriate high-level goals from user actions and requests and take actions to achieve these goals. The intelligent software agent is a computational entity that can adapt to the environment, making it capable of interacting with other agents and transporting itself across different systems in a network.

Chapter 13 entitled, "Impacts of Software Agents in E-Commerce Systems on Customer's Loyalty and on Behavior of Potential Customers" by Juergen Seitz, Eberhard Stickel and Krzysztof Woda of Viadrina University (Germany) analyzes the possible consequences of new push and pull technologies in e-commerce, which are jockeying for customers' loyalty. The active technologies enabling customers to purchase efficiently and force merchants to offer highly personalized, value-added and complementary products and services in order to stay competitive. This chapter provides examples of such services and of personalization techniques, which aid in sustaining one-on-one relationships with customers and other actors involved in e-commerce. Finally, it discusses the additional cost and benefits for suppliers and customers using electronic payment systems.

Chapter 14 entitled, "Internet Payment Mechanisms: Acceptance and Control Issues" by Ulric Gelinas and Janis Gogan of Bentley College (USA) reviews several mechanisms of online payment mechanisms. It assesses the control issues associated with each of them, and the authors use the Diffusion of Innovations theory to assess the perceived benefits and risks of each of the payment mechanisms. It concludes that the success of online payment mechanisms is largely due to their perceived relative advantage, compatibility and trialability. It further concludes that these perceived characteristics are in turn affected by consumers', bankers', merchants', and regulators' understanding of the security and control surrounding them.

Chapter 15 entitled, "Approaches to a Decentralized Architecture for an Electronic Market—A Study for the Air Cargo Business" by Freimut Bodendorf and Stefan Reinheimer of the University of Erlangen-Nuremberg (Germany) proposes a decision support model for electronic markets using software agents. The model is based on the value chain concept applied to interorganizational information technology (IT), and the consideration of new coordination mechanisms to increase the efficiency of business processes. The proposed framework is used to design an electronic air market. In recent years, the companies of the air cargo arena have neglected to adapt to their customers' needs in a timely manner. This chapter suggests that the decentralized implementation of software agents to support the transaction processes will support users and allow them to accomplish the needed phases involved in business transactions ranging from information gathering to negotiation.

Chapter 16 entitled, "A Web Usability Assessment Model and Automated Toolset" by Shirley Becker, Anthony Berkemeyer and Natalie Roberts of the Florida Institute of Technology (USA) speculates that an e-commerce site will be most useful when consumer usability attributes (e.g., performance, design layout, navigation) drive its development. This chapter describes a web usability assessment tool that is being developed to provide usability feedback on a particular Web site. This tool incorporates a set of usability attributed with user profile data and organizational goals for ongoing assessment of the effectiveness of a Web site.

Chapter 17 entitled, "Categorizing the Supplier Content of Public Web Sites," by Dale Young of Miami University of Ohio (USA), identifies the supplier communication and supplier diversity content on public Web sites of the firms on the 2000 Fortune 500 list and creates a categorization scheme for that content. The chapter concludes that public Web sites are largely underutilized as a means of interacting with potential suppliers from a diverse population. The chapter also indicates the most common supplier diversity content for prospective suppliers on Fortune 500 public Web sites: certification requirements, online applications and a contact name/title for the diversity manager.

Chapter 18 entitled, "Multi-Dimensional B2B Auctions for Electronic Commerce" by Marilyn T. Griffin and France Belanger of the Virginia Polytechnic University and Craig Van Slyke of the University of Central Florida (USA) argues that early online auctions were based on price alone, but businesses must now consider shipping, storage, financing and insurance costs. These multiple variables have increased the complexity of B2B auctions and have led to the implementation of multidimensional B2B auctions. This chapter discusses the development of these multidimensional auctions and predicts that B2B online business will become increasingly more saturated with auction mechanisms in the near future. The chapter further shows that B2B market places will only succeed if they offer value-added services and are able to meet their customers' expectations in the areas of privacy, trust, and security.

Chapter 19 entitled, "Mobile Agents, Mobile Computing and Mobile Users in Global E-Commerce" by Roberto Vinaja of the University of Texas Pan American (USA) examines the implication of mobility in three aspects: mobile code, mobile hardware and mobile users. The chapter also analyzes the impact of mobility on electronic commerce in the areas of security issues, export controls, legal jurisdiction, taxation and international issues. Mobile agent technologies and mobile computers will play an important role in the new cyberspace economy; however, the chapter indicates that many issues must be addressed before this technology can be fully implemented and discusses these important issues.

Chapter 20 entitled, "Evaluation of Electronic Commerce Adoption Within SMEs" by Marco Tagliavini, Aurelio Ravarini, and Alessandro Antonelli of Universita Cattaneo (Italy) aims to support SMEs in choosing the most suitable electronic commerce approaches according to their peculiarities and strategic goals. First, it identifies five EC approaches that support various business activities. The chapter further describes the business variables involved in any e-commerce project and identifies four SME profiles characterized by different values of these variables. Finally, a cross analysis between the e-commerce approaches and SME profiles allows developing a framework and suggesting the most suitable e-commerce solution for each business profile. This paper provides SMEs with a simple, easy to use tool to perform a *qualitative* evaluation of e-commerce opportunities.

Chapter 21 entitled, "The Cost of Email Within Organizations" by Thomas Jackson and Ray Dawson of Loughborough University and Darren Wilson of the Danwood Group (UK) details a pilot exercise on the cost-benefit analysis of the use of internal email performed at the Danwood Group. This exercise was part of a larger endeavour to evaluate computer communication to help enhance performance throughout the organization. The chapter resulted in the creation of an internal email costing process showing when it begins to become a more efficient means of communication. In the study, the time taken to read, write and perform other functions with email were measured from a sample of employees. The email content was also monitored to determine which emails were business-related. It was found that nearly two-thirds of all emails were not business-related at the start of the research, but this decreased to a consistent 43% towards the end.

Chapter 22 entitled, "Electronic Commerce: Determining B2C Web site Functions," by Bijan Fazlollahi of Georgia State University discusses requirements for web site functions from the point of view of both the firm and the customer. The firm's business strategies and customer decision support needs are mapped into web site functionalities. Two existing web sites of firms in the building industry are analyzed for illustrative purposes.

Electronic commerce and its implementations—enterprise resource planning, online shopping, mobile agents—are prominent areas of research that are revolutionizing the face of organizations throughout this world. The collections of essays in this work detail the most important issues surrounding electronic commerce as they address the way different cultures deal with e-commerce and the different methods to implement electronic commerce. The chapters also look at electronic commerce's impact on different types and sizes of organizations. The authors of this timely new book address issues important to consumers and providers in ways that will prove to be useful to academicians, researchers, students and business people alike.

IRM Press
October 2001

Chapter 1

Cyber Shopping and Privacy

Jatinder N. D. Gupta and Sushil K. Sharma
Ball State University, USA

INTRODUCTION

As we enter a new millennium, we find cyber shopping has become the order of the day. Consumers find it easier to cyber shop than to take time from their schedules to visit malls. One can shop any time depending upon availability of time. Many working couples order the items as they leave from their workplaces and receive deliveries right when they reach home. Some people shop late at night and receive items the very next morning. Cyber shopping is exciting because: 1) one can shop directly from home or the workplace, and 2) the cost of items may be cheaper than the traditional buying. Considering these conveniences, many people prefer cyber shopping. Also, there are very many exciting sites such as E-auction etc. on the Net which otherwise are not available.

Some consumers consider cyber shopping as unsafe. They argue that: 1) giving credit card information on the net may bring problems if credit card information falls into the wrong hands; 2) the net does not provide the expected level of security; and 3) companies may record all their purchases, purchasing habits, etc., and may pass on or sell this information to other potential marketers who in turn may solicit the customer (Handerson, 1999).

The growing popularity of cyber shopping means information can be transmitted all around the globe with just one click of the mouse (Manes, 2000). However, it also means that some information that was thought to be private, such as medical records or financial data, is now out in the public domain for all to see and there are people who are actually hacking them all the time. Those hackers or companies know an individual's name, address, phone number, marital status, age and

Previously Published in *Managing Business with Electronic Commerce: Issues and Trends* edited by Aryya Gangopadhyay, Copyright © 2002, Idea Group Publishing.

approximate income level. They know what publications people read, what catalogs they receive, what Web sites they visit and what products they buy both online and off. The ability of marketers to track customers' surfing and buying patterns can lead to abuses. Before the advent of cyber shopping, direct-mail marketers would at times collect information and threaten privacy, but they didn't have the breadth of information now available on the Internet (Lawton, 1998).

Today, when a customer goes online for rentals, credit card purchases, airline reservations and other such electronic transactions, s/he is required to complete a form which contains personal information that defines or represents his/her habits. This information is collected and can be passed to other marketing companies to market their product and services without their knowledge. Many believe that too much personal information is being collected when they go online (Caudill, 2000). Others are not willing to use credit card numbers to purchase items on the Internet. The strange contradiction is that people like to use the Internet for cyber shopping while at the same time they do not trust it. Millions of people are using the Internet everyday, for work, play, learning, business and for social interaction. As we depend on and enjoy it more, we are worried if and how others or organizations may be secretly watching us and collecting information for purposes that we are unaware. "Spamming," which is the practice of sending out unsolicited e-mail, is growing because it costs so little to send out millions of messages or advertisements electronically. Many prominent high-technology companies have already been caught attempting to quietly collect information about their customers via the Internet. DoubleClick, a popular supplier of online advertising services, and RealNetworks, the producer of the RealPlayer line of multimedia software, were subjects of a scandal when their millions of trusted users learned that their personal information was being collected without their consent (Kling, 1996; Gurak, 1997). Privacy can be defined as an individual's right to be left alone, free from interference or surveillance from other parties. Privacy requires security mechanism, policy and technology to provide control over information.

The way sites handle personal information is a concern to the general public. The general population is very cold to the idea of having personal information distributed without the knowledge of the individuals in question. It is an issue because of the risk of taking adverse actions based on inaccurate information, i.e., spam, phone call (Gillin, 2000a). Internet privacy is clearly controversial and can be confusing. As mentioned above there are companies who are keeping track of the Net users. Most of the time they do that with the help of a unique identifier called a cookie, usually a string of random-looking letters, that a Web server places on a computer's hard drive. Cookies enable Web sites to track usage patterns and deliver customized content to visitors.

At times, privacy issues are perceived as a part of security issues, therefore, let us differentiate them. **Security** refers to the integrity of the data storage, processing and transmitting system and includes concerns about the reliability of hardware and software, the protection against intrusion or infiltration by unauthorized users. **Privacy**, on the other hand, refers to controlling the dissemination and use of data, including information that is knowingly or unknowingly disclosed. Privacy could also be the by-product of the information technologies themselves (Cate, 1997).

Over the past decade, numerous surveys conducted around the world have found consistently high levels of concern about privacy. Many studies (Dorney, 1997; Allard, 1998; Harris and Westin, 1999) found that more than 80% of Net users are concerned about threats to their privacy while online. The Federal Trade Commission discovered (Privacy online: A report to Congress/Federal Trade Commission, United States, Federal Trade Commission, 1998) that many Web sites collect personal information and release the same without the users' knowledge and permission.

There are methods (Adam et al., 1996; Verton, 2000; Wen, 2001; McGuire, 2000; Feghhi, 1999) that make cyber shopping secure, although consumers may still have concerns about security aspects of cyber shopping. How can one keep information about his/her Internet browsing habits to oneself? It's a challenge in this era of technological advancements. In this chapter, we focus exclusively on privacy issues that arise in cyber shopping. In the recent past, many articles on privacy have appeared in journals. In this chapter, we review these publications on privacy.

PRIVACY CONCERNS

Privacy is currently front-page news and is the focus of much legislative activity. The privacy issue has been dominant since the passage of the Federal Privacy Act and similar state laws in the mid -70s and has created a legal battleground of conflicting expectations. On the one hand, employees assert that their privacy rights are being trampled upon by employers, while employers claim the need to protect business assets from employee abuse. The ability to shop online—anytime, anywhere—is drastically changing the way consumers shop and have added more dimensions to privacy. Privacy refers to controlling the dissemination and use of data, including information that is knowingly disclosed as well as data that are unintentionally revealed or a by-product of the information technologies themselves (Cate, 1997).

Cyber shopping is growing every year, and it is estimated that by 2010, 55% of retail sales will come from cyber shopping. While this may be great for consumers, it presents an enormous challenge for retailers and consumers. Further growth of the Internet will make the cyber-shopping experience much easier, faster and cheaper. This may reduce the cost of cyber shopping for consumers but at the same time may also benefit the companies by reducing the cost of gathering information about consumers to practically zero. Due to these low costs of data entry, computer processing, storage and communications, companies would be more encouraged to record every detail of their interactions with customers for later use and these details may be for sale. Loss of privacy is the price consumers pay for the convenience of shopping online. Web sites take personal information and use it themselves, sell it to other operations and sometimes have it stolen from them. Thus, privacy has become a key issue in the digital age because technological advances make it easier than ever for companies to obtain personal information and to monitor online activities, thus creating a major potential for abuse (Sykes, 1999). People are concerned about privacy, particularly on the Internet. The study conducted by Harris and Westin (1999) confirms this concern. Online privacy concerns focus on the protection of "customer identifiable" information, which an individual or other customer reasonably expects to be kept private. As the term suggests, "customer identifiable" information is information that can be associated with a specific individual or entity, including, for example, a customer's name, address, telephone number, e-mail address and information about online activities that are directly linked to them.

It is common practice and often a necessity for companies, governments or other organizations to collect customer-identifiable information in order to conduct business and offer services. For example, a telecommunications provider may collect customer-identifiable information, such as name, address, telephone number and a variety of other information in the course of billing and providing telephone service to a customer. Some activities on the Internet follow very familiar patterns. Consumers signing up for an Internet access service, for example, are usually asked to provide name, address, telephone number and credit card and other information that is typical when the consumer orders a product or service. Similarly, business Web sites may ask visitors to supply information about themselves, particularly when information, services or merchandise are requested, but often simply to be able to better target the company's services to the customer's interests and requirements (Blotzer, 2000). All instances cited above are examples of how consumers provide much information about themselves to companies that may misuse this information, thus creating concerns for privacy. Table 1 highlights the main privacy concerns surrounding cyber shopping and suggested remedies.

Spamming-Unsolicited Commercial E-Mail

When consumers receive many e-mails from unknown friends and organizations, this privacy intrusion is known as "spam" or receiving unsolicited commercial

Table 1: Privacy concerns

Type of Concern	Description	Remedies
Spamming	*Unsolicited commercial E-mail*	*Never respond to junk E-mail,*
Unauthorised Access/Surveillance	*Employers monitoring E-mail, computer and Internet use in the workplace*	*Review workplaces, ISP and Web site privacy policies*
Collection of Information through Cookies	*Cookies - Documenting consumers' buying habits etc. from their on-line interactions*	*Block cookies and manage their cookie files . Internet users can access free programs such as IDcide, AdSubtract, and Naviscope are free programs available at <http://www.pcworld.com/downloads > to help block cookies.*
Selling Personal information by Information brokers	*Desire to control the collection, compilation and transfer or sale of one's personal information to others*	*Opt out of profiling and market research services.*
Intellectual Property Rights (IPR)	*Copying, editing, morphing and otherwise manipulating information; S/W piracy - unlicensed distribution of copyright music*	*Use disclaimers to discourage, be prepared to file a law suit.*
Privacy and Children's On-line Activities	*Companies at times target children on-line for collecting information*	*Controlling children's access to on-line environment by their parents and educating them about on-line environment abuses.*

e-mail. Spamming is growing because it costs so little to send out millions of messages or advertisements electronically. Many prominent high-technology companies have already been caught attempting to quietly collect information about their customers and pass it to potential marketing companies who in turn send junk mail to market their products. Junk e-mail is becoming very pervasive, with one bulk e-mailer, Cyber Promotions, boasting that it sends 1.5 million messages a day (Smith, 1996). The users who receive junk mail can request the cyber shopping company from whom they have purchased to remove them from their e-mailing list and the company not to distribute the user's identity. E-mail service providers and browsers also offer a utility to block unwanted e-mail. One should use these utilities to protect oneself from an onslaught of undesired mail.

Unauthorized Access/Surveillance-Employee Monitoring

Some employers utilize workplace surveillance technology to ensure that they are getting the most out of their workers. Estimates indicate that employers eavesdrop on about 400 million telephone calls between employees and customers every year. It is particularly prevalent in the insurance, telecommunications and banking industries. Employer eavesdropping on electronic mail transfer is also widespread and currently not banned by federal wiretapping law (Kling, 1996). The key in this issue is the trade off between productivity versus employee comfort and morale. There isn't much doubt that monitoring will improve employee output, but at what cost? Workers may be under more stress and may generally be more edgy while at work. Employees may dread coming in to work, and absenteeism may be more frequent. It is more effective to have employees that want to be there and are comfortable working in their environments. The benefits of employee monitoring can be achieved by proper supervision from management. If the employer must secretively listen in on conversations or read employee e-mail, then he/she really doesn't know the worker too well and should get to know them better. On the other hand, one can also argue that reading employees' e-mail or eavesdropping on their telephone calls is not an invasion of worker privacy because, after all, they are being paid for working. Employers have the right to determine if the employee is not meeting expectations (Hubbart, 1998).

The issue of e-mail and e-mail monitoring has received a great deal of attention, both in the media and in legal writing, especially in the United States. Moreover, with increasing frequency, employers and employees alike are seeking answers to the question: may employers legally monitor employee e-mail and Internet use? A 1999 American Management Association (AMA) survey reveals that 67.3% of major U.S. firms monitor their employees by reviewing their e-mail, tracking their Internet usage, looking over their phone logs or even installing video cameras. And they often do this without letting their employees know. The computer, the telephone lines and the office space all belong to the company, and the company has a legal right to monitor its own property. Managers can use them as grounds to fire someone.

The forms of surveillance that employers use are diverse, generally inexpensive and are likely being used at the office. Several software can track the network server for keywords and if found can pass on the related material to the management. This kind of surveillance has become quite common in many companies. At times, management has taken harsh actions by firing the employee who was found to be spending a lot of time on e-mail and Internet use. All this monitoring may seem insidious, but in the opinion of legal experts, employers have a legitimate right to know about employees and the way employees spend their time in workplaces. This way, companies not only ensure productivity but also ensure that their trade secrets are not passed on to competitors.

Sending e-mail-Is it safe?

If employees know that their e-mails are monitored, then why do the employees use the e-mail facility of a company? Do the employees not understand that e-mails are not secure and network servers keep track of every bit of mail that employees send out or every Web page they view? There are two possible answers to these questions: one is that employees know these facts but still feel that employers may not take it seriously, and second is that the employee believes if they have passwords, it is secure. Whereas, the fact is that it is not only employers who can access this mail, but this mail is vulnerable to abuse by eavesdroppers because e-mail messages travel from the originating host computer to the destination and often pass through several relaying hosts. Administrators of any of these hosts can easily eavesdrop on the mail traffic.

How to protect e-mail invasion of privacy?

There are preventive measures which could be applied to avoid embarrassment or possibly even being fired for e-mail abuse:

1. It is better to have a personal account at home with an Internet service provider and direct all confidential messages to be sent to the home computer Internet account and not to the by workplace account.
2. E-mail should be selective and purposeful. It is not recommended to send any confidential or personal information.
3. E-mail accounts require proper management such as deleting old mail and sensitive mail, etc. One can also employ encryption technologies offered by e-mail service providers to avoid eavesdropping.
4. It is desirable that employees check the company e-mail policy before they start using e-mail.

Collection of Information Through Cookies

Many advertising and market research companies collect information from consumers through their online interactions. The companies can then create a database of preferences, habits and choices of consumers to be used to market their products and services. This is not a new phenomenon, but due to the breadth and speed of the Internet, it creates concerns for consumers.

How do these companies collect information?

As discussed earlier, companies often ask consumers to provide their personal details through online interaction. The more dominant method used by companies to collect information is to use "Cookies." Cookies are the most common privacy invader as they can store and even track down information about online travels and shopping without the user's knowledge (Bass, 2000). Cookies enable Web sites to track usage patterns and deliver customized content to visitors. Cookies are short pieces of data, usually a string of random-looking letters, that a Web server places on a computer's hard drive. They are planted on the consumer's computer by the Web sites which are visited or surfed. Cookies help to know the movements of consumers while surfing on the Web site. This information can be used by companies to figure out the buying habits and tastes of consumers, and at times can even be sold to third-party agencies for potential marketing.

Most consumers are blissfully unaware of the electronic footprint they leave when they surf Web sites. There are sites available such as www.privacy.net which help to know how cookies keep details of the consumers. Cookies keep information about computer's identity (referred to as the IP address), computer's configuration, the route from computer to the destination computer system, the last Web pages accessed and so on. Privacy campaigners fear that using cookies could lead to senders' identities being easily traceable.

While cookies don't give a Web site any personal information, such as an individual's name or address, they create a unique identity for the browser so that a site can recognize a person if he visits again using the same computer terminal. In some ways, cookies benefit Web surfers; without them, people would have to enter a user name and password over and over to see any personalized content on the Web. However, cookies actually act like hidden cameras or microphones capturing computer users' movements.

Cookies are meant to help consumers. Detailed marketing databases enable companies to better match their products and services to consumer demands. By performing statistical analysis of database information on consumers, the companies can target their products in a more focused manner and consumers can get their wish list items without spending the time searching for it.

How do advertising companies benefit from cookies?

When a browser sends a request to a server, it includes its IP address, the type of browser being used and the operating system of the computer. This information is usually logged in the server's log file. A cookie sent along with the request can add only that the same server originally sent information. Thus, there is no additional personal information explicitly sent to the server by allowing cookies. On multiple client sites being serviced by a single marketing site, cookies can be used to track browsing habits on all the client sites. The way this works is a marketing firm contracts with multiple client sites to display its advertising. The client sites simply put a tag on their Web pages to display the image containing the marketing firm's advertisement. The tag does not point to an image file on the client's machine but contains the URL of the marketing firm's advertisement server and includes the URL of the client's page.

The advertising firm sends a cookie along with the advertisement, and that cookie is sent back to the advertising firm the next time someone views any page containing one if its advertisements. If many Web sites support the same advertising firm, that firm will be able to track an individual's browsing habits from page to page within all the client sites. The firm will not be able to see what an individual does with the pages which he views; it will only know which pages are viewed, how often are viewed and the IP address of the computer. This information can be used to infer the things people are interested in and to target advertising to those people based on those inferences.

How to avoid cookies?

No files are destroyed or compromised by cookies. Cookies contain only text and cannot damage any computer. It is easy to block cookies. The new browsers have the capability to turn off the cookies and the computer can stop accepting any cookies. There are number of programs such as Webwasher, Cache and Cookiewasher which can remove footprints. These programs are available and can be easily downloaded from the Internet. Encryption and Decryption can also ensure personal privacy over the Net. In fact it is more desirable that companies make use of encryption method during their online interactions (Smith, 1996).

Blocking all cookies prevents some online services for cyber shopping. Also, preventing a browser from accepting cookies does not make the consumer anonymous, it just makes it more difficult to track usage. IDcide, AdSubtract and Naviscope are free programs available at www.pcworld.com/downloads that can help to block cookies. Users can also make their computer undetectable by using ZoneAlarm, a firewall free for personal use.

Selling Personal Information by Information Brokers

Many companies act as information brokers and collect information from various public record online databases and sell the information to various interested parties. At times, this is done for information entrepreneurialism (Kling, 1996) which refers to the dynamic attempts of organizations to take advantage of technology and principal social relationships to gain both organizational and competitive advantage. Computer-based information entrepreneurialism made significant strides in the early 1990s (Ackerman et al., 1996). Many companies consider personal data of customers to be a corporate asset that can be sold (Borrus, 2000; Lehman, 2000). Information broker companies use data-intensive techniques like profiling and data mining to aid in precision marketing. This has led organizations to sell information as a good or service much like how magazines can sell their mailing lists. The key issue here is, should these companies sell the personal information of consumers without their consent? Should the profits that information broker's companies earn be shared with the consumer because it is consumers' data? This may be serious concern for privacy because if this data is changed or gets into the wrong hands, it can lead to serious consequences for consumers. Another main problem, as stated by Jeffrey Rosen, legal affairs editor of the *New York Times* newspaper, is that information on individuals gained from computers creates a fractionalized image of the computer user. When agencies, companies and others make conclusions that are based on fragmentary information, society as a whole loses out, leading to potentially small-minded and dangerous results.

It has been observed that in an online environment, there is much unreliable information available. Researchers (Linowes, 1996) found that more than 70% of Net users always provide false information about themselves and hide their real identity. They see this as the convenient way to protect their privacy. While it may be a convenient way to protect privacy, it may allow an information broker to divulge wrong information about them that can create problems. That is why even today many data miners do not fully trust the Internet as a good resource of information because they feel that the information divulged is not accurate.

Knowing all these online privacy concerns of consumers, it is expected that companies will move toward self-regulation and mutual cooperation (Wazeka, 2000). Many companies have taken initiatives toward this, but the Enonymous.com survey, released in April 2000, revealed that among the 1,000 busiest Web sites, 63% post some sort of policy, but many do not provide a great deal of protection (Lehman, 2000). In May 2000, the Federal Trade Commission (FTC) recommended to Congress that it extend new powers to control the way companies collect and use personal information through the Internet because most of the Web sites are not implementing self-regulatory measures and are defying core privacy principles. It is expected that the FTC will play an important role in auditing cyber shopping sites and will set the guidelines from time to time in the future (Gillin, 2000b).

Intellectual Property Rights (IPR)

IPR includes copying, editing, morphing software piracy, unlicensed distribution of copyright music and otherwise manipulating information. Everyday there are millions of people who download or copy information without acknowledging the authors. At times the same information is modified and sold under a different name. Software piracy is another menace and yet still prevalent. Net users are becoming aware that Web sites may be encroaching on their privacy by collecting information thus infringing upon IPR. Realizing that the subject of IPR and copyrights need to be protected, Internet privacy requires federal and state politicians to introduce new bills aimed at safeguarding consumers' personal information from aggressive advertisers and direct marketers (Cate, 1997). Although, there are existing laws aimed at providing Internet privacy, they are not enough. The recent case of Napster is a good example of IPR as a privacy concern. There are many such legal issues which are yet to be resolved (Adam et al., 1996).

Privacy and Children's Online Activities

As the culture of cyber shopping grows, it also attracts the attention of children. Children may be encouraged to use online environments for educational and entertainment resources and certainly, it can be an important and useful tool to help enrich and educate children. Most of the schools have introduced computers at early stages, and children are capable of using the Internet for personal use. In the last few years, computer literacy increased and more children are joining the cyber space world for their day-to-day activities. Interactive online communications provides tremendous opportunities for children (United States Congress Senate Committee on Commerce, 1998), but at the same time, it presents unique challenges for protecting the privacy of young children.

When children go online, companies may lure them to play a few games, solve a few puzzles and attract them with offers of free gifts, free trips or awards, etc., and as a result may collect personal information from them. Unlike adults, they may not be fully capable of understanding the consequences of giving out personal information online. Parents will not always have the knowledge, the ability or the opportunity to intervene in their children's choices about giving personal information. Therefore, companies at times target children online for collecting information and create a serious threat for privacy. One remedy for this concern could be controlling children's access to the online environment by their parents and educating the children about online environment abuses. Another way could be thought of whether Internet service providers themselves can give options to parents to restrict interactions with sites that may be in the business of collecting information.

REMEDIES AND FUTURE TRENDS

As long as consumers look for online environments for cyber shopping, the privacy concern up to a certain extent will remain unresolved. As consumers look for convenience, companies may exploit these situations to collect personal information.

Possible Remedies

There could be two methods to resolve the privacy concern. The first method would be for the companies to enforce a self-regulated privacy policy as suggested by the Federal Trade Commission. The second method could be to use encryption technology (Encryption-the process of hiding the meaning of a readable message [clear text] in an incomprehensible text [cipher text]) for any cyber shopping interactions. Using a secure browser that complies with industry standards, such as Secure Sockets Layer (SSL) or Secure Hypertext Transfer Protocol (S-HTTP), would ensure that data cannot be read by undesired persons even if it is accessed. The standards such as SSL and Secure Electronic Transactions (SET) provide enough measures to protect the consumers' data from unauthorized access.

SSL and SET are the technology used to make cyber shopping transactions secure. For the cyber shopping experience, it is recommended to use a secure server. A secured server will use Secure Sockets Layer (SSL) technology to provide a safe way to transmit sensitive information, such as credit card numbers, online banking, e-mail messages, surveys and other personal information. Only authorized people or organizations can access consumers' data once the transactions are carried over the secure channel. It has been reported by some experts that if consumers use Secure Sockets Layer for online transactions, it would take $100,000 worth of computer equipment 100,000,000,000,000,000,000 years (10 to the 19 power of years), when a 128-bit key is used to decrypt the transaction information. Even when only an 80-bit key were used, it is estimated that it would take $100,000 worth of computer equipment 70,000 years to break the code used to encrypt credit card data.

Most up-to-date Web browsers have a small picture of a key or padlock indicating an SSL port. On a secure site, the key or padlock is usually located in the lower left corner of the browser. Secure sites are always listed as https:// at the beginning of the address of the Web page, instead of the more common, insecure http://. Using a secure channel would help to make sure that the information stays private.

Future Trends: The Clipper Chip
To make sure that every piece of information which goes out of consumers' computers or networks is secure, it would be desirable to implement encryption standards right at machine level. The clipper chip is an encryption device that could be used at every computer to provide a means to scramble communications. It is envisaged that in the near future all computers, hand-held devices such as personal digital assistants and even telephone sets would have clipper chips embedded in them to provide a secure communication channel. Any data sent by computers or any home call made by a telephone with a clipper chip, will go encrypted and the device on the other side having a similar clipper chip would decrypt the message.

The chip would employ "escrowed encryption" meaning that a third-party (Denning, 1996), in this case the government, would hold the encryption keys. There are concerns expressed by a few groups that the clipper chip would keep record of every transaction and the government could take advantage of the information for tax raids to catch sensitive information. These fears are real to a certain extent, but the advantages to consumers outweigh the fear of loss. This technology cannot be easily cracked, as it is not software based but rather a physical piece of hardware (Rapalus, 1997). One of the concerns that may arise out of the clipper chip is the cost to consumers when purchasing cellular phones and other telecommunication devices and services. Still, the U.S. Department of Justice and the Federal Bureau of Investigation are making amendments to existing laws to take advantage of this new technology in the future.

CONCLUSION AND FUTURE DIRECTIONS

The growing popularity of cyber shopping means information can be beamed around the globe with just one click. However, it also means that some information that we believe to be private, such as medical records or financial data, is now in the public domain for all to see. Each time someone visits a Web site to get information or make a purchase, the site operator, as well as other third parties, can surreptitiously collect many types of information about that person. With more consumers buying books and music online and more new media companies, the power to track what people read and listen to will be in the hands of a few very large firms. These firms keep track of people while leaving a cookie in their system. Most of the companies have been doing this for years and they have developed intensive databases of the people surfing the Net. Employers are keeping an eye on their employees while reading their mail, and check which sites they click during official working hours. Later on, they may use them to fire a person. Even the Internet service providers keep track of the sites visited by their customers.

As cyber shopping grows, organizations may attempt to gather new and more revealing consumer data. Organizations like banks, credit card associations, direct mail marketers and other organizations started mining personal data for profit long before the Net burst into prominence. However, public concern about privacy protection today tends to focus on the Internet or online environments. Since we are interested in having more interactions with the online environment, maybe we need to question how much one is prepared to accommodate for the sake of convenience. It will also be worthwhile to research issues through empirical studies to determine if privacy concerns will have a direct impact on the number of cyber shopping transactions. Although many studies indicate that cyber shoppers list privacy as their concern for online shopping, further research is needed on whether the privacy concerns have a strong influence to convert cyber shoppers to traditional shoppers.

The question remains whether is it legal to track the personal behaviour of other people? Do these companies have a legal right to keep track of their customers and consumers? These issues will be debated for many years to come. Many are so controversial because they are "catch-22" situations. Gains are made on one front but losses occur on the other. Maybe even more government regulation is required to help clean up our information environment.

REFERENCES

Ackerman, M. S., Allen, J. P. and Kling, R. (1996). Information entrepreneurialism In Kling, R. (Ed.), *Computerization and Controversy*, 2nd ed. San Diego: Academic Press.

Adam, N. R., Dogramaci, O., Gangopadhyay, A., and Yesha, Y. (1999). *Electronic Commerce-Technical, Business and Legal Issues*. Prentice Hall.

Allard N. W. (1998). Privacy online: Washington report. *Hastings Communications and Entertainment Law Journal*, 20, 511-540.

American Management Association Report. (1999).

Bass, S. (2000). Fight for your online privacy, *PC World*. November 18(11), 45.

Blotzer, M. (2000). Privacy in the digital age. *Occupational Hazards*, July, 62(7), 29-31.

Borrus,-A. (2000). Online privacy: Congress has no time to waste, *Business Week*, September 18, (3699), 54.

Cate, F. H. (1997). *Privacy in the Information Age*. Washington, DC: Brookings Institution Press.

Caudill, E. M. and Murphy, P. E. (2000).Consumer online privacy: Legal and ethical issues. *Journal of Public Policy and Marketing*, Spring, 19(1), 7-19.

Denning, D. E. (1996). Clipper chip will reinforce privacy, In *Computerization and Controversy*, 2nd Ed, edited by Rob Kling. San Diego, CA: Academic Press.

Dorney, M. S. (1997). Privacy and the Internet. *Hastings Communications and Entertainment Law Journal*, 19, 635-660.

Electronic Communication Privacy Policy Disclosures. (2000). Government Publication.

Evans, J. (2000). Paranoids, unite!, *The Computer Paper*, 44. www.canadacomputers.com/v3/story/1.1017.3302.00html.

Feghhi J. (1999). Digital certificates: Applied Internet security, Reading, MA: Addision-Wesley.

Gillin, D. (2000a). How privacy affects us all: Friction between the researcher's need for information and a respondent's privacy grows. *Marketing Research*, Summer, 12(2), 40-41.

Gillin, D. (2000b). The Federal Trade Commission and Internet privacy. *Marketing Research*, 12(3), 39-41.

Gurak, L. J. (1997). *Persuasion and Privacy in Cyberspace–The Online Protests Over Lotus Marketplace and the Clipper Chip*. New Haven, CT: Yale University.

Handerson, H. (1999). *Privacy in the Information Age*. New York: Facts on File.

Harris, L. and Westin, A. F. (1999). *Harris-Equifax Consumer Privacy Survey*. Atlanta, GA: Equifax Inc.

Hubbart, W. S. (1998). The new battle over workplace privacy. *Business-Insurance*, April, 32(15), 18.

Kling R. (Ed.). (1996). Information technologies, and the continuing vulnerability of privacy. In *Computerization and Controversy*, 2nd ed. San Diego, CA: Academic Press.

Lawton G. (1998). The Internet challenge to privacy, *Computer*, June, 16-18.

Lehman, DeW. (2000). Privacy policies missing at 77% of Web sites. *Computerworld*, April, 34(16), 103.

Linowes, D. F. (1996). Your personal information has gone public. In Kling, R. (Ed.), *Computerization and Controversy*, 2nd ed. San Diego, CA: Academic Press.

Manes, S. (2000). Private lives? Not ours! *PC World*, June, 18(6), 312.

McGuire, B. L. and Roser, S. N. (2000). What your business should know about Internet security. *Strategic Finance Magazine,* 82(5), 50-4.

Privacy Online: A Report to Congress/federal Trade Commission, (1998). United States, Federal Trade Commission.

Rapalus, P. (1997). Security measures for protecting confidential information on the Internet and intranets. *Employment Relations Today*, Autumn, (24), 49-58.

Smith, H. J. (1994). *Managing Privacy*, Carolina Press.

Smith, W. (1996). How to get rid of all your junk e-mail. *Money*, July, (25), 21.

Sykes C. J. (1999). *The End of Privacy*. New York: St. Martin's Press.

United State Congress Senate Committee on Commerce, Science and Transportation. (1998). *Subcommittee on Communication*, Children's Online Privacy Protection Act of 1998.

Verton, D. (2000). How companies can enhance Web security, *Computerworld,* November, 34(46), 141.

Wazeka, R. (2000). Internet privacy. *Success*, September, 47(4), 64-65.

Wen, H. J. and Tarn, J. M. (2001). The impact of the next-generation Internet protocol on e-commerce security. *Information Strategy,* 17(2), 22-28.

ONLINE RESOURCES

Beyond Concern; Understanding Online Privacy Concerns. Available on the World Wide Web at: http://www.research.att.com/resources/trs/TRs/99/99.4/99.4.3/report.htm.

Canada Newswire, Privacy Code in Canada. Available on the World Wide Web at: http://www.newswire.ca/releases/September1998/18/c4437.html.

Consumer World. Available on the World Wide Web at: http://www.consumerworld.org.

Electronic Privacy Information Center. Available on the World Wide Web at: http://www.epic.org/.

Federal Trade Commission. Available on the World Wide Web at: http://www.ftc.gov.

Fraud on the Internet. Available on the World Wide Web at: http://www.emich.edu/public/coe/nice/fraudr1.html.

Georgetown Internet Privacy Policy Study. Available on the World Wide Web at: http://www.msb.edu/faculty/culnanm/gippshome.html.

Internet Privacy Coalition. Available on the World Wide Web at: http://www.privacy.org.

Keeping Secrets on the Internet. Available on the World Wide Web at: http://www.cme.org/priv698.html.

Securities and exchange Commission. Available on the World Wide Web at: http://www.sec.gov/consumer/cyberfr.htm.

Student Internet Privacy Guidelines. Available on the World Wide Web at: http://www.4j.lane.edu/4jnet/privacyguide.html and http://www.anu.edu.au/people/Roger.Clarke/DV/Surveys.html.

Tips for Online Privacy for Kids and Consumers. Available on the World Wide Web at: http://www.privacyalliance.org/join/background.shtml.

World Intellectual Property Organization. (WIPO). Available on the World Wide Web at: http://www.wipo.org.

Chapter 2

Structural Influences on Global E-Commerce Activity

M. Lynne Markus
City University of Hong Kong, Hong Kong

Christina Soh
Nanyang Technological University, Singapore

An important line of research on global information management examines the effects of national culture on IT development, operations, management and use. This paper argues that global information management researchers should not lose sight of structural conditions related to business-to-business and business-to-consumer e-commerce activity. Structural conditions are physical, social and economic arrangements that shape e-commerce business models and influence individual and organizational use of the Internet. Examples include geography (which affects the physical distribution of goods purchased online), space (which influences the choice of access technology for e-commerce) and financial infrastructure (which is related to credit card use). Structural conditions differ from country to country—and even from location to location within country, but they are not necessarily related to dimensions of natural culture. Therefore, valid explanations of global differences in e-commerce activity require a careful assessment of relevant structural factors.

INTRODUCTION

IS research interest in the global aspects of IT use is growing, partly owing to the efforts of publications like *JGIM*. A popular type of study examines the effect of national culture on IT development, operations, management and use (Gallupe

Previously Published in the *Journal of Global Information Management, vol.10, no.1*, Copyright © 2002, Idea Group Publishing.

and Tan, 1999), where national culture is frequently understood in terms of Hofstede's (1983, 1991) concepts and operationalizations (Davison, 1996).

This essay reminds the IS community not to neglect the structural conditions (Orlikowski, 1992; Markus and Benjamin, 1997) within which IT use occurs. Structural conditions are physical, social, and economic arrangements that shape e-commerce business models and influence individual and organizational use of the Internet. Examples include geography (which affects the physical distribution of goods purchased online), space (which influences the choice of access technology for e-commerce) and financial infrastructure (which is related to credit card use). Structural conditions differ from country to country—and even from location to location within country, but they are not necessarily related to dimensions of natural culture. Therefore, analysis of cultural differences alone is unlikely to provide a satisfactory explanation of global differences in e-commerce activity. Valid explanations of global differences require a careful assessment of relevant structural, as well as cultural, factors.

To make this point, we examine a few of the structural conditions likely to influence e-commerce activity that are significantly different in various parts of Asia than they are in the U.S.A. The next two sections of the paper describe structural conditions related to business-to-consumer and business-to-business electronic commerce activity. The discussion section identifies implications for future research.

BUSINESS-TO-CONSUMER ELECTRONIC COMMERCE

In this section, we address the adoption of B2C e-commerce by individuals and the development of B2C e-commerce business models by firms.

Structural Factors in Individual B2C e-Commerce Adoption

One structural factor likely to affect IT adoption and e-readiness is the urban-rural distribution of a country's population. People in rural districts generally have lower levels of access to the IT infrastructure necessary to sustain ordering over the Web; long distances may make "delivery to order" difficult, if not impossible. In North America urban dwellers comprise 77% of the population; in Asia as a whole the figure is 37% (United Nations Population Division, 1998). But within Asia, there are huge differences. The percent urban is 100% in Singapore, 95% in Hong Kong, 81% in South Korea, 78% in Japan, 54% in Malaysia, 30% in China, 27% in India, and 20% in Thailand (http://www.xist.org/global/urban.htm). It is not surprising therefore that the latest Economist Intelligence Unit's survey ranks largely urban countries or territories like Singapore and Hong Kong high on e-readiness while relatively developed countries with a greater proportion of rural population like Taiwan, Japan, and South Korea rank lower (Yang, 2001). Similarly, A. Chen (2001) points out that "while packages in the US can be shipped cross-country in a matter of days…, in China the roads—or lack thereof—mean that, even if B2B e-commerce were to take off, there is no efficient way to deliver products." (The same holds true for B2C.)

By contrast, the big cities of Asia—Hong Kong, Singapore, Taipei, Tokyo, Seoul—differ from most western urban areas in another dimension that inhibits the proliferation of B2C e-commerce—the *vertical* dimension. Most people in Asian cities are housed in high-rise building complexes that are miniature cities. (The Mongkok district of Hong Kong is said to be the most densely populated place on earth.) At the base of residential and office buildings, people have access to public transportation and a myriad of conveniences—restaurants and stores selling food, sundries, entertainment items (reading matter, music, videos), clothing, housewares, furniture, jewelry, and more. People hardly need to travel at all to obtain either the necessities or the luxuries of life. And when they do, the businesses they buy from will usually deliver—a practice made practical by the geographic compactness of many Asian cities.

The homes in which Asian people live are, on average, extremely small by US standards. In Hong Kong the typical government-provided flat is a mere 300 square feet—and that flat may accommodate a family of three generations. Even when family income is sufficient to buy a PC, there is often no place at home to put one. Anyway, for obvious reasons, people don't spend much time in their homes. In Singapore, for example, many families take most of their meals in the public eating houses on the ground floors of their housing estates. As a result of such living arrangements, home PC penetration in parts of Asia is low[1] (Dedrick and Kraemer, 2000), and Internet use is often more likely to occur in public places than in the home. About half of the people with Internet access in China, for example, log on from Internet cafes (a big business in Beijing!) or other public places—a factor believed likely to dampen prospects for online purchasing (Smith, 2001).

Even in Singapore, where 44% of the population has access to the Internet, only 16% of Internet users have conducted purchase transactions online (Kuo et. al, 2001). In the US, where almost two-thirds have access to the Internet, over 50% have transacted online (Cole et al, 2000). The ease of access to most shopping facilities in compact Asian cities reduces the impact of the convenience afforded by Internet shopping. The lack of prior experience with traditional catalog shopping also makes online catalog shopping an unfamiliar proposition. Martinsons (forthcoming) describes the case of Medcox Lane, a Shanghai-based online retailer: the company was founded in 1996 as one of the first mail order businesses in China.

Other structural dimensions contribute to low levels of online purchasing in Asia. By comparison to the US, credit cards are used much less in Asia (Dedrick and Kraemer, 2000). In Hong Kong, for example, the generally poor consumer protection regime extends to credit cards: Many Hong Kong consumers are liable for the entire amount charged to a stolen credit card before it is reported—there is no $50 limit as in the US. (This is also the case in China.) In Hong Kong stores that accept credit cards, the buyer is often asked if she will pay by cash—even when the amount far exceeds what most American consumers would carry on their person. Daily cash withdrawal limits on Hong Kong ATMs are HK$20,000 (roughly US$2,500)—far higher than they are in the US.

Ironically, for many *small* purchases, Asians are much more likely to use electronic payments than people in the US. Smart card use for public transportation is widespread in both Hong Kong and Singapore. In Singapore, "Cashcards" are used in all vehicles as part of the country's electronic road pricing scheme where readers mounted on road gantries automatically make deductions from the Cashcard based on the time of day and traffic flow. The ubiquity of Cashcards for both private and public transportation has led to businesses finding other uses for the card, such as for payment in public parking facilities. Hong Kong is also seeking alternative uses for its Octopus transportation payments card, e.g., for food and sundries in transportation-adjacent shopping facilities.

While consumption taxes are increasingly being levied in Asia (Australia and Singapore are two recent examples), electronic purchasing does not confer the same tax advantages that it does in the US. Both Australia and Singapore, for example, collect GST on Internet purchases from abroad over a certain amount, and, within Australia, all electronic purchases are subject to GST (Jordan, 2000). The costs of shipping to Asia from the US and within Asia are also much higher than within the US. Typically, shipping costs for consumer purchases from the US to Singapore add another 20% to 25% to the purchase cost. In Hong Kong, Internet purchases also have no tax advantages, but for a different reason: there is no sales tax on purchases in retail outlets.

Another important structural dimension is the distribution of education levels across age groups. The developed countries in the West have a more even distribution of education across age groups, while in Asia people 40 and older often did not have the opportunity to pursue tertiary education. In Singapore, for example, the proportion of those above 40 years old with a tertiary education is about 5%, compared to 25% for the developed countries in the West. Hence, when we compare Internet use across age groups between Singapore and the US, we find that, for the 18-24 age group, usage rates are quite similar, around 85% for both countries. However, when we compare the 45-55 age group, usage rates are 14% for Singapore and about 70% for the U.S. (Kuo et al., 2001; Cole et al., 2001).

In contrast to the adoption of PCs and the Internet, the penetration of mobile technology is much *higher* in Asia than in the US (Dedrick and Kraemer, 2000). People on the street, in public transportation, in stores, in places of entertainment, even in classrooms, use mobile devices for interpersonal communication, games, and access to information services such as stock quotes and movie listings. Interestingly, there are substantial differences even within Asia as to how these devices are used. In Hong Kong and Singapore, for example, mobile phones ring during every public lecture—even after the usual request for people to turn them off. In Japan, by contrast, people are said to be too polite to offend others by talking on mobile telephones. But the DoCoMo short messaging service is wildly popular there as a way to communicate unobtrusively during long train commutes to work.

Altogether then, there are very different structural conditions surrounding individual business-to-consumer e-commerce adoption in Asia than in the US. In the US, many people both live and work far from convenient shopping. They have convenient access to PCs both at home and at work, where they can browse electronic catalogs, order using credit cards, and get a tax advantage for doing so. The average education level is higher. Not surprisingly, many people order and pay for everything from books and groceries to computer equipment electronically.

In rural Asia, the barriers to individual e-commerce adoption are great. In Asian cities, many people both live and work close to convenient shopping. While they may not have convenient access to a PC or to the Internet in either location, they may be quite willing and able to use mobile devices for ordering goods and services. They may have a strong preference for paying in cash and would receive no tax advantage from ordering electronically. A large proportion of the population 40 years of age or older is relatively less educated and also less exposed to information technology. Not surprisingly, relatively few people purchase online, but use of mobile electronic information services has great potential.

B2C e-Commerce Business Models

Successful Asian B2C e-commerce business models look very different than that of Amazon.com. For example, Japan's Internet bookstore e-Shopping!Books allows people to pick up their online purchases at Seven-Eleven stores, and some 75% of them do (*The Economist*, 2000). 7Dream.com—Seven-Eleven Japan's own e-commerce venture—involves Internet-based ordering from in-store multimedia terminals that are capable of producing custom music MiniDiscs, printed digital photos, and concert tickets (Williams, 2000).

As another example, the Bank of East Asia (BEA), a Hong Kong based leader in consumer electronic banking, found it necessary to develop seven different technology platforms—in addition to traditional ATMs—to address the structural conditions found in Hong Kong and China (Hui, 2000).

- *Cyberbanking*. Cyberbanking is an online banking service, accessible by PCs and an Internet connection.
- *Telephone banking.* Telephone banking has been widely accepted in Hong Kong since it was first introduced in 1989. BEA's fully automated voice response system is integrated with its call center.
- *Mobile phone banking.* With one of the highest mobile phone penetration rates in the world, mobile banking is a promising service, and BEA offers access through two major telecommunications operators (PCCW and Hutchison Telecom).
- *In-bank kiosks.* BEA was the first bank in HK to launch kiosks for banking transactions; the touch-screen device is located in branches and other high traffic locations.
- *PowerPhones*. PowerPhones are multimedia payphones located in subway and train stations, at the airport, and in shopping malls. In addition to payphone service, they provide free access to the Bank's Websites and electronic banking services.
- *"Web TV" banking.* iCare Internet-on-TV requires a set-top box for home access to e-banking services.
- *Cyber Active Transaction Stations*. These Internet-enabled kiosks, which provide direct access to the Bank's Web sites, are being pilot tested in two 24 hour convenience stores.

In Internet-savvy Hong Kong, this proliferation of banking platforms seems costly and unnecessary. However, the bank plans to expand in China, where PC ownership and personal Internet access are much lower than in Hong Kong. For tapping the China market, mobile phones, kiosks, webTV and CATS terminals are likely to be better e-banking platforms, at least in the short term.

One of these platforms is "Cyberbanking" using PC-based Internet access (*http://www.hkbea-cyberbanking.com/index.htm*). Many of BEA's Cyberbanking services are familiar to customers in North America and Europe, e.g., balance inquiry, securities trading, bill payment, funds transfer. But some of BEA's online services are more advanced than those available elsewhere. In the US, for example, e-banking customers cannot directly transfer funds to another unrelated person's account or into their own accounts in other financial institutions. BEA's customers can do so, in multiple currencies. This feature fits Hong Kong's small geographic size and mobile, international population and reflects the relatively high concentration of banks in Hong Kong compared to the US.

Two other BEA Cyberbanking services deserve mention. One is online loan application and approval. BEA claims a fully automated online application, qualification and approval service for personal loans. All loan processing is done automatically from the customer's online input; customers are only required to enter a branch and sign forms in person *after* the loan has been approved. BEA has been gratified by customer acceptance of online lending. In contrast to the often-cited preference of Chinese people to do business in person, it appears that they prefer the face-saving aspects of applying (and learning whether they qualify) for loans anonymously.

It is also possible to be qualified and approved for mortgage loans online at BEA. Again, the Bank claims that processing is fully automatic: human intervention is required only when loan documents are signed at the branch. An interesting twist is that customers can also get property valuations online and at no charge via the Bank's partnership with *www.house18.com*. House18 maintains a database of a large number of residential properties in Hong Kong. The consumer can type in the address of a property one wishes to buy and receive a valuation that the Bank will accept as the basis for a mortgage loan. Various calculators enable the consumer to estimate payments on mortgages of various terms; it's a simple step to applying for the mortgage loan. House18 also supports a consumer's "dream house search" –identification of listed properties meeting various requirements. Other features provide advice and directory listings in such matters as decoration and removals. All in all, BEA provides its customers with a complete *real estate* package— everything from finding the right property to closing the loan. This capability suits the bank's Hong Kong clientele, for whom real estate is a favorite investment vehicle.

In short, just as structural conditions in Asia promote very different patterns of consumer e-commerce behavior than in the US, structural conditions in Asia promote very different B2C business models. While cultural factors undoubtedly play a role in these e-commerce activity patterns, structural factors also exert independent influences on the observed behavior. The next section examines structural conditions in the context of business-to-business electronic commerce.

BUSINESS-TO-BUSINESS ELECTRONIC COMMERCE

In the realm of business-to-business electronic commerce also, notable structural differences exist between Asia and North America. They include the disproportionate contribution of direct goods to final products (80% versus 60% in the US), relatively inefficient and fragmented supply chains, smaller domestic markets, and less developed infrastructure for electronic commerce (Dhawan et al., 2000). Each of these structural differences has a significant influence on the patterns of B2B e-commerce emerging in Asia.

B2B E-commerce Business Models—Asian e-Marketplaces

Consider e-markeplaces. Many of the more successful Asian B2B e-marketplaces deal in direct goods (that is, primary raw materials), whereas many

US e-marketplaces deal in indirect goods (such as office supplies, lubricants, and travel services). Direct goods often pose greater challenges in product specification and cataloging than indirect materials, and e-marketplace operators necessarily develop capabilities in this domain. The potential benefits e-marketplaces— increased supply chain efficiency through reducing the number of intermediaries or through informating the supply chain—are greater in Asia than in the West, where there are already fewer intermediaries and more efficient supply chains. Many Asian e-marketplaces target Asian MNCs and large buyers from the West and seek to link them with smaller Asian suppliers. Finally, the lack of supporting infrastructure in much of Asia means that e-marketplaces have to provide numerous complementary services in the areas of logistics, payments, assurance, and credit checks for a successful launch.

These differences are well illustrated by an industry important in both locales—nonferrous metals (e.g., aluminum and copper) (Hempel and Kwong, 2001). In this industry, key structural characteristics plausibly related to e-commerce business models and e-business adoption differ sharply in China and the US—industry consolidation/fragmentation, spot versus systematic sourcing patterns, and e-commerce infrastructure.

Industry concentration is an important structural condition likely related to e-commerce activity, because fragmentation (of buyers, suppliers, or both) is believed to promote the formation of electronic marketplaces and exchanges (Kaplan and Sawhney, 2000). In the US, the ten largest companies account for 70% of aluminum extrusion production. In China, the ten largest companies produce only 30%; about 600 small companies account for roughly half of all production. Therefore, one would expect that electronic marketplaces would be more successful in the highly fragmented Chinese nonferrous metals industry than in the US, where the industry is quite concentrated.

Industry sourcing patterns—systematic versus spot—are also plausibly related to e-commerce activity, since widespread use of spot purchasing is believed favorable to the use of electronic exchanges (Kaplan and Sawhney, 2000). In the US, systematic sourcing of nonferrous metals predominates, whereas spot purchasing is more common in China. Again, one would expect electronic marketplaces to be more successful in China.

However, while both industry fragmentation and spot sourcing patterns favor e-marketplace activity, the quality of e-commerce infrastructure does not. The quality of the e-business infrastructure differs greatly between China and the US in a direction that bodes ill for the use of electronic marketplaces in China. For example, China lacks a well-functioning electronic payment system (Silwa, 2001). Most business funds transfers involve currency: business checks are uncommon, and use of credit cards is considered an unsound practice. Business interruption insurance is unknown; banks do not provide escrow services to facilitate large transactions; and inventory financing is unavailable (that is, banks do not accept warehouse receipts as collateral for business loans). Chinese businesses have been quite loath to adopt ERP systems and other technologies that formalize and routinize business practices (Martinsons and Hempel, 1995; Silwa, 2001). And Chinese managers are relatively unversed in some modern business practices, such as the use of hedging in the metals industry. These factors would lead one to expect that electronic marketplaces would be much less successful in the Chinese nonferrous metals industry than in the US.

These differences in structural conditions mean that a successful electronic marketplace for the nonferrous metals industry in China would have to undertake the development of infrastructure that its US counterparts could take for granted. And, indeed, this pattern of activity can be observed in i-Metal.com, a wholly-owned subsidiary of Global Applied Technologies Holdings (GAT—China's largest aluminum extruder and fabricator, headquartered in Hong Kong), founded in 2000 to operate an exchange for the nonferrous metals industry (Hempel and Kwong, 2001; Lincoln, 2000; Trepp, 2000).

i-Metal.com provides members a full range of commercial services (some still under construction), including industry news and market information, online futures trading via the Shanghai Futures exchange, online spot trading of primary and scrap metal, catalog and quotation model purchasing and ancillary services such as transportation and payment. Today, i-Metal.com is well on its way to success. The exchange has over 100 member companies, and trades worth over 1B renminbi (US$120M) have been conducted through the site. But getting there has been challenging. i-Metal.com had to partner with three leading Chinese financial institutions to overcome the barriers to e-commerce in the Chinese financial services industry:

- i-Metal.com partnered with a leading bank to develop a Web-based payment system and to implement procedures for freezing funds (to emulate escrow arrangements—a service not offered by Chinese banks). The company is also working with banks to introduce more flexible inventory financing.
- i-Metal.com worked with a leading futures brokerage to enable electronic funds transfers to brokerage accounts for online futures trading.
- i-Metal.com worked with the Shanghai futures exchange to develop new business practices that would ensure that buyers and sellers would honor their online transactions despite the high price volatility that gives them an incentive to renege.
- i-Metal.com worked with warehousing and transportation companies to support critical services ancillary to the online purchasing of physical metals.

- i-Metal.com is working with China Telecom to introduce the use of digital certificates.

The point of this example is that there are important aspects of cross-cultural B2B e-commerce activity (both in business model creation and in the adoption or success of these business models) that one cannot understand solely through cultural comparisons. Existence of a supportive banking infrastructure and comfort with credit financing are relevant factors that are not captured in measures of national culture. Like i-Metal.com, many Asian e-marketplaces have had to partner extensively in order to assemble the requisite level of supporting infrastructure. Even within a specific area of service, such as logistics or financing, the e-marketplace may have to forge multiple partnerships in order to obtain pan-Asian coverage, and the required degree of functionality. By contrast, in the US, many e-marketplaces can take the existence of a supportive infrastructure for granted and devote greater attention to attracting buyers and sellers. The likely consequences for e-marketplace success are clear.

Other Structural Factors in B2B e-Commerce Activity

Another two important structural dimensions of the Asian business context are language and family businesses. Billboards (advertising IS consulting services) in the Hong Kong airport and elsewhere in Asia point out that by the year 2007, Chinese will be the #1 language of the Web. But which Chinese? Although there are many spoken Chinese dialects, there is only one written Chinese language—or, there *was* only one, until Mao introduced a "simplified" Chinese character set to increase peasant literacy. By now, the two written languages have diverged to such an extent that many overseas Chinese (e.g., Hong Kongers, Taiwanese) who have learned the traditional written language frequently have to guess the meaning of simplified Chinese. Some 20 years ago, Singapore began teaching simplified Chinese in schools—as part of the country's strategy for building relations with China. In the process, something of a literacy gap has developed between younger and older generations. Clearly, then, the language of an e-business Web site is a plausible structural factor in its success. (i-Metal.com, the e-marketplace described earlier, supports business in traditional Chinese, simplified Chinese and English.)

Another small, but interesting, structural factor related to language concerns the structure of people's names. Whereas western names are given first, middle, last, Chinese names are given last, first middle, and Vietnamese immigration documents require names to be reported last, middle, first. To add to the confusion, when Hong Kong people have both Western and Chinese given names, the names are listed in the following order: [western first name] [Chinese last name] [Chinese first names]. Not surprisingly, customer service workers often have great difficulty parsing names—a factor important in their ability to successfully use software developed in the West (Soh et al., 2000).

Other, more important, structural factors include the role of family business in Asia, which interacts with the important cultural concepts of guanxi (or quanzi, loosely "connections") (Chen, 2001; Hempel and Chang, 2000). Family businesses account for a large proportion of businesses in Asia. In Hong Kong and Singapore for example, considerably more than 90% of businesses have fewer than 100 employees. Asian family businesses differ systematically from the typical mature Western business. For example, Hempel and Chang's (2000) summary of overseas Chinese business characteristics includes:

- Simple organizational structures
- Growth by opportunistic expansion
- A high degree of strategic adaptability
- Centralized decision making, usually by the founder or his immediate family
- Very few written guidelines and formal control measures
- Low trust in subordinates

Family businesses tend to be slow in adopting sophisticated information technology, so that B2B e-commerce has not reached many of these companies. The reliance on guanxi also means that there may be a high level of discomfort with the often anonymous or arms-length nature of some types of B2B activity. Similarly, Berger and Lester (1997) note that most business financing in Hong Kong comes from relatives and family connections—a factor that places important constraints on patterns of investment and technological innovation.

A final important structural difference concerns national policies that may promote or inhibit business-to-business e-commerce. China's attempts to regulate Internet content are well known (Chen, 2001). And differences in national policy regimes have been credited with the greater early success of electronic custom and trade declarations in Singapore than in Hong Kong (Damsgaard and Lyytinen, 1997).

In short, as is the case with B2C e-commerce, structural conditions in Asia lead to significantly different B2B e-commerce business models and patterns of e-commerce activity than can be found in the US. Cultural factors certainly play a role in these outcomes, but they cannot provide as satisfactory an explanation alone as they can in combination with structural conditions.

DISCUSSION AND CONCLUSION

The examples presented above suggest that global e-commerce activity is strongly shaped by structural conditions—physical, social, and economic factors—*in addition to* the dimensions of national culture. Examples of key structural conditions are:

- Financial infrastructure (e.g., electronic payment systems, credit financing)
- Legal and regulatory infrastructures (e.g., consumer protection legislation, taxation)

- National policies about promoting or regulating Internet usage and e-commerce
- Space and logistics (e.g., home size, distance to shopping, transportation, warehousing)
- Telecommunications infrastructure and prices; IT penetration; types of IT use (e.g., PC versus mobile)
- Local business practices (e.g., purchasing, payment, financing)
- Language and education
- Firm size, structure and control systems
- Industry concentration

These structural conditions vary from country to country and even within country.[2] They are not fully captured in measures of national culture (Hofstede, 1983, 1991), and they may not co-vary with measures of national culture. In other words, while the cultural orientations of people in Beijing and Singapore might be similar, the structural conditions in these two locales differ considerably—and so does electronic commerce activity. Therefore, while Hofstede's cultural measures capture to some extent the differences between eastern and western business practices (Davison, 1996), they do not provide adequate insight into *how* (in what ways and the processes by which) and *why* e-commerce activity differs in various parts of the world. For that one also needs an understanding of structural factors.

Just how important it is to look beyond broad characterizations of national culture is amply demonstrated by a study of organizational control practices in Chinese joint ventures: Robins and Zhiang (2000) found significant differences between Sino-American and Sino-Japanese joint ventures, indicating that the multinational parent, not just the local culture, is an important explanatory factor.

The conclusion is that national culture alone does not make a satisfying explanation of e-commerce activity. Further, an accurate understanding of cross-country (and cross-location within countries) electronic commerce behavior requires careful attention to local structural factors. These observations have several implications for future global information management research.

First, the line of argument presented in this paper suggests the value of systematic research on the relationship between structural factors and various measures of e-commerce activity. Further, one wants to know to what extent do structural factors exert an effect *independent of cultural dimensions* on e-commerce activity. One type of study addressing such issues would be a multivariate analysis of individual e-commerce purchasing behavior in different locales with average home size, home Internet access, credit card penetration rates, taxation benefits and cultural dimensions as dependent variables. Another would be a quasi-experimental design in which locales are selected for cultural homogeneity but variation on structural factors—hypotheses about effects of structural factors would be tested by pattern matching.

Second, an exciting direction for future research is the relationship between certain structural conditions and cultural dimensions. For example, to what extent do local business practices and control systems reflect cultural values; to what extent are they independent of cultural values?

In short, structural conditions have important and understudied influences on global e-commerce activity; the study of structural conditions can complement research on cultural factors. Systematic empirical investigation is needed to address this promising line of global information management research.

ENDNOTES

[1] However, this is not the case in Singapore and Hong Kong.

[2] In China, there are vast differences in structural conditions important for e-commerce (e.g., telecommunications access, banking services) between the Southern and Eastern coastal regions and the Northern and Western interior regions.

REFERENCES

Berger, S., & Lester, R K (Eds.). (1997). *Made By Hong Kong*, Oxford, UK: Oxford University Press.

Chen, A. (2001, June 18). Scaling the Wall. *eWeek*. Retrieved August 7, 2001 from http://www.zdnet.com/eweek/stories/general/0,11011,2773643,00.html

Chen, M-Y. (2001). *Inside Chinese Business: A Guide for Managers Worldwide*. Boston, MA: Harvard Business School Press.

Cole, J. I., & Suman, M. (2000). *The UCLA Internet Report: Surveying the Digital Future*. Retrieved August 7, 2001 from University of California, Los Angeles, Center for Communication Policy: http://www.ccp.ucla.edu./pages/internet-report.asp

Damsgaard, Jan, & Kalle Lyytinen. (1997). Hong Kong's EDI Bandwagon: Derailed Or On the Right Track? In T. McMaster, E. Mumford, B. Swanson, B. Warboys, & D. Wastell (Eds.) *Facilitating Technology Transfer through Partnership: Learning From Practice and Research* (pp. 39-63). London: Chapman and Hall.

Davison, R. M. (1996). *National Cultures, Organisational Forms and Group Support Systems*. Retrieved August 7, 2001 from City University of Hong Kong Web site: http://www.is.cityu.edu.hk/Research/Publication/paper/9607.pdf

Dedrick, J., & Kraemer, K. L. (2000). *Japan E-Commerce Report*. Retrieved August 7, 2001 from University of California, Irvine, Center for Research on Information Technology and Organizations (CRITO) Web site: http://www.crito.uci.edu/git/

Dhawan, R., P. Mangaleswaran, A. Padhi, S. Sankhe, K. Schween, & P. Vaish. (2000). The Asian Difference in B2B. *McKinsey Quarterly (Asia)*, 4. Retrieved August 7, 2001 from http://www.mckinseyquarterly.com

Gallupe, R. B., & Tan, F.B. (1999). A Research Manifesto for Global Information Management. *Journal of Global Information Management, 7(3)*, 5-18.

Hempel, P. S., & Chang, C-Y. D. (2000). *The Changing Management Culture of Taiwan: Reconciling Traditional Chinese Management with High-Technology Business.* Working Paper 2000-007, Department of Management, City University of Hong Kong.

Hempel, P. S., & Ying K K. (2001). *B2B e-Commerce in Emerging Economics: i-Metal.com's Nonferrous Metals Exchange in China.* Unpublished paper, City University of Hong Kong.

Hofestede, G. (1983). The Cultural Relativity of Organizational Practices and Theories. *Journal of International Business Studies, 63,* 75-89.

Hofstede, G. (1991). *Cultures and Organizations: Software of the Mind.* New York: McGraw Hill.

Hui, V. (2000, November 10). *Electronic Banking at the Bank of East Asia.* Presentation given at the City University of Hong Kong.

Jordan, E. (2000, October 26). *Leading Edge E-commerce in Australia.* Presentation given at the City University of Hong Kong.

Kaplan, S. & Sawhney, M. (2000). E-hubs: The New B2B Marketplaces, *Harvard Business Review, 78(3)*, 97-200+.

Kuo, E., Choi, A., Mahizhnan, A., Lee, W-P., & Soh, C. (2001). *Singapore Internet Project: Key Findings of 2000 Adult Survey.* Nanyang Technological University.

Lincoln, A. (2000, October). Bank to the Future. [Electronic version]. *CFO Asia.* Retrieved August 7, 2001 from http://www.cfoasia.com/archives/200010-45.htm

Markus, M. L., & Benjamin, R. I. (1996). Change Agentry- The Next IS Frontier. *MIS Quarterly, 20 (4)*, 385-407.

Martinsons, M. G. (Forthcoming). Electronic Commerce in China: Theory and Emerging Success Stories, *Information and Management.*

Martinsons, M. G., & Hempel, P.S. (1995). Chinese Management Systems: Historical and Cross-Cultural Perspectives. *Journal of Management Systems, 7(1),* 1-11.

Orlikowski, W. (1992). The Duality of Technology—Rethinking the Concept of Technology in Organizations. *Organization Science,* 3(3), 398-427.

Robins, J. A., & Zhiang L. (2000). Institutional Influences on Organizational Control: A Comparative Examination of Agency Theory In Sino-Japanese and Sino-American Joint Ventures. *Advances in International Comparative Management, 12*, 119-148.

Seven-Eleven Japan: Blending E-commerce with Traditional Retailing. (2000, May 24). *The Economist*. Retrieved August 7, 2001 from http://www.ebusinessforum. com/index.asp?layout=rich_story&doc_id=3544

Silwa, C. (2001, May 28). China: The Web's Next Frontier, *Computerworld*. Retrieved August 7, 2001 from http://www.computerworld.com/cwi/story/ 0,1199,NAV47_STO60907,00.html

Smith, C. S. (2001, July 6). Across China, New Economy is Being Absorbed Into the Old. *The New York Times on the Web*. Retrieved August 7, 2001 from http:/ /www. nytimes.com

Soh, C., Sia, S-K., & Tay-Yap, J. (2000). Enterprise Resource Planning: Cultural Fits and Misfits: Is ERP a Universal Solution? *Communications of the ACM, 43(4)*, 47-51.

Trepp, L. (2000). *i-Metal.com: China's First Mover in Futures Trading and Spot Procurement of Nonferrous Metals Over the Internet*. Philadelphia, PA: Electronic Market Center, Inc. Retrieved August 7, 2001 from http:// www.netmarketmakers.com

United Nations Population Division. (1998). *Urbanization Prospects 1998 Revision- Key Trends*. Retrieved August 7, 2001 from http://www.undp.org/ popin/wdtrends/wdtrends.htm#Population & Development

Yang, M. (2001). Asia: e-Ready or Not? *MISweb Online*. Retrieved August 7, 2001 from http://www.misweb.com/

Williams, M. (2000, January 6). Seven Eleven Japan, Others to Launch E-Commerce JV. *IDG.net*. Retrieved August 7, 2001 from http://www.idg.net/ ec?idgns_path=% 2Fidgns%2F2000%2F01%2F06%2FSevenEleven JapanOthersToLaunch%2Eshtml

Chapter 3

Social Issues in Electronic Commerce: Implications for Policy Makers

Anastasia Papazafeiropoulou and Athanasia Pouloudi
Brunel University, United Kingdom

The revolutionary development of network technologies launched electronic commerce as a global phenomenon. Consequently, the policy issues that arise from its use create new responsibilities for policy makers world-wide. Apart from the technical (e.g. fast and reliable networks) and regulatory (e.g. legal frameworks and standardization) challenges that need to be tackled there are a number of social concerns that also need consideration. It is important for policy makers to see Internet use and electronic commerce as a social as well as a technical phenomenon. In this paper we examine how social concerns such as trust and digital democracy pertain to all levels of Internet and electronic commerce policy, posing dilemmas and influencing the construction of an effective and socially responsible strategy for electronic commerce.

INTRODUCTION

Policy implementation for electronic commerce is a complex process since policy makers, national governments in their majority, have to act in a fast changing environment. They need to balance special national demands with international cooperation (Papazafeiropoulou and Pouloudi, 2000). One of the areas that policy makers have to tackle is dealing with barriers that have been reported in the adoption of electric commerce today. These barriers are mostly derived from factors such as lack of awareness about the opportunities offered by electronic

Previously Published in the *Information Resources Management Journal, vol.14, no.4*, Copyright © 2001, Idea Group Publishing.

commerce as well as lack of trust toward network security. Additionally the current legislative framework, drawn before the advent of electronic commerce, is perceived as outdated, thus impeding the expansion of on-line transactions. Policy makers, therefore, find it increasingly critical to update commerce legislation (Owens, 1999; Shim et al., 2000; The White House, 1999) and take other measures to facilitate the uptake of electronic commerce.

As the need for appropriate policy measures that support the information society is increasing, it is important to prevent a predominantly technical, commercial or legal approach that neglects the broader social issues related to policy making. To this end, this paper examines social issues related to electronic commerce policy making and is structured as follows. In the next section we present two fundamental social concerns that are related to policy making in electronic commerce: trust and digital democracy. In Section 3 we discuss these concerns in the light of different policy issues arising from the use of network technologies, and in Section 4 we present their implications for policy making in electronic commerce. The paper concludes with the importance of a holistic approach to policy making and suggestions for further research.

SOCIAL CONCERNS

The introduction of technologies such as the Internet in everyday life has resulted in a debate about its relative merits and disadvantages. Some of the social concerns are illustrated in the study conducted by the Stanford Institute for the Quantitative Study for Society (SIQSS, 2000) concerning the social implications of Internet use. The findings of the study indicate that the Internet is an "isolating technology" that could seriously damage the social fabric of communities as users interact physically with other people less. The social implications of the Internet can be witnessed in organizational processes, the nature of work, learning and education, innovation and competition, electronic democracy, privacy and surveillance (Dutton, 1996). This section considers the social concerns related to the use of Internet technologies by focusing on two of the most frequently discussed social issues in electronic commerce. These are *trust*, a social issue underlying the business use of the Internet, and *digital democracy*, a term underlying the use of Internet technology in the society as a whole. The following paragraphs consider each in detail.

Trust

Lack of trust in on-line transactions is one of the main reasons reported for the relatively low electronic commerce adoption today. Trust is a key issue and its existence among the business community and the end consumers will increase the willingness of trading partners to expand their electronic transactions (e.g., Hart and Saunders, 1997; Miles and Snow, 1992; Ratnasingham, 1998; Wilson, 1997). The low level of trust in electronic commerce can be attributed partly to the lack of face-to-face interaction between trading partners in conjunction with the general uncertainty of users in taking advantage of network technologies (Ratnasingham, 1998). According to Johnston (1999), there are a number of actions that can be taken to respond to user uncertainty. First, users should be educated about privacy and security issues. Second, the necessary legislation framework that protects trading partners must be developed. Third, the perceptions about technology as a tool that can threaten trust need to change to acknowledge that technology can also be applied for the users' protection, for example, through the effective use of encryption mechanisms.

Digital Democracy

Information and communication technologies offer opportunities for governments and citizens to be brought into closer dialogue; they also facilitate political organization and debate (Raab, et al., 1996). However, the extent to which the information superhighway can fully enable citizens to participate in this emerging 'digital democracy', has been heavily debated. First, at a conceptual level, our understanding of democracy is "as bounded in time as it is rooted in space" (Nguyen & Alexander, 1996, p. 120), which means that the term digital democracy is inherently problematic in 'cyberspace'. Importantly, there is a concern that if citizens are not able to have access to on-line services, because they do not have the means or the knowledge to do so, existing patterns of inequalities will be reinforced. The digital democracy is threatened by "information aristocracy" (Carter, 1997). In particular, there is evidence of a gender and race gap in the use of the Internet as well as differences for users with different levels of income and education (Hoffman and Novak, 1999; Kouzmin et al, 1999). While policy makers at an international level are concerned about access to electronic commerce, the burden falls mostly upon local authorities, which are responsible for the provision of access to network facilities through the use of public access centers, kiosks or tele-working centers. At a global level, the penetration of electronic commerce in developing countries is also an outstanding issue related to the "haves" and "have-nots" in cyberspace, (e.g. Bhatnagar, 1997; Blanning et al., 1997; Clark and Lai, 1998; Kim and Hong, 1997). Easy global information access, however, is also problematic as it has been described as threatening both cultural identity and the regulatory sovereignty of the state, especially when used in less powerful economies (Shields, 1996). Finally, as privacy protection is a major concern in electronic commerce there is a concern on whether 'cyberspace' can promote democracy while protecting privacy. The free information flow of democracy and the users' need to control the flow of personal data can be seen as zero-sum alternatives that may (or may not) be balanced (Raab, 1997). This generates several policy dilemmas, which are reviewed in the following sections.

EMERGENT POLICY ISSUES

The Internet is the most popular means for the implementation of electronic commerce systems. Its fast expansion in the last decade was exceptional, forcing policy makers to speed up their efforts for its governance and regulation. The policy issues described in this section have to be addressed in order to facilitate the development of a safe and well-defined environment for electronic commerce, addressing the social concerns outlined in the previous section. These policy issues are presented following the six levels of Internet policy architecture including infrastructure, governance, security, privacy, content and commerce. These have been defined by the Global Internet Project (GIP), a group of senior executives from leading companies around the world (Patrick, 1999; www.gip.org). The second part of the section presents the dilemmas in addressing policy issues, leading on to a discussion of the implications for policy makers in the remainder of the paper.

Policy Issues at Six Levels of Internet policy
Infrastructure

The infrastructure level aims at addressing "the challenge of meeting the demand for reliable and scaleable access to the Internet" (Patrick 1999, p. 106). The speed, the quality, the reliability and the cost of the networks used for on-line transactions, are very important factors that can either boost or obstruct evolution of electronic commerce. One of the top priorities of governments is the support of the telecommunication industry so that it can offer better quality services in terms of speed, reliability, continuous access and interconnectivity between sub-networks (Patrick, 1999). The American government, for example, aims at the provision of on-line services to the majority of American households not only through desktop computers connecting to the Internet but also through devices such as television, cellular phones and portable digital assistants (US Department of Commerce, 1998). The liberalization of the telecommunication market is a relevant directive of the European Union (EC, 1997) and OECD (1997b) to their member states. It demonstrates the intention of international policy making organizations to reduce the cost and improve the robustness of the telecommunication infrastructure worldwide.

In relation to the social concerns discussed in the previous section, policies that support the infrastructure level contribute towards better *trust* in terms of Internet performance. The availability of appropriate infrastructure and the capability to access it, however, as a prerequisite for the *digital democracy*, are contingent on the resources available within a particular region or country. Thus, global coverage is a major concern for policy makers today (Hudson, 1999). Within a national context, the quality of the telecommunication infrastructure in rural areas is particularly significant, when the accessibility to alternative means of obtaining information is very limited. Overall, as the role of the nation state declines in providing access to telecommunications networks, it may be up to independent bodies to support citizens gaining access to Internet-delivered services (Keenan & Trotter, 1999). At an international level, also, it may be up to independent bodies and international organizations to facilitate the development of Internet and technological infrastructure in developing countries. National governments also take initiatives to improve the adoption and use of information technologies but they do not always succeed (e.g., Walsham, 1999).

Governance

The Internet is characterized by its ability to expand without central governance. The Internet is the 'place' where the free economy can blossom and this presents immense opportunities for electronic commerce. It is the intention of the policy makers at an international level to support industry leadership and self-regulation for electronic commerce (The White House 1999; EC 1997; OECD, 1997b). Specifically, there is a tendency to minimize government involvement and avoid unnecessary restrictions on electronic commerce.

However, as electronic commerce use becomes mature its international nature creates the need for global governance in certain areas. For example, several legal cases have been reported that involved Web site owners and consumers or other companies. The conflict usually derives from the lack of certainty about where a Web company is physically located and thus under which country's legal system the company works (Aalberts and Townsend, 1998). Taxation is a specific concern for companies that intend to invest in new technologies and for governments that want to control electronic commerce similarly to traditional commerce. There is a wide range of proposals concerning the administration of taxes in electronic commerce (Johnston, 1999; Owens, 1999). At one extreme there is the idea of absolute 'tax-free' electronic commerce that has already been implemented for transactions taking place among US states, until February 1998 when the US public administration reaffirmed its commitment to making cyberspace a free-trade zone (Negroponte, 1999). At the other end there are proposals for introduction of special new taxes for electronic commerce. OECD (1997a) proposes an intermediate solution, directing its members to apply existing tax principles in electronic transactions. OECD, in co-operation with the European Union, the World's

Customs Organization and the business community, has defined a set of framework conditions to govern the taxation of electronic commerce. These are neutrality, effectiveness and fairness, certainty and simplicity, efficiency and flexibility, factors that are naturally important to traditional commerce as well. Thus it is necessary to define the 'rules' that govern electronic commerce and ensure that regulations can be enforced.

Overall, the governance level of Internet policy presents a challenge for national policy makers as they realize it is difficult, if not impossible, to control electronic transactions. Also, it is debatable what is within a specific jurisdiction or how 'net-laws' will be enforced or who will pay for enforcement (Shim et al., 2000). Additionally, policy makers are also keen to promote electronic commerce with minimal intervention, as they want to attract investors that will contribute to economic growth. North American countries, the European Union and Japan for example have realized that it is in their best interest to collaborate in order to create market conditions of *trust*. However, the interests of specific countries may at times prevail, and the compromises reached may be at a cost for *digital democracy*. A characteristic example is the difference between European and American provisions for personal data protection and its impact on electronic transactions between the two areas. This issue is addressed in further detail at the security and privacy levels in the next paragraphs.

Security

Network security and especially Web security is one of the most sensitive issues identified in the electronic commerce literature (e.g., Crocker, 1996; Kosiur, 1997; Liddy, 1996). A recent survey of Australian firms (Dinnie, 1999), "among the world's earliest adopters" of electronic commerce, reports that network security is a continuing concern and companies are more concerned about external threats. The survey reports that "sixteen per cent of firms have suffered, or believe they may have suffered, at least one break-in via the Internet" (p. 112). Despite their perceptions of external threats, however, thirty per cent of businesses admitted that their organization had no formal information security policy. More generally, the anxiety about security is expected to increase in coming years as web-based applications are increasingly used for financial transactions. As the number of computers, networks, data and information multiply every day, the need for better security practices that protect information systems from malicious attacks and at the same time preserve the civil liberties, will increase in the future (Hurley, 1999).

Cryptography is put forward as a powerful technological solution to network fraud. At an international level it can be applied with the collaboration of governments, the business community and trusted third parties (Denning, 1996). The required use of public and private keys in cryptography methods, raises several public policy issues surrounding the encryption of data and who should hold the keys that unlock the encrypted information (Patrick, 1999; Pouloudi, 1997). Policy makers can play an important role in the implementation of a security policy, acting as trusted third parties or defining the legal framework for such organizations (Froomkin, 1996). There are multiple models concerning the role of governments in security policy. At one extreme, public authorities may have ultimate access to information and at the other, they may leave the responsibility for security of the data to the information owner (Patrick, 1999). What seems to be urgently required today is better education and awareness of security of information systems and good security practices for companies and individuals (Hurley, 1999).

Privacy

Computer technologies like the Internet facilitate the exchange of personal information that can be collected, aggregated and sold across the world. As companies can easily take advantage of personal information that becomes accessible on information networks, e.g., through direct marketing (Wang, *et al.,* 1998), several issues are at stake. The most important concern is whether information is collected, aggregated or sold with the individual's explicit consent. There are several private organizations (Better Business Bureau onLine (BBBOnLine), Worldwide Web Consortium (W3C), TRUSTe) that try to address the issue by giving a privacy 'seal' to Web sites that are fulfilling some set criteria of privacy protection. These include the responsibility to make visitors to web sites aware of what data is collected and giving them choice about making this data available to third parties. The TRUSTe white paper (http://www.truste.org/about/about_wp.html) also emphasizes that Web sites bearing their Privacy Seal "must provide reasonable security to protect the data that is collected". Security is seen as the technological aspect of the broader social issues that are related to privacy.

Privacy is particularly important for the protection of sensitive personal data such as medical records, credit records, government data and personal data about children. The US government has taken an untied regulatory approach to protect such information. In other words the aim is to enable Internet users to choose for themselves what level of privacy protection they want (Nelson, 1999). In Europe, in contrast, data protection is stricter and has been articulated at a pan-European level (Allaert & Barber, 1998). In the United States, the EU directive (EC, 1995) has been perceived as being overprotecting for European companies, raising barriers to the free exchange of electronic data between Europe and other countries (Swire and Litan, 1998). Indeed, the European directive on data protection challenged electronic transactions and data exchanges internationally, as it banned the export of personal data from the EU to those countries without strict federal data protection laws. This included the U.S., and resulted in severe trade disputes at an international level, which have been resolved recently with the Safe Harbor Privacy Arrangement. This is a mechanism with which, through an exchange of documents, EU is able to certify that participating U.S. companies meet the EU requirements for adequate privacy protection. Participation in the safe harbor is voluntarily. Privacy advocates, however, argue that privacy is a profound and fundamental concept, hence "it merits extra-ordinary measures of protection and overt support" (Introna, 1997, p. 259).

The political nature of privacy is also evident within national boundaries, in particular in terms of the power that national regulators have: "what we should fear is the growth of government databases" (Singleton, 1998). Privacy therefore clearly raises social concerns in terms of *trust*, *digital democracy* as well as *employment*, particularly in relation to the rights of employers to access or monitor personal information of their employees (ranging from email messages to medical records), often without their explicit consent or even their knowledge. Finally, the difficulties of updating databases and business processes and the challenges to comply at a technical level when using some contemporary information technologies (Lycett & Pouloudi, 2001) signify that privacy protection remains a challenge for policy makers.

Content

As electronic commerce is an international phenomenon it is impossible for policy makers to control the content of the information transferred on-line. While the exposure to all this information can be beneficial, for example expanding people's learning horizons (Forcheri et al., 2000), governments and citizens are concerned about the publication of offensive material (Nelson, 1999). As the complaints from parents and educators about the influence of the Internet on children become more frequent, there are several civil liberties organizations devoted to protecting users from exposure to inappropriate on-line material. Such groups include the Electronic Frontier Foundation (EFF), which supports legal and legislative action to protect the civil liberties of on-line users and the Computer Professionals for Social Responsibility (CPSR), which aims to protect privacy and civil liberties. The World Wide Web Consortium (W3C) has developed a technical platform that allows user-defined, customized access to the Internet (Patrick, 1999; www.w3.organisation/PICS) and has enabled the creation of rating services and filtering software, for use by concerned parents. While the need for filtering of some information is generally considered as appropriate, there are also attempts at censorship. For example certain Asian countries place restrictions on the use of the Internet. The use of censorship on the information highway is debatable, both in terms of its technological feasibility but also in terms of its moral foundation (Ebbs & Rheingold, 1997).

Other content related issues in electronic commerce are the protection of copyright and intellectual property rights. The essence of copyright is to prevent the unauthorized copying, but works stored in a digital format can easily be copied or altered, while they can also be transmitted speedily through electronic networks (Brett, 1999). The practical problems that owners of digital data face are very important for governments trying to apply or extend existing copyright laws to digital means. At an international level the World Intellectual Property Organization (WIPO) facilitates the protection of property rights. According to its general director, Dr. Kamil Idris, the organization's aim is to ensure that "expertise is provided when laws or systems need upgrading to take into account novel areas of invention (such as providing protection for the fruits of genetic research) or of medium (such as the Internet)". As with other policy issues, intellectual property involves multiple stakeholders with different interests (Radcliffe, 1999), which makes it difficult to resolve at a global level.

Underlying the discussion in terms of content are also issues of *trust*, in terms of access to 'suitable' material but also in terms of authenticity and issues related to the concept *digital democracy*, depending on who, if any, decides what constitutes 'suitable' material.

Commerce

Electronic commerce is at the top of the policy architecture pyramid of the Global Internet Project, as it is perceived to be a critical factor driving the growth of the Internet. Although electronic commerce has revolutionized the way of conducting business, it is still a business activity that has to conform to certain rules and work under specific standards (Negroponte, 1999). The European Union was the first official body that considered a supranational policy on electronic commerce, in its effort to advance the integration process and to create a single market (Mc Gowan, 1998). However, there are several organizations working at a supranational level trying to enable global seamless communication such as the International Organization for Standardization (ISO) and the World Trade Organization (WTO). This is because standardization is recognized as an important issue in electronic commerce, since the establishment of EDI applications (e.g., Chatfield and Bjorn-Andersen, 1998; Faltch, 1998; Sokol, 1995; Tan, 1998). Standardization however can be problematic, as it needs to balance multiple interests in an area where competition has international dimensions and differs considerably from traditional commerce. The extent to which certain stakeholders are privileged has an impact on the role of electronic commerce in facilitating the *digital democracy*. The importance of *trust* at this level cannot be understated since, as discussed in Section 2, it is one of the main reasons why electronic commerce has not reached its current potential.

The discussion in the previous five levels of the policy architecture demonstrates that issues of trust are relevant at all levels and indeed underpin the development and use of electronic commerce. The problem is that most of these policy issues are related to social concerns and cannot be easily resolved as they bring about conflicts amongst stakeholder groups and policy dilemmas. These dilemmas are discussed in detail below in the context of electronic commerce policy-making.

Dilemmas in addressing policy issues

Previous research has argued that the policy objective of promoting deregulation and competition is in conflict with other policy priorities, in particular the desire to provide open networks and open access and the aspiration to provide universal service to citizens (Graham, 1995). As electronic commerce expands, the dilemmas for the stakeholders of the information society increase. The review of policy issues at different levels in the previous section has revealed some of the dilemmas that policy makers face today:

- Should governments give priority to the protection of national identity and language or to international compliance?
- Should they promote their own interests or provide assistance to developing countries?
- Is governance about protection or restriction? (For example, at an individual level: is censorship desirable? At a business level: is taxation desirable?)
- Where should priority be given: to the protection of personal data or to competitiveness (to the extent that the free exchange of information and personal data supports electronic transactions and business practices)?
- What is more important, data and intellectual property protection or the free exchange of ideas and data?

These dilemmas relate to the appropriate use of regulation, although in some cases policy makers may have little choice as only some options are realistic (e.g., the Internet is used even though the legal context is unstable). Thus, one important observation is that some dilemmas may no longer be a matter of choice, particularly for less powerful stakeholders, such as individuals, or governments of developing countries. A further observation is that in many cases these dilemmas imply *a conflict between the commercial and social interests of various stakeholder groups*. However, it is very difficult to draw some general conclusions about when either interest is at stake. Research in management (e.g., Pettigrew, 1985) and information systems (e.g., Walsham, 1993) as well as in law studies (e.g., as evident in the importance of case law) has stressed the importance of *context*. However, in 'cyberspace' the context, whether temporal or spatial, is elusive, making policy making for electronic commerce more challenging. In view of these issues, the following section presents implications for policy makers, with emphasis on the policies that are relevant at the business and the societal level.

IMPLICATIONS FOR POLICY MAKERS

The challenge that policy makers face today in order to implement an efficient electronic commerce policy while addressing the dilemmas outlined above is twofold. Firstly, they need to provide the business community with a robust technical infrastructure and an efficient legislation framework. Secondly, they need to accommodate the social concerns rising from the use of electronic commerce, in order to create a 'digital literate' society that will fully exploit the technology at hand while preserving their social interests and cultural identities.

A very important aspect of a national electronic commerce strategy is diffusion of knowledge to business and society at large. Damsgaard and Lyytinen (1998) use, in their analysis on the diffusion of EDI (business-to-business electronic commerce), six government strategies defined by King et al. (1994). These are knowledge building, knowledge deployment, subsidy, mobilization, innovation directive, and standard setting. We extend these strategies for the diffusion of electronic commerce, where apart from business, individuals are also the targets of the government intervention. Thus, a grid can be created (see Table 1) with the combination of these strategies and their target groups (business, society).

Companies are usually the direct beneficiaries of electronic commerce policies. This is why all the diffusion strategies are applicable (see far right column in Table 1). Policy makers try to persuade enterprises to invest in new technologies and take advantage of the opportunities the new means can offer. The governments may use a great number of the strategies to influence companies and help them in the implementation of electronic commerce technologies and practices. Companies can first be made aware of the new technologies (*knowledge deployment*), receive

Table 1: Target groups of an electronic commerce strategy

Policies	Individuals-Societal level	Companies-Business level
Knowledge building	✔	✔
Knowledge deployment	✔	✔
Subsidy		✔
Mobilization		✔
Innovation directive		✔
Standard/regulation setting		✔

financial support for investing in new technologies (*subsidy*), be encouraged to use technology in the 'best way' (*mobilization*), be provided with examples of electronic commerce use (*information directive*) and finally follow standards (*regulation setting*). This part of the electronic commerce diffusion practice is related to technical and commercial aspects, which as we will explain in the next paragraph can be conflicting with social issues.

Individuals acting as consumers (such customers of virtual stores) or citizens (as users of on-line government services) are in need of information. Governments can use traditional means such as the media to make their wide audience aware of the usefulness of the new medium and build confidence in electronic commerce transactions. *Knowledge deployment* and *mobilization* are the strategies that can best fit government's intention to create awareness about electronic commerce, as well as about the rights of individuals in this new environment. Issues such as awareness about privacy protection and trust toward electronic means should be considered by policy makers when they apply knowledge building and deployment practices. The education of the public on one hand can help the electronic commerce marketplace to reach a critical mass of users. On the other hand, a "digital literate" society can use electronic means to perform "electronic activism" and express disappointment about business practices (see, for example, Badaracco and Useem, 1997). Additionally, they might refuse the exchange of personal data through electronic means, although this is a practice that is very useful to companies for marketing purposes. Thus, regulators should balance the needs of the business community with the social concerns related to the use of electronic means. It is expected that when the social issues such as trust and digital democracy are addressed satisfactorily, electronic commerce is more likely to become the predominant business practice.

The "education" of individuals within the business environment (business level) is essential. In this field the help of professional bodies such as chambers of commerce and trade associations is essential. While most of policy research concentrates on the role of governments or international organizations, the role of players, such as trade associations, that can act as policy intermediaries is very important: they have knowledge of the local context and thus can complement the general national or international policies. As discussed earlier in the paper, other policy intermediaries that become increasingly involved in policy issues in the information society include independent private organizations as well as civil liberties and professional groups who wish to promote the interest of a particular group or the net-citizens at large. Schools and universities also face pressures to support the 'workforce of the future' and try to promote the use of information and communication technologies, thus contributing to knowledge building and deployment strategies. Finally, the Internet empowers individuals to draw their own policies at a micro-level, e.g., choosing as parents which Internet sites they allow their children to access, deciding whether to make their personal information available and so on. While the Internet enables people as citizens and consumers to take action (e.g., Badaracco & Useem, 1997), people are not necessarily aware of the opportunities and risks of cyberspace or they may not have the power and access to make a difference, hence the importance of knowledge building and deployment strategies. Policy makers, whether local or national, government or private, need to recognize the prevalence and importance of social issues and encourage the debate for appropriate policymaking among stakeholders.

CONCLUSIONS

Policy makers have recognized the viability of electronic commerce and the opportunities it offers for business and citizens. While several ethical and security issues arise from the use of the new technologies, there is a general consensus that the benefits are substantial and justify the investment in electronic commerce. There are several efforts in this direction by policy makers at a national and international level. The paper has argued that technology alone is not sufficient for the successful implementation of complex electronic commerce strategies but the examination of social and political issues is crucial for a holistic approach on the subject. Indeed there are several dilemmas related to policy issues, making the role of the policy makers critical. We considered a general framework for policy making that could be used at a national or international level as a starting point for considering social issues in the context of electronic commerce strategies.

Further research in the area may include the investigation of electronic commerce policies implemented in different national settings and social environments since, in practice, different countries have different priorities. The case of developing countries would be of particular interest as technical infrastructure and stakeholder awareness and involvement can be substantially different. Research also needs to be continued in specific areas that are affected by the extensive use of electronic commerce. Because of their social importance, of particular interest are the areas of health and education where issues of Internet use and electronic commerce become increasingly relevant (e.g., through tele-health or distance learning applications). A study of alternative national policies in these areas can lead to an informative debate about the underlying assumptions concerning the duties and social responsibility of policy makers towards different stakeholder groups.

ACKNOWLEDGMENTS

The financial support of EPSRC (grant GR/N03242) is gratefully acknowledged.

REFERENCES

Aalberts, R., and Townsend, A. (1998). The threat of long-arm jurisdiction to electronic commerce. *Communications of the ACM*, 41(12), 15-20.

Allaert, F.-A., & Barber, B. (1998). Some systems implications of EU data protection directive. *European Journal of Information Systems*, 7 (1), 1-4.

Badaracco, J. L., Jr, & Useem, J. V. (1997). The Internet, Intel and the Vigilante Stakeholder. *Business Ethics: A European Review*, 6 (1), 18-29.

Bhatnagar, S. (1997). Electronic commerce in India: The untapped potential. *Electronic Markets*, 7(2), 22-24.

Blanning, R., Bui, T., and Tan, M. (1997). National information infrastructure in Pacific Asia. *Decision Support Systems*, 21, 215-227.

Brett, H. (1999). Copyright in a digital age. Masters of the wired world, A. Leer, ed., Financial Times Pitman Publishing, London, 162-171.

Carter, D. (1997). 'Digital democracy' or 'information aristocracy' economic regeneration and the information economy. The Governance of Cyberspace, B. Loader, ed., Routledge, London, 136-152.

Chatfield, A., and Bjorn-Andersen, N. (1998). Reengineering with EDI. A Trojan horse in circumventing non-tariff barriers to trade. EDI and Data Networking in the Public Sector, K. V. Andersen, ed., Kluwer Academic publishers, 155-172.

Clark, J., and Lai, V. (1998). Internet comes to Morocco. *Communications of the ACM*, 41(2), 21-23.

Damsgaard, J., and Lyytinen, K. (1998). Governmental intervention in the Diffusion of EDI: Goals and conflicts. EDI and Data Networking in the Public Sector, K. V. Andersen, ed., Kluwer Academic publishers, 13-41.

Daniel, J. (1999). The rise of the mega-university. Masters of the wired world, A. Leer, ed., Financial Times Pitman Publishing, London, 333-342.

Dinnie, G. (1999). The Second Annual Global Information Security Survey. *Information Management & Computer Security*, 7 (3), 112-120.

Doukidis, G., Poulymenakou, A., Terpsidis, I., Themistocleous, M., and Miliotis, P. (1998). The Impact of the Development of Electronic Commerce on the Employment Situation in European Commerce. Athens University of Economics and Business, Athens.

Dutton, W. H. (Ed.). (1996). *Information and Communication Technologies: Visions and Realities*. Oxford: Oxford University Press.

Ebbs, G., & Rheingold, H. (1997). Censorship on the information highway. *Internet Research: Electronic Networking Applications and Policy*, 7 (1), 59-60.

EC. (1995). Directive 95/46/EC of the European Parliament and the Council of 24 October 1995 on the protection of individuals with regard to the processing of personal data and on the free movement of such data. *Official Journal of the European Communities*, L281(23 Nov 1995), 31.

EC. (1997). A European Initiative in Electronic Commerce' (COM (97) 157 final), EC (European Commission), Brussels.

Faltch, M. (1998). EDI in the Public Sector: Building on lessons from the private sector. EDI and Data Networking in the Public Sector, K. V. Andersen, ed., Kluwer Academic publishers.

Forcheri, P., Molfino, M. T., & Quarati, A. (2000). ICT driven individual learning: new opportunities and perspectives. *Educational Technology & Society*, 3 (1), 51-61.

Froomkin, A. (1996). The essential role of Trusted Third Parties in Electronic Commerce. Readings in Electronic Commerce, R. Kalakota and A. Whinston, eds., Addison-Wesley.

Graham, A. (1995). Public policy and the information superhighway: the scope for strategic intervention, co-ordination and top-slicing. In R. Collins & J. Purnell (Eds.), *Managing the information society* (pp. 30-44). London: Institute for public policy research

Hart, P., and Saunders, C. (1997). Power and trust critical factors in the adoption and use of electronic data interchange. *Organization Science*, 8(1), 23-41.

HCWD. (2000). Work Trends Survey, Nothing but Net: American workers and the Information Economy, Heldrich Center for Workforce Development, 10 February 2000.

Hoffman, D., and Novak, T. (1999). The evolution of the digital divide: Examining the relationship of race to Internet access and usage over time. Conference on *Understanding the Digital Economy: Data, Tools and Research*, 25-26 May 1999, Washington, USA.

Hudson, H. (1999). Access to the digital economy: issues in rural and developing regions. Conference on *Understanding the Digital Economy: Data, Tools and Research*, 25-26 May 1999, Washington, USA.

Hurley, D. (1999). Security and privacy laws. The showstoppers of the Global Information Society. Masters of the wired world, A. Leer, ed., Financial Times Pitman Publishing, London, 247-260.

Introna, L. D. (1997). Privacy and the computer: why we need privacy in the information society. *Metaphilosophy*, 28 (3), 259-275.

Johnston, D. (1999). Global electronic commerce-realizing the potential. Masters of the wired world, A. Leer, ed., Financial Times Pitman Publishing, London, 228-237.

Keenan, T. P., & Trotter, D. M. (1999). The changing role of community networks in providing citizen access to the Internet. *Internet Research: Electronic Networking Applications and Policy*, 9 (2), 100-108.

Kim, E., and Hong, P. (1997). The government's role in diffusion of EC in Korea. *Electronic Markets*, 7(2), 6-8.

King, J., Gurbaxani, V., Kraemer, K., McFarlan, F., Raman, F., and Yap, F. W. (1994). Institutional factors in information technology innovation. *Information Systems Research*, 5(2), 139-169.

Kouzmin, A., Korac-Kakabadse, N., & Korac-Kakabadse, A. (1999). Globalization and information technology: vanishing social contracts, the "pink collar" workforce and public policy challenges. *Women in Management Review*, 14 (6), 230-251.

Lycett, M.G, & Pouloudi, A. (2001) Component-based development: issues of data protection. In Dhillon, G. (ed.) *Social responsibility in the information age*. Hershey: Idea Group Publishing (Forthcoming).

Martin, J. (1999). Building the cyber-corporation. Masters of the wired world, A. Leer, ed., Financial Times Pitman Publishing, London, 324-332.

Mc Gowan, L. (1998). Protecting competition in a global market: the pursuit of an international competition policy. *European Business Review*, 98(6), 382-339.

Miles, R., and Snow, C. (1992). Causes of failure in network organizations. *California Management Review*, summer, 53-72.

Murison-Bowie, S. (1999). Forms and functions of digital content in education. Masters of the wired world, A. Leer, ed., Financial Times Pitman Publishing, London, 142-151.

Negroponte, N. (1999). Being digital in the wired world. Masters of the wired world, A. Leer, ed., Financial Times Pitman Publishing, London, 386-394.

Nelson, M. (1999). Politics and policy-making in the electronic marketplace. Masters of the Wired world, A. Leer, ed., Financial Times Pitman Publishing, London, 261-269.

Nguyen, D. T., & Alexander, J. (1996). The coming of cyberspacetime and the end of the polity. In R. Shields (Eds.), *Cultures of Internet: virtual spaces, real histories, living bodies* (pp. 99-124). London: Sage.

OECD. (1997a). The Communication Revolution and Global Commerce: Implications for tax policy and administration, OECD (Organization for Economic Co-operation and Development).

OECD. (1997b). Global Information infrastructure-global information society (GII-GIS), Policy requirements, OECD (Organization for Economic Co-operation and Development).

Owens, J. (1999). Electronic commerce: taxing times. Masters of the wired world, A. Leer, ed., Financial Times Pitman Publishing, London, 286-295.

Papazafeiropoulou, A., and Pouloudi, A. (2000). The Government's Role in Improving Electronic Commerce Adoption. In H.R. Hansen et al., (Eds.) Proceedings of the European Conference on Information Systems 2000 vol. 1, (pp. 709-716). July 3-5. Vienna, Austria.

Patrick, J. (1999). The opportunity and the challenge to sustain rapid Internet growth. Masters of the wired world, A. Leer, ed., Financial Times Pitman Publishing, London, 105-112.

Pettigrew, A. M. (1985). Contextualist research and the study of organisational change processes. In E. Mumford, R. Hirschheim, G. Fitzgerald, & T. Wood-Harper (Eds.), *Research Methods in Information Systems* (pp. 53-78). Amsterdam: Elsevier Science Publishers, North-Holland.

Raab, C. (1997). Privacy, democracy, information. The Governance of cyberspace, B. Loader, ed., Routledge, London, 155-174.

Raab, C., Bellamy, C., Taylor, J., Dutton, W. H., & Peltu, M. (1996). The Information Polity: Electronic Democracy, Privacy, and Surveillance. In W. H. Dutton (Eds.), *Information and Communication Technologies* (pp. 283-299). Oxford: Oxford University Press.

Radcliffe, M. (1999). Intellectual property and the global information infrastructure. Masters of the wired world, A. Leer, ed., Financial Times Pitman Publishing, London, 105-112.

Ratnasingham, P. (1998). The importance of trust in electronic commerce. *Internet research: Electronic Networking Applications and Policy*, 8(4), 313-321.

Shade, L. R. (1996). Is there Free Speech on the Net? Censorship in the Global Information Infrastructure. Cultures of Internet Virtual Spaces, Real Histories, Living Bodies, R. Shields, ed., Sage, London.

Shields, R. (Ed.). (1996). *Cultures of Internet: virtual spaces, real histories, living bodies*. London: Sage.

Shim, J. P., Simkin, M. G., & Bartlett, G. W. (2000). NetLaw. *Communications of the Association for Information Systems*, 4 (4).

Singleton, S. (1998). *Privacy as censorship: a skeptical view of proposals to regulate privacy in the private sector* (Cato Policy Analysis No. 295).

SIQSS. (2000). Internet and society, Stanford Institute for the Quantitative Study for Society, 17 February 2000.

Sokol, P. (1995). *From EDI to Electronic Commerce*, McGraw-Hill.

Swire, P. P., and Litan, R. E. (1998). *None of your business. World Data Flows, Electronic Commerce, and the European Privacy Directive*, Brookings Institution Press, Washington, D.C.

Tan, M. (1998). Government and private sector perspective of EDI: The case of TradeNet EDI and Data Networking in the Public Sector, K. V. Andersen, ed., Kluwer Academic Publishers, 131-153.

The White House. (1999). Facilitating the growth of electronic commerce, The White House, Washington.

US Department of Commerce. (1998). The Emerging Digital Economy, US Department of Commerce, Washington.

Walsham, G. (1993). *Interpreting Information Systems in Organizations*. Chichester: Wiley.

Walsham, G. (1999). GIS for district-level administration in India: problems and opportunities. *MIS Quarterly*, 23 (1), 39-66.

Wang, H., Lee, M. K. O., & Wang, C. (1998). Consumer privacy concerns about internet marketing. *Communications of the ACM*, 41 (3), 63-70.

Wilson, S. (1997). Certificates and trust in electronic commerce. *Information Management & Computer Security*, 5(5), 175-181.

Chapter 4

Identifying Motivations for the Use of Commercial Web Sites

Thomas F. Stafford
Texas Woman's University, USA

Marla Royne Stafford
University of North Texas, USA

The uses and gratifications theoretical framework has continued to prove useful in the study of new and emerging media. In previous research on television as a medium, motivations for media use have been grouped into either process gratifications (motivations associated with using the medium, like channel surfing) or content gratifications (motivations related to information or entertainment delivered by the medium, like watching the evening news for information). This study applies the uses and gratifications perspective to better understand the factors motivating commercial Web site use, and identifies a new media use gratification unique to the Internet: socialization (using the medium to communicate with people). Through the cooperation of two major on-line companies, this research reports the results of a two-part study that begins with the identification of 179 motivations for Web use and subsequently reduces those to five primary underlying factors. These factors are discussed and related to three key indicators: frequency of Web use, frequency of computer use, and affinity with the computer. Implications for new social gratifications for Internet use are discussed, and directions for future research are proposed.

Previously Published in the *Information Resources Management Journal, vol.14, no.1*, Copyright ©
2001, Idea Group Publishing.

INTRODUCTION

Information forms the underpinnings of modern society (Ball-Rokeach & Reardon, 1988; Rogers, 1986), and since media are required for the transmission of information at any level other than the interpersonal, the new medium represented by the World Wide Web might be considered the vanguard of the information society (Stafford & Stafford, 1998). The marketing strategies of industry are evolving into a mediated process that will support the commercial viability of "segments of one" in the form of direct-to-consumer commerce over computer networks (Rogers, 1986; Sheth, 1992). As this evolution takes place, the marketing communication flows that support commercial activity are reversing from marketer-consumer to consumer-marketer (Sheth, 1992); consumers are beginning to seek out the companies and products that interest them rather than relying on traditional mass marketing activities to inform and persuade them about opportunities.

As this idea of the segment of one develops in practice, it seems clear that the World Wide Web will present potent capabilities for reaching and commercially serving consumers (Drèze & Zufryden, 1997). However, throughout this evolutionary process, it also seems clear that marketers must begin asking questions about the unique characteristics of this new commercial medium; one critical question will concern the nature of motivations, which bring consumers to *utilize* this new medium for commercial purposes (Stafford & Stafford, 1998). This consideration implies not only a need to understand what might motivate consumers to attend to marketing efforts on the Web, but also what might motivate them to use commercial Web sites, in general. In short, what are consumers' uses for, and associated gratifications in use of, commercial Web sites?

The Internet is experiencing phenomenal growth; it is growing so fast that researchers have a hard time simply keeping up with its current size and likely future growth. In previous years, the growth rate was estimated at between ten percent (Rubenstein, 1995) and twenty percent *per month* (Thomsen, 1997), with early estimates of the Internet audience suggesting that there were between 30 and 50 million users (Fox, 1995; Kambil, 1995). Audience size was expected to be near 150 million by the millennium (Barker & Groenne, 1997), but more current reports (Applegate, McFarlan & McKenney, 1999) placed 1995 audience levels at 40 million, with 100 million consumers logged on in 1998 and estimates of one billion Internet users by 2005. As of 1999, at least one home in four in the U.S. had Internet access (Clark, 1999), and the number of registered Internet commerce sites nearly tripled, from 600,000 to 1.7 million, in a one-year period monitored between 1996 and 1997 (Applegate et al., 1999).

This combined pattern of growth among both consumers and businesses in the use of the Internet underscores its obvious utility for making connections between buyers and sellers. The Web promises to be a potent marketing vehicle, combining the power of promotional communications with the instant gratification of on-line purchases. A better understanding of the motivations which bring consumers to specific sites and the uses consumers might make of those sites can assist marketers in the design of more effective and compelling offerings in the new Internet medium. Consequently, the overall purpose of this paper is to report a study that examines consumer motivations that drive Web site use.

MOTIVATIONS FOR WEB USE

Previous research suggests that motivations for the use of media, in general, tend to be dichotomous, split between what are known as process and content gratifications. The preference for media content (i.e., a content gratification) might be analogous to a television watcher who wishes to watch the nightly news to learn about local events, while television watchers who routinely video tape shows in order to enjoy the ability to fast forward through commercials in later viewing are motivated by the actual *use* of the medium — a process gratification (Stafford & Stafford, 1996). Correspondingly, in the Internet medium, some people may enjoy the *process* of randomly browsing the Web for enjoyment (Hoffman & Novak, 1996), while others may prefer to seek out and use specific Internet sites primarily to access site-related informational *content* (Stafford & Stafford, 1998). These are the modern analogs of process and content gratifications in the new Internet medium.

In the formative days of uses and gratifications research, McGuire (1974) noted that it seemed less important to know how a user came *to* a medium than to understand how the medium could *hold* a user once browsing had its intended effect, and Internet scholars voice this same concern with regard to the "holding power" of Web site content (Barker & Groenne, 1997). Hence, while browsing might be considered a general motivation for Internet use, what a commercial Web site specifically offers in terms of content appears to be a key factor that will determine if that site has influence with potential consumers.

USES AND GRATIFICATIONS FOR WEB SITES

In the Internet marketplace, understanding the motivations which bring consumers to a site, can be a success characteristic, since the "segment of one" approach can only be profitable if a marketer can reliably attract and serve *numerous* individual customers (Stafford & Stafford, 1998). Hence, knowledge of what consumers desire and benefit from in accessing commercial Web sites will provide Internet marketers with the ability to better [more profitably] serve their audiences. To that end, uses and gratifications theory can be diagnostic in understanding consumer motivations for using the Web (Newhagen & Rafaeli, 1996; Rafaeli, 1988).

Some say that the Web will simply serve as an additional tool to be integrated with traditional advertising and marketing processes (Peterson, Balasubramanian & Bronnenberg, 1997; Philport & Arbittier, 1997). Others consider the Internet to be a genuinely new medium for communication between buyers and sellers, and suggest that the uses and gratifications approach (U&G) will be useful for examining emerging trends in the commercial use of the Web (Eighmey, 1997b; Newhagen & Rafaeli, 1996). U&G theory has already been demonstrated in business-to-business Internet applications (Eighmey, 1997a; 1997b), and preliminary U&G work on consumer Web site applications has shown much promise (e.g., Stafford & Stafford, 1998).

USES AND GRATIFICATIONS FOR MEDIA

The basic premise of the U&G paradigm focuses on what people do *with* the mass media (Klapper, 1963). It has long been known that individuals have particular motives for media use (Katz, 1959), and that individuals' media choices are motivated by particular self-defined uses and goals (Lin, 1977). In the case of the Internet, U&G provides the theoretical framework for understanding motivations that drive Web use.

The Active Audience

A basic tenet of uses and gratifications theory is the active audience (Katz, Blumler & Gurevitch, 1974; Rubin, 1981), and this concept of active involvement is particularly important when investigating the emerging Internet medium, where communication is best conceptualized as a *reversed* flow, and the individual user controls the process by simple virtue of initiating access (Stafford & Stafford, 1998). To paraphrase Klapper, what people do with the Web is to use it to their own *personal* ends.

Active audiences are selective and make their own choices (Levy & Windahl, 1984), so understanding the activities prized by audience members is critical, since these activities are representative of the underlying motivations which influence selective and individual media access. Hence, the Web site marketer is best served by a clear understanding of those activities and motivations, which influence audience members who electronically access and use Internet resources. Audience activity is axiomatic in emerging Internet media—Web sites are *designed* for active use, since undirected viewing does not engage search engines or access information packets (Stafford & Stafford, 1998).

Content and Process Gratifications

As noted previously, motivations to access media are generally considered to be either content related or process related. Content gratification includes *use* of the messages carried by the medium, and process gratification relates to enjoyment of the *act* of using the medium, as opposed to interest in its content (Cutler & Danowski, 1980). While it has been posited that that the mere act of Web surfing, itself, is inherently gratifying (Hoffman & Novak, 1996), there currently is a great deal of concern about Web site content, with indications that users may be quite motivated by content in their choice of specific sites to visit, as opposed to the recreational act of browsing (Drèze & Zufryden, 1997; McDonald, 1997; Stafford & Stafford, 1998). In short, it may be that what a site offers content-wise may be the attraction, which serves to bring consumers to the site, so that commercial transactions might take place.

Potential Factors Motivating Web Users

According to Stafford and Stafford (1998), Web site use might be character-ized initially by process gratifications in recognition of the "Web surfing" phenom-enon which has the potential to expose new users to site content. However, while initial and accidental exposure could often be due to some random browsing effect, content gratifications seem more likely to represent the reason for continued site access, a perspective in line with McGuire's (1974) "holding power" arguments.

Aimless surfing is an apt Internet characterization of McGuire's process gratification, but bookmarking a site might be more representative of motivations arising from content gratifications. When a user finds a site compelling enough to mark the return passage for a later visit, this is probably indicative of strong content interest. Researchers have expressed concern about the ability to hold the attention of Web site users (Barker & Groenne, 1997), and it appears that site designers should be working on ways to increase a user's involvement with Web sites--motivating users to use sites actively and mark them for additional later use, rather than working out ways to enhance the users' browsing experience.

Researchers have already compared the Web to television in terms of potential effects and uses (Eighmey, 1997b; McDonald, 1997), an ironic analogy, since what is known about uses and gratifications theory comes from studies of television in its infancy (Stafford & Stafford, 1996). In some cases, the television metaphor is directly applicable, as in the case of Eighmey (1997a; 1997b), who investigated corporate Web sites to determine user motivations with scales developed in earlier U&G studies of television. Certainly, television research has provided a broad understanding of general commercial media user motivations (Rubin, 1981), and the broad paradigm of uses and gratifications arising from these previous media studies can be adapted very nicely in modern application (e.g., Eighmey, 1997b; Newhagen & Rafaeli, 1996; Peterson et al., 1997). Yet, relying on methods based only on commercial television research may limit the understanding of Web-based motivations. In short, there has been little empirical work to specifically adapt the U & G perspective to commercial Web use. To that end, the objectives of this study are:

1) to develop a U & G approach specifically for examining the use of the World Wide Web.

2) to identify key factors representing consumer motivations for utilizing specific Web sites.

3) to link these factors to key indicators related to the computer and the Web.

METHOD

As demonstrated in previous television studies, the general approach to building a U&G profile is to determine key motivations for using (i.e., gratifications sought from) a particular medium. The current research accomplished this through a traditional factor analytical procedure, which is consistent with the work of Bantz (1982) and Levy and Windahl (1984). First, a list of descriptors that were representative of Web use and gratification were identified. Second, principal components analysis was used to reduce this list of descriptors into key underlying motivation dimensions.

In this research design, the unit of analysis was at the individual level, concerning user motivations to access Internet resources. The sampling frame of each of the two parts of the study consisted of current Web site users who self-selected themselves for participation in a convenience sample. Non-response issues were not feasible to address, given the self-selection process and our commitment to participating site operators to not contact their Web site visitors. However, given the richness of the actual site user data, the tradeoffs involved were considered reasonable in exchange for access to current customers of Internet Service Providers (Benbasat & Zmud, 1999).

PART 1

The first part of the study sought to develop a list of descriptive adjectives corresponding to the specific motivations of Web users. In order to accomplish this, cooperation was obtained from HotWired, a major Internet-themed Web site.

Table 1: Initial Motivations Items Identified in Stage 1

Item	Overall Frequency of Response
Information	114
Email	49
Research	45
News	41
Software	31
Chatting	24
Entertainment	24
Communication	23
Fun	20
Access	17
Work	15
People	13
Web Sites	12
Speed	12
Updates	12
Freedom	11
Interaction	11
Games	11
Knowledge	11
Surfing	11
New	10
Technology	9
News Groups	9
Resources	9
Education	8
Interesting	8
Easy	8
Stocks	7
Answers	7
Browsing	6
Variety	6
Learning	6
Weather	6
Progressive	5
Friends	5
Shopping	5
Search Engines	5
Relaxing	4
Sports	4
Ideas	4
Money	4
Searching	4
Current	4
Homework	4
Government	4

HotWired agreed to place an open-ended questionnaire on their site, and this questionnaire was available for one week to all individuals signing on to the HotWired site; registered site users self-selected themselves for participation.

The questionnaire included four open-ended questions that were designed to elicit a thorough list of uses and gratifications associated with the site. As proposed by Szalay and Deese (1978) and Friedmann and Fox (1989), word association techniques help in understanding the cognitive schemata of subjects. To obtain the most thorough list possible, four questions were asked to capture all potential uses and gratifications of respondents. These four questions were: 1) What is the first thing that comes to mind when you think about what you enjoy most when accessing the Web? 2) What other words describe what you enjoy about interacting with the Web? 3) Using single, easy-to-understand terms, what do you use the Web for? and 4) What on-line activities are most important to you?

Results

A total of 98 individuals completed the questionnaire during the week. To encourage ready participation, personal information was not solicited, so demographic characteristics cannot be reported; however, relatively recent information on Web users suggests that the average Web site visitor has a college degree (67%), is reasonably affluent ($69,000 average income), and is married with children (Gupta, 1997).

The respondents provided a total of 179 individual descriptive terms. Of these 179 items, 45 were mentioned a total of four times or more. These items and their total number of mentions are shown in Table 1. The other 134 items were mentioned three times or less. To maintain a manageable number of items in the subsequent analysis, the 45 items mentioned four times or more were used in the questionnaire for the second part of the research.

PART 2

The Questionnaire

A questionnaire was developed that included the 45 items identified in the first stage of the research. For each of the 45 items, respondents were instructed to indicate their perceived level of importance for each item with regard to their motivations in accessing the Web. A scale of one to seven, with seven being the most important, was used.

To better understand the different motivations related to use of the technological interface with the Internet (i.e., personal computers), three additional measures were included in the questionnaire. The first was a five-item "affinity for the computer" measure adapted from Rubin's (1981; 1984) affinity for television scale. The second measure was a single item that assessed frequency of Web use, and the last measure was a single item that captured frequency of computer use.

The Sample

Digital Marketing Services (DMS), an America Online subsidiary, agreed to participate in this research project. DMS administers AOL's on-line marketing research, and is actively engaged in the determination of motivations for commercial Internet use. The questionnaire was placed in the Opinion Place section of the America Online member services screen. Individuals were randomly selected from a pool of customer volunteers who were compensated for their participation with free on-line time for use in their AOL accounts. The questionnaire was active for this data collection over a one-week time period. This was a convenience sample, even though subjects assigned to this task were randomly selected from a pool of available respondents for projects that DMS was administering. Members of the Opinion Place participant pool at AOL self-select themselves for participation in researcher activities in exchange for a reward, so the construction of a sample from this pool was not truly random.

A total of 343 usable on-line questionnaires were collected. The subjects ranged in age from 18 to over 55, and included a mix of 165 men and 178 women. Fifty-seven respondents were in the 18-24 age category, 72 were 25-34, 68 were 35-44, 70 were 45-54, and 76 were 55 or older.

ANALYSIS AND RESULTS

Initially, data on the 45 individual gratifications were subjected to principal components analysis. Factor scores for the dimensions of Web use identified in the analysis were then calculated and used as the independent variables in a multiple regression analysis. In order to provide an opportunity to better understand which sort of motivations were indicative of distinctive types of computer users (i.e., high use/low use), the affinity for the computer, computer use frequency and Web use frequency measures were specified as dependent variables.

Principal Components Analysis

The principal components analysis was conducted with varimax rotation, and specified the retention of factors with eigenvalues greater than one. This resulted in a total of 11 initial factors. Scree plot analysis (e.g., Hair, Anderson, Tatham, & Black, 1998) indicated a natural break after the fifth factor, and of the five retained factors, when reliability coefficients were calculated, it was noted that coefficient

Table 2: Exploratory Factor Analysis Results, Factor Loadings

Factor	Search Factor	Cognitive Factor	New and Unique Factor	Social Factor	Entertainment Factor
Eigenvalue	10.96	3.0	2.28	2.0	1.7
Variance explained	24.36%	7.32%	5.06%	4.43%	3.80%
Reliability (Cronbach's Alpha)	.82	.76	.80	.74	.73
Variable					
Resources	**.575**	.395	.005	.006	-.173
Search Engines	**.686**	.102	.003	.104	-.124
Searching	**.685**	.254	.125	.003	-.105
Software	**.557**	.200	.008	.111	.291
Surfing	**.590**	-.004	.306	.123	.117
Technology	**.661**	.219	.009	.004	.008
Updates	**.529**	.141	.174	.104	.160
Web sites	**.551**	.200	.314	.002	.156
Education	.122	**.671**	-.009	.123	.194
Information	.266	**.683**	.368	-.001	.002
Learning	.210	**.734**	.285	.007	.001
Research	.204	**.597**	.195	.000	-.009
Ideas	.240	.390	**.574**	.174	-.001
Interesting	.164	.230	**.703**	.115	.002
New	.224	.241	**.552**	.233	.008
Progressive	.291	.360	**.518**	.208	.000
Relaxing	.006	.009	**.613**	.162	.318
Chatting	.000	-.001	.002	**.776**	.131
Friends	.003	-.003	.002	**.686**	.199
Interaction	.247	.007	.203	**.718**	.136
Newsgroups	.127	.167	.280	**.500**	.206
People	.149	.126	.362	**.711**	.109
Entertainment	.007	-.001	.131	.296	**.711**
Fun	.113	.002	.007	.229	**.718**
Games	.006	.004	.006	.007	**.784**

alpha levels dropped noticeably beyond the fifth factor. All coefficients in these first five factors were above the acceptable level of .70 (Nunnally, 1978), and the five retained factors together accounted for about 45% of the total variance. Table 2 presents these results and reliability coefficients.

Factor One:

Factor one is characterized as a Search Factor. This theme was chosen based on key loadings for the variables of search engines, searching software and Web sites. Other variables loading on this factor include technology, updates and resources. Together, this suggests that the motivation underlying this dimension relates to using the Internet medium and its sites to search for the latest in informational updates and resources. The combination of key variables representative of both searching (a key Internet *process*) and informational resources (a notable *content* of the medium) implies that this initial factor represents a synergistic combination of both process and content gratifications (e.g., Stafford and Stafford, 1998; Cutler and Danowski, 1980). In short, it appears that users are *process* motivated to search for specific *content*.

Factor Two:

Factor two represents a theme of thinking and knowledge, and we characterize it as the Cognitive Factor. Variables loading on this factor include education, information, learning and research. This mix of variables appears to represent a primary motivation of Web-based learning and information seeking, which is highly content-specific.

Factor Three:

The third factor is termed "New and Unique," because all but one of the items loading on it seem to signify the new and unique things that are available on the Web. The variables that comprise this factor include ideas, interesting, new, progressive and relaxing. While this last item, relaxing, does not appear to be as thematic as the others, it is possible that finding new and unique things on the Internet is relaxing to some people. In general, this appears to be a content-based factor.

Factor Four:

Factor four is clearly the Social Factor, with variables such as chatting, friends, interaction, newsgroups, and people all loading strongly here. It appears that some people are motivated to use the Web simply for social purposes and thus receive important *social* gratifications. This factor appears to represent a new sort of motivation: one that is neither content nor process dominant.

Factor Five:

The final factor appears to be an Entertainment Factor. Three related items (entertainment, fun and games) all load nicely here, indicating that people might obtain gratifications from the Web simply by taking advantage of the fun, games and other entertainment offered on the Web. Interestingly, this appears to be the case of a process-motivated gratification that depends on site content.

Multiple Regression Analysis

As noted, a regression analysis was conducted with the five factors (represented by the factor scores of their signifying items) as independent variables and affinity with the computer, frequency of Web use, and frequency of computer use

Table 3: Multiple Regression Results, Parameter Estimates (F-tests)

	Multivariate F-Statistic	Affinity w/the Computer	Frequency of Web Use	Frequency of Computer Use
Adjusted R²		.104	.211	.055
Independent Variable				
Search Factor	23.60 [c]	.931	.577	.219
		(3.77[c])	(7.74[c])	(4.56[c])
Cognitive Factor		.169	.002	-.002
	.327	(.684)	(.282)	(-.556)
New & Unique Factor	5.09[b]	.604	.244	-.001
		(2.443[a])	(3.28[b])	(-.256)
		.888	.102	.007
Social Factor	4.65[b]	(3.59[a])	(1.37)	(1.51)
Entertainment Factor	9.61[c]	.820	.363	.005
		(3.32[b])	(4.87[c])	(1.23)

[a] = p < .05
[b] = p < .01

as dependent variables. This analysis allows us to determine if certain motivations for using the Web potentially result in differences in Web and computer use and affinity with the computer. Multi-collinearity tests were conducted, and all variance inflation factors were equal to one, indicating that multi-collinearity was non-problematic. Results of the regression analysis are presented in Table 3.

As shown, the multivariate tests for four of the five independent variables were significant. For the Search Factor, the multivariate F statistic was 23.60 (p<.001), for the New & Unique Factor, the multivariate F statistic was 5.09 (p < .01), for the Social Factor, the multivariate F statistic was 4.65 (p < .01) and for the Entertainment Factor, the multivariate F statistic was 9.61 (p < .001). For the Cognitive Factor, the F-test was not significant (F=.327, p>.10).

The univariate tests provide further understanding and details. For example, the searching motivation was significant (p<.001) for all three dependent variables. That is, respondents with a higher motivation to search had a higher affinity with the computer and appeared to use the computer and the Web more. Respondents with motivations relating to finding new and unique things on the Web had a higher affinity with the computer (F = 2.443, p < .05) and used the Web more frequently (F = 3.28, p<.01), but there was no significant relationship between this factor and frequency of computer use (F = -.256, p > .10)

Social motivations had a positive and significant relationship with affinity with the computer (F=3.59, p<.05), but not with the two frequency measures. Finally, entertainment motivations had a positive and significant relationship with both affinity with the computer ($F = 3.32$, $p < .05$) and frequency of Web use ($F = 4.87$, $p < .001$) but not with frequency of computer use ($F = 1.23$, $p > .10$).

DISCUSSION

This paper applied the uses and gratifications paradigm to develop an understanding of general consumer motivations for accessing commercial areas of the World Wide Web. The investigation identified five key underlying dimensions of Web use motivation: Searching, Cognition, New and Unique, Socialization, and Entertainment. Interestingly, the three dimensions of motivation represented by the searching, new/unique and entertainment factors appear to represent various mixtures of the two general media gratifications of process and content.

Moreover, the analysis indicates that four out of five underlying motivations are related to high affinity for computers, and three of those motivations are significantly related to more frequent use of the Web. Interestingly, only one the motivations (search) is significantly related to frequency of computer use. Thus, it seems that respondents motivated by searching on the Web tend to like and need the computer and use it frequently to search the Web.

However, respondents motivated by entertainment or new and unique things on the Web seem to have a high need for and liking of the computer and spend a lot of time using the Web, but not necessarily the computer itself. Although this might initially seem contradictory since computers are used to access the Internet, this finding might indicate that individuals see themselves as using the Web quite a bit for new and entertaining things, and like and need their computer for that specific use, but they don't see themselves as using the computer much, otherwise.

The one positive and significant relationship for the social factor was with affinity for the computer. It is possible that those seeking social gratifications for Web use see the computer as a telecommunications device to contact peers, and that it represents a social outlet, much like a phone. Moreover, it is possible that those individuals who have a higher affinity for the computer may actually be more interested in using their *computers* to interface with their peers (or, perhaps, find it more *convenient* or even *prefer* to do so), as compared to direct interpersonal social interactions and entertainment activities. The characterization of an "Internet Hermit" comes to mind in this regard; for these individuals, the Web may be a primary source of socialization and fun.

There are interesting implications to these results, since they appear to suggest a case of socialization made possible *through* a commercial mass medium. The only other communication medium that even partially affords this possibility is the telephone. However, it is readily apparent that the telephone is nothing like the Internet for social purposes. For one thing, the Web provides a *rich* audio-visual environment of multimedia presentations and information transmissions, including processes that enhance mediated interpersonal interaction, such as two-way video, interactive gaming, instant messaging, and voice transmission. For another thing, telephone socialization generally takes the form of direct, identified, interpersonal contact, whereas the Internet facilitates numerous interpersonal interaction formats that can range from direct/identified, direct/anonymous (chat rooms, for example) and indirect and/or time-shifted formats (such as e-mail and bulletin boards).

A Third General Area of Media Gratification

A rich tradition of previous U&G research has brought a generalization that gratifications generally fall into two specific areas: process-related or content-related (e.g., Cutler & Danowski, 1980). Based on the current study, we are suggesting the existence of a new, Internet-specific, media gratification: socialization.

There are powerful implications for this third general gratification: the Internet is at once an interpersonal *and* a mass exposure medium, and this new medium can provide simultaneous commercial *and* noncommercial opportunities for parties to any interaction. "Personal ads" in newspapers are presented as "interpersonal" messages in a commercial format, but it is *not* an interactive venue. The telephone is highly interactive, and conference calls are available for group interaction, but there are generally no commercial applications during private phone calls.

However, Web-based interpersonal interactions carry the potential for exposure to all manner of site-based advertising and promotional messages during interpersonal encounters between one or more individuals on-line. Marketers may find commercial Web opportunities analogous to the "personal ads" of print media, by offering sites that facilitate interpersonal interaction; a handy example is America Online's "push" for user participation in Instant Messaging technologies during sign-on processes. The Internet is the first true interactive commercial medium, and it appears that the general gratifications frequently identified in studies of non-interactive media must now be supplemented with the third general media gratification of socialization.

LIMITATIONS, FUTURE RESEARCH AND CONCLUSIONS

While this study began the process of identifying key underlying uses and gratifications of the World Wide Web, there are limitations. First, self-selection in on-line research is a potential problem, but this is an issue that applies generally to on-line studies where volunteers must be recruited for participation. Moreover, in Part Two of our study, those who volunteered to participate were further qualified based on previous participation in on-line studies and/or demographic character-istics. Our questionnaire was included with a standard Digital Marketing Service AOL user satisfaction survey, which had respondent targets and qualifications designed to more fully represent the makeup of the AOL user base. Thus, our data collection process can in no way be construed as random, although it was widespread and reached diverse groups of Internet users. More to the point, we feel a nice balance between rigor and relevance is achieved. Although we sacrifice a small amount of rigor, we gain highly desirable access to a relevant technological context and actual technology users (e.g., Benbasat & Zmud, 1999, p. 5)

Another problem inherent in on-line research is the inability to calculate traditional response rates, or even estimate non-response, as compared to survey research through the mail. It is not impossible to assess the exact number of individuals who have access to a Web site and thus, who represents a sampling frame for response rate calculations. However, our commercial on-line research partners have generally been less concerned with response rates than response quality; they have no trouble recruiting participants for their studies. The primary issue is obtaining samples that are consistent demographically with their key audiences.

A related concern is the limited number of respondents in both parts of the study. Given that just under a 100 respondents participated in Part One and 343 in Part Two, the findings from this study should be verified with a larger sample to increase generalization. Another limitation is that the data in both stages of the study were obtained from respondents at individual Web sites (HotWired in Part 1 and AOL in Part 2). Although the results do not appear to be biased in any site-specific way, future research on uses and gratifications for the World Wide Web should attempt to reach users through a wider range of sites.

Nevertheless, the initial list of 179 potential uses and gratifications presented here, along with the five underlying dimensions, provide a basis from which to move forward in future research on uses and gratifications for the Web. For example, future research can use the current study's results for classic U&G measure development (e.g., Bantz, 1982; Levy & Windahl, 1984) or to segment Web and computer users based on their individual motivations.

Moreover, this research began the process of attributing certain motivations to users with a higher affinity for the computer and those individuals who use the Web more frequently. Results suggest both process and content gratifications are important, and different motivations relate to affinity with the computer and frequency of Web and computer use. Results also suggest that process and content gratifications may combine synergistically to motivate use. Finally, a social motivation emerged and this motivation was significantly related to affinity with the computer. Consequently, a key conclusion of this study is that Webmasters and others who manage organizational Web sites need to understand their customers in terms of their personal and social Web usage and their feelings toward the computer. Such concepts appear to be highly important in determining what an individual hopes to gain by visiting a particular spot located on the World Wide Web.

REFERENCES

Applegate, L.M., McFarlan, F.W., & McKenney, J.L. (1999). *Corporate Information Systems Management*. Boston: Irwin McGraw-Hill.

Ball-Rokeach, S.J., & Reardon, K. (1988). Monologue, dialogue and telelogue: Comparing an emerging form of communication with traditional forms. In R. Hawkins, S. Wieman, & S. Pingree (Eds.), *Advancing Communication Science: Merging Mass and Interpersonal Processes*. Newberry Park, CA: Sage.

Bantz, C.R. (1982). Exploring uses and gratifications: A comparison of reported uses of television and reported uses of favorite program types. *Communication Research,* 9 (July), 352-379.

Barker, C., & Groenne, P. (1997). Advertising on the web. http://www.samkurser.dk/advertising/research.html.

Benbasat, I., & Zmud, R.W. (1999). Empirical research in information systems: The practice of relevance. *MIS Quarterly,* 23(1), 3-16.

Clark, D.D. (1999). High speed data races home. *Scientific American,* 281(4), 94-99.

Cutler, N.E., & Danowski, J.A. (1980). Process gratification in aging cohorts. *Journalism Quarterly,* 57 (Summer), 269-77.

Drèze, X., & Zufryden, F. (1997). Testing web site design and promotional content. *Journal of Advertising Research,* 37 (2), 77-91.

Eighmey, J. (1997a). On the web: It's what you say and how you say it. http://eighmey.jlmc.iastate.edu/.

Eighmey, J. (1997b). Profiling user responses to commercial web sites. *Journal of Advertising Research,* 37 (May/June), 59-66.

Fox, B. (1995). Retailing on the Internet: Seeking truth beyond the hype. *Chain Store Age,* 71 (September), 33-46, 68, 72.

Friedmann, R., & Fox, R. (1989). On the internal organization of consumers' cognitive schemata. *Psychological Reports,* (65), 115-126.

Gupta, S. (1997). Consumer survey of WWW users. http://www-personal.umich.edu/~sgupta/hermes/survey3/summary.html.

Hair, J.F., Jr., Anderson, R.E., Tatham, R.L., & Black, W.C. (1998). *Multivariate Data Analysis,* 5th Edition. Upper Saddle River, NJ: Prentice Hall.

Hoffman, D.L., & Novak, T.P. (1996). Marketing in hypermedia computer-mediated environments: Conceptual foundations. *Journal of Marketing,* 60 (July), 50-68.

Kambil, A. (1995). Electronic commerce: Implications of the Internet for business practice and strategy. *Business Economics,* 30 (October), 27-33.

Katz, E. (1959). Mass communication research and the study of popular culture: An editorial note on a possible future for this journal. *Studies in Public Communication,* (2), 1-6.

Katz, E., Blumler, J.G., & Gurevitch, M. (1974). Uses of mass communication by the individual. In W. Davison, & F. Yu (Eds.), *Mass Communication Research: Major Issues and Future Directions*, New York: Praeger.

Klapper, J.T. (1963). Mass communication research: An old road resurveyed. *Public Opinion Quarterly*, 27, 515-527.

Levy, M.R., & Windahl, S. (1984). Audience activity and gratifications: A conceptual clarification and exploration. *Communication Research,* 11 (January), 51-78.

Lin, N. (1977). Communication effects: Review and commentary. In B. Ruben (Ed.), *Communication Yearbook* 1, New Brunswick, NJ: Transaction Books.

McDonald, S.C. (1997). The once and future web: Scenarios for advertisers. *Journal of Advertising Research,* 37 (2), 21-28.

McGuire, W.J. (1974). Psychological motives and communication gratification. In J. Blumler, & E. Kaatz (Eds.), *The Uses of Mass Communications: Current Perspectives on Gratifications Research,* Beverly Hills: SAGE Publications, Inc.

Newhagen, J., & Rafaeli, S. (1996). Why communication researchers should study the Internet: A dialogue. *Journal of Communication,* 46 (1), 4-13.

Nunnally, J. (1978). *Psychometric Theory.* New York: McGraw-Hill.

Peterson, R.A., Balasubramanian, S., & Bronnenberg, B.J. (1997). Exploring the implications of the Internet for consumer marketing. *Journal of the Academy of Marketing Science*, 25 (4), 329-346.

Philport, J.C., & Arbittier, J. (1997). Advertising: Brand communication styles in established media and the Internet. *Journal of Advertising Research,* 37 (2), 68-78.

Rafaeli, S. (1988). Interactivity: From new media to communication. In R. Hawkins, J. Wieman, & S. Pingree (Eds.), *Advancing Communication Science: Merging Mass and Interpersonal Processes*. Newberry Park, CA: Sage.

Rogers, E.M. (1986). *Communication Technology: The New Media in Society*. New York: Free Press.

Rubin, A.M. (1981). An examination of television viewing motivations. *Communication Research,* 8 (April), 141-165.

Rubin, A.M. (1984). Ritualization and instrumental television viewing. *Journal of Communication,* 34 (Summer), 67-78.

Rubinstein, E. (1995). The retail superhighway: Take a ride on the net. *Discount Store News,* 34 (August), 79-81.

Sheth, J.N. (1992). *Marketing's Sacred Pigs. Presentation to the Marketing Ideas Consortium*, Athens, GA.

Stafford, M.R., & Stafford, T.F. (1996). Mechanical commercial avoidance: A uses and gratifications perspective. *Journal of Current Issues and Research in Advertising,* 18 (Fall), 27-38.

Stafford, T.F., & Stafford, M.R. (1998). Uses and gratifications of the World Wide Web: A preliminary study. In D. Muehling (Ed.), *The Proceedings of the 1998 American Academy of Advertising Conference,* Pullman, WA: Washington State University.

Szalay, L.B., & Deese, J. (1978). *Subjective Meaning and Culture: An Assessment through Word Association*. Hillsdale, NJ: Lawrence Erlbaum Associates.

Thomsen, M.D. (1997). *Advertising on the Web*. http://www.samkurser.dk/advertising/thomsen.html.

Chapter 5

Signalling Intentions and Obliging Behavior Online: An Application of Semiotic and Legal Modeling in E-Commerce

James Backhouse
London School of Economics

Edward K. Cheng
Harvard Law School

Electronic commerce has the potential to deliver goods and services to customers more quickly, cheaply, and conveniently than ever before. But before performance the obligations have to be created. This paper explores the semiotic and legal aspects of online contracts. It reviews speech act theory from philosophers such as Austin and Searle to explain how words and actions can create legal obligations. It then examines English contract law and its requirements to find an abstract basis upon which contract creation can be modeled. Using semiotics and law, the paper thereafter creates a model of the contract creation process and applies it to electronic commerce in intangible goods. Since electronic commerce is so pervasive and extends beyond any particular jurisdiction, the need is destined to increase for high-level abstraction and for a model for comparison and cross reference.

By establishing agreements and expectations regarding future actions, contracts enable business to be conducted in a stable context. For example, contracting parties know when to expect deliveries of raw materials, and can thus optimize their manufacturing processes, making gains in efficiency. In

Previously Published in the *Journal of End User Computing, vol.12, no.2*, Copyright © 2000, Idea Group Publishing.

addition, if something goes awry and a party breaches the contract, the injured party can seek legal recourse.

In traditional commerce, people create commercial contracts in-person, and the courts and legislature have developed an extensive body of contract law to govern these transactions. Among the legal requirements are the four elements of any contract: offer, acceptance, consideration, and intent to create legal relations, as discussed in Part II. However, these requirements are not merely for the benefit of jurists and legal scholars. Merchants incorporate contract law into their standard business practices not only to satisfy the law, but also to conform with informal norms and to prevent misunderstandings with customers. The four elements of the legal contract derive largely from the fundamentals of any negotiating process. The law has merely formalised the elements and the process. Furthermore, businesses often use the ceremonial aspects of the contract creation process for their "cautionary effect, thereby deterring hasty, premature or ill-considered contracts from being made."[1] People understand that signing a document creates legal obligations and that it should not be taken lightly. However, rituals in the virtual world with similar significance have yet to be established.

The legal and social aspects of contracts have similarly important roles to fulfill in the new world of electronic commerce. Merchants need contracts not only to secure their legal rights, but also to prevent consumer misunderstandings. But contract law and standard business practices have had little time to adjust and develop to handle the virtual and ephemeral nature of cyberspace. Will the long-held traditions and principles of English contract law be flexible enough to accommodate this new commercial medium? Will on-line contracts be accepted and enforced by the courts?

Even more importantly, will contract law be consistent with commercial norms and practices and will consumers readily comprehend the meaning and consequences of their actions online? A mismatch between law and practice could result in misunderstandings, injustices, inefficiencies, and added costs. Even more so than mail order catalogue transactions, on-line transactions in intangible goods predominantly gain competitive advantage through lower prices from the reduction of distribution, intermediary, and overhead costs. Therefore, the margins in electronic commerce will most likely be razor thin and unable to absorb the costs of consumer misunderstandings, disputes, and particularly litigation. Electronic commerce will demand the utmost legal and commercial certainty in on-line contracts, otherwise its enormous potential will not be fully realized.[2] This means that there will need to be certainty and understanding about the significance of online behaviour, both from the merchant and customer side.

The complementarity between the semiotic approach taken here[3] and law in contracts forms the focus of this paper. Semiotics can be applied to informal matters: how people interpret on-line actions, how certain signs or actions can lead to contractual obligations, and what assumptions there are about contractual terms and conditions. Contract law, on the other hand, specifies only the formal requirements of contracts. In addition, the law considers outward appearances rather than actual intentions in making contractual rulings, and also frequently considers the assumptions of a 'reasonable man.'

For the most part, this paper will address consumer contracts for intangible goods made by means of the World Wide Web.[4] Consumers (parties conducting transactions outside the course of business) are most likely to be confused and unaware of the developing norms, conventions, and laws in electronic commerce. Technically speaking, intangible goods (e.g., software, video, music, and other digital information content) could be equally classified as digitised services, and English contract law does draw distinctions between goods and services.[5] However, in order to avoid these legal niceties, more generally applicable principles for transacting and contracting online will be discussed.

The first section of the paper discusses the principles of semiotics, and how the use of particular signs, symbols, or actions in a particular context can create moral, social and legal obligations. This section will concentrate principally on the philosophies of John Searle and J. R. Austin. The next section examines the English law requirements for contract formation, specifically the phenomena of offer and acceptance, as well as consideration, the intent to create legal relations, and the presentation of contractual terms. As previously mentioned law and semiotics are intimately related, and later the paper brings them together to create a semiotic model for the 'traditional' contract. This model suggests what principles should be observed and what elements should be present during the formation of an online contract. Finally, using the model, we make recommendations and compares them to the purchasing process found on the Web site of an online retailer of intangible goods.

Signs and Negotiation of Obligations

Semiotics is "the process of analyzing signs and how they function."[6] In the past, research in the information systems field, including Stamper (1987),[7] Backhouse (1991),[8] Dhillon(1996),[9] and Backhouse(1996)[10] have applied semiotics attempting to highlight the role of meaning and culture in communication as traditional work environments move toward the use of information

Figure 1: Application of four branches of semiotics to contracts.

	Branch of Semiotics	Application to Contracts
Epistemic	Pragmatics (intentions)	Context, commercial norms and culture, and common practices which affect the expectations, assumptions, and intentions of the contracting parties
	Semantics (meanings)	Understandings, agreements and obligations derived from the utterances, gestures, etc. in a given context
Ontological	Syntactics (formalisms)	Contracting procedures such as offer and acceptance, or formal requirements such as writing and signatures
	Physical/Empirics (signals/codes)	The physical signs used in the contracting process: verbal utterances, gestures, written letters, actions performed on Web sites, etc.

technology. The success of these studies suggest that semiotics could provide valuable insights into constructing on-line contracting environments.

Liebenau and Backhouse (1990) divide the concerns of semiotics into four levels for analyzing 'speech acts,' communication acts such as stating, asking, and most importantly to this discussion, making promises and contracts.[11] The four branches are: pragmatics, which addresses the culture and context of the speech act; semantics, which studies its meaning; syntactics, which deals with form and formal rules; and empirics, which examines codes and signal transmission.[12] Above and below these concerns lie respectively those of the business itself and those of the physical world.

As mentioned in the introduction, the primary motivation of this paper is to study contractual misunderstandings between consumers and merchants in electronic commerce. Thus, semiotics, with its focus on signs and meaning, provides an instructive view of the phenomenon of contract. After all, at the most fundamental level, the contractual process is an exchange of certain signs or symbols (empirics) between two parties. The signs, if performed in accordance with an accepted procedure (syntactics) under the given context (pragmatics), convey meanings (semantics) from which contractual obligations arise, which is the purpose of the process. This basic semiotic deconstruction of the contractual process is summarized in Figure 1.[13]

Interestingly, using the perspective gained from the above analysis, the contractual process can be split into two major semiotic divisions: ontological and epistemic.[14] On the ontological or physical side, contracts involve formal procedures (syntactics) and physical utterances (empirics). However, on the epistemic or 'thought' side, contracts require a consumer's tacit assumptions, which arise from the context (pragmatics), as well as the meanings (semantics) that consumers derive from the procedures and signs.

How do the epistemic aspects of contracts arise from the ontological? In other words, how do contracting parties create moral, social and legal obligations by following an accepted procedure when uttering, writing, or electronically displaying appropriate words? These questions are at the heart of contract formation, and the contributing theories of Austin and Searle suggest possible insights.

Performatives

To help understand how words can create obligations (doing things with words), Austin offers the concept of a 'performative utterance.' As Austin suggests, a performative utterance, or more simply a 'performative,' "indicates that the issuing of the utterance is the performing of an action – it is not normally thought of as just saying something."[15] Performatives 'do things' rather than merely state the facts, and can be expressed in the first person singular present indicative active, such as 'I give' (in the context of a will), 'I name,' 'I bet,' and more important to this discussion, 'I promise,' and 'I agree to.'[16] Performatives can be accomplished using other sentence structures or even non-linguistic actions (gestures, signs, etc.), but will almost always reduce to the explicit form above (first person singular present indicative active). For example, by signing one's name on a contract or shaking hands on a deal, a party may not necessarily explicitly say 'I promise,' but implicitly he/she does so nonetheless.

In the execution of a performative, a person attempts to create a new element of social reality, such as an obligation or an expectation that previously did not exist. Naturally, this process is the essence of contract. However, whether the performative act is successful and recognized by others depends on whether the circumstances and context are appropriate. Austin proffers three necessary conditions for a performative to be effective.

a) A conventional procedure must exist for achieving the effect desired, and the circumstances must be appropriate for using the procedure.
b) The parties must execute the procedure fully and correctly.
c) If the procedure requires certain attitudes or mindsets (e.g. sincerity), the participants must have them, and act in accordance with them in the future.[17]

Violating the conditions results in 'infelicities,' situations in which the performative either fails to achieve its purpose or is defective in some manner. Infelicities apply to all performatives, verbal and non-verbal; it "is an ill to which *all* acts are heir which have the general character of ritual or ceremonial…"[18] For example, in the case of contracts, the law sets a conventional procedure for contract creation, which requires *inter alia*, offer and acceptance. If the procedure and associated requirements are fulfilled completely and correctly, then a valid contract exists. However, if the circumstances are inappropriate (e.g. the party is under duress, or the subject matter is unconscionable or against public policy), then the contract will be invalid.

Another example of an infelicity is where at least one participant may be insincere or may lack intent—"I did not really mean it, I was only joking". In this latter case, the 'locutionary' act, the actual words uttered and the meanings conveyed, conflicts with the 'illocutionary' act, the force or intent behind it, creating a defective performative. Because the law recognizes outward appearances rather than internal intent, a valid contract forms. However, the inconsistency between locutionary and illocutionary acts may create disputes and litigation, clearly still an undesirable or 'unhappy' result.

In his own analysis on the process of promising, Searle offers a different, more specific set of necessary conditions.

Though more specific and detailed, Searle's analysis is highly consistent with Austin's broader framework (presented earlier). At first glance, two minor deficiencies may seem to appear in Searle's necessary conditions, but they are easily resolved. First, unlike Austin, Searle does not explicitly require the existence of a conventional or well-accepted procedure for promising. However, as previously mentioned, Searle implicitly assumes that the procedure exists, and given the familiar nature of promising, the standard procedure for promising (i.e., the utterance of certain words, such as 'I promise that') seems obvious enough. Second, since Searle's analysis specifically pinpoints intent and sincerity rather than broadly encompassing all proper mindsets, it does not seem to preclude other infelicities such as duress. However, a closer examination shows that the broadly constructed condition 1, normal input and output conditions, quickly disposes of this problem. The notion of normal implies a preexisting practice or pattern of behaviour, which is present in traditional commerce but still awaited in e-commerce.

Institutional facts and constitutive rules

The concept of a performative sentence provides a useful analytical perspective by showing how certain words, if uttered under appropriate circumstances, can create contractual obligations. However, the discussion still does not fully answer the original question of how utterances or actions lead to contractual obligations. After all, who sets Austin's conventional procedure? And how does a society come to recognize an individual's actions as constituting a promise or contract? To resolve these questions, one needs to build on performative acts and examine Searle's concepts of institutional facts and constitutive rules.

Searle distinguishes between two types of facts: 'brute facts' and 'institutional facts.'[19] Brute facts exist independently of any human institution. For example, the ink and paper with which some contracts are written have intrinsic chemical properties. Those properties are brute facts; they exist irrespective of the observer.

By properly uttering performatives, people can create institutional facts such as contracts. But how do simple performatives such as 'I promise' lead to serious contractual obligations? To accomplish this transformation, society uses the power of 'constitutive rules.' Unlike 'regulative rules' which limit or prohibit actions that people can intrinsically perform (i.e. rules or laws against robbery or burglary), constitutive rules enable people to create new social institutions or institutional facts.

Constitutive rules have the form "X counts as Y in C."[20] At the most basic level, a constitutive rule allows X, some brute fact or physical action under certain contexts and circumstances C, to simply 'count as' Y, some institutional fact.[21]

Owing to the requirement of collective intentionality, only society (or any collective group) has the power to recognize institutional facts. Consequently, society necessarily also has the power to determine the constitutive rules and the conditions under which an institutional fact may be created. In the case of contracts, the law embodies the constitutive rules. Contract law specifies the requirements and conditions (C) under which certain utterances, writings, or gestures (X) constitute a legally binding contract (Y).

This last observation has led to a slightly surprising, but very desirable result. Normally, as in the case of more informal institutional facts such as promises, the constitutive rules are not codified or formalized, but nevertheless exist. Consequently, the requirements are often vague and require more broadly defined necessary conditions, such as those found in Searle's conditions for promise. However, a contract is different. A contract is a formal, legal concept with its constitutive rules perforce well-codified in contract law. Undoubtedly the formal legal concept of contract was preceded by millennia of less formally determined agreements, replete with attendant misunderstandings and unpleasant retribution: think of the centuries of domestic conflict turning on betrothal promises, presumed and denied.

This conclusion suggests that any semiotic model of the contracting process can confidently use the abstract legal requirements of contract as a bridge between the traditional practices of the business world and electronic commerce. Therefore, a useful tool for abstracting a semiotic model for contracts is, appropriately enough, English contract law.

Contract Law

As we have seen, English law requires four elements to form a valid contract: offer, acceptance, consideration (something of value), and an intent to create legal relations. The courts often view these four elements as fundamental to contract, so even though they are not absolute requirements,[22] failure to satisfy any one of them often results in a court refusing to enforce the contract.

To allay fears regarding formalisms, such as writing or signatures,[23] English contract law has few rigid requirements. Contracting parties typically may form contracts in any available manner, including verbally in-person, by telephone, written document, telex, fax, and even by conduct.[24] Accordingly, English law will not debar people from forming legally binding contracts through electronic mail (e-mail) or the World Wide Web as part of an electronic commerce transaction.

English courts will often rule that if a reasonable person were to interpret a particular action or communication as a contractual element, then it is binding, regardless of whether the party intended it or not: there is assumed to be a rational connection between actions and intentionality.

Agreement . . . is not a mental state but an act, and, as an act, is a matter of inference from conduct. The parties are to be judged, not by what is in their minds, but by what they have said or written or done.[25]

The rationale behind this doctrine principally stems from a court's inability to judge what a person internally intends. The only feasible method for determining intent is through external manifestations, and thus appearances are legally more important than the actual intent. However, if intent belies external appearance, then disputes and misunderstandings will arise.

To prevent such miscues, traditional business practices utilize contracting procedures that extirpate any semantic[26] uncertainty. Merchants will often use the four elements of contract as procedural or ceremonial devices to reinforce and ensure that customers understand the full import of their actions. Thus, a further examination of contract law, in both legal and procedural/ semiotic senses, is necessary before one can develop a model to aid electronic commerce transactions.

Offer

An offer expresses the desire to enter into a contract on the understanding that if the other party accepts the offer, the agreement will be legally binding. Just like the contracts they help form, offers can be made using virtually any medium of communication. Contracting parties can make offers by post, fax, telex, telephone, etc. In cyberspace, these methods extend to e-mail and the World Wide Web.

A fine distinction separates offers from invitations to treat, which are merely "offers to receive offers."[27] Promotional devices such as advertisements, price lists, and store displays are invitations to treat, not offers in themselves, as the court held in *Pharmaceutical Society of Great Britain v Boots Cash Chemists (Southern) Ltd.* [28]

The concept of an invitation to treat allows merchants to retain control, because they alone have the final decision on whether to create a contract or not. A number of good reasons exist, including supply constraints, refusing certain categories of customers and possible transmission faults, for online merchants to conform to this present commercial practice and to ensure that their advertisements, price lists, and preconstructed order forms on the Web are construed as mere invitations to treat.

To maintain the traditional invitation to treat distinction, online merchants could use simple disclaimers defining the on-line advertisements or displays as invitations to treat and not offers. However, textual legalese in cyberspace is often not seen (because it falls outside the viewable window) or ignored, and here custom and practice is gradually still being set. Therefore, even though this solution may absolve the merchant of any legal liability, it does not prevent consumer misunderstandings or disputes. Hence the formal requirements of legal niceties are satisfied, but the practical and informal realities are not. To ensure consistency, the disclaimers will need to be supplemented by on-line ordering procedures that mimic or are analogous to those found in the traditional environment.

Acceptance

If the offeree accepts an offer, a contract is formed.[29] An acceptance is an unconditional agreement to the offer presented. It cannot be a message merely notifying the offeror that the offer has been received (c.f. acknowledgement), nor can the acceptance attempt to change the contractual terms (cf. counter offer). Again, just as in the case of an offer, an acceptance can be communicated using any viable method, as long as it is 'reasonable' under the circumstances. Consequently, if a consumer makes an offer through a Web site, the merchant (offeree) can validly accept the offer through a variety of methods, including the following:

Automated acceptance. Under English law, the merchant can automate the acceptance process.[30] Consumers can misconstrue poorly constructed "thank you for your order" confirmation Web pages or e-mails as acceptances, even though none was intended. Again, since the legal liability hinges on external acts and not internal intent, careless merchants could find themselves liable. In addition, even if no legal obligation exists, misunderstandings can lead to consumer dissatisfaction, disputes, and litigation - contingencies that merchants obviously wish to avoid.

Acceptance by conduct. For the sale of immediate intangible goods or digitised services, the Web merchant can accept offers like a traditional mailorder house. The consumer submits the offer via the Web, and then Web server accepts by beginning the transfer of the software, video, music, etc. to the customer. As affirmed in *G. Percy Trentham Ltd v Archital Luxfer Ltd and Others*, "a contract can be concluded by conduct."[31]

Acceptance by click-wrap. Further, acceptance can be effected through 'click-wrap' agreements. A click-wrap is where the contract is presented in a window online, and the customer is asked to click an 'I accept' (or more preferably, an 'Offer') button to accept (or offer) a contract. Web merchants of software may prefer this method of acceptance since it forces the consumer to agree to specific licensing terms. Although English courts have not yet dealt with click-wrap agreements, a United States District Court in *Hotmail Corporation v Van Money Pie Inc.*[32] implicitly held them to be enforceable in America. Based on the similarity of contract doctrine between American and English law, an English court will probably similarly recognise click-wrap contracts.

All the above methods of acceptance for on-line merchants have analogs in traditional commerce. Automated acceptance is found at car parks and vending machines. As already mentioned, acceptance by delivery is common practice among mail-order merchants. Click-wrap is similar to reading an agreement or credit card receipt and signing it, although arguably it does not have the same ceremonial weight. Therefore, using these acceptance methods may lessen the possibility of disputes and litigation in electronic commerce.

Consideration

Consideration is the element which typically transforms a mere promise into a legally binding contract, embodying the common law belief that only bargains should be enforced.[33] It is often defined as the exchange of something of value, but may also include any detriment to the promisee or benefit to the promisor. In order for a binding contract to exist, the promisee must pay or give something to the promisor in return for the assurances, goods, services, or other benefits which he/she receives.

Historically, English courts have broadly interpreted the consideration requirement, and often will even 'invent consideration,' or regard something as consideration even though the promisor did not necessarily want it.[34] In addition, the amount of consideration is irrelevant; determination of what constitutes 'proper' compensation is left to the contracting parties.[35] Consequently, the requirement of consideration is usually easy to satisfy. Indeed, for normal commercial transactions (both traditional and electronic), consideration will almost never pose a threat to contract validity. The digital 'goods' (or services) provided by the on-line merchant and the payment given by the customer fully satisfy the requirement of consideration.

Intention to create legal relations

The final criteria for contract formation, the intent to create legal relations, is also easily satisfied under most circumstances. Indeed intention is automatically presumed in a commercial transaction with an explicit contract, and the onus of proving otherwise "is on the party who asserts that no legal effect is intended, and the onus is a heavy one."[36]

Beyond the procedures already discussed to ensure intent (e.g., a well-defined offer/acceptance process and the ceremonial use of consideration), on-line merchants might consider another device to avoid disputes — a 'last chance' screen. After proceeding through the sequence of Web pages concerning the transaction, the consumer should be presented with a 'last chance' screen that includes all of the major terms (digital service requested, price total, credit card number, etc.). At this point, the consumer either submits the offer or cancels it without any legal implications. Establishing this purchasing framework will prevent misunderstandings of meaning and intention, and lead to greater legal enforceability as well.

Presentation of terms

One final concern in the contractual process is the presentation of contractual terms.[37] Most consumer contracts do not form after prolonged discussions and negotiations over specific terms and clauses. Rather, they are generally standard form contracts, pre-drafted by the merchant to protect his/her own interests. The consumer receives the terms only at the time of purchase.

However, the terms and conditions in a standard form contract will have no effect unless the customer is given 'notice' of them before the contract is formed.[38]

For example, in *Olley v Marlborough Court Ltd*, the court held that a contract for a hotel room, having been agreed to and signed at the hotel's reception desk, was not subject to terms found on a notice inside the bedroom.[39] As suggested by Lord Denning MR in *Thornton v Shoe Lane Parking*, "the customer is bound by the . . . conditions if he knows that the ticket [contract] is issued subject to it; or if the company did what was reasonably sufficient to give him notice of it."[40]

In traditional commerce, giving a consumer 'notice' of the terms was usually a straightforward task. Often, merchants print the terms on the back of the order form, and in some cases, may require consumers to sign underneath, signifying that they have read and understood them. In other instances, the sales representative may explicitly state important conditions of the sale. These traditional methods of giving 'notice' are well-known and understood by consumers, and thus present little in the way of semiotic ambiguity.

In order to maintain similar levels of semiotic certainty, the electronic commerce environment needs to develop analogous methods for giving 'notice.' The following list describes a number of possible methods in increasing order of substantiality (i.e. greater notice to the customer).

Reference statement with hyperlink. Merchants can include a statement such as "This contract subject to Company's standard terms and conditions" at the bottom of the online order form. This statement would be linked to a page detailing the standard terms. The technique is popular with many current web merchants because it achieves some legal credibility without substantial disruption of the promotional or commercial aspects of the order form or web page.

However, the legal and semiotic benefits of this method are debatable. In one sense, it alerts the customer to the existence of terms and makes them available for inspection. Thus, the reference statement with hyperlink is similar to the 'See back' notice in *Parker v South Eastern Railway*.[41] In *Parker*, the court held that the statement 'See back' on the front of a ticket with the terms on the back constituted sufficient notice. Alternatively, one could criticize the reference statement with hyperlink method because the hyperlink seemingly hides the terms from the customer. The mere accessibility of the terms does not necessarily induce a consumer to examine them. The situation may be comparable to the U.S. case of *Microstar v Formgen*,[42] where the court admonished the merchant for putting restrictive terms in a separate file, LICENSE.DOC, that the customer did not necessarily view.

Display terms at bottom of page. Instead of hyperlinking the standard terms and conditions, the merchant could stream the whole text at the bottom of the order form or Web page. Since the terms are conspicuously displayed, the method has greater legal and semiotic weight. However, it could easily make the Web page visibly unattractive, and the consumer could miss the terms (because they are off the immediate screen) or ignore them. Furthermore, users still remain passive participants, and do not demonstrate that they have had the opportunity to read the terms and conditions.

Dialogue box. Perhaps one of the most elaborate display mechanisms is to create a dialogue box that forces the user to scroll through the terms and conditions before clicking 'I agree' or 'I have reviewed these terms.' This method is analogous to the traditional process of presenting a customer with the terms and conditions and then requesting a signature to signify that the customer has reviewed them.[43]

However, the method is legally and semiotically powerful. Consumers are not just given the opportunity to review the terms; indeed, they are forced to review them, and even have to agree through a positive action, the 'click.' Although there is the ever-present danger of customers simply "going through the motions" in a mechanical fashion, they would clearly recognise that the contract was subject to certain terms and conditions, reducing the probability of dispute or misunderstanding to a minimum.

A Model for Consumer Contracts

So far, the principal problem has been ensuring consistency between the empirical and syntactical (procedural and formal) aspects of the contractual process and the actual meanings that a customer derives from them. Signs by themselves do not have inherent meanings.[44] The meanings surface over time through an evolutionary process, and are associated with certain contexts and other informal cues. In the traditional commercial world, consumers understand and are familiar with the procedures involved in forming a contract or making a transaction. The meanings that each person derives from those procedures are essentially uniform, and thus relatively few semiotic problems are encountered. However, electronic commerce represents a new, unexplored, and unfamiliar commercial environment. The standard contracting procedures themselves are not widely known (or not yet developed), and thus the probability of semantic ambiguity is high.

One way for merchants to reduce misunderstandings and disputes is to ensure that the on-line contracting process is reasonably similar or analogous to the traditional. Using English contract law as a basis, analysis can abstract the traditional contractual process into its essential elements. The resulting model can then be used to guide decisions and recommendations on how to construct a semiotically consistent and legally effective online contracting process. As previously mentioned, the study of semantics[45] deals with meanings, or to what signs refer. One effective technique for performing semantic analysis is to create a schema or framework showing the relationships among all elements involved. Because of its abstract form, a schema is

Figure 2: Generic and Abstracted Speech Act in particular contexts

Abstracted Speech Act	Traditional Face-to-face	Mail Order
Invitation to treat	Store display	Catalogue or advertisement
Offer	Selection of merchandise and presentation to cashier	Filling out and posting the order form, or requesting item over the phone
Acceptance	Cashier accepts payment	Delivery of goods

generally applicable and offers a lot of stability. From the generalized speech acts, modelling can describe most contract formation processes. For example, in a traditional, face-to-face contract, the generic act of "invitation to treat" is represented in the "store display;" "offer" becomes "selection and presentation of merchandise;" and acceptance becomes "cashier accepts payment." Thus, the schema could aid online businesses wishing to design clear and complete Web sites. Figure 2 shows this transformation, as well as the application of the model to mailorder purchases.

Avoiding confusion and lack of understanding about the implications of actions online is a paramount concern for electronic merchants. The key actions include invitation to treat, offer, acceptance, consideration, intent, and the presentation of terms. Figure 3 sets out an ontology chart of these constructs. If miscommunication occurs at any of these points, disputes will likely arise, or worse still, the contract may be legally invalid. To minimize the possibility of these problems occurring in electronic commerce, the list below provides a number of suggestions culled from existing practice for each action.

Invitations to treat – Alluding to the traditional practice of selecting products off the shelf (whose price tags are invitations to treat), some form of on-line 'shopping cart' could prove useful. Currently, a number of on-line stores of tangible goods, such as Amazon Books,[46] have electronic shopping carts, which store all selected items until the customer proceeds to the 'checkout.' On-line merchants of intangible digital services may wish to use a similar scheme. In addition, to stop unwanted customers (whether by virtue of age, place of residence, etc.), an online business might consider a home page banner such as "U.S. Residents only," or "Adults only."

Offer – To emphasize that the consumer (and not the merchant) is making the offer, the web site might consider an online order form, reminis-

Figure 3: Semantic Analysis of contract formation

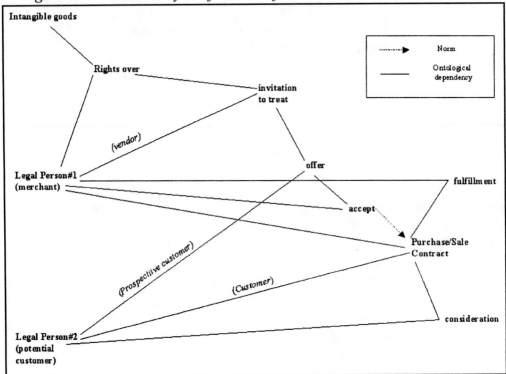

cent of mail order purchases. Merchants could also mark submission buttons as 'Submit order' or 'Submit offer,' rather than the ambiguous 'Yes' or 'OK.'

Presentation of terms – In order for standard terms and conditions to be valid, online merchants need to present them to customers prior to or at the time of ordering. Currently the most effective method is to create a dialogue box where customers must scroll down and then click a button signifying that they have reviewed the terms. In any case, the key concern is that standard terms should be available and prominent.

Acceptance – In most cases, digital services will require automated acceptance and performance, since transfer of the digital information will commence immediately. However, where possible, such as in the case of subscription services, merchants should delay acceptance to maximize their ability to screen customers. In these delayed cases, acceptance would follow from later notification (probably through e-mail), and thus any confirmation web page should clearly specify that it is an acknowledgment of the order only and not an acceptance.

Consideration – For most web sites, consideration will not present a problem. However, providers of digitized services should ensure that prices are displayed and credit card numbers (or electronic cash) are received before transmitting data.

Intent – If all the above steps are rigorously followed, intent is probably unquestionable. However, as a final safety catch, the web site might provide the consumer with a 'last-chance' page. On this page, the consumer can verify all the details of his/her order and then either submit the order or cancel it with no residual legal ramifications.

CONCLUSION

In summary, this paper has explored the semiotic and legal aspects of traditional and on-line contracts. It first applied semiotic and speech act theory from philosophers such as Austin and Searle to explain how words and actions can create legal obligations. Essentially, people use certain speech acts called performatives to create institutional facts, constructs that have no physical basis and exist only by societal recognition. The creation of these institutional facts is governed by constitutive rules, which for the case of contracts are codified in contract law. This result suggests that the legal requirements for contracts provide a theoretically suitable structure for modeling the contract creation process.

"A Model for Consumer Contracts" examined English contract law and its requirements: offer, acceptance, consideration, and the intent to create legal relations. One other significant requirement is that contractual terms must be presented prior to agreement. These five areas constitute a standard sequence of events leading to contract formation and thus ensure, with appropriate account taken to avoid semiotic uncertainties, that both parties understand the legal ramifications of their actions.

The junction between semiotics and law examined in this paper offers many opportunities for future study. Most significantly, the models of contract creation are still very limited and preliminary, and need to be further expanded in scope. In addition, the success and applicability of the models remains undetermined. Future work could perform case studies, testing the applicability of the model to different firms and industries. Alternatively, studies could look at the long-term success of using a semiotic model for constructing an on-line contracting process.

The mantra is intoned time and again: electronic commerce has the potential to fundamentally change the business landscape. With its lower overhead and transaction costs, electronic commerce will enable consumers to obtain goods and services cheaper, faster, and more conveniently. However, in order for those savings to become a reality, on-line business will need to reduce their profit margins and thus will not be able to absorb the costs related to dispute resolution and litigation. By applying a combination of semiotic and legal theory, models can help on-line businesses reduce the probability of misunderstanding, making life easier for both consumers and businesses. More clarity will also encourage new users to explore the cyberspace market, helping to bring nearer the day that global electronic commerce becomes reality.

CASES CITED

Carlill v. Carbolic Smoke Ball Co [1893] 1 QB 256.

Edwards v. Skyways Ltd [1964] 1 WLR 349.

G. Percy Trentham Ltd v. Archital Luxfer Ltd and Others [1993] 1 Lloyd's Rep 25.

Hotmail Corp v. Van$ Money Pie Inc, et al., 47 U.S.P.Q.2d 1020 (N.D. Cal. 1998)

L'Estrange v. Graucob [1934] 2 KB 394.

Microstar v. Formgen, 942 F.Supp. 1312 (S.D. Cal 1996).

New Zealand Shipping Co Ltd v. A M Satterthwaite & Co Ltd [1975] AC 154.

Olley v. Marlborough Court Ltd [1949] 1 KB 532.

Parker v. South Eastern Railway (1877) 2 CPD 416.

Pharmaceutical Society of Great Britain v. Boots Cash Chemists (Southern) Ltd [1951] 2 QB 795.

Thornton v. Shoe Lane Parking [1971] 1 All ER 686.

REFERENCES

Alston, W. P. (1963). Meaning and Use, *Philosophical Quarterly 13*, 107-24.

Austin, J. L. (1962). *How to Do Things with Words*, Oxford: Oxford University Press.

Backhouse, J. (1991). *The Use of Semantic Analysis in the Development of Information Systems*, Ph.D. Dissertation, London School of Economics.

Backhouse, J. and Dhillon, G. (1996). Structures of responsibility and security of information systems, *European Journal of Information Systems 5*, 2-9.

Beniger, J. R. (1986). *The Control Revolution*, London: Harvard University Press.

Bentham, J. (1948). *The Principles of Morals and Legislation,* New York: Hafner Press.

Bostad, F. (1994). What happens to writing when texts in 'a world on paper' are replaced by messages in 'virtual space?', *1994 Research Congress of the Nordic Association for Semiotic Studies*, http://www.hf.unit.no/anv/wwwpages/Finn/Finn.html.

Campbell, D. (1997). *The Law of Online Business*, London: Sweet and Maxwell.

Cheng, E. (1997). *Security in Cyberspace: Preparing the Information Infrastructure for the 21ˢᵗ Century*, B.S.E., Princeton University.

Chissick, M. (1997). *Internet Law*, London, Financial Times Law and Tax.

Dhillon, G. and Backhouse, J. (1996). Risks in the Use of Information Technology Within Organizations, *International Journal of Information Management, 16:1*, pp. 65-74.

Fried, C. (1981). *Contract as Promise: A Theory of Contractual Obligation*, London: Harvard University Press.

Furmston, M. P. (1996). *Cheshire, Fifoot and Furmston's Law of Contract*, 13ᵗʰ ed., London: Butterworths.

Furmston, M. P. et al. (1998). *Contract Formation and Letters of Intent*, London: Wiley.

Gringras, C. (1997). *The Laws of the Internet*, London: Butterworths.

Guest, A. G. (Ed.) (1994), *Chitty on Contracts*, London: Sweet and Maxwell.

Holdcroft, D. (1964). Meaning and Illocutionary Acts, *Ratio 6*, 128-43.

Jackson, B. S. (1985). *Semiotics and Legal Theory*, Liverpool: Deborah Charles Publications.

Kant, I. (1965). *The Metaphysical Elements of Justice,* London: Collier Macmillan.

Kelman, A. and Chissick, M. (1999). *Electronic Commerce: Law and Practice*, London: Sweet and Maxwell.

Lehrer, A. and Lehrer, K. (eds.) (1970). *Theory of Meaning*, Englewood Cliffs (NJ): Prentice Hall.

Lehtinen, E. and Lyytinen, K. (1986). Action Based Model of Information System, *Information Systems 11:4*, pp. 299-317.

Liebenau, J. and Backhouse, J. (1990), *Understanding Information*, London: Macmillan.

Lloyd, I. J. (1997). *Information Technology Law*, 2ⁿᵈ ed., London, Butterworths.

Morris, C. (1964). *Signification and Significance*, Cambridge (MA): MIT Press.

Perritt, H. H., Jr. (1996). *Law and the Information Superhighway*, Chichester: Wiley.

Searle, J. R. (1969). *Speech Acts*, Cambridge: Cambridge University Press.

Searle, J. R. (1970). Meaning and Speech Acts, in Lehrer, Adrienne, and Keith Lehrer, eds. *Theory of Meaning*, Englewood Cliffs (NJ): Prentice Hall.

Searle, J. R. (1995). *The Construction of Social Reality,* London: Free Press.

Smith, G. J. H. (1998). *Internet Law and Regulation*, London: FT Law and Tax.

Stamper, R. et al. (1987). Semantic Normal Form? *ASLIB Conference Proceedings*, Cambridge: Cambridge University Press.

Smedinghoff, T. J. (Ed.) (1996). *Online Law*, Harlow: Addison Wesley.

Wells, R. (1970). Meaning and Use, in Lehrer A and Lehrer K, eds., *Theory of Meaning*, Englewood Cliffs (NJ): Prentice Hall.

ENDNOTES

[1] A G Guest (1994), *Chitty on Contracts*, 4-001. (Hereafter, *Chitty*) *Chitty* here refers to the requirement of writing, but the concept is nonetheless applicable to procedural requirements of contract.

[2] The authors thank Mr. Alistair Kelman for this point.

[3] The study of semiotics concerns signs and meaning, and how people communicating meaning through a sequence of signs and symbols.

[4] E-mail can provide another possible medium for contracts, but the trend is increasingly toward web based commerce since it provides a graphical interface and allows instant, interactive contact. This trend is particularly true for intangible goods.

[5] For example, implied contractual terms for the sale of goods and the sale of services differ. Under the Sale of Goods Act 1979, goods are expected to be of satisfactory quality and fit to the purpose for which they are commonly intended. Services, on the other hand, under the Supply of Goods and Services Act 1982 must be performed with reasonable care and skill to the degree expected of an ordinary person in the profession. This two definitions have implications for, *inter alia,* liability (determination of negligence) and warranties.

[6] J Liebenau and J Backhouse (1990), *Understanding Information*, London, Macmillan, p. 14.

[7] R Stamper, *et al.* (1987), "Semantic Normal Form?" *ASLIB Conference Proceedings*, Cambridge, Cambridge University Press.

[8] J Backhouse (1991), *The Use of Semantic Analysis in the Development of Information Systems*, Ph.D. Dissertation, London School of Economics.

[9] G Dhillon and J Backhouse (1996), "Risks in the Use of Information Technology Within Organizations," *International Journal of Information Management*, 16:1 pp. 65-74.

10   J Backhouse and G Dhillon (1996), "Structures of responsibility and security of information systems," *European Journal of Information Systems* 5, pp. 2-9.

11   J Searle (1969), *Speech Acts*, Cambridge, Cambridge University Press, p. 16.

12   Liebenau and Backhouse (1990), p. 13.

13   *Ibid.*, p. 14.

14   J R Searle (1995), *The Construction of Social Reality*, London, Free Press, p. 8.

15   J R Austin (1962), *How to do things with Words*, Oxford, Oxford University Press, p. 6.

16   *Ibid.*, p. 5.

17   *Ibid.*, pp. 14-15.

18   *Ibid.*, p. 19.

19   Searle (1990), p. 27.

20   *Ibid.*, p. 43.

21   Constitutive rules can build upon each other to create increasing complex social realities. Thus on a subsequent level, X could be a basic institution or institutional fact (e.g. a citizen) and Y could be a more abstract institutional fact (e.g. President or candidate) with C changing appropriately (e.g. winning an election). Searle(1990).

22   *New Zealand Shipping Co Ltd v A M Satterthwaite & Co Ltd* [1975] AC 154.

23   English law generally no longer requires the use of writing or signatures in contracts (ever since the Statute of Frauds 1677 was repealed by the Law Reform (Enforcement of Contracts) Act 1954). Thus, the semiotic aspects of contractual formalisms such as writing and signatures will not be discussed in this paper. They may, however, prove an interesting study in the future.

24   M Chissick (1997), *Internet Law*, London, Financial Times Law and Tax.

25   M P Furmston (1996), *Cheshire, Fifoot and Furmston's Law of Contract*, 13th ed., London, Butterworths., p. 29. (Hereafter *Cheshire*)

26   Here, 'semantic' is used because it deals with the study of meaning. 'Semiotic' is the entire sign process.

27   *Carlill v Carbolic Smoke Ball Co* [1893] 1 QB 256.

28   *Pharmaceutical Society of Great Britain v Boots Cash Chemists (Southern) Ld.* [1951] 2 QB 795.

29   Depending on how the courts interpret a web site or other on-line advertisement (as either an invitation to treat or an offer), the consumer's

placement of an order could be either an acceptance or an offer. However, future discussion will assume that proper construction of the Web site will necessitate that the consumer makes the offer, and the merchant has the option of accepting.

30   The court in *Thornton v Shoe Lane Parking* ruled that customers could contract with car park machines, which represented the car park owners. *Thornton v Shoe Lane Parking* [1971] 1 All ER 686.

31   *G. Percy Trentham Ltd v Archital Luxfer Ltd and Others* [1993] 1 Lloyd's Rep. 25.

32   Hotmail Corp v Van$ Money Pie Inc, et al., 47 U.S.P.Q.2d 1020 (N.D. Cal. 1998)

33   *Cheshire*, p. 74.

34   *Chitty*, 3-008.

35   Fried (1981), p. 29.

36   *Edwards v Skyways Ltd* [1964] 1 WLR 349 at 355, cited in *Chitty* 2-106.

37   In keeping the discussion in this section relevant to semiotic aspects, it will only examine the procedures for presenting contractual terms, and not the contents of the terms, which are equally important.

38   *Chitty,* 12-009.

39   *Olley v Marlborough Court Ltd* [1949] 1 KB 532.

40   *Thornton v Shoe Lane Parking,* [1971] 2 QB 163 at 170.

41   *Parker v South Eastern Railway* (1877) 2 CPD 416.

42   *Microstar v Formgen,* 942 F.Supp. 1312 (S.D. Cal. 1996).

43   Under *L'Estrange v Graucob* [1934] 2 KB 394, if the customer signs the contract, then all specified terms are effective, regardless of whether the customer is given notice. Legally, whether a button-click is equivalent to a written signature (in terms of its assent, not authentication function) is unknown. Semiotically, a button-click is probably a weaker procedure compared to a written signature, since button-clicks are required for mundane tasks (i.e. hyperlinking, closing windows, etc.) in addition to serious contractual tasks.

44   *Ibid.*, p. 43.

45   For a detailed analysis and explanation on semantic analysis, the reader is referred to Backhouse (1991).

46   http://www.amazon.com.

Chapter 6

Customer Loyalty and Electronic Banking: A Conceptual Framework

Daniel Tomiuk and Alain Pinsonneault
McGill University, Canada

In this paper, we present a conceptual framework that helps to better understand and assess the impacts of information technology on customer loyalty in retail banking. To do so, we define the concept of customer loyalty and identify its antecedents. A conceptual framework describing the impacts of information technology on loyalty is developed based on the literature in marketing, social psychology, and communication. The framework suggests that electronic banking might have different effects on loyalty depending on the type of customer. Research in social psychology indicates that customers can be either communally-oriented or exchange-oriented. Loyalty is thus likely to be generated differently in each case: for communally-oriented customer loyalty is likely to be generated based on social and personal interactions, whereas for exchange-oriented customers, loyalty is enhanced by service efficiency and reliability. Because it reduces the amount of face-to-face interactions customers have with bank personnel, electronic banking is likely to lead to lower levels of loyalty for communally-oriented customers and to higher levels of loyalty for exchange-oriented customers.

INTRODUCTION

Today's banking industry is increasingly turbulent and competitive. While some North American banks such as Citibank now derive more than half of their

Previously Published in the *Journal of Global Information Management, vol.9, no.3*, Copyright © 2001, Idea Group Publishing.

income from abroad, several international banks (e.g., Hong Kong Bank, Banque de Paris) have recently entered the North American market. Similarly, London-based Standard Chartered Bank has recently either taken control or bought out banks in Thailand, New Zealand, and Australia. Over half of all banking sector assets are now under foreign control in Chile and Argentina (The Economist, 2000). Likewise, in Central Europe, foreign banks have increased their ownership in bank assets from 10% to more than 50% in the last five years (The Economist, 2000). In addition, numerous firms are now entering in the banking industry by offering financial products and services (e.g., Toyota's credit card, GM's auto financing, Merrill Lynch investments, Fidelity's and Investors' mutual funds).

To compete in such an environment, banks have adopted a strategy that focuses on trying to instill, build, and maintain the loyalty of clients through customer segmentation, product differentiation, cross-selling, product bundles, and establishing a long-term relationship through personal contacts. This strategy is expected to lead to increase post-purchase consumer communications (e.g., positive word of mouth) (Reichheld, 1996), decrease search motivation (Holbrook, 1978), diminish resistance to counter-persuasion (Wood, 1982), increase frequency of purchase (Reichheld and Sasser, 1990), lower price sensitivity (Krishnamurthi and Raj, 1991), and give more time for companies to respond to competitors' actions (Aaker, 1991). The importance of establishing a relationship that fosters customer loyalty is reinforced by the fact that it can be five to ten times more expensive to win a customer than to keep an existing one (Rosenberg and Czepiel, 1984). In retail banking, the benefits associated with increasing customer retention includes a three year increase in average customer lifetime when customer retention increases by five percent, a reduction of defection rates, and an increase in account usage (Council of Financial Competition, 1995; Reichheld and Sasser, 1990; Rust and Zahorik, 1993). A significant association between customer-oriented measures such as satisfaction, repurchase intention, perceived quality, perceived value, and loyalty and financial performance measures such as ROA, market-to-book ratio, and price-earnings ratio (Anderson, Fornell, and Lehmann, 1994; Murphy, 1996).

In parallel, in an effort to offer better services and to reduce operating costs, banks invest important amounts of money into Electronic-banking (E-banking from now on). In 1998, U.S. banks invested $21 billion (US) in information technology (Ernst and Young, 1998). Worldwide, the global market for automatic teller machine (ATM) services and equipment is expected to rise from $5.6 billion (US) in 1999 to $13.3 billion (US) by 2002, and the number of ATMs is expected to surpass 1.15 million in 2004 (Cochran, 2000). Banks have also used information technology to facilitate Direct Deposit/payment (automatic deposits/withdrawals into and from bank accounts), Pay-by-Phone Systems (payment of bills and transfer of funds by telephone), Personal Computer Banking (ability to conduct banking transactions such as view account balances, transfer funds, and pay bills electronically), and Web-based banking (IFG Inc., 2000). E-banking grew from 6 to 27.5 million users between April 1998 and March 2000 in the United States alone (Yasin, 2000). Also, Sakura Bank in collaboration with Fujitsu and several other partners has recently opened Japan's first pure virtual bank – Japan Net Bank. In spring 1999, Citibank reported that 60% of all customer transactions in Hong Kong were done via ATMs or using the telephone and that, less than six months following the introduction of services over the Internet, six percent of all transactions had already moved to this new channel (Bickers, 1999). Hong Kong's Bank of East Asia indicated that the number of customers having opened on-line accounts grew to more than 100,000 only six months after its opening (Granitas, 2000). By the end of 2002, the total number of on-line accounts is expected to reach 250 million worldwide (Lafferty Online, 2000). The end result of these dramatic changes is that more people now use self-service IT in retail banking and fewer go to branches, where the bank can establish and nurture a personal contact with clients. Consequently, a key question arises: What is the impact of E-Banking on customer loyalty? The present paper addresses this issue by developing a conceptual framework which suggests that the impact of self-service banking fundamentally depends on the type of relationships customer desire to maintain with a firm.

Research in social psychology and marketing indicates that customers vary in the type of relationship they wish to maintain with service providers such as banks. Individuals may desire to establish relationships that are more personal and friendship-like (communally-oriented customers) while others seem to value efficiency of service and prefer more impersonal and 'at arms-length' associations (exchange-oriented customers) (Clark and Mills, 1979, 1993). Therefore, for those customers that derive social and psychological benefits from establishing close and personal relationships with bank employees, repeat face-to-face inter-action with front-line personnel may be intrinsic in establishing customer loyalty in retail banking. For these customers, human interaction during service provision may represent more than simply a conduit for service delivery, but rather, may have strong affective connotations. Largely devoid of human interaction, E-banking environments may, therefore, have detrimental effects on customer loyalty for these patrons. Conversely, it is suggested that for customers whose relationship with banks is primarily anchored in the efficiency of its services (i.e., the employee's ability to provide reliable, accurate, and timely service), traditional and E-banking environments may be perceived as being highly substitutable. It is suggested that, for these customers, salient factors affecting their loyalty will largely be cognitive, based on technological innovation, IT performance, and the breadth of services offered over electronic channels.

In the following section, we define loyalty and identify its antecedents. In the next section, we propose a conceptual framework that describes how E-Banking is expected to affect loyalty and its antecedents. The paper ends by presenting a discussion of the framework and presenting its implication for research and practice.

CUSTOMER LOYALTY

Despite the reported benefits of loyalty and its links to financial performance, a review of marketing literature indicates that there has long been disagreement about what represents customer loyalty and how it should be measured. Generally, assessing customer loyalty to a seller, manufacturer, or service provider has often consisted of using either actual purchase behavior or customer self-reports. For instance, Newman and Werbel (1973) consider loyalty as *repurchase behavior* and Tellis (1988) equates loyalty with *repeat purchase frequency*. Massey, Montgomery, and Morrison (1970) see loyalty as a *probability of purchase* while both Cunningham (1966) and Neal (1999) view loyalty as a *proportion of a customer's purchases*. Segal (1989) has gone as far as to suggest that a customer is loyal if more than about 90% of his / her purchases are to a single supplier. It has been suggested that behavioral data is easier and less costly to collect (Dekimpe, Steenkamp, Mellens, and Abeele, 1990) and that it may be superior to attitudinal data because it represents how customers actually behave instead of how they merely feel (Colombo and Morrison, 1989). Nonetheless, behavioral measures are not problem-free. Several authors have cautioned against using and interpreting behavioral data to gauge loyalty and have criticized the setting of arbitrary cut-off margins to assess whether a customer can be classified as loyal or not. In addition, customer loyalty is often conceptualized as a dichotomous variable (i.e., either 'on' or 'off'). However, several authors have argued against this and have suggested that loyalty represents a dynamic, temporal, and continuous concept. For instance, Fournier and Yao (1997) suggest that, often consumers are classified as loyal or disloyal based on some arbitrary cutoff in purchase-share qualifications, which precludes attention to loyalty levels and types. Finally, using purely behavioral definitions and measures of loyalty tends to overestimate true levels of loyalty. In fact, by simply observing overt behavior one cannot differentiate whether a customer's loyalty is true or spurious (Zabava Ford, 1998). Simply put, because behavioral measures cannot successfully differentiate whether a customer that has remained with the same bank over several years has done so out of real loyalty, simply because no competitor has established a presence close to the customer's home or place of work, or alternatively, because the customer perceives little

Figure 1: Dick and Basu's (1994) framework suggests that loyalty is the relationship between relative attitude and repeat patronage

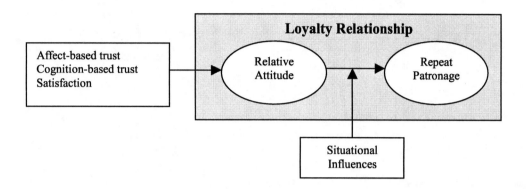

difference between competitors and, therefore, does not recognize any advantages in switching (i.e., customer indifference or inertia). Consequently, behavioral definitions of loyalty have been criticized as focusing solely on outcomes because they fail to identify what important factors underlie the actual behavior (Jacoby and Chestnut, 1978; Huang and Yu, 1999).

Several authors have suggested that loyalty be considered as a composite of both attitude and behavior (e.g., Day, 1969). Figure 1 presents this conceptualization of loyalty.

Recent conceptual work by Dick and Basu (1994) construes loyalty as the relationship between attitude towards the target relative to available alternatives and patronage behavior. Consequently, 'true loyalty' is said to exist only when strong relative attitudes are associated with high levels of repeat patronage while a 'no loyalty' condition exists when both relative attitude and repeat purchase behavior are low[1]. Therefore, in order to be considered as loyal, a customer must exhibit the behavior of continued patronage, which must be intentional and founded on relative positive customer feelings and evaluations regarding the particular service provider. Importantly, Dick and Basu's (1994) conceptualization of loyalty includes cognitive, affective, and conative factors as antecedents to relative attitude and recognizes that situational factors mediate the relationship between relative attitude and behavior (See Figure 1). Situational factors are believed to moderate the 'relative attitude—repeat patronage relationship. For instance, before the advent of E-banking, branch location may have strongly dictated what bank a customer patronized.

Figure 2: Models suggesting the impact of E-banking on customer loyalty

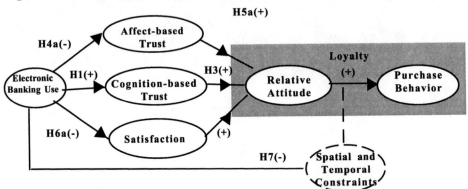

Model A. Communally-Oriented Customers (DCR)

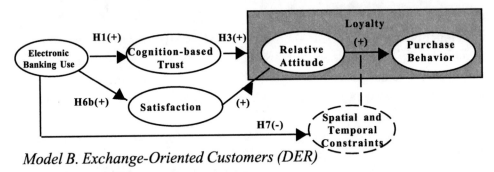

Model B. Exchange-Oriented Customers (DER)

Note: (+) denotes that a positive relationship has been empirically demonstrated in the literature

THE IMPACT OF E-BANKING ON CUSTOMER LOYALTY

In this section we present two conceptual models describing how E-banking affects customer loyalty (See Figure 2). Importantly, our analysis acknowledges customer heterogeneity. Model A suggests how E-banking affects customers who value more personal, communal-like relationships with a financial institution. Model B, on the other hand, describes how E-banking may affect customers who value establishing relationships that are more utilitarian and functional in nature. Our analysis suggests that the impact of substituting E-banking to traditional environments may be different for both groups. The components of our models are discussed below.

TRUST AND LOYALTY

Trust has been linked to loyalty. For instance, it seems that a negative relationship exists between trust and a customer's propensity to leave (Morgan and Hunt, 1994). Moreover, trust was found to positively influence anticipated future interactions (Doney and Cannon, 1997) and expected relationship continuity (Anderson and Weitz, 1989). Trust is said to develop over time as a cumulative process as one person amasses knowledge about another person or thing through experience (Lewicki and Bunker, 1995; Wilson and Mummalaneni, 1986; Ford, 1981). Accordingly, a relationship between trust and the frequency of personal interaction (or object use) seems to exist. In traditional service settings, as face-to-face encounters cumulate over time, trust begins to form when the customer feels confident that experienced-performance thus far, represents a good indicator for expected future performance. Similarly, in E-banking environments, a relationship between use and trust is also apparent. Mazanet (2000) reports that ATMs have become so reliable that, in the United States, it is expected that more than 60 billion transactions will occur in the upcoming year using this technology, demonstrating that the trust customers place in this and similar technologies continues to grow. Aside from direct customer experiences, factors such as reputation, positive word of mouth, and endorsement may also affect the development of trust. For instance, third party endorsement (e.g., Trust-E) can be considered as a trust booster in the area of Web-retailing. In fact, although trust usually develops from personal experience with people or objects, trust can develop through a transference process (Doney, Cannon and Mullen, 1998) when the information comes from a trusted "proof source." For the banking industry, the services provided range from low-involvement services such as opening savings or checking accounts to high-involvement services such as long-term savings and investment products (i.e., financial advising). The importance of employees in establishing customer trust may be especially significant in the delivery of the latter type of service. When seeking financial advice, customers may place themselves in a vulnerable position due to the long-term nature of savings and investment products and because of imperfect and asymmetric information. Consequently, because assessing advice quality is very difficult for customers, the establishment of trust and confidence plays a crucial role when providing financial advice (Palmer and Bejou, 1994).

Recent research indicates that trust is a multidimensional construct made of a cognitive and an affective component (McAllister, 1995, Johnston, 1996). Cognition-based trust develops when a consistent pattern of good performance is believed to exist. Cognition-based trust can, therefore, be considered as a predictive mechanism regarding future performance. In the context of commercial exchanges, cognition-based trust can be linked to the role-based performance of the employees (i.e., competency and expertise in service delivery), the reputation of the service provider, the reliability of the technology, the robustness of its supporting applications and the accuracy of the information these provide. In other words, cognition-based trust is linked with the assurance that, in future encounters, a certain degree of consistent performance will be delivered by the service provider. Conversely, affect-based trust is said to develop from the affective bonds that develop between individuals (i.e., between the customer and the front-line employee). McAllister (1995) and Johnston (1996) suggest that cognition-based trust may be necessary in order for affect-based trust to develop. In the early stages of a commercial relationship, the supplier cultivates trust with the customer by demonstrating reliability and quality (Johnston, 1996). At this stage, the development of trust is synonymous with the development of confidence in the consistency of the quality of service delivered; in other words, the customer wants to know whether he/she can count on the firm's and its employees' professionalism. At latter stages, as interpersonal relationships often develop between the customer and one or more service employees, trust begins to take on affective overtones similar to those encountered in friendships[2]. The development of affect-based trust (i.e., the feeling that the customer is cared about) may create a particularly strong bond between the customer and the representatives of an organization. Macintosh and Lockshin (1997) suggest that the interpersonal relationships between customers and salespeople act as a bonus, making customers more loyal. Similarly, Iacobucci and Ostrom (1996) note that although a relationship can occur between the customer and the store and between the customer and a salesperson (interpersonal), that customers may see the former are less enduring, less intense, and more distant than the latter. The relationships that develop between persons may represent a stronger type of bond. According to the authors' results, customers who had personal relationships with salespeople were found to have a more positive attitude about the store and were more loyal. However, it seems that banks have traditionally failed to recognize the importance of their branch personnel in helping to establish customer trust. Survey results reported in the February 1999 issue of the *ABA Banking Journal* show that only 4.4% of the banks surveyed in the United States indicated that they used incentives to encourage employees to work hard to hold onto existing customers.

E-BANKING, TRUST, AND TYPE OF RELATIONSHIP DESIRED

Research indicates that the factors that influence the development of trust in salespeople include likeability, similarity, and frequency of contact (Doney and Cannon, 1997). Likewise, a sense of familiarity with the service employee has been shown to play an important role in the customer's assessment of the service experience (Czepiel, 1990; Price, Arnould, and Tierney, 1995). Studies that have collected data directly from customers rather than service providers offer a more accurate picture of what actual service characteristics lead to higher quality assessments in retail banking. Research indicates that "continuity and comfort of the relationship" (Stafford, 1994) and "rapport" (Gremler and Gwinner, 1998) positively influence customer's evaluation of loyalty. In other words, customers experience rapport when both they and the employee 'click' together or have good 'chemistry' – a definition closely approaching that of affect-based trust.

However, although research has evidenced that the formation of personal relationships between employees and customers can have positive effects on customer retention, several authors suggest that the generalizability of such assertions may be questionable. In fact, several researchers have noted that attempts on the part of the service provider to get close may be viewed by the customer as intrusive and may be rejected (Adelman, Ahuvia, and Goodwin, 1994). What a customer considers a warm, close, friendly relationship, can be considered as stifling and unnecessary by another customer who prefers a more distant relationship characterized by much less warmth (Price and Arnould, 1999). Studies in the field of social psychology seem to shed some light on this inconsistency. In fact, several studies have evidenced important differences between *communal* and *exchange* relationships (Batson, 1987; Batson & Oleson, 1991; Clark & Mills, 1979, 1993; Mills & Clark, 1994). Communal relationships are often exemplified by relationships with friends and family, whereas, exchange relationships are exemplified by relations between strangers. The distinction between exchange and communal relationships is based on the rules and norms that govern the giving and receiving of benefits (Clark & Mills, 1993, p. 684). Importantly, according to McAllister (1995), the formation of affect-based trust and communal relationships are fundamentally linked to one another. Communal relationships in service contexts are related to what marketing researchers call 'commercial friendships' (Price and Arnould, 1999). Research indicates that certain service encounters are liable to be more similar to a meeting between friends than merely economic transactions (Price and Arnould, 1999). Similarly, Goodwin and Gremler (1996) drew upon the distinction between both types of relationships (i.e., communal versus exchange), by noting that, for certain customers, bartenders often serve as part of a their social support network. They noted that behaviors associated with communal relationships during the service encounter may be separated from the actual delivery of services (i.e., bartender's performance gauged by speed of service and his / her knowledge of drink ingredients and proportions).

Research suggests that customers vary in the type of relationships they wish to maintain with their service provider. Reynolds and Beatty (1999), for instance, suggest that relationships have both functional and social benefits and Gwinner et al. (1998) argue that customer may vary on the value they place on these benefits. In fact, in a study conducted by Beatty et al. (1996), the authors report that those customers who did not have a 'close' relationship with the salesperson did not consider that it would be beneficial to have one. Alternatively, others may rely on relations in the marketplace as a source of human contact and for whom the retailing encounter is not merely a commercial transaction, but has value as a surrogate social contact in which a familiar face and casual conversation offered by a store owner or employee may be a source of comfort, adding a sense of community to an otherwise transient local social landscape (Forman and Srivam, 1991). Also, in a study on retail banking (Barnes, 1997), the study results imply that different segments exist in the retail banking market depending on the type of relationship the customer wishes to have with a bank. Some customers may be very satisfied with the relationship they have with their banks, and yet may feel relatively low levels of closeness. These customers may simply not wish to have a close relationship with their bank, preferring to maintain minimal contact, likely characterized by a desire to use technology and to experience efficiency rather than more personal staff interaction.

Given that E-banking environments are largely devoid of face-to-face human interaction, one could reasonably infer that establishing and sustaining customer loyalty may be more difficult in such environments. Although services may continue to be delivered very reliably with the aid of technology, thus helping to build customers' cognition-based trust, such depersonalized environments do little to promote affect-based trust, suggesting a potential negative impact on loyalty. In fact, empirical evidence in communications suggests that the choice of communication channel may affect how relationships develop. Computer-mediated communication (CMC) was found to be less personal and socio-emotional than face-to-face exchanges (Hiltz, Johnson, and Turoff, 1986). Because many of the cues that are present during face-to-face communication are not available in CMC, differences in affective and relational patterns may evolve. Similarly, research on the Information Richness Theory indicates that face-to-face communication is a better medium to transmit complex messages essential to establish a personal contact (e.g., personal communications, social interactions) than other less-rich media such as e-mail (Daft and Lengel, 1986). Likewise, Social-Presence Theory suggests that 'social presence', which is defined as the degree of salience of another person in an interaction and the consequent salience of an interpersonal relationship may be very low in CMC when compared to face-to-face communication (Walther and Burgoon, 1992, p. 52). During face-to-face exchanges, participants can use both verbal and non-verbal cues, and feedback is instantaneous as opposed to, for instance, e-mail. Because of the physical presence of the interactants and immediate exchange of verbal and nonverbal cues, face-to-face communication is personal in nature (Westmeyer, DiCioccio, and Rubin, 1998). Research indicates that when social cues are missing, communication becomes impersonal (Westmeyer et al., 1998). Research has shown that during CMC, there are fewer spontaneous questions and more formal expression (Kiesler, Zubrow, Moses, and Geller, 1985). Furthermore, bonding especially develops during face-to-face interactions (Czepiel, 1990), and, consequently, if creating an interpersonal atmosphere is important, the medium should stress social presence (Westmeyer et al., 1998). We suggest that the lesser degree of 'richness' and 'social presence' of E-banking environments (compared to traditional, face-to-face retail banking settings) will significantly affect the bank's ability to create trusting relationships between its customers and its employees. However, the impact of E-banking on the formation of customer trust can be expected to be different for customers who desire more communally-oriented relationships (DCR) when compared to customers desiring exchange-oriented relationships (DER). For both models we postulate the following hypotheses:

H1: The relationship between the use of E-banking and the customer's belief that consistent and reliable service performance will continue to be delivered in the future (cognition-based trust) is positive.

H2: The greater the use of E-banking technology, the less significant the relationship between frequency of personal contact and cognition-based trust will be.

H3: The relationship between cognition-based trust and relative attitude is positive.

Hypotheses 1 and 2 imply a 'substitutability effect'. It is suggested that frequency of contact with front-line employees becomes less significant in establishing customer confidence in E-banking environments. In other words, E-banking represents a viable alternative to customer-employee contact in order to establish cognition-based trust (i.e., fostering a belief in the customer that a consistent level of good service performance will continue to be delivered in the future), and this for both exchange- and communally-oriented customers. Conversely, hypotheses 4a and 5a (below) pertain solely to model A (customers desiring a communally-oriented relationship) while hypothesis 5b concerns only model B (customers desiring an exchange-oriented relationship).

H4a: For communally-oriented customers, the relationship between use of E-banking and affect-based trust is negative.

H5a: For communally-oriented customers, the relationship between affect-based trust and relative attitude is positive.

H5b: For exchange-oriented customers, the relationship between affect-based trust and relative attitude is non-significant.

As discussed above, the occurrence of affect-based trust is closely related to the development of commercial friendships. Although our models suggest that E-banking (a service environment which substitutes people for technology) will not deter from the bank's ability to foster cognition-based trust, they also suggest that the use of E-banking will have a negative effect on a bank's ability to generate affect-based trust. The loss of affect-based trust should translate into a negative impact on relative attitude and, thus, loyalty for customers desiring a communally-oriented relationship.

E-BANKING AND OVERALL SATISFACTION

Satisfaction has been defined as a general customer evaluative judgment based on the total purchase and consumption experience with a good or service over time (Anderson, Fornell, and Lehmann, 1994; de Ruyter and Wetzels, 2000). It is the pleasurable fulfillment of a need (Oliver, 1999) or the positive emotional response resulting from a customer's evaluation of a product or service (Woodruff, 1997). Satisfaction is said to be a function of expectations and actual experience (Oliver, 1980). When customer expectations are positively disconfirmed, satisfaction is believed to arise. Conversely, dissatisfaction occurs when the service experience is below what was expected by the customer.

Research indicates that customer satisfaction is a an important affective and emotional antecedent to loyalty (Dick and Basu, 1994; Mittal and Lassar, 1998; Newman and Werbel, 1973; LaBarbera and Mazursky, 1983). Crosby and Stephens (1987) found that overall satisfaction was related to whether or not insurance customers allowed their policies to expire and Anderson and Sullivan (1990) found that repurchase intentions were strongly influenced by product satisfaction among Swedish consumers. Research in social psychology suggests that, although E-banking environments may provide all customers with important functional benefits (e.g., more convenience and service reliability), for communal customers, it can break existing interpersonal bonds that have been established between customers and front-line personnel and thus reduce satisfaction. However, for customers that care little about developing interpersonal relationships with front-line personnel (i.e., exchange-oriented customers), E-banking may provide considerable value because these customers focus predominantly on the functional benefits such environments provide. Clark and Taraban (1991) suggest that when an exchange relationship is desired, expression of emotion may be reacted to negatively because it suggests the other party desires a type of relationship one does not want. Clark and her colleagues indicate that the greater a person's desire for a communal or exchange relationship (the more a person polarizes to either extreme), the more distressing violations of the norms appropriate to that relationship will seem. This suggests that in an E-banking environment, overall satisfaction depends on whether one experiences a relationship that closely matches the type of relationship one desires to have. We postulate the following hypotheses:

   H6a: For communally-oriented customers, the relationship between use of E-banking and overall satisfaction is negative.

   H6b: For exchange-oriented customers, the relationship between use of E-banking and overall satisfaction is positive.

SITUATIONAL FACTORS: MODERATORS

   The conceptual model of loyalty discussed previously (See Figure 1) suggests that loyalty is the relationship between relative attitude and patronage behavior (Dick and Basu, 1994). Situational factors are believed to affect this relationship and explain why customers may or may not behave accordingly to their attitudinal dispositions (i.e., why some customers continue patronizing institutions for which they harbor weak attitudes, and vice-versa). Traditionally, for financial service providers, the location of branches has been the most important factor in distributing their services effectively (Riggins, 1998). Proximity to home or work and operating hours have been identified as being central reasons dictating what bank customers choose (Keaveney, 1995; Rust and Zahorik, 1993). Because E-banking reduces switching costs such as spatial and temporal constraints, it should entail customers to behave more consistently with their relative attitudes. Moreover, because E-banking increases customer choice (i.e., more alternatives are now available to customers because of globalization), the impact of relative attitude should become more important in predicting behavior. Overall, assuming that relative attitude does not diminish following the customer's adoption of E-banking, this technology should allow banks to attract and retain their customers. Consequently, we suggest the following hypothesis:

   H7: E-banking use will be negatively related to perceived spatial and temporal constraints (i.e., limited operating hours, distance).

DISCUSSION

   In an E-banking environment, patronage behavior should become more consistent with relative attitude. However, as our analysis suggests, it is likely that relative attitude will change. The added convenience and flexibility of E-banking in conjunction with their high level of reliability should help banks generate cognition-based trust in both communally- and exchange-oriented customers. However, research suggests that the benefits customers derive from commercial relationships are not merely functional but may be social as well. Because E-banking environments are less rich and have less social presence than traditional, face-to-face service settings, the use of this technology may impact customer loyalty differently for communally- and exchange-oriented customers. In fact, we have argued that communally-oriented customers may experience difficulty in establishing the friendship-like (affect-based) relationships they value. In fact, although E-banking technology may provide customers with a service environment that is highly reliable and high in functional quality, these environments are largely devoid of human interaction. Without the communication richness and social presence intrinsic to traditional retail banking settings, it may be difficult for banks to effectively attract and hold onto communally-oriented customers who may be less satisfied in an E-banking environments. Because alternatives become increasingly available and switching costs are reduced, customer volatility is likely to increase.

Although we have suggested that E-banking environments should lead to greater satisfaction and the ability to establish trust for exchange-oriented customers, the lack of richness or social presence in such environments may potentially also have negative consequences. The lack of richness/social presence may become salient to exchange-oriented customers if service failure occurs. Primarily, this is because richer communication channels (i.e., face-to-face) may be more effective in responding to customer queries and in dealing with service failures. Smith et al. (1999) suggest that, because service failure induces a negative emotional response, customers get more emotionally involved and watchful of the actions taken by the organization to remedy the failure. Failure to remedy may actually bring about more dissatisfaction than the failure itself. Lovelock (1994) has suggested that this effort to gain back disgruntled customers may actually win their loyalty because it represents a demonstration of service excellence. The availability of rich (as opposed to lean) communication channels may enable the bank to better understand the problem at hand and guide its recovery efforts more effectively and in a more timely manner. However, without such a trigger (i.e., failure), the ability to generate trust in exchange-oriented customers should remain unabated. Consequently, when dealing with exchange-oriented customers, it is possible for banks to build customer loyalty in E-banking environments. However, our analysis also suggests that the type of loyalty that emerges in these technology-supported environments (which may be termed as 'E-loyalty') may be particularly sensitive to negative deviations in service performance because of the predominance of technological rather than emotional/interpersonal bonds. Particularly, for banks operating in pure E-banking environments, increased attention will be needed to ensure that the services provided via the technology is flawless. If not, disgruntled exchange-oriented customers may readily switch to another financial institution.

CONCLUSIONS

We used a definition of customer loyalty that recognizes the relationship between relative attitude and patronage behavior (Dick and Basu, 1994). When both are high, true loyalty exists. We identified overall satisfaction and trust as important antecedents to customer loyalty and suggested that trust is multidimensional having both a cognitive and an affective dimension. Furthermore, based on research in both social psychology and marketing, which indicates that customers vary in the types of relationships they wish to establish with service providers, we suggested that high relative attitude may wane with the use of E-banking for customers who desire communally-oriented relationships with their bank. We argued that this may occur because it is difficult to establish affect-based trust in E-banking environments. Such trust occurs with interpersonal exchanges that traditionally occurred when customers and front-line employees met face-to-face. At present, most banks that offer services through E-banking technology rely mainly on lean communication media with very little social presence. These environments are not conducive to social interaction. Furthermore, because communally-oriented customers may become particularly aware of their inability to derive social benefits (i.e., interpersonal bonds) in E-banking, the impact on overall satisfaction may be negative. Consequently, we suggest that for communally-oriented customers, relative attitude may falter, which may have negative effects on loyalty.

Conversely, exchange-oriented customers may focus strongly on the added convenience and flexibility such technology offers, and thus, may experience increased overall satisfaction. For these customers, establishing trusting relationships depends largely on cognitive aspects (i.e., performance) such as reliability. For these customers, the use of E-banking technology may enable them to by-pass the traditional customer-employee encounters without any negative consequence. In the absence of service failure, our analysis suggests that banks may effectively foster loyalty in exchange-oriented customers in E-banking environments.

Also, we argued that the type of loyalty that emerges in E-banking environments may be different than that in traditional settings. In these environments, positive relative attitude is dominantly founded on performance aspects rather than socio-emotional bonding. Consequently, it is unlikely that customers will be ready to solve service problems while an ever-increasing number of service providers offering similar technology are available.

REFERENCES

Aaker, D. A. (1991). *Managing Brand Equity*. New York: The Free Press.

Adelman, M. Ahuvia, A. & Goodwin, C. (1994). Beyond Smiling: Social support and service quality. In R.T. Rust and R. L. Oliver (Eds.), *Service Quality: New Directions in Theory and Practice* (pp. 138-172). London: SAGE Publications.

Anderson, E. W., Fornell, C., & Lehmann, D. R., (1994). Customer satisfaction, market share and profitability. *Journal of Marketing*. 58, 53-66.

Anderson, E. W. & Sullivan, M. W. (1990, September). Customer satisfaction and retention across firms. Paper presented at the TIMS College of Marketing Special Interest Conference on Services Marketing, Nashville, TN.

Anderson, E. W., & Weitz, B. (1989). Determinants of continuity in conventional industrial channel dyads. *Marketing Science*. 8 (Fall), 310-323.

Barnes, J. G. (1997). Closeness, Strength, and Satisfaction: Examining the Nature of Relationships Between Providers of Financial Services and Their Customers. *Psychology and Marketing*. 14 (8), 765-790.

Batson, C.D. (1994). Prosocial motivation: Why do we help others? In A. Tesser (Ed.), *Advanced Social Psychology* (pp.333-381). Boston: Mcgraw-Hill.

Batson, C.D., & Oleson, K.C. (1991). Current status of the empathy-altruism hypothesis. In M.S. Clark (Ed.), *Prosocial Behavior* (pp. 62-85). Newbary Park, CA: Sage Publications.

Beatty, S. E., Mayer, M. L., Coleman, J. E., Reynolds, K. E., & Lee, J. (1996). Customer-sales associate retail relationships. *Journal of Retailing*, 72 (fall), 223-247.

Bickers, C. (1999). *Net Returns. Far Eastern Economic Review*, 162 (18), 48-49.

Clark, M. S., & Mills, J. (1979). Interpersonal attraction in exchange and communal relationships. *Journal of Personality and Social Psychology*. 37, 12-24.

Clark, M. S., and Mills, J. (1993). The difference between communal and exchange relationships. *Personality and Social Psychology Bulletin*. 19, 684-691.

Clark, M. S., & Taraban, C. (1991). Reactions to and willingness to express emotion in communal and exchange relationships. *Journal of Experimental Social Psychology*. 27, 324-336.

Cochran, R. M. (2000). ATM market update – the new millennium. *Business Communications Review*. 30 (9), 52-58.

Colombo, R. A., & Morrison, D. G. (1989). A brand switching model with implications for marketing strategies. *Marketing Science*. 8 (1), 89-99.

Council of Financial Competition (1995). *Perfecting Customer Retention and Recovery – Overview of Economics and Proven Strategies*. Washington, DC: Advisory Board Company.

Crosby, L. A, & Stephens, N. (1987). Effects of relationship marketing on satisfaction, retention, ad prices in the life insurance industry. *Journal of Marketing Research*. 24 (Nov), 404-411.

Cunningham, S. M. (1966). Brand loyalty – What, where, how much? *Harvard Business Review*. 34 (January-February), 116-128.

Czepiel, J. A. (1990). Service encounters and service relationships: Implications for research. *Journal of Business Research*. 20 (1), 13-21.

Daft, R. L., & Lengel, R. H. (1986). Organizational information requirements, media richness, and structural design. *Management Science*. 32, 554-571.

Day, G. S. (1969). A two-dimensional concept of brand loyalty. *Journal of Advertising Research*, 9, 29-35.

Dekimpe, M. G., Steenkamp, J. B., Mellens, E. M., & Abeele, P. V. (1997). Decline and variability in brand loyalty. *International Journal of Research in Marketing*. 14, 405-420.

de Ruyter, K. & Wetzels, M. G. M. (2000). The impact of perceived listening behavior in voice-to-voice service encounters *Journal of Service Research*. 2 (3), 276-284.

Dick, A. S., & Basu, K. (1994). Customer loyalty: Toward an integrated conceptual framework. *Journal of the Academy of Marketing Science*. 22, 99-113.

Doney, P. M., & Cannon, J. P. (1997). An examination of the nature of trust in buyer-seller relationships. *Journal of Marketing*. 61, 35-51.

Doney, P. M., Cannon, J. P., & Mullen M. R. (1998). Understanding the influence of national culture on the development of trust. *Academy of Management Review*. 23(3), 601-620.

Ernst and Young, Fifth Annual Special Report on Technology in Banking, *Creating the Value Network*, 1998.

Ford, D. (1981). The development of buyer-seller relationships in industrial markets. *European Journal of Marketing*, 14, 339-53.

Forman, A. M., & Srivam, V. (1991). The depersonalization of retailing: Its impact on the "lonely" consumer. *Journal of Retailing*, 67 (2), 226-243.

Fournier, S. & Yao, J. L. (1997). Reviving brand loyalty: A reconceptualization within the framework of consumer-brand relationships. *International Journal of Research in Marketing*, 14, 451-472.

Hiltz, S. R., Johnson, K., & Turoff, M. (1986). Experiments in group decision making: Communication process and outcome in face-to-face versus computerized conferences. *Human Communication Research*, 13, 225-252.

Holbrook, M. B. (1978). Beyond attitude structure: Toward the informational determinants of attitude. *Journal of Marketing Research.* 15 (November), 545-556.

Huang, M-H, & Yu, S. (1999). Are consumers inherently or situationally brand loyal? - A set intercorrelation account for conscious brand loyalty and nonconscious inertia. *Psychology & Marketing.* 16 (6), 523-544.

Granitas, A. (2000). Tangled in the Web. *Far Eastern Economic Review.* 163 (18), 48-50.

Gremler, D. D., & Gwinner, K. P. (1998). Connecting with customers: An examination of rapport in service industries. In *American Marketing Association. Conference Proceedings*, Vol. 9 (pp. 161-162). Chicago, IL.

Goodwin, C., & Gremler, D. D. (1996). Friendship over the counter: How social aspects of service encounters influence consumer service loyalty. In T. A. Swartz, D. E. Bowen, and S. W. Brown (Eds.), *Advances in Services Marketing and Management,* Vol. 5, (pp. 247-282). Greenwich, CT: JAI.

Gwinner, K., Gremler, D. D., & Bitner, M. J. (1998). Relational benefits in service industries: The customer's perspective. *Journal of the Academy of Marketing Science.* 26 (Spring), 101-114.

Iacobucci, D., & Ostrom, A. (1996). Commercial and interpersonal relationships: Using the structure of interpersonal relationships to understand individual-to-individual, individual-to-firm, and firm-to-firm relationships in commerce. *International Journal of Research in Marketing.* 13, 53-72.

IFG Inc. (2000). Electronic banking basics. Retrieved April, 22, 2000 from the World Wide Web: http://www.ifg-inc.com/Consumer_Reports/ElectBank.shtml

Jacoby, J., & Chestnut, R. W. (1978). *Brand Loyalty: Measurement and Management.* New York: Wiley, Chichester.

Johnston, C. J. (1996). *Beyond customer satisfaction to loyalty.* The Conference board of Canada.

Keaveney, S. (1995). Customer switching behavior in service industries: An exploratory study. *Journal of Marketing.* 59 (April), 71-82.

Kiesler, S., Zubrow, D., Moses, A. M., & Geller, V. (1985). Affect in computer-mediated communication. *Human Computer Interaction.* 1, 77-104.

Krishnamurthi, L., & Raj, S. P. (1991). An empirical analysis of the relationship between brand loyalty and consumer price elasticity. *Marketing Science.* 10 (2), 172-183.

LaBarbera, P. A., & Mazursky, D. (1983). A longitudinal assessment of consumer satisfaction/dissatisfaction. *Journal of Marketing Research.* 20, 393-404.

Lafferty Report (2000). E-Banking a global strategic and statistical analysis of online banking. Retrieved January 15, 2001 from the World Wide Web: http://www.lafferty.com/manreports/ebank.shtml

Lewicki, R. J., & Bunker, B. B. (1995). Trust in relationships: A model of trust development and decline. In B. B. Bunker and J. Z. Rubin (Eds.), *Conflict, Cooperation and Justice* (pp. 133-173). San Francisco, CA: Jossey-Bass.

Lovelock, C. (1994). *Product Plus: How Product + Service = Competitive Advantage.* New York: McGraw-Hill.

Macintosh, G., & Lockshin, L. S. (1997). Retail relationships and store loyalty: a multi-level perspective. *International Journal of Research in Marketing.* 14, 487-497.

Massey, W. F., Montgomery, D. B., & Morrison, D. G. (1970). *Stochastic Models of Buyer Behavior.* Cambridge: MIT Press.

Mazanet, S. (2000). Online ATMs enhance member relationships. *Credit Union Magazine.* 66 (11), 66-68

McAllister, D. J. (1995). Affect- and cognition- based trust as foundations for interpersonal cooperation in organizations, *Academy of Management Journal.* 38 (1), 24-59.

Mills, J., and Clark, M. S. (1994). Communal and exchange relationships: Controversies and research. In R. Erber and R. Gilmour (Eds.), *Theoretical Frameworks for Personal Relationships* (pp. 29-42). Hillsdale, NJ: Erlbaum.

Mittal, B. & Lassar, W. M. (1996). The role of personalization in service encounters. *Journal of Retailing.* 72 (1), 95-109.

Mittal, V., Ross, W. T. Jr., & Baldasare, P. M. (1998). The asymmetric impact of negative and positive attribute-level performance on overall satisfaction and repurchase intentions. *Journal of Marketing.* 62 (January), 33-47.

Morgan, R. M., & Hunt, S. D. (1994). The commitment-trust theory of relationship marketing. *Journal of Marketing.* 58, 111-124.

Murphy, J. A. (1996). Retail banking. In F. Buttle (Ed.), *Relationship Marketing: Theory and Practice* (pp. 74-90). London, England: Paul Chapman Publishing Ltd.

Neal, W. D. (1999). Satisfaction is nice but value drives loyalty. *Marketing Research.* 11 (1), 21-24.

Newman, J. W., & Werbel, R. A. (1973). Multivariate analysis of brand loyalty for major household appliances. *Journal of Marketing Research.* 10, 404-409.

Oliver, R. L. (1980). A cognitive model of the antecedents and consequences of satisfaction decisions. *Journal of Marketing Research.* 17 (November), 460-469.

Oliver, R. L. (1999). Whence consumer loyalty? *Journal of Marketing.* 63, 33-44

Palmer, A. & Bejou, D. (1994). Buyer-seller relationships: a conceptual model and empirical investigation. *Journal of Marketing Management.* 10 (6), 495-512.

Price, L. L., & Arnould, E. J. (1999). Commercial friendships: Service provider-client relationships in context. *Journal of Marketing.* 63 (October), 38-56.

Price, L. L., Arnould, E. J., & Tierney, P. (1995). Going to extremes: Managing service encounters and assessing provider performance. *Journal of Marketing.* 59 (April), 83-97.

Reichheld, F. F. (1996). *The Loyalty Effect: The Hidden Force Behind Growth, Profits, and Lasting Value,* Boston, Massachusetts: Harvard Business School Press.

Reichheld, F. F., & Sasser, E. (1990). Zero defections: quality comes to services. *Harvard Business Review.* 68, 105-111.

Reynolds, K. E. & Beatty, S. E. (1999). A relationship customer typology. *Journal of Retailing.* 75 (4), 509-523.

Riggins, F. J. (1998). Developing a Web-Based Strategy for the Delivery of Online Banking Services. Retrieved May 20, 2000 from the World Wide Web: Http://riggins-mgt.iac.gatech.edu/papers/banking.html

Rosenberg, L. J. & Czepiel, J. A. (1984). A Marketing Approach to Customer Retention. *Journal of Consumer Marketing.* Spring, 45-51.

Rust, R., & Zahorik, A. J. (1993). Customer satisfaction, customer retention, and market share. *Journal of Retailing.* 69 (2), 193-215.

Segal, M. N. (1989). Implications of single vs. multiple buying sources. *Industrial Marketing Management.* 18, 163-178.

Smith, A. K., Bolton, R. N., & Wagner, J. (1999). A model of customer satisfaction with service encounters involving failure and recovery. *Journal of Marketing Research.* 36 (3), 356-372.

Stafford, M. R. (1994). How customers perceive service quality. *Journal of Retail Banking Services.* 17 (2), 29-38.

Tellis, G. J. (1988). Advertising exposure, loyalty, and brand purchase: A two-stage model of choice. *Journal of Marketing Research.* 25 (March), 134-144.

The Economist, (2000, Nov 4). Emerging-market indicators: Foreign banks, 118.

Walther, J. B., & Burgoon, J. K. (1992). Relational communication in computer-mediated interaction. *Human Communication Research.* 19 (1), 50-68.

Westmeyer, S. A., DiCioccio, R. L., & Rubin, R. B. (1998). Appropriateness and effectiveness of communication channels in competent interpersonal communication. Journal of Communication. 48 (3), 27-48.

Wilson, D. T., & Mummalaneni, V. (1986). Bonding and commitment in buyer-seller relationships: A preliminary conceptualization. *Industrial Marketing and Purchasing.* 1 (3), 44-58.

Wood, W. (1982). Retrieval of attitude-relevant information from memory: effects on susceptibility to persuasion and on intrinsic motivation. *Journal of Personality and Social Psychology.* 42 (May), 798-810.

Woodruff, R. B. (1997). Customer value: The next source of comparative advantage. *Journal of the Academy of Marketing Science.* 25 (Spring), 139-153.

Yasin, R. (2000). E-Bank enters crowded waters. InternetWeek, 834 (11). Retrieved January 16, 2001 from the World Wide Web: http://www.internetwk.com/

Zabava Ford, W. S. (1998). Communicating with Customers. Cresskill, New Jersey: Hampton Press, Inc.

ENDNOTES

[1] Aside from the 'true loyalty' and 'no loyalty' conditions, the model also suggests that two additional loyalty conditions may occur. This is because repeat patronage may occur without the existence of prior positive attitude, or that, strong relative attitude may not necessarily be accompanied by repeat patronage. 'Spurious loyalty', or customer inertia, emerges when the customer perceives little difference between alternatives (i.e., relative attitude is low) but purchases one brand more consistently than others. 'Latent loyalty' is categorized by high relative attitude and low repeat patronage. Such a condition may occur when situational and social factors intervene strongly and counter the effects of relative attitude.

[2] Accordingly, it is interesting to note that by dichotomizing trust as being both cognitively or affectively oriented, it becomes evident that recent attention to the question of establishing trust in virtual commercial environments pertains mainly to establishing cognition-based trust (e.g., Trust-E). Whereas the impacts of electronic commerce on affect-based trust remain largely unexplored.

ACKNOWLEDGEMENTS

Financial support for this research was provided by the Social Sciences and Humanities Research Council of Canada.

Chapter 7

Electronic Commerce and Strategic Change Within Organizations: Lessons from Two Cases

Robert D. Galliers
London School of Economics, United Kingdom

Sue Newell
Royal Holloway, University of London, United Kingdom

This article reviews and contrasts the experiences of two major companies in attempting significant change projects incorporating information and communication technologies. It does so by utilizing and critiquing the MIT "Management in the 1990s" model and by reflecting on socio-technical approaches to organizational change. It makes the point that while much of current attention is on electronic commerce as it pertains to industry transformation and inter-organizational relations, it is nonetheless a phenomenon that can impact complex internal relations and communication in addition. Additionally, conclusions are drawn with respect to the process of change and the need for further longitudinal studies when researching change projects of this kind.

INTRODUCTION

It goes without saying that electronic commerce has been a major topic of interest in recent years, with considerable importance being placed on the opportunities provided by information and communication technologies (ICTs) to improve coordination between businesses and with customers. Electronic commerce resonates as a potential means of finding solutions to some of the inter-

Previously Published in the *Journal of Global Information Management, vol.9, no.3*, Copyright © 2001, Idea Group Publishing.

organizational communication issues that confront modern-day businesses. However, with globalization, companies are themselves increasingly widely dispersed geographically so that internal communications are also more difficult and complex. ICTs can therefore also potentially improve communication between individuals and groups within an organization. This suggests that we might usefully broaden and unpack the concept of electronic commerce to include intra-organizational collaboration and partnerships. For example, corporate intranets, ERP systems, corporate databases and even internal email systems are all examples of electronic commerce that are increasingly used within a company. These ICTs enable data, knowledge and information to be shared even when the individuals involved are widely distributed. However, while intra-organizational electronic commerce can provide a communication link between people who are functionally, hierarchically or geographically separated, this does not necessarily mean that the social and psychological barriers between groups will be broken. The cases reported in this paper demonstrate very clearly that technology per se will not automatically improve communication between groups where long-standing barriers exist.

The importance of breaking down functional and hierarchical barriers has long been recognized in the information systems world. In academia, our roots in systems thinking provide us with a conceptual base for viewing organizational issues from a process orientation, with information requirements being associated with those activities necessary to achieve a desired purpose (e.g., Checkland, 1981). This so-called infological approach has been paralleled by what might be called a datalogical perspective, where the focus is on an analysis of the data entities – and their relationships - required to provide necessary information (Martin, 1982). These concepts have found practical form in such phenomena as database technologies and approaches, and more recently in business process reengineering (BPR), and knowledge management and knowledge management systems (KMS) (see, for example, Davenport, 1993; Alavi & Leidner, 1999).

This paper describes research concerning two companies that have been seeking to improve collaboration and communication internally across functional and departmental boundaries through the use of ICT. In one case the development and introduction of the ICT-based system leads to unintended, negative effects; in the other, there is preliminary evidence to suggest that the results have been much more positive. The experiences of the two companies help to reinforce lessons that have been known for some time[1] as well as providing new insights. The fact that these two cases are contemporary and that there appears to be evidence that some of the lessons of the past have been forgotten or have remained unheard, suggests that the comparison may be enlightening.[2]

The paper is structured as follows. Following this introduction, we will describe the methodology followed in the research upon which the case studies are based. Then we will briefly outline important aspects of each case, the first concerning the experiences of a major multinational bank in implementing KMS, and the second describing the somewhat more emergent and holistic approach adopted by a major international airline. In the next section, we will attempt to extract from the two cases those features that appear to be key. The concluding section provides something of a reflection on more general lessons, in terms of what remains to be done in the current research effort, and of potentially useful directions for future research in this area.

METHODOLOGY

Qualitative methods were used to explore the impact of ICTs on intra-organizational processes since these methods allow the researcher to examine the phenomenon of interest in its natural setting. Case studies were considered most appropriate since they allow for the adoption of multiple data collection methods (Yin, 1984), which was thought to be important in order to develop the rich case descriptions needed to build theoretical understanding. Case studies generate insightful stories, rather than statistical information, and permit a better understanding of organizational complexity from an insider's viewpoint (Mitchell, 1983) allowing the researcher to formulate a more holistic perspective on the studied phenomenon (Van Maanen, 1979). The cases reported in this paper were drawn from a larger pool of cases that have focused on investigating innovation processes in both manufacturing and service organizations across Europe. These two cases have been selected because they allow some interesting comparisons in relation to intra-organizational electronic commerce. Exploring the contextual similarities and differences between the cases is useful for examining their impacts on intra-organizational electronic commerce (Orlikowski, 1993).

Methods of data collection included interviews, on-site observation and documentation. Adopting multiple methods is important not only to enhance the richness of the findings but also to ensure validity through the process of triangulation (Stake, 1995). The research in each case was conducted over a period of approximately 18 months. This included four visits to the bank during this period and two to the airline. The interviews, in both cases, were conducted primarily with project team members and sponsors and included individuals from various hierarchical levels and divisions. The interviews were conducted face-to-face, using a semi-structured interview schedule, and tape-recorded and later transcribed. The interviews varied in length, but most were between one-and-a-half and two hours. The on-site observation took place during visits to the companies and allowed informal conversations with project members during coffee and lunch breaks. In the bank a two-day workshop was attended which greatly increased the opportunity for informal as well as formal research material to be collected. This allowed the researchers to make sense of the situation from an insider point of view (Evered & Louis, 1981). The on-site interviews at the airline were supplemented by telephone discussions, and further clarification regarding specific issues was provided via e-mail communication. Documents, such as minutes, reports and intranet sites related to the projects were used to further enhance the richness of the material collected. Observation of subsequent developments has taken place through study of media articles, press releases and the like.

As is typical in inductive studies, writing the case studies was an iterative process in which the data were constantly revisited. Triangulation across the different sources of primary and archival case material revealed a high level of consistency so that the 'story' described in each case can be said to be valid. While there were no preconceived hypotheses at the outset of the inquiry, patterns emerged from the data which suggested the potential for using the MIT model (Scott Morton, 1991; p. 20) to compare the two cases in relation to their electronic commerce projects (see below).

CASE 1: THE BANK

The bank has around 70,000 employees and operates in approximately 70 countries worldwide, with its headquarters in Europe. The bank was formed from a merger of two banks from the same country and has subsequently grown via the acquisition of banks in the various countries in which it now operates. ICT has always been an important priority in the bank, as evidenced by the fact that it is the fifth highest spender on IT in Europe. Its structure and functioning is highly decentralized, with resources allocated to the independent divisions and with very few resources retained at the center. It consists of a number of different product divisions including domestic, international and investment banking.

A problem that was exercising the minds of top management in this bank was that they had recently lost a key account thanks to the perceived inability of the bank to adopt similar procedures and provide similar services in the countries in which the global client company was operating. Exasperated by the bank's apparent inability to present a 'common face' worldwide (despite this being a stated strength in its marketing literature), the client company took its business to a rival. The bank's reaction to this event was to set up a pilot intranet project. This pilot project was a key part of its "Vision 2000" strategy, which was aimed at creating "The Networked Bank". The strategic intent of this project was thus to create a network across the bank so that knowledge and information could be shared more effectively across functions and geographically dispersed sites. This, it was assumed, would lead to the common adoption of defined 'best practices' and so stimulate the integration of procedures and services across the bank. However, in direct contrast to the stated strategy, the actual impact was that the existing boundaries between functions and dispersed business units were reinforced. This was because, during the 18 month life of the pilot, in excess of 150 known intranets had been set up by individual departments in individual countries.

Once this became evident, the bank called together representatives (both banking and IT) from its major national sites worldwide with a view to investigating how to coordinate this emerging web of intranets and achieve the stated strategic objectives. The idea was that this might help reduce response variety in the different countries. The meeting took place over two days at the bank's headquarters. Two problems emerged almost instantaneously. First, the banking representatives were "too busy" to attend both days - having attended the first "strategic focus" day, they left their IT colleagues to "sort out the technical details" on the second day. Second, the IT representatives on the second day focused exclusively on technical solutions and came to the conclusion that the way forward was to create a corporate portal through which individuals could navigate the myriad of intranets. However, these national IT representatives were so energized as a result of these discussions that many of them set about designing their very own 'corporate' portal. Within ten days the Bank was the 'proud owner' of six or seven 'corporate' portals, each with its own characteristics and idiosyncracies – and there were more on the way. In other words, the bank's knowledge management system (KMS) turned out to be many KMSs and the original objective of presenting a common client interface was lost. Additionally, while making available a considerable quantity of apparently usable and useful data, few of the bank's employees found their KMS to be particularly useful in their dealings with clients – or anything else for that matter. In one department in one country – and this appeared to be the most established of the intranets - the best that anyone could come up with when asked how it was being used, was "to look up the company bus timetable."

A key problem in this case was that the vision of a 'global' bank was in stark contrast to the existing culture and structure of the bank. The bank had grown largely through acquisition and merger, and each of these acquired banks had been left very much to operate using their home-grown procedures, offering the particular services they had historically provided. There had been no attempt to standardize, and indeed the culture of decentralization was built into the distribution of resources and the performance management measures used. Thus, when the pilot intranet project was started, each nationally-located bank and department recognized the potential usefulness of this technology for improving its own internal efficiencies. However, there was no reason for each to consider the potential of the technology for communicating and sharing information and knowledge across the existing internal boundaries since there was no real incentive for them to do so. Thus, while all were aware of the stated vision, and indeed during interviews related their own intranet initiatives to this globalizing vision, each unit was most concerned with using its own resources for establishing internal efficiencies. Collaborating with other units would take time and resources away from this focus, at least in the short-term. The result was that a strategy aimed at coordinating knowledge and information across the bank actually resulted in a great deal of reinvention as each unit developed its own applications for sharing across its own uniquely developed intranet. There were examples given during interviews of how significant sums of money (c.$500,000) had been spent on developing intranet applications for knowledge sharing in one department, only for those involved to later find that similar sums had been spent by other units developing very similar if not identical applications elsewhere.

CASE 2: THE AIRLINE

The second case is of one of the world's largest international passenger airlines, based in Europe. It had 356 aircraft in December 1999, operating over one thousand flights a day and flying 45 million passengers in 1998-99. It has approximately 64,000 staff worldwide, 80% of them based in Europe. Originally a publicly-owned company, it was privatized in 1987. It is now owned entirely by private investors with around 265,000 shareholders, including 71% of the company's own employees. The airline market has become increasingly fierce and had led to a drop in profits for the company in both 1998-99 and 1999-2000. The company's response was to target profitable passenger segments and to work more closely with other airline companies in global alliances. These partnerships give the airline a presence in all major world markets.

The issue confronting this airline was that many of its central departments were housed in different buildings with consequent inefficiencies and complex communications. A new headquarters was therefore planned, presenting an opportunity to upgrade systems and communications, utilizing the very best in modern ICT, and to house the c.3000 employees involved. A project team was set up, with a representative from each of the departments affected by the proposed office move. The chair of the project team reported to a steering committee comprising senior executives and chaired by a Main Board member. The initial major objective was for the move – a $320m investment – to reap annual savings of at least $25m through streamlined procedures, reduced paper usage and reductions in headcount. The project was quickly perceived (by both the steering committee and the project team members) as representing an opportunity not only to save money but to improve communications across departmental boundaries and to enable creative, innovative thinking to take place. This did result in significant savings with, for example, 89 tons of paper having been saved in the first five months of operation in the new building. In addition, however, further benefits ensued.

Primarily a partnership between those responsible for office design and the IT and Human Resource Management departments, the project's scope soon expanded to include new ways of working, streamlined procedures and extensive training programs for all involved in the move – including the CEO. Everyone was expected to participate and ideas about potential innovations were actively sought: the very process of preparing for the move set the tone for the new working environment with knowledge sharing and knowledge creation being both encouraged and rewarded. Those involved recognized that the potentially disruptive and unsettling experience of a major office move, combined with new procedures, new technology and systems, not to mention downsizing, could be perceived in a much more positive light were the approach to be inclusive and participative. Furthermore, excitement and pride might actually be generated in looking forward to the new opportunities available in the new working environment. The fact that the media also took considerable interest in the project added to the sense of expectancy being generated by the move. Communication was seen to be key throughout and this was achieved through face-to-face briefings, discussion groups, training programs, videos, newsletters and the like.

The new headquarters was designed to enable informal, ad hoc meetings to take place in, for example, coffee bars located on either side of the main thoroughfare. Individual offices and meeting rooms are few and far between (even the CEO did not have his own office), with 'hot desking' being the norm, and mobile cell-phones being used to ease mobility and communication. The intranet is used extensively, for example, for booking travel (and for claiming the related travel expenses), for gleaning information on both corporate and individual customers— either in response to inquiries or proactively for direct marketing purposes, and for communicating with company offices and major client organizations worldwide in addition.

It is too early to judge the longer term benefits (and disbenefits) of the move which has not been without its teething problems of course. For example, the hot desking concept has not been entirely successful with individuals deliberately leaving their belongings behind on 'their' desk in an attempt to reserve their own space. In addition, others have been somewhat unsettled by the lack of a 'home' given their need to 'belong', while the continuing need to drive down costs even further has raised tensions. From the systems perspective, it is clear that further modifications to user interfaces may be required since infrequent use leads to forgetfulness, which in turn has a tendency to raise frustrations about 'the technology'. Further, the initial euphoria attaching to the move to the new building which, as already indicated, had attracted considerable media interest and critical acclaim, died down considerably over time. This perfectly natural decline in enthusiasm was exacerbated for example, by adverse market and media reaction to certain of the airline's high profile strategic decisions and the subsequent replacement of the CEO. Despite this and some of the problems mentioned above, many of the sought-after benefits have been achieved and communication appears to be more open and streamlined, with informality having been retained despite the new formal procedures. Morale remains high despite the company's somewhat disappointing financial results and the continuing intense competition it faces.

REFLECTIONS: KEY ISSUES

While considerably more research has to take place in both organizations in order properly to reflect on the widely differing experiences of the two companies, some initial comments can be made. The two cases are clearly rather different, but in both the focus was on using ICT to facilitate communication and knowledge sharing across their dispersed operations. In other words, both organizations were attempting to use electronic commerce to transform intra-organizational relations, in particular by encouraging greater coordination and collaboration across departments and business units. In both cases, top management was committed to change and saw each project as being strategically important from the point of view of the business. While both change projects were to be enabled by ICT, both were essentially 'business-driven'. In the case of the bank, however, it would seem that the project was initially conceived, and remained, one of *superimposing* an ICT on to an existing organizational structure, with little in the way of changed work practices. For example, departmental boundaries and authority remained untouched, with each department remaining responsible for its own "slice of the action". An ICT-based KMS was perceived to be the answer, with it being 'parachuted' on top of the existing organization. Making apparently useful data available for everyone would lead to the common client interface that was considered essential to retain key customers. For the airline, what was initially an office move, conceived for the purposes of cost reduction and greater efficiency, soon became an opportunity radically to streamline office procedures, reduce paperwork and improve communication – both internally and externally. What *emerged* was what we might view as a socio-technical design for the new building *and the people in it*. Perhaps the irony in this comparison is that while the bank actively sought improved customer relationship management and internal communication, the airline achieved it without planning to do so. We might characterize the bank's approach as a case of 'top-down', business–driven planning, while the airline's management gave their project team broad guidelines (and tough financial targets), but the freedom to be creative and the ability to allow ideas to *emerge* from knowledge sharing.

It has often been said that it is easier to effect change when there is a sense of crisis. Paradoxically, however, it was the bank that saw itself as facing a crisis, while the airline simply wanted to become more competitive by being more efficient – seeing the issue as simply the on-going business of competing in what is a cut-throat industry. In addition, it is clear that while the bank expected that the mere provision of a KMS would lead to the improvements they sought, the airline took considerable steps to inform, motivate and energize those concerned, both before the move and afterwards.

Utilizing the MIT "Management in the 1990s" model (Scott Morton, 1991), we can map the alternative approaches adopted by the two case companies. Figure 1 illustrates the MIT model in outline, while Figure 2 provides a comparison of the paths followed by the bank and the airline. Essentially, the original model attempts to illustrate the nature of strategic change and fit. The model emphasizes (after Leavitt, 1965) that a change in any of the five elements will have an impact on the other four elements. It also reminds us that there is more to the management of change than the early advocates of business process reengineering would have had us believe (Galliers & Swan, 1999), given their emphasis on process innovation on the back of ICT alone (e.g., Davenport, 1993). While Figure 1 might be seen as an idealized version of an holistic approach to organizational change and fit, Figure 2 represents the stark reality of the approaches adopted in the two case companies.

The model in Figure 1 depicts all the elements as being interrelated, but in practice the dominant assumption has been that technology must be aligned to the established strategy-structure fit (Scott Morton, 1991). In other words, a firm must

Figure 1: The MIT Model of Strategic Change and Fit

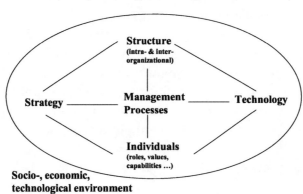

Figure 2: The two approaches compared

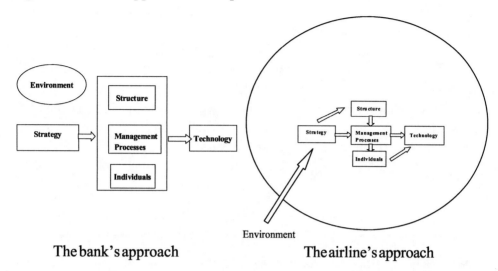

The bank's approach   The airline's approach

first develop its strategy, then design the structure to support this strategy, and finally build new management processes, align IT and ensure that appropriate roles are created and individuals are trained (McGee & Prusak, 1993). Comparing the two cases against these normative assumptions it is clear that neither case company operated according to this 'best practice' prescription.

Essentially the bank's approach was little more than identifying a technological solution to a perceived business problem. It was assumed that, having articulated the strategy, all that was necessary was to align the selected ICT with this strategy. Unfortunately, this ignored the existing management processes and individual roles and skills, as well as leaving the organizational structure unchanged. Recall, too, that the individual national banks were essentially operating in opposition to the newly defined strategy. Hence, the approach ignored the organizational environment, let alone the wider socio-economic environment. In this situation, as the MIT model would suggest, the impact of the ICT (in this case intranet technology used as a KMS) was limited and certainly did not result in the strategic changes intended.

In contrast, the airline, taking into account the socio-economic environment in which it was operating, initially converted its strategy (i.e., to improve efficiency and cut costs by moving disparate functional units into a single location) into required changes in structure and business processes. Shortly after its formation, members of the project team saw the wider opportunities afforded by the move, more specifically in terms of a new working environment, enabled by ICT (in this case an intranet/KMS), and the pressing need to develop new roles and skills. Importantly, the development of the technology support for the new strategy, as well as the roles and management processes, was much more emergent than is suggested by the MIT model. There was never any explicit attempt to align the ICT available with the strategy. What is more, and this is not adequately illustrated by the MIT model, the process by which they went about the change project was key, with participation and inclusiveness being the watchwords. In other words, the *process* of IT implementation management in the airline appeared to be crucial to the success experienced, especially in terms of involving potential users as widely as possible and letting solutions emerge and evolve as individuals interacted and learned about the available technologies. Similarly, Yetton (1997) argues that successful IT management is often more evolutionary than the strategic alignment approach advocated.

CONCLUSIONS AND FUTURE RESEARCH

In many ways, the message from this comparison is not new – i.e., that we should not expect business improvements to come from ICT alone but that we should see such change projects as being essentially about human beings, about social systems ... albeit with a technological component. After all, this has been the mantra of the socio-technical school for the past 50 years or so. Having said that, the fact that we can observe such differing experiences in implementing change on the back of ICT at the beginning of the 21st century suggests that much has still to be learned in this respect. This is perhaps particularly true now, given that such flexible ICT as intranet technology is both commonplace and accessible, and its promise is well known among even the most troglodyte of business executives. In selling solutions as the IT industry is prone to do, it is not unreasonable to expect that executives might be lulled into a false sense of security when investing in those solutions. We have seen here that a business-driven, top-down approach, even with top management commitment, may well be necessary but not sufficient to effect change that brings about business benefits. We have also seen that a broader conception of an IS change project (taking into account people and their modes of working and communicating) seems more likely to bring about beneficial results – even unexpected ones. Creating the conditions for emergence and serendipity appears to hold considerable promise in this context. The related concepts of 'bricolage' (Ciborra, 1992) and improvisation (Orlikowski, 1996; 1997) have recently been introduced in the context of ICT management, and the airline case certainly appears to support the argument of letting ICT applications evolve as people use and experiment with them.

The use of the term 'evolve' is both deliberate and important in this context. Often, debate in the field of business strategy has focused on the two schools of thought concerned with emergent and deliberate strategies (cf., Mintzberg, 1989).

This finds form in the IS literature in addition (e.g., Orlikowski, 1996). In both cases considered here, however, the strategy was evidently deliberate and emanated from 'the center'. In the case of the bank, the strategy was limited to the development of a technological solution imposed on an 'alien' culture. It therefore failed, at the time of writing at least, to bring about the desired results. Conversely, in the case of the airline, a more broadly based, but nonetheless deliberate strategy was formulated. In contrast to the bank, however, an appreciative climate was fostered, enabling greater acceptance of the proposed strategy. Additionally, a climate of mutual learning developed, thus enabling the strategy to *evolve* in the light of experience.

While the findings here support a socio-technical view of organizational change, they also take us beyond this since even here the *process* of change has been under-examined. For example, both companies involved multi-functional project teams in implementing the change programs. However, there was a significant difference in how these teams operated – i.e., in their processes. In the bank, the different functions worked essentially independently, even when they were supposedly working on a joint project. This was demonstrated most clearly at the two-day workshop. Knights and Wilmot (1997) refer to this as mechanistic pooling, which they define as occurring where "each member of the pool takes a different 'slice' of the project and the work then proceeds with the minimum of communication between its members" (p. 19). In the airline, on the other hand, the project team was much more clearly engaged in joint knowledge production, where the knowledge from the different functional specialists was shared and integrated to produce new solutions which were accepted by those involved. These micro-level processes appeared to be essential to the relative success of the two cases but are not captured by static and more messo-level models of organizational change.

The MIT model may provide a useful starting point for examining the impact of intra-organizational electronic commerce but what is now needed is longitudinal research that tracks and monitors the messy and sometimes tortuous *process* by which this change takes place. In this vein, on-going research in the two case study companies is taking place with a view to ascertaining more clearly the repercussions of the two initiatives, over time, both in terms of intended and unintended effects. We cannot assume that the only outcomes in the case of the bank are entirely negative, nor that in the case of the airline, they are entirely positive. Pennings (1998), for example, has highlighted the lagged effects of ICT investments and Pettigrew (1990) counsels longitudinal research in the context of change projects. While the research described here was clearly longitudinal (being conducted over a period of 18 months) the projects which are being considered here are on-going in the sense that in neither case has the technology been fully appropriated. Appropriation occurs when a new technology that has been implemented has become routine (Clark & Staunton, 1989). With complex technologies implemented in large global companies this is likely to take a very long time, if indeed it ever happens. So, here we have considered the *initial* impacts only of two ICT implementation projects. However, with the pressure on academics to publish, and with the limits to research funding available, it is often very difficult to conduct longitudinal research over extended periods, covering the entire innovation process from agenda formation (when the idea for implementing a particular new technology is first tabled) through to appropriation. This means that many of our research findings are likely to provide only a snapshot (or at least only a small movie extract) of the ICT management process. Given the importance noted here of emergence and evolution, this suggests a problem for those interested in this area, and poses a significant challenge for IS research more generally. Discussion and debate as to how to resolve this problem is urgently needed so that we prevent oversimplification of ICT-based change which tends to highlight the failures rather than the successes. Successes are likely to take considerable time to emerge and not be captured by the snapshots that commonly get taken through the research process conducted in real time. On the other hand, retrospective accounts suffer from post-hoc rationalizing and justification so that much of the emergent and messy process of ICT-based change is concealed (Lanzarra, 1999).

There is some additional learning that might potentially be gleaned from this comparison. The lack of a cumulative tradition in IS has been highlighted and criticized for some time (e.g., Keen, 1980). More recently, and in a similar vein, one of the authors of this paper has expressed his concern regarding our propensity in the IS field to study emerging phenomena in isolation. In doing so, he highlighted as examples, KMS and electronic commerce at this point in the development of our subject area (Galliers, 1999). It would seem, certainly on the face of it, that the experience of both the airline and the bank would lend some weight to further research in which electronic commerce and KMS are considered as related phenomena in the context of the kind of strategic change reported on here.

Finally, in relation to intra-organizational electronic commerce per se, there is an important difference between the two cases that needs to be considered. Specifically, while the bank relied wholly on a virtual space (the intranet) to facilitate improved internal communication and collaboration, the airline incorporated an improved physical as well as virtual space as part of its change program. The new building designed by the airline not only co-located individuals from the different functional areas but also created places where people could meet, either formally and informally. Nonaka and Konno (1994) develop the concept of 'Ba' to highlight the need for 'space' in the knowledge creating company. While some of these 'Bas' are virtual, others require a shared physical space. It is tempting to argue that the airline was relatively more successful precisely because its change strategy that encouraged greater interdepartmental collaboration, perhaps serendipitously, gave employees access to both a virtual and a physical space in which to interact with colleagues. This suggests that intra-organizational electronic commerce will need to be carefully integrated with face-to-face opportunities for interaction for the benefits of such virtual communication to be more fully exploited.

REFERENCES

Alavi, M. & Leidner, D. E. (1999). Knowledge Management Systems: Issues, Challenges, and Benefits. *Communications of the Association for Information Systems,* 1(7), February. http://cais.isworld.org/articles/1-7/article.htm

Bjerknes, G., Ehn, P. & Kyng, M. (Eds.) (1987). *Computers and Democracy: A Scandinavian Challenge.* Aldershot, UK: Avebury.

Bostrom, R. P. & Heinen, J. S. (1977a). MIS Problems and Failures: A Socio-Technical Perspective, Part 1: The Causes. *MIS Quarterly,* 1(3), September.

Bostrom, R. P. & Heinen, J. S. (1977b). MIS Problems and Failures: A Socio-Technical Perspective, Part 2: The Application of Socio-Technical Theory. *MIS Quarterly,* 1(4), December.

Checkland, P. B. (1981). *Systems Thinking. Systems Practice.* Chichester, UK: Wiley.

Ciborra, C. U. (1992). From Thinking to Tinkering: The Grassroots of Strategic Information Systems, *The Information Society,* 8, 297-309.

Clark, P. & Staunton, N. (1989). *Innovation in Technology and Organization.* London, UK: Routledge.

Coakes, E., Willis, D. & Lloyd-Jones, R. (Eds.) (2000). *The New Socio-Tech: Graffiti on the Long Wall.* London, UK: Springer-Verlag.

Davenport, T. H. (1993). *Process Innovation. Reengineering Work through Information Technology.* Boston, MA: Harvard Business School Press.

Evered, R. & Louis, M. R. (1981). Alternative Perspectives in the Organizational Sciences: "Inquiry from the Inside" and "Inquiry from the Outside", *Academy of Management Review,* 6, 385-395.

Galliers, R. D. (1999). Towards the Integration of e-Business, Knowledge Management and Policy Considerations within an Information Systems Strategy Framework. *Journal of Strategic Information Systems,* 8(3), September, 229-234.

Galliers, R. D. & Swan, J. (1999). Information Systems and Strategic Change: A Critical Review of Business Process Re-engineering. In W L Currie & R D Galliers (Eds.) *Rethinking Management Information Systems: An Interdisciplinary Approach,* Oxford, UK: Oxford University Press, 361-387.

Keen, P. G. W. (1980). MIS Research: Reference Disciplines and a Cumulative Tradition, *Proceedings*: 1st International Conference on Information Systems, Philadelphia, PA, December, 9-18.

Knights, D. & Wilmott, H. (1997). The Hype and Hope of Interdisciplinary Management Studies, *British Journal of Management*, 8, 9-22.

Lanzarra, G. (1999). Between Transient Constructs and Persistent Structures: Designing Systems in Action, *Journal of Strategic Information Systems*, 8(4), 331-350.

Leavitt, H. J. (1965). Applying Organizational Change in Industry: Structural, Technological and Humanistic Approaches. In J G March (Ed.), *Handbook of Organizations*. Stokie, IL: Rand McNally.

Martin, J. (1982). *Strategic Data Planning Methodologies*, Englewood Cliffs, NJ: Prentice-Hall.

McGee, J. & Prusak, L. (1993). *Managing Information Strategically*. New York, NY: Wiley.

Mintzberg, H. (1989). Strategy Formation: Ten Schools of Thought. In: J Fredricson (Ed.), *Prospectus on Strategic Management*. New York, NY: Ballinger.

Mitchell, J. C. (1983). Case and Situation Analysis. *Sociological Review*, 31, 186-211.

Mumford, E. (1983). *Designing Human Systems: The ETHICS Approach*. Manchester, UK: Manchester Business School.

Mumford, E. (1987). *Sociotechnical Systems Design: Evolving Theory and Practice*. In: Bjerknes et al. (Eds.), *op cit.*, 59-76.

Nonaka, I. & Konno, N. (1998). The Concept of 'Ba': Building a Foundation for Knowledge Creation, *California Management Review*, 40(3), 40-54.

Orlikowski, W. J. (1993). CASE Tools as Organizational Change: Investigating Incremental and Radical Changes in System Development, *MIS Quarterly*, 17, 309-340.

Orlikowski, W. J. (1996). Improvising Organizational Transformation Over Time: A Situated Change Perspective, *Information Systems Research*, 7(1), 63-92.

Orlikowski, W. J. (1997). An Improvisational Model of Change Management: The Case of Groupware Technologies, *Sloan Management Review*, Winter.

Pennings, J. (1998). Innovations as Precursors of Organizational Performance. In R. D. Galliers & W. R. J. Baets (Eds.). *Information Technology and Organizational Transformation: Innovation for the 21st Century Organization*. Chichester, UK: Wiley, 153-178.

Pettigrew, A. M. (1990). Longitudinal Field Research on Change: Theory and Practice, *Organization Science*, 1(3), 267-292.

Sauer, C., Yetton, P. W. & Associates (1997). *Steps to the Future. Fresh Thinking on the Management of IT-Based Organizational Transformation*. San Francisco, CA: Jossey-Bass.

Scott Morton, M. S. (Ed.) (1991). *The Corporation of the 1990s: Information Technology and Organizational Transformation.* New York, NY: Oxford University Press.

Stake, R. (1995). *The Art of Case Study Research.* London, UK: Sage.

Van Maanen J. (1979). Reclaiming Qualitative Methods for Organizational Research, *Administrative Science Quarterly*, 24, 520-526.

Yetton, P. W. (1997). False Prophecies, Successful Practice, and Future Directions in IT Management. In Sauer, Yetton & Associates, *op cit.*, 27-54.

Yetton, P. W., Johnston, K. D. & Craig, J. F. (1994). Computer-Aided Architecture: A Case Study of IT and Strategic Change. *Sloan Management Review,* 35(4), 57-67.

Yin, R. K. (1984) *Case Study Research - Design and Methods.* London, UK: Sage.

ENDNOTES

[1] Through, for example, the work of those associated with the socio-technical school of thought (e.g. Mumford, 1983; 1987), particularly in relation to Information Systems (IS) failures (e.g. Bostrom & Heinen, 1977a,b) and a more balanced, non- technologically deterministic and emanicapatory approach to IS development and implementation. (e.g. Bjerknes, *et al.*, 1987)

[2] The fact that a new book (Coakes, *et al.*, 2000) has recently been published on new thinking and contemporary accounts of the socio-technical approach suggests that we are not alone in this belief.

Chapter 8

Trust in Internet Shopping: Instrument Development and Validation Through Classical and Modern Approaches

Christy M. K. Cheung and Matthew K. O. Lee
City University of Hong Kong, China

Despite the phenomenal growth of Internet users in recent years, the penetration rate of Internet shopping is still low and one of the most often cited reasons is the lack of consumers' trust (e.g. Hoffman et al., 1999). Although trust is an important concept in Internet shopping, there is a paucity of theory-guided empirical research in this area. In this paper, a theoretical model is proposed for investigating the nature of trust in the specific context of Internet shopping. In this model, consumers' trust in Internet shopping is affected by propensity to trust and two groups of antecedent factors, namely, "trustworthiness of Internet vendors" and "external environment". Trust, in turn, reduces consumers' perceived risk in Internet shopping. As an important step towards the rigorous testing of the model, the necessary measurement instrument has been developed with its reliability and validity empirically tested. The psychometric properties of the measurement instrument have been investigated using both a classical approach (based on Cronbach's alpha and exploratory factor analysis) and a contemporary approach (based on structural equation modeling techniques), as a way of methods triangulation for validating instrument properties. The resulting instrument represents a rigorously developed and validated instrument for the measurement of various important trust related constructs. This research contributes to the

Previously Published in the *Journal of Global Information Management, vol.9, no.3,* Copyright © 2001, Idea Group Publishing.

development of trust theory in e-commerce and add to the repository of rigorous research instruments for IS survey researchers to use.

INTRODUCTION

The growth of the Internet and its user base in recent years has been truly phenomenal. As of November 2000, the estimated number of people online has exceeded 407 million[1] and the annual growth rate remains high. Enormous potential therefore exists for the use of the Internet for the purchase of goods and services ("Internet Shopping"). However, this potential remains largely untapped as market surveys[2] have confirmed that many Internet users are still reluctant to make purchases on the Internet. One of the most often cited reasons for consumers not purchasing from Internet shops is the lack of trust, which stops or discourages consumers from entering into exchange relationships with Internet shops (e.g. Hoffman et al., 1999). Despite the importance of trust in consumer-based electronic commerce, little theory-guided empirical research has been undertaken to understand the nature of trust, its antecedents and consequences in the specific context of Internet shopping. The few research papers available (e.g. Jarvenpaa et. al., 1999) tend to focus on very small models, ignoring many potentially important constructs (e.g. trust propensity, privacy and security) suggested by the rich but distant literature on trust. Thus, more research is called for. In addition, the study of e-commerce trust has been hampered by a lack of validated measurement instrument in the literature. As a step towards bridging this gap, this paper proposes a research model of trust in Internet shopping and presents the development of an empirically validated measurement instrument for testing the trust model.

This paper is presented as follows. The first section reviews the literatures on Trust. Then we present the research model and propositions and describe the instrument development and validation process, and results. Finally, conclusions of the findings and suggestions for future research are provided.

TRUST

The notion of trust has been examined under various contexts over the years, e.g. in bargaining (Schurr & Ozanne, 1985), industrial buyer-seller relationships (Doney & Cannon, 1997), distribution channels (Dwyer, Schurr & Oh, 1987), partner cooperation in strategic alliances (Das, 1998) and the use of market research (Moore et al., 1993). Different theoretical perspectives have been used in these studies, which may be aggregated into three categories (Lewicki & Bunker, 1995):

1. The views of personality theorists, conceptualizing trust as a belief, expectancy, or feeling which is deeply rooted in the personality and has its origins in the individual's early psychological development.
2. The views of sociologists and economists, conceptualizing trust as a phenomenon within and between institutions, and as the trust individuals put in those institutions.
3. The views of the social psychologists, characterizing trust in terms of the expectation and willingness of the trusting party engaging in a transaction, the risks associated with and acting on such expectations, and the contextual factors that serve to either enhance or inhibit the development and maintenance of that trust.

Although the social-psychological perspective appears to be most relevant in the understanding of consumer trust in Internet shopping as this perspective focuses on transactions, the other perspectives also contribute to our understanding of trust in this context in their unique ways. For example, it would be insufficient to consider consumers' trust in Internet shopping without examining the trust propensity (which is a personality trait) of the consumers concerned.

The distant literature on trust across a wide variety of disciplines provides a useful basis on which to investigate consumer trust, its antecedents and consequences in the context of Internet shopping. However, most of the literature still suffers from the problems identified by Mayer and Davis (1995). Confusions between trust and its antecedents still abound. For example, in Kini and Choobineh (1999) the definition of trust included the sources of trust itself. In addition, most of the literature does not contain empirical supporting evidence. In the context of consumer trust in Internet shopping, theory-guided empirical study is rare. This severe lack of theory-guided empirical studies is critically impeding our understanding of consumers' trust in Internet shopping.

RESEARCH MODEL AND PROPOSITIONS

This research synthesizes the diverse literature on trust in order to develop an integral research model of consumer trust in Internet shopping (CTIS). According to Hardin (1992), trust is a three-party relation involving properties of a trustor, attributes of a trustee, and a specific context in which trust is conferred.

As depicted in Figure 1, trust in Internet shopping is affected by: a consumer's propensity to trust; the trustworthiness of an Internet vendor; and relevant external environmental factors impacting Internet shopping transactions. Limerick and Cunnington (1993) also argued that trust can reduce uncertainty about the future and is a necessity for a continuing relationship with participants who have

Figure 1: A conceptual model of trust in Internet shopping

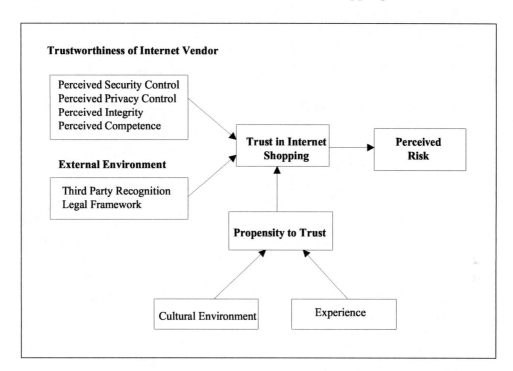

opportunistic behavior. The essence of risk is uncertainty about the future. Thus, the formation of trust, in turn, reduces consumers' perceived risk of Internet shopping.

Trustworthiness of Internet Vendor

The perceived trustworthiness of a party is often suggested as an important antecedent of trust. There is a long line of research (summarized in, for example, Mayer et al. (1995)) examining the influence of perceived trustworthiness on the building of trust. Mayer et al. (1995) found that three factors – ability, integrity, and benevolence – are consistently related to trust in most previous studies. Hence, these factors are included in our model. In addition, in the specific context of this study, two new factors are added to the model to reflect the specific nature of Internet shopping. These two factors are Perceived Security Control (PSC) and Perceived Privacy Control (PPC).

PSC and PPC are critical characteristics of Internet shopping transactions affecting the development of Internet users' trust in Internet shopping. Previous studies find that these two factors are the major concerns of Internet users. In particular, privacy is the number one consumer issue facing the Internet (Benassi, 1999; Hoffman et al., 1999; Wang et al., 1998).

Perceived Security Control (PSC)

In this study, perceived security control refers to the Internet users' perception on the Internet vendors' ability to fulfill security requirements, such as authentication, integrity, encryption, and non-repudiation. Consumers tend to have a better trust in Internet shopping if a higher level of security is believed to exist. Therefore, the proposition is:

Proposition 1: The perceived security control of Internet vendors is positively related to CTIS.

Perceived Privacy Control (PPC)

In this study, perceived privacy control is conceived as the Internet users' perception on the ability of Internet vendors in protecting consumers' personal information collected from its electronic transactions from unauthorized use or disclosure. Consumers tend to have a better trust in Internet shopping if they perceive their privacy information as being well protected. Therefore, the proposition is:

Proposition 2: The perceived privacy control of Internet vendors is positively related to CTIS.

Perceived Integrity (PI)

In this study, perceived integrity refers to the perception of Internet users on the honesty of Internet vendors. For instance, whether they have consistent actions, whether their actions are congruent with their own words, and whether their transactions with consumers are fair. Integrity gives rise to trust. Therefore, the proposition is:

Proposition 3: The perceived integrity of Internet vendors is positively related to CTIS.

Perceived Competence (PC)

Perceived competency, in this study, is defined as the Internet consumers' perception on the skills, abilities, and expertise of Internet vendors. Consumers tend to have a higher trust in Internet shopping if they think Internet vendors are competent. Therefore, the proposition is:

Proposition 4: The perceived competence of Internet vendors is positively related to CTIS.

External Environment

According to Lewicki and Bunker (1996), trust is context specific. In the faceless world of electronic commerce, third party recognition and a legal framework are two key environmental and contextual factors affecting the formation of consumers' trust. Benassi (1999) argued that third party recognition, such as that provided by organizations such as TRUSTe, can help build consumers' trust on the Internet and in turn, accelerate the growth of the Internet. The Graphics, Visualization, & Usability Center's (GVU) 10th WWW User Survey [3] also reported that a majority (over 70%) of Internet users worldwide wanted more new laws to protect their privacy online.

Third Party Recognition (TPR)

In this study, third party recognition refers to the assurance of the trustworthiness of Internet vendors by third party recognition bodies. Thus, the proposition is:

Proposition 5: The perceived effectiveness of the third party recognition is positively associated with CTIS.

Legal Framework (LF)

In this study, legal framework refers to the law and code of practice established to protect Internet shoppers during electronic transactions. An effective legal framework can enhance consumers' trust in Internet shopping. Thus, the proposition is:

Proposition 6: The perceived effectiveness of the legal framework is positively associated with CTIS.

Propensity to Trust (PTT)

Propensity to trust is a stable, within-party factor that affects the likelihood that a party will trust another party. People with different cultural backgrounds, personality types, and developmental experiences vary in their propensity to trust (Hofstede, 1980). People living in an environment with a strong culture of trust tend to have a higher propensity to trust. People who have a positive experience with the Internet also tend to be more trusting of Internet transactions. This propensity to trust is viewed as a personality trait that leads to generalized expectations about the trustworthiness of others. Mayer et al. (1995) have suggested that trust propensity has a direct impact on the formation of trust. Thus, the propositions are:

Proposition 7: The strength of a Trusting Cultural Environment is positively associated with PTT.

Proposition 8: Prior positive Personal Experience in Internet usage is positively associated with PTT.

Proposition 9: PTT is positively associated with CTIS.

Consequence of Trust: Perceived Risk (PR)

Perceived risk is very powerful in explaining consumers' behavior since consumers tend more often to avoid mistakes than to maximize utility in purchasing (Mitchell, 1998). In particular, perceived risk is higher in Internet shopping than in the traditional mode of shopping because, for instance, a consumer will not be able to physically examine the appropriateness of a product before a purchase decision is made. Peter and Ryan (1976) argued that perceived risk generally consists of two components, one related to an uncertainty or probability of loss notion and the other related to a consequence or the importance of the notion of loss. In this study, perceived risk refers to the Internet users' perception on the possibility of yielding unexpected outcomes with undesirable consequences. Many prior studies (Dion et al., 1995; Doney & Cannon, 1997; Morgan & Hunt, 1994) have discovered a strong relation between risk and the concept of trust. As suggested by Selnes (1998), perceived risk in a buyer-seller relationship is reduced by trust. Therefore, the proposition is:

Proposition 10: CTIS is negatively associated with perceived risk in Internet shopping.

INSTRUMENT DEVELOPMENT

A systematic and rigorous approach of developing measurement instruments is strongly advocated in the IS discipline. IS scholars (e.g. Bailey & Pearson, 1983; Ives et al., 1983; Doll & Torkzadeh, 1988; Davis, 1989) have claimed that constructs with strong theoretical justification and measures with high degrees of reliability and validity are prerequisites to cumulative knowledge in IS research. Since this study is one of the first empirical studies of trust in Internet shopping, a large part of the measurement instrument had to be developed from scratch, rather than be borrowed from the literature. The process of instrument development in this study is mainly divided into three stages, they are: (1) item creation, (2) scale development, and (3) instrument testing.

Stage 1: Item Creation

Churchill (1979) recommended a series of techniques in generating measurement items, including literature searches, experience surveys, critical incident analysis, focus groups, and in-depth interviews. The use of these methods can enable the generation of measurement items with a relatively high degree of content validity (Moore & Benbasat, 1991). In this study, forty-one items were generated using the following three methods and all these measurement items are listed in Appendix 1.

1. Literature searches – five validated measurement items were obtained from the literature.
2. Focus groups – the items were generated through the discussion of the research topic with eight academic staff in the business faculty of a large university.
3. In-depth interviews – the items were obtained from personal interviews with six research students in the IS department of a local university.

Stage 2: Scale Development

In this study, four judges who were experts in IS were requested to do the card sorting. As there were eleven constructs and forty-one items in the sample item pool, the card-sorting process was simplified with labels and definitions of constructs provided for categorization. Theoretically, if an item was correctly placed in a particular category, it was considered to display initial convergent validity with the related construct, and discriminant validity with the others.

Two measurements, Cohen's (1960) Kappa and item placement ratio, were computed to assess the reliability of the sorting procedures and the construct validity of the scales. With reference to previous studies (Vessey, 1989; Jarvenpaa, 1989; Todd & Benbasat, 1989), an acceptable score of Kappa should be greater than 0.65. In addition, high degree of "correct" placement of items within them can be considered to demonstrate a high degree of construct validity. In this study, the average inter-judge agreement score is 0.96 and the overall placement ratio of items to target constructs is 95.73%. In sum, a high level of agreement is found among the judges and a high degree of convergent and discriminant validity of the scale is obtained. (Details of the two measurements are reported in Appendix 2)

Stage 3: Instrument Testing

Pilot Test

A self-administrated questionnaire was distributed to 40 research students and academic staff (who were not involved in the previous stages of instrument development) in the faculty of business of a large university. Item-to-total score correlation and the effects of deleting items on Cronbach's alpha were worked together to determine candidate items for further studies. Synthesizing all the previous procedures and iteration results, five items were removed from the item pool. As illustrated in Table 1, one item was removed from each of the five constructs, including *"Perceived Security Control", "Perceived Privacy Control", "Perceived Integrity", "Perceived Competence", and "Cultural Environment"*.

In accordance with Hair et al. (1998), Cronbach's alpha for each construct should be greater than 0.70. As shown in Table 1, most of these constructs have a Cronbach's alpha larger than 0.70, except the construct *"Perceived Security Control"* with an alpha of 0.68.

Table 1: Cronbach's Alpha of the eleven Constructs in Pilot Study

Construct	No. of Items	Cronbach's Alpha	Item(s) Removed
Perceived Security Control	3	0.68	Internet vendors have the ability to verify Internet shoppers' identity for security purpose.
Perceived Privacy Control	3	0.81	Internet vendors will sell my personal information to the third parties without my permission.
Perceived Integrity	3	0.73	I will not be overcharged by Internet vendors during sales transactions.
Perceived Competence	3	0.90	Most Internet vendors have a good reputation.
Propensity to Trust	4	0.93	None
Cultural Environment	3	0.74	A high degree of trust exists in my family.
Experience	3	0.89	None
Third Party Recognition	3	0.85	None
Legal Framework	3	0.85	None
Trust	4	0.70	None
Perceived Risk	4	0.82	None

Field Test

A refined self-administered questionnaire was distributed to the management information systems (MIS) students from the school of business in a large university and a total of 405 usable questionnaires were collected.

Before the scales were subjected to any statistical analysis, a thorough examination of the psychometric properties of measuring items was performed. The instrument validation process consisted of both classical approach (item-to-total score correlation, Cronbach's alpha, and exploratory factor analysis) and contemporary approach (structural equation modeling) (Bagozzi, Yi, & Phillips, 1991). The aims of using these approaches as a way of method triangulation were to ensure the development of a rigor measurement instrument.

Classical Approach

Similar to the pilot test, item-to-total score correlations and Cronbach's alpha were applied to evaluate the reliability. In accordance with Table 2, all Cronbach's alphas exceed 0.70 and all item-to-total correlations are greater than 0.70 (except 1 item in the construct "Cultural Environment"). For assessing the validity of the

Table 2: Psychometric properties of measurement instrument (classical approach)

* Item does not load into its target construct.

	Item	Item-to-total score correlation	Factor loading to "target" construct
Propensity to Trust (α = 0.88)			
	a1a	0.88	0.83
	a1b	0.87	0.83
	a1c	0.86	0.82
	a1d	0.83	0.81
Cultural Environment (α = 0.75)			
	a2a	0.89	0.89
	a2b	0.86	0.85
	a2c	*0.68*	0.59
Experience (α = 0.88)			
	a3a	0.88	0.86
	a3b	0.92	0.92
	a3c	0.90	0.89
Perceived Security Control (α = 0.76)			
	b1a	0.84	0.85
	b1b	0.85	0.83
	b1c	0.78	0.49
Perceived Privacy Control (α = 0.81)			
	b2a	0.84	0.72
	b2b	0.86	0.78
	b2c	0.86	0.70
Perceived Integrity (α = 0.79)			
	b3a	0.83	0.73
	b3b	0.87	0.73
	b3c	0.83	0.75
Perceived Competence (α = 0.85)			
	b4a	0.84	0.63
	b4b	0.89	0.82
	b4c	0.90	0.86
Third Party Recognition (α = 0.79)			
	c1a	0.82	0.70
	c1b	0.85	0.81
	c1c	0.86	0.75
Legal Framework (α = 0.83)			
	c2a	0.78	0.63
	c2b	0.91	0.88
	c2c	0.89	0.87
Trust (α = 0.85)			
	d1a	0.86	0.68
	d1b	0.88	0.64
	d1c	0.83	0.60
	d1d	0.75	0.70
Perceived Risk (α = 0.86)			
	d2a	0.89	-0.71
	d2b	0.85	-0.73
	d2c	0.76	*-0.41**
	d2d	0.86	-0.66

Table 3: Psychometric properties of measurement instrument (contemporary approach)

	Item	Factor Loading	Standard Error	t-statistic
Propensity to Trust				
ρ=0.92	a1a	0.88	0.02	43.78
σ=0.73	a1b	0.88	0.01	62.92
	a1c	0.85	0.02	43.78
	a1d	0.81	0.03	29.91
Cultural Environment				
ρ=0.85	a2a	0.88	0.03	33.30
σ=0.66	a2b	0.88	0.02	38.92
	a2c	0.66	0.08	8.54
Experience				
ρ=0.92	a3a	0.89	0.26	3.45
σ=0.80	a3b	0.94	0.22	4.35
	a3c	0.85	0.25	3.38
Perceived Security Control				
ρ=0.85	b1a	0.77	0.10	7.39
σ=0.65	b1b	0.79	0.07	10.82
	b1c	0.86	0.04	21.01
Perceived Privacy Control				
ρ=0.88	b2a	0.81	0.03	28.67
σ=0.72	b2b	0.84	0.02	40.25
	b2c	0.89	0.02	52.83
Perceived Integrity				
ρ=0.88	b3a	0.80	0.03	24.09
σ=0.71	b3b	0.88	0.02	35.64
	b3c	0.84	0.03	25.24
Perceived Competence				
ρ=0.91	b4a	0.84	0.02	36.37
σ=0.76	b4b	0.90	0.02	45.81
	b4c	0.88	0.03	33.50
Third Party Recognition				
ρ=0.88	c1a	0.83	0.19	4.29
σ=0.71	c1b	0.88	0.25	3.49
	c1c	0.81	0.24	3.42
Legal Framework				
ρ=0.90	c2a	0.83	0.04	22.51
σ=0.74	c2b	0.89	0.03	29.20
	c2c	0.86	0.04	21.19
Trust				
ρ=0.90	d1a	0.87	0.02	46.65
σ=0.70	d1b	0.89	0.02	59.45
	d1c	0.83	0.02	44.62
	d1d	0.74	0.04	20.87
Perceived Risk				
ρ=0.91	d2a	0.89	0.01	76.72
σ=0.71	d2b	0.87	0.02	52.89
	d2c	0.75	0.04	17.22
	d2d	0.85	0.03	30.48

$$\text{Composite Reliability} (\rho) = \frac{(\sum_{i=1}^{p} \lambda_i)^2}{(\sum_{i=1}^{p} \lambda_i)^2 + (\sum_{i=1}^{p} Var(\varepsilon_i))}$$

$$\text{Variance Extracted} (\sigma) = \frac{\sum_{i=1}^{p} \lambda_i^2}{\sum_{i=1}^{p} \lambda_i^2 + \sum_{i=1}^{p} Var(\varepsilon_i)}$$

Note: λ = Factor loading; ε = Measurement error instrument, the 36 items were subjected to exploratory factor analysis (EFA). In an attempt to improve the interpretation and to obtain some theoretically meaningful factors, orthogonal rotational, EQUIMAX rotation[4] was applied to these items and an eleven-construct solution with a total of 74.63% variance extracted was obtained. Except for one item in the construct *"Perceived Risk"* that loaded higher on the construct *"Trust"*, all the remaining items loaded on their respective theoretical constructs correctly. The factor loading matrix is shown in Appendix 3.

Contemporary Approach

Structural equation modeling (SEM) techniques are very useful in validating measurement instruments (Steenkamp & Trijp, 1991). LISREL (LInear Structural RELations) and PLS (Partial Least Squares) are two commonly used second-generation multivariate techniques to test psychometric properties of measurement instrument through SEM. Because of the ability to estimate latent model under conditions of non-normality and small sample sizes, PLS has been widely adopted in IS research (Chin, 1998; Compeau & Higgins, 1995; Vandenbosch & Higgins, 1996). In this study, we will evaluate the measurement model of PLS for instrument validation.

Composite reliability and average variance extracted are used to assess the reliability of the constructs and they are reported in Table 3. The acceptance value of composite reliability is 0.70 (Hair et al., 1998) and it is found that all constructs have a high degree of internal consistency. Another reliability measure, average variance extracted, reflects the overall amount of variance in the items accounted for by the latent construct. According to Fornell & Larcker (1981), average variance extracted is a more conservative measure than composite reliability and their suggested acceptable level of average variance extracted is 0.50 or above for a construct. As shown in Table 3, all average variance extracted of constructs are greater than 0.50.

Fornell and Larcker (1981) suggested that average variance extracted can also be used to evaluate discriminant validity. To demonstrate the discriminant validity of the constructs, average variance extracted for each construct should be greater than the squares of the correlations between the constructs and all other constructs. By examining Table 4, it is obvious that all squared correlations between constructs are smaller than the average variance extracted of their respective constructs.

In view of the results obtained from classical and contemporary approaches, two problematic items are found in the constructs *"Cultural Environment"* and *"Perceived Risk"*. First, a relatively low item-to-total scores correlation (0.68) is found in the item *"I am living in a high trust society"* of the construct *"Cultural Environment"*. Second, exploratory factor analysis indicates that the item *"There*

Table 4: Squared correlations between constructs (Diagonal elements are average variance extracted)

	PTT	CE	EXP	PSC	PPC	PI	PC	TPR	LF	Trust	PR
PTT	**0.73**										
CE	0.15	**0.66**									
EXP	0.00	0.03	**0.80**								
PSC	0.05	0.02	0.03	**0.65**							
PPC	0.04	0.01	0.04	0.41	**0.72**						
PI	0.00	0.00	0.04	0.25	0.21	**0.71**					
PC	0.03	0.00	0.07	0.19	0.19	0.30	**0.76**				
TPR	0.06	0.03	0.01	0.10	0.14	0.04	0.18	**0.71**			
LF	0.01	0.02	0.02	0.13	0.17	0.10	0.03	0.12	**0.74**		
Trust	0.01	0.00	0.00	0.10	0.21	0.21	0.10	0.02	0.09	**0.70**	
PR	0.00	0.00	0.00	0.10	0.13	0.09	0.04	0.05	0.10	0.59	**0.71**

Keys:
PSC = Perceived Security Control
PPC = Perceived Privacy Control
PI = Perceived Integrity
PC = Perceived Competence
PTT = Propensity to Trust

CE = Cultural Environment
LF = Legal Framework
TPR = Third Party Recognition
PR = Perceived Risk
EXP = Experience
Trust = Trust

are negative outcomes on Internet shopping" of the construct "*Perceived Risk*" loaded higher to the construct "*Trust*".

Despite the problems identified, the two items will still be retained for further analysis. According to Chin (1998), factor loading of 0.50 or 0.60 may still be acceptable if there exist additional indicators in the block for comparison basis. "*Cultural Environment*" is a three-item construct and the factor loading of the problematic item is 0.68, which is acceptable and should be retained. In contrast, item "*Perceived Risk*" identified as problematic in the exploratory factor analysis fits well in the structural equation modeling analysis. In particular, it exhibits a relatively high factor loading to its own construct (0.75) and the average variance extracted of its construct is (0.71) higher than all the squared correlations of other constructs. As suggested by Segars and Grover (1993), one of the shortcomings of exploratory factor analysis is that it tends to search for factors in an exploratory way and the factor solution obtained is just one of an infinite number of possible solutions. Thus, all the 36 items validated through structural equation modeling techniques should be retained in the instrument.

CONCLUSIONS

Drawing from findings of recent electronic commerce research and integrating trust theories from the fields of marketing, psychology and sociology, this study proposes a conceptual model for the investigation of trust, its antecedents and consequences in the context of Internet shopping. Also, a 36-item measurement instrument with high reliability and validity for the trust model was developed systematically and validated using both classical and contemporary approaches. Consistent results from both approaches provide users with additional confidence in the desired psychometric properties of the instrument.

This proposed research model improves our understanding of trust and electronic commerce, and adds to the existing literature. Now that the research model is developed and the measurement instrument has been validated, the stage is set for the empirical testing of the theoretical model, which is an obvious area of future work. The results of such testing will help to clarify and enrich the relevant theories and extend their boundaries. In addition, the results can inform the management of Internet shops how they can manipulate trust antecedents to increase consumers' trust and hence improve the chances of consumer purchasing from their Internet shops. Finally, the validated research instrument adds to the repository of rigorous research instruments for IS survey researchers to use, thus helping to develop a cumulated tradition for research in the IS discipline.

REFERENCES

Bagozzi, R.P., Yi, Y., & Phillips, L.W. (1991). Assessing Construct Validity in Organizational Research. *Administrative Science Quarterly*, 36(3), 421-458.

Bailey, J.E. & Pearson, S.W. (1983). Developing a Tool for Measuring and Analyzing Computer Satisfaction. *Communications of the ACM*, 26(10), 785-793.

Benassi, P. (1999). TRUSTe: An Online Privacy Seal Program. *Communications of the ACM*, 42(2), 56-59.

Chin, W.W. (1998). *The Partial Least Squares Approach for Structural Equation Modeling. Modern Methods for Business Research*. Marcoulides G.A. Hillsdale, NJ: Lawrence Erlbaum Associates, 295-336.

Chow, S. & Holden, R. (1997). Toward an Understanding of Loyalty: the Moderating Role of Trust. *Journal of Managerial Issues*, 15(3), 275-298.

Churchill, G.A. (1979). A Paradigm for Developing Better Measures of Marketing Constructs. *Journal of Marketing Research*, (16), 64-73.

Cohen, J.A. (1960). A Coefficient of Agreement for Nominal Scales. *Educational and Psychological Measurement*, (20), 37-46.

Compeau, D.R. & Higgins, C.A. (1995). Application of Social Cognitive Theory to Training for Computer Skills. *Information Systems Research*, (6), 118-143.

Das, T.K. (1998). Between Trust and Control: Developing Confidence in Partner Cooperation in Alliances. *The Academy of Management Review*, 23(3), 491-513.

Davis, F.D. (1989). Perceived Usefulness, Perceived Ease of Use, and User Acceptance of Information Technology. *MIS Quarterly*, 13(3), 319-340.

Dion, P., Easterling, D. and Miller, S.J. (1995). What is really necessary in successful buyer-seller relationships? *Industrial Marketing Management*, 24(1), 1-9.

Doll, W.J. & Torkzadeh, G. (1988). The Measurement of End-User Computing Satisfaction. *MIS Quarterly*, 12(2), 259-274.

Doney, P.M. & Cannon, J.P. (1997). An Examination of the Nature of Trust in Buyer-seller Relationships. *Journal of Marketing*, (61), 35-51.

Dwyer, R.F., Schurr, P.H. & Oh, S. (1987). Output Sector Munificence Effects on the Internal Political Economy of Marketing Channels. *Journal of Marketing Research*, (24), 347-358.

Fornell, C., & Larcker, D.F. (1981). Evaluating Structural Equation Models with Unobservable Variables and Measurement Error. *Journal of Marketing Research*, (18), 39-50.

Hair, J.F., Anderson, R.E., Tatham, R.L. & Black, W.C. (1998). *Multivariate Data Analysis*, 5th ed. Englewood Cliffs, NJ: Prentice-Hall.

Hardin, R. (1992). The Street-level Epistemology of Trust. *Politics and Society*, (21), 505-529.

Hoffman, D.L., Novak, T.P. & Peralta M. (1999). Building Consumer Trust Online. *Communications of the ACM*, 42(4), 80-85.

Hofstede, G. (1980). Motivation, Leadership, and Organization: Do American Theories Apply Abroad? *Organizational Dynamics*, 9(1), 42-63.

Hulland, J., Chow, Y.H., and Lam, S.(1996). "Use of Causal Models in Marketing Research: A Review", *International Journal of Research in Marketing* (13), . 181-197.

Ives, B., Olson, M.H., & Baroudi, J.J. (1983). The Measurement of User Information Satisfaction. *Communications of the ACM*, 26(10), 785-793.

Jarvenpaa, S.L. (1989). The Effect of Task Demands and Graphical Format on Information Processing Strategies. *Management Science*, 35(3), 285-303.

Jarvenpaa, S.L., Tractinsky, N. & Vitale, M. (1999). Consumer trust in an Internet store. *Information Technology and Management*, 1(1/2), 45-72.

Kini, A. & Choobineh, J. (1998). Trust in electronic commerce: definition and theoretical considerations. *Proceedings of the 31st Hawaii International Conference on System Sciences* (HICSS), 51 – 61.

Lewicki, R.J. & Bunker, B.B. (1995). Trust in Relationships: A Model of Trust Development and Decline. *Conflict, Cooperation, and Justice.* San Francisco: Jossey-Bass.

Lewicki, R.J. & Bunker, B.B. (1996). Developing and Maintaining Trust in Work Relationships. *Trust in Organizations: Frontiers of Theory and Research:* Sage Publications.

Limerick, D. & Cunnington, B. (1993). *Managing the New Organization.* San Francisco: Jossey-Bass.

Mayer, R.C. & Davis, S.F. (1995). An Integrative Model of Organizational Trust. *Academy of Management Review, 20*(3), 709-734.

Mitchell, V.W. (1999). Consumer Perceived Risk: Conceptualizations and Models. *European Journal of Marketing, 33*(1/2), 163-195.

Moore, C., Deshpande, R. & Zaltman, G. (1993). Factors Affecting Trust in Market Research Relationships. *Journal of Marketing,* (57), 81-101.

Moore, G.C. & Benbasat, I. (1991). Development of an Instrument to Measure the Perceptions of Adopting an Information Technology Innovation. *Information Systems Research, 2*(3), 192- 222.

Morgan, R.M. & Hunt, S.D. (1994). The Commitment-trust Theory of Relationship Marketing. *Journal of Marketing,* (58), 20-38.

Peter, J.L. & Ryan, M.J. (1976). An Investigation of Perceived Risk at the Brand Level. *Journal of Marketing Research,* (13), 184-188.

Schurr, P.H. & Ozanne, J.L. (1995). Influences on Exchange Processes: Buyers' Preconceptions of a Seller's Trustworthiness and Bargaining Toughness. *Journal of Consumer Research,* (11), 939-953.

Segars, A.H. & Grover, V. (1993). Re-examining Perceived Ease of Use and Usefulness: A Confirmatory Factor Analysis. *MIS Quarterly, 17*(4), 517-525.

Selnes, F. (1998). Antecedents and Consequences of Trust and Satisfaction in Buyer-seller Relationships. *European Journal of Marketing, 32*(3/4), 305-322.

Steenkamp, J.E. M. & Trijp H.C.M. van. (1991). The Use of LISREL in Validating Marketing Constructs. International *Journal of Research in Marketing,* (8), 183-199.

Subramanian, A. and Nilakanta, S. (1994). "Measurement: A blueprint for theory building in MIS", *Information and Management, 26*(1), 13-20.

Todd, P.A. & Benbasat, I. (1989). An Experimental Investigation of the Impact of Computer Based Decision Aids on the Process of Preferential Choice. Working Paper, School of Business, Queen's University.

Vandenbosch, B. & Higgins, C.(1996). Information Acquisition and Mental Models: Investigation into the Relationship between Behaviour and Learning. *Information Systems Research, 7*(2), 198-214.

Vessey, I. (1984). An Investigation of the Psychological Processes Underlying the Debugging of Computer Programs. Unpublished PhD Dissertation, Department of Commerce, University of Queensland.

Wang, H.Q., Lee M.K.O. & Wang, C. (1998). Consumer Privacy Concerns about Internet Marketing. *Communications of the ACM*, 41(3), 63-70.

ENDNOTES

[1] http://www.nua.ie/surveys/how_many_online/

[2] Neilsen//NetRatings e-Commerce ratio, Q4, 2000, http://www.eratings.com

[3] GVU 10th WWW User Survey Report, May 14, 1999: http://www.gvu.gatech.edu/user_surveys/survey-1998-10/graphs/privacy/q59.htm

[4] In practice, the objective of all methods of rotation is to simplify the rows and columns of the factor matrix to facilitate interpretation. The EQUIMAX approach is a compromise between two frequently used methods, QUARTIMAX and VARIMAX approaches. Rather than concentrating either on simplification of the rows or on simplifications of the columns, it tries to accomplish some of each.

ACKNOWLEDGMENT

The work described in this paper was partially supported by grants from the Research Grants Council of the Hong Kong Special Administrative Region, China [Project Nos. CityU 1191/98H and CityU 1204/97H].

APPENDIX 1

Construct	Item	Sources
Perceived Security Control		
a1a	Internet vendors implement security measures to protect Internet shoppers.	New item
a1b	Internet vendors have the ability to verify Internet shoppers' identity for security purpose.	New item
a1c	Internet vendors usually ensure that transactional information is protected from accidentally altered or destroyed during transmission on the Internet.	New item
a1d	I feel secure about the electronic payment system of Internet vendors.	New item
Perceived Privacy Control		
a2a	Internet vendors will sell my personal information to the third parties without my permission.	New item
a2b	Internet vendors concern about consumers' privacy.	New item
a2c	Internet vendors will not divulge consumers' personal data to other parties.	New item
a2d	I feel safe about the privacy control of Internet vendors.	New item
Perceived Integrity		
a3a	Internet vendors will not charge Internet shoppers more for Internet shopping.	New item
a3b	Internet vendors are honest to their consumers.	Moorman et. al. 1993
a3c	Internet vendors act sincerely in dealing with customers.	Moorman et. al. 1993
a3d	I will not be overcharged by Internet vendors during sales transactions.	New item
Perceived Competence		
a4a	Internet vendors have the ability to handle sales transactions on the Internet.	New item
a4b	Internet vendors have sufficient expertise and resources to do business on the Internet.	New item
a4c	Internet vendors have adequate knowledge to manage their business on the Internet.	New item
a4d	Most Internet vendors have a good reputation.	Doney & Cannon 1997
Propensity to Trust		
b1a	It is easy for me to trust a person/thing.	New item
b1b	My tendency to trust a person/thing is high.	New item
b1c	I tend to trust a person/thing, even though I have little knowledge of it.	New item
b1d	Trusting someone or something is not difficult.	New item
Cultural Environment		
b2a	A high degree of trust exists in my family.	New item
b2b	People of my community trust each other.	New item
b2c	I am living in a high trust society.	New item
b2d	My friends are generally trustworthy.	New item
Experience		
b3a	Using the Internet has been a good experience to me personally.	New item
b3b	I have positive experiences of using the Internet.	New item
b3c	I have good experiences of using the Internet.	New item
Third Party Recognition		
c1a	There are many reputable third party certification bodies available for assuring the trustworthiness of Internet vendors.	New item
c1b	I think third party recognition bodies are doing a good job.	New item
c1c	Existing third party recognition bodies are adequate for the protection of Internet shoppers' interest.	New item
Legal Framework		
c2a	The existing business code of conduct is sufficient for the protection of Internet shoppers' interest.	New item
c2b	The existing law is adequate for the protection of Internet shoppers' interest.	New item
c2c	The existing legal framework is good enough to protect Internet shoppers.	New item
Trust in Internet Shopping		
d1a	Internet shopping is unreliable.	New item
d1b	Internet shopping cannot be trusted, there are just too many uncertainties.	New item
d1c	In general, I cannot rely on Internet vendors to keep the promises that they make.	Chow & Holden 1997
d1d	Anyone trusting Internet shopping is asking for trouble.	Chow & Holden 1997
Perceived Risk		
d2a	Internet shopping is risky.	New item
d2b	Shopping on the Internet entails uncertainty or vulnerability.	New item
d2c	There are negative outcomes on Internet shopping.	New item
d2d	I find it dangerous to shop on the Internet.	New item

APPENDIX 2

Interviewer	Interviewer	Degree of Agreement
		Kappa
1	2	0.97
1	3	0.95
1	4	0.97
2	3	0.97
2	4	0.95
3	4	0.95

Table of Degree of Agreement – Kappa Coefficient

TARGET CATEGORY	ACTUAL CATEGORIES											TOTAL	TOTAL %
	PSC	PPC	PI	PC	PTT	CE	LF	TPR	PR	EX	T		
PSC	16											16	100.00
PPC		16										16	100.00
PI	2		13				1					16	81.25
PC				16								16	100.00
PTT					16							16	100.00
CE						16						16	100.00
LF		2	2				8					12	66.67
TPR								12				12	100.00
PR									16			16	100.00
EX										12		12	100.00
T											16	16	100.00
Total Placement: 164				Hits:	157			Overall Hit Ratio:		95.73%			

Table of item placement ratio

Keys:
PSC = Perceived Security Control
PPC = Perceived Privacy Control
PI = Perceived Integrity
PC = Perceived Competence
PTT = Propensity to Trust
CE = Cultural Environment
LF = Legal Framework
TPR = Third Party Recognition
PR = Perceived Risk
EX = Experience
T = Trust

APPENDIX 3: FACTOR LOADING OF THE MEASUREMENT INSTRUMENT

Rotated Component Matrix [a]

	Component										
	1	2	3	4	5	6	7	8	9	10	11
a1a	.831	.122	9.882E-02	-3.94E-03	.116	5.117E-02	5.372E-02	7.308E-02	9.618E-02	7.412E-02	.155
A1B	.827	.100	-1.11E-02	2.713E-02	7.889E-02	9.908E-02	6.082E-02	.121	4.567E-02	1.358E-02	.207
A1C	.822	3.339E-02	.129	2.421E-03	5.303E-02	7.023E-02	.155	2.046E-02	3.877E-02	4.405E-02	.138
A1D	.809	-3.20E-02	-5.65E-03	.118	1.445E-02	6.023E-02	3.872E-02	.101	1.058E-02	8.637E-02	.148
A2A	.144	-.120	4.401E-02	5.652E-02	4.248E-02	4.978E-02	2.781E-03	3.080E-02	3.769E-02	5.936E-02	.889
A2B	.198	-4.98E-02	.145	2.419E-02	4.984E-02	-8.56E-02	6.279E-02	5.243E-02	9.067E-02	.102	.846
A2C	.117	.355	-.308	.177	3.747E-02	.185	7.060E-02	8.984E-02	2.794E-02	-5.64E-02	.591
A3A	2.914E-02	-5.00E-04	-1.98E-02	.856	-1.31E-02	7.749E-02	-1.18E-03	1.967E-03	2.230E-02	8.579E-02	.107
A3B	6.256E-02	1.653E-02	-8.03E-03	.919	-3.69E-02	1.712E-02	3.167E-02	4.432E-02	6.927E-02	5.309E-02	5.628E-02
A3C	3.163E-03	-7.30E-03	9.607E-03	.891	-4.57E-02	8.194E-02	2.637E-02	8.863E-03	4.233E-02	6.459E-02	1.581E-02
B1A	3.815E-02	5.747E-02	-1.81E-02	.119	4.600E-02	.153	8.721E-02	.118	9.068E-02	.847	7.353E-02
B1B	1.378E-02	2.753E-02	1.328E-02	8.866E-02	.135	.123	.218	5.998E-02	4.609E-02	.828	5.824E-02
B1C	.149	-.115	.388	-3.00E-02	.101	8.840E-02	.409	8.803E-02	.136	.491	2.102E-02
B2A	7.851E-02	.111	-2.38E-02	.140	.145	.186	.716	9.165E-02	.155	.277	3.967E-02
B2B	3.039E-02	.136	-1.24E-02	-1.98E-02	.166	.159	.779	.152	.164	.118	.117
B2C	-.133	1.847E-02	.269	-3.35E-02	.268	8.921E-02	.697	.176	.239	.201	-3.85E-03
B3A	-7.56E-03	.127	6.384E-02	4.135E-02	8.737E-02	.262	.169	-6.24E-03	.732	1.427E-02	9.843E-02
B3B	4.556E-02	2.937E-02	.193	2.552E-02	.161	.191	.322	.156	.733	9.630E-02	2.800E-02
B3C	7.703E-02	.137	6.363E-02	.105	.134	.184	8.016E-02	.157	.751	.193	9.496E-02
B4A	6.529E-02	.129	-2.37E-02	5.577E-02	3.029E-02	.628	.150	.278	.352	.132	-4.07E-03
B4B	8.445E-02	5.019E-02	7.344E-02	8.206E-02	.114	.823	.185	.129	.208	.115	.120
B4C	6.088E-02	1.137E-02	5.956E-02	5.266E-02	8.641E-02	.860	8.681E-02	.165	.147	.188	-2.55E-02
C1A	9.701E-02	5.907E-02	-2.34E-02	2.379E-02	.154	9.582E-02	.129	.702	.200	.343	.137
C1B	1.940E-02	.110	7.573E-02	-7.58E-03	.153	.191	.164	.810	8.012E-02	2.180E-02	1.889E-03
C1C	.123	-8.83E-02	.148	2.879E-03	.211	.214	.133	.750	1.803E-02	5.158E-02	.101
C2A	.128	.128	-3.95E-02	-8.37E-02	.628	.135	.140	.322	.235	7.741E-02	-3.79E-02
C2B	5.703E-02	-8.36E-03	.104	-2.45E-02	.881	2.354E-02	.177	.122	9.793E-02	.103	7.032E-02
C2C	1.220E-02	-1.99E-02	7.552E-02	-5.38E-02	.873	9.061E-02	.184	.105	4.408E-02	9.886E-02	9.713E-02
D1A	.110	.680	.401	-3.41E-02	.122	3.894E-03	.124	-4.81E-02	.157	.137	3.823E-02
D1B	7.726E-02	.637	.479	1.606E-03	.165	7.306E-02	.109	2.618E-02	.155	.115	9.312E-03
D1C	5.060E-02	.599	.430	6.883E-02	.116	4.344E-02	7.068E-02	-2.40E-02	.169	.156	-7.37E-02
D1D	2.448E-02	.701	.227	3.021E-02	-8.26E-02	.187		.147	.197	-3.99E-02	-6.07E-04
D2A	-8.57E-02	-.425	-.709	3.045E-02	-.133	-7.16E-02	-8.96E-02	-.103	-.139	-5.33E-02	-6.11E-02
D2B	-9.78E-03	-.410	-.727	-5.50E-02	-.151	-2.60E-02	-7.65E-02	-8.20E-02	-.136	-6.64E-02	-7.70E-02
D2C	-.108	-.526	-.412	-2.60E-02	4.752E-02	-.145	-8.40E-02	-.269	-4.30E-02	9.851E-02	-2.08E-02
D2D	-9.87E-02	-.365	-.664		-3.19E-02	-.122	-.140	-.184	-.154	-6.05E-02	-2.27E-02

Extraction Method: Principal Component Analysis.
Rotation Method: Equamax with Kaiser Normalization.
a. Rotation converged in 12 iterations.

Chapter 9

Electronic Broker Impacts on the Value of Postponement in a Global Supply Chain

William N. Robinson
Georgia State University, USA

Greg Elofson
Fordham University, USA

Global and electronic markets are increasingly forcing manufacturing enterprises to become more competitive. As a result, many manufacturing enterprises are seeking to manage their supply chains more effectively. Product differentiation timing is one important factor in supply chain management. Under an early product differentiation process, finished products are manufactured and stored in a distribution center until delivery. Under a delayed product differentiation process, partially completed product components are manufactured and stored in a distribution center; later, based on demand information, finished products are completed from the product components. The difference in value between early product differentiation and delayed product differentiation is the value of postponement. Prior research has analytically shown that the value of postponement is affected by information precision in demand forecasts. In this article, we investigate whether adding a market-making electronic broker to a supply chain increases the value of postponement. We hypothesize that it may do so by providing greater accuracy in demand forecasting. We test this relationship by comparing the results of agent-based simulations that vary between early and late differentiation strategies and the use of an

Previously Published in the *Journal of Global Information Management, vol.9, no.4*, Copyright © 2001, Idea Group Publishing.

electronic broker. In each simulation, the effects of demand correlation, demand variability, and demand pooling are considered. The simulations show that an electronic broker increases inventory cost savings (compared to a non-broker) and increases the value of postponement in the face of increasing demand variability, increasing demand pooling, and decreasing demand correlation. Moreover, an electronic broker may, through its own actions, increase demand variability and demand pooling, while decreasing demand correlation, thereby creating the environment in which is best operates.

INTRODUCTION

As global sourcing increases (Kotabe, Murray & Javalgi, 1998), decisions about supply chain design become more complex. For multi-national corporations with international product lines and supply chains, the careful designation of vendors, services and components, timing and transportation has continually broadened to include an ever-enlarging landscape of contingencies and alternatives. Further magnifying the scope of this task is the rapid deployment of Information Technology, which has lowered transaction costs (Williamson, 1975) and raised flexibility in global sourcing opportunities. Thus, increases in global sourcing requires that the stream of research involving issues of supply chain management must necessarily continue to grow.

The use of information technology is an important research issue for global supply chain management. A supply chain involves a sequence of organizations, each fulfilling some function, as part of an overarching process of providing value to the customer. Increasingly, customers are pressuring suppliers to reduce costs and increase quality. Such pressures are being felt by each organization within a supply chain. At the same time, reduced transaction costs have enabled the formation of global supply chains. Yet, coordination is more problematic in a global supply chain. To support the interactions among globally distributed organizations, information strategies and information technologies have become critical issues.

To date, supply chain management has already received some considerable attention. Beginning with early research on channel structure (Bucklin, 1965; Dixon & Wilkinson, 1986) and coordination (Gaski, 1984; McGuire & Staelin, 1986), the scope of supply chain considerations has broadened to include, for example, communication strategies in supply chains (Mohr & Nevin, 1990), multi-market coordination issues (Anand & Mendelson, 1997), as well as material management concerns (Lee & Billington, 1992). Global supply chain management considerations now reach across the personal computer industry, clothing, and the automobile manufacturing industry, to name a few (Feitzinger & Lee, 1997; Fisher, Hammond, Obermeyer & Raman, 1994; Fuller & O'Conor, 1998). And the role of information technology is now recognized as an important and valuable component of supply chain effectiveness (Malone & Crowston, 1994).

Of particular interest in this paper is the role of information technology in delayed product differentiation in a global supply chain. The value of delayed product differentiation was originally posited by Alderson, who suggested that demand information might better be used later in the distribution channel where it was presumed to be more accurate to guide the form, identity and distribution of products. This stream of research has continued, so that recently Lee and Tang (1997) have modeled the costs/benefits of redesign strategies for delayed differentiation, and Anand and Mendelson (2000) have modeled delayed differentiation in a supply chain to analyze the effects of information in postponement strategies.

In this paper, we employ a simulation approach to analyze the impact of an electronic broker (Elofson & Robinson, 1998; Robinson, 1997) on the *value of postponement* in a supply chain (defined as the difference in profits between early and late product differentiation). We focus on the impact of an electronic broker because it increases the precision of demand information, and in doing so may affect postponement strategies in the distribution channel. We assume that the organizations in the supply chain are distributed; however, the results also apply to geographically localized supply chains that have time delays in their channels.

This paper is organized as follows: In the next section, we discuss the issues related to delayed product differentiation. In the following section, *The Electronic Broker Model*, we describe our electronic broker model, called a customer mass-production broker. In *Impacts of an Electronic Broker*, we list hypotheses that are later tested. In *Methodology*, we discuss the methods we use to test our hypotheses, the use of simulations as well as the benchmarking of our model. In *Experiments*, we present the results of our study. Finally, in the *Discussion* section, we discuss the implications of our research findings.

THE VALUE OF POSTPONEMENT

Demand uncertainty is increasing in a number of markets. Because of increased product proliferation, diminished lead times, global differences in product specifications and preferences, the requirements for firms to produce more product variations with less forecasting information are increasing. Anand and Mendelson point out that these developments are particularly salient for fast clock-speed industries such as hi-tech, as well as industries with long production and lead times such as the fashion industry (Anand & Mendelson, 2000). Product proliferation has a large impact on hi-tech industries because quickly diminishing value of inventories makes managing the supply chain through maintaining large amounts of safety stock highly expensive. In the case of the fashion industry, long production lead times require that the creation of clothing is done before sufficient demand information is available for making style decisions that are compatible with the upcoming seasons.

One consideration in obviating the demand uncertainty problems associated with the above examples is known as postponement, or delayed product differentiation (Shapiro & Heskett, 1985; vanDoremalen & Flueren, 1991; Zinn & Bowersox, 1988; Zinn, 1990; Lee & Tang, 1997). Under postponement, the differences that make up product variety are added as late in the supply chain as is possible, in order to take advantage of better and more recent demand information. Thus, with postponement, laser printers sent to Europe are not fitted with the appropriate power supply until after their destination is decided. So, too, with the laser printers that are sent to locations in the United States, with the appropriate power supply added later as well.

The difference in profits between early differentiation (e.g., making finished laser printers before their destination is identified) and delayed differentiation (e.g., making finished laser printers only after their destination is identified) is known as the value of postponement. The value of postponement for a given production process is contingent on a variety of factors such as demand correlation, demand variation, demand pooling, and information precision and timing (Anand & Mendelson, 2000). So, for example, in the case of demand correlation, the value of postponement is very small when product demand is highly correlated (e.g., when roughly equal demand exists for both European and American versions of a laser printer, making the demand for one region's products a good predictor of the demand for another region's products). Concerning demand variation, when overall product demand changes sharply from period to period, the value of postponement is high.

In the remaining sections, we consider the impact of an electronic broker on the value of postponement, and juxtapose our finding to those of Anand and Mendelson's analytical results.

THE ELECTRONIC BROKER MODEL

The model of an electronic broker used in our research is based on the Custom Mass Production (CMP) model discussed in Elofson & Robinson (1998). Fundamentally, the model entails joining together buyers with locally unique preferences, in a global electronic format, to form a market that suppliers can serve in a cost-effective way. The model was characterized as an electronically brokered

Figure 1: An illustration of the assistance provided by a custom mass-production broker. The two computer users, Bob and Carol, are assisted by the CMP-broker in the definition of a common product specification, followed by negotiation with the manufacturer to produce their products

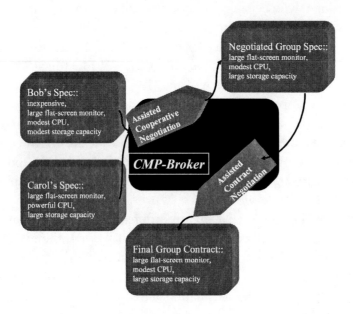

CMP channel that allowed buyers to acquire customized products at prices that reflected economies of scale. This was achieved through buyer consolidation: using collaborative filtering to identify like-minded buyers, negotiating satisfactory product configurations to allow for self-generated market niches, and negotiating contracts with various suppliers. The model assumed that there were more similarities in buyers' custom preferences than traditional market research methods could detect or suppliers could exploit through traditional distribution channels. The CMP broker, then, represents individual buyers in a multi-stage bargaining action.

An example of how the CMP broker is used is shown in Figure 1. In the figure, Bob and Carol are one of *n* number of like-minded buyers who are seeking to buy a personal computer that primarily supports surfing on the Web. They are customers of a global computer selling supply chain. They, like the suppliers and manufacturers of the supply chain, may reside anywhere in the world. Carol wants lots of CPU power, a large flat screen monitor, and substantial storage capacity. Bob wants a large flat-screen monitor, modest CPU power to save money, and modest storage capacity Together, Bob and Carol—along with *n* other like-minded global buyers—engage in a negotiation over the sought after PC's product specification until it is agreed that they will try to buy a PC with a large flat-screen monitor, modest CPU power, and large storage capacity. Once this agreement has taken place, the PC specification, along with the number of orders, is submitted to one or more world-wide suppliers for pricing and a deal is made.

The goal of a CMP broker, therefore, is to facilitate the process of providing buyers with products that are better suited to their needs, but without the penalty of higher prices—that is, to consolidate buyer-purchasing decisions and achieve better results through lower search costs and higher bargaining power.

A more detailed sequence of the steps that a CMP Broker must take to create a custom order, the procedural account of interaction between the collaborative filtering module, the negotiation engine, and the supplier-order-generation module is given below.

(1) Start: A buyer states a request for a PC.
(2) Preference Acquisition: Buyer specifies PC preferences, usage information, and price preference.
   (a) Many other buyers contribute their buying preferences.
(3) Collaborative filtering module finds group of like-minded buyers.
(4) Based on buyer group characteristics, the negotiation module suggests existing product(s) as a straw-man from which to begin customization (e.g., Pentium 3, 1 gigabyte hard drive, 17" flat screen, DVD).
(5) Buyer Feedback: Buyer requests deal improvement mediated by negotiation module.
(6) Contract Restructuring: Negotiation module restructures to create new contracts for Buyers to examine.
(7) Iterative Restructuring: Repeat steps 4 - 6.
(8) Proposal Submission: Buyer requests PC deal.
(9) Basic Matching: Auction module offers custom product to suppliers for bid.
(10) Deal Creation: Buyers and suppliers agree to deal: End.

Thus, the events that are mediated by the CMP broker are: 1) a buyer decides to look into a product purchase, 2) the CMP broker finds other people interested in making a similar purchase, 3) a negotiation session among buyers to agree on a specific set of product characteristics takes place, and 4) the custom product specification goes out for bid.

The result of such a session is a completed specification of n number of PC orders to be filled by a given supplier. Whether or not suppliers can reasonably offer to fill these orders at prices that are lower than standard make-to-order prices, and whether suppliers are better off postponing product differentiation in conjunction with a CMP broker, is the subject of the sections that follow.

IMPACTS OF AN ELECTRONIC BROKER

Within the bounds of global supply chain management, a CMP broker changes the characteristics of Information Precision. We assume that because a CMP broker helps define product configurations that are agreed upon by a group of individuals, individual make-to-order requests may instead become batched, make-to-order requests. In the case of information precision, we assume that information precision in demand forecasting becomes certain insofar as large scale orders are made through buyer consolidation, and forecasting for non-stock items is obviated with the presence of a CMP broker.

With regard to global supply chain management, and particularly focusing on the value of postponement, we are interested in evaluating the effects of a CMP broker along several dimensions: 1) inventory costs in early and late differentiation, 2) lead times in early and late differentiation, and 3) the overall value of postponement. We are also interested in evaluating whether early or delayed differentiation is the best strategy to use when a global supply chain is enabled by a CMP broker.

Within this realm of inquiry, we ask three questions. First, we consider the role of *demand variability*—the degree to which the quantity ordered varies over time. Anand and Mendelson (2000) showed that the value of postponement increased in demand variability and information precision. Further, because a CMP-broker facilitates greater information precision in demand forecasting, we believe it is likely that an CMP-broker enabled supply chain will increase the value of postponement over a non CMP-broker supply chain. Thus, in our first hypothesis, we state:

- **H1:** A CMP-broker enabled supply chain will, in the face of increasing demand variability, produce a greater value of postponement than a non-brokered supply chain.

Second, we consider the role of *demand correlation*—the degree to which the order quantities of different products are similar, or the same. Anand and Mendelson (2000) showed that the value of postponement falls with demand correlation, but that it increases with information precision. Thus, we believe it is likely that a CMP-broker enabled supply chain will have a greater value of postponement as demand correlation decreases than a non-brokered supply chain. This is because of the additive effect anticipated by a CMP-broker's greater information precision regarding demand forecasting. Thus, our second hypothesis is as follows:

- **H2:** A CMP-broker enabled supply chain will, in the face of decreasing demand correlation, produce a greater value of postponement than a non-brokered supply chain.

Third, we consider the role of *demand pooling*—the degree to which a large number of small orders becomes a small number of large orders. Lee(1996) and

Lee and Tang (1997) showed that the value of postponement increases with demand pooling. Thus, we believe it is likely that a CMP-broker enabled supply chain will have a greater value of postponement as demand pooling increases than a non-brokered supply chain. Our third hypothesis is as follows:

- **H3:** A CMP-broker enabled supply chain will, in the face of increasing demand pooling, produce a greater value of postponement than a non-brokered supply chain.

METHODOLOGY

To evaluate the effects of a CMP-broker on a supply chain, we employ a simulation methodology. The use of simulations in research has broadened over time to include a widening range of applications, ranging as far as to evaluate descriptions of bounded rational but adaptive economic systems (Cyert & March, 1963; Crecine, 1969), normative implications characterized by intentional rational economic behavior (Nelson, 1982) as well as issues as complex as organizational learning (Lant & Mezias, 1990; Levinthal & March, 1988). Within the topic of this paper, simulations have also been used to evaluate supply chain characteristics (Fulkerson & Staffend, 1997).

The limitations of simulations include the fact that they are dependent upon researchers' theoretical assumptions and the initializing values of the independent variables. Some of these concerns may be obviated by changing the assumptions of the model or by altering the initial variables or both, and performing a sensitivity analysis over the manifold versions of the model. The problems of simulations generally include, as with any abstraction, their omission of detail, limiting somewhat the complexity of individuals and decisions and processes. Additional problems include attempting to verify the models under consideration.

To capture the salient characteristics of the supply chain in our study, we began by recognizing that there are five elements of a simulation (Whicker & Seligman, 1991).

- Researcher specified assumptions about the model being tested
- Parameters (fixed values and control variables)
- Inputs, or independent variables
- Algorithms, or process decision rules that convert input values to outputs
- Outputs, or dependent variables

We explain these elements in the sections that follow, and detail the Swarm implementation tool kit, which we used as a simulation platform, in the appendix.

Modeling Assumptions

Our simulation model of a supply chain is based on a simple, three-node chain described in Anand & Mendelson (2000). The supply chain model is abstract. In it, each node can represent a work station within the context of job scheduling in a production facility. Alternatively, each node can represent a site within multinational cooperating companies. Thus, times and costs are relative within the abstract model.

Using the simple, three-node chain, Anand and Mendelson compared Inventory, Sales, and Profits under delayed and early differentiation to quantify the value of postponement (VOP) (Anand & Mendelson, 2000). Our model defines VOP in terms of inventory holding costs; that is, the quantity of each inventoried item multiplied by its holding period and storage costs. Like Anand and Mendelson, this model does not consider production efficiencies, production line setup time, or other factors related to profits. Thus, (the inverse of) our inventory holding costs allows us to define a VOP that is comparable to VOP as described in Anand & Mendelson (2000). Additionally, they (as we) assumed the same demand and cost environments for early and delayed differentiation, and found the following relationships (which we used to benchmark and verify our simulation model):

(1) Delayed differentiation (DD) reduces inventory costs
(2) DD increases VOP
(3) VOP increases in demand variability
(4) Profits fall with demand variability[1]
(5) VOP falls with demand correlation
(6) DD reduces average inventory
(7) Profits increase under DD with increased information precision

All of the above relationships were benchmarked and confirmed with our simulation model.

Fixed Simulation Parameters

We created models for both instances of differentiation: early and delayed. The two models vary in the way products are manufactured; delayed differentiation relies on an intermediate product—see Figures 2 and 3. Both models have parameters that were identically fixed during all simulations. They included the following parameters.

- *Model parameters*. In addition to the basic structure of the supply chain, both models also define how orders and parts move between and within nodes of the supply chain. Numeric values define the order and part forwarding times, production times, inventory costs, and startup inventory quantity. In the simulations, the startup inventory quantity was zero. Early differentiation initial production time was 0.02 hours for each part, and the customization time was 0.02 hours for each part. Delayed differentiation was similar with 0.03 and 0.01 production times. Inventory costs were computed as the holding time multiplied by a fixed cost: (PartexitTime - PartarrivalTime) * cost. For all nodes, the cost was $1.00 per part.

- *Order and part parameters*. All orders originate at customers, pass through a broker, arrive at the distribution node and then are passed onto the manufacturing nodes. All parts originate at a supplier and are passed onto the manufacturing nodes.
- *Part parameters*. In the DD model, finished product A is manufactured from parts 2 and 6, where 2 is manufactured from parts 0 and 1. The ED (early differentiation) model has a similar fixed structure. (See Figures 2 and 3.)
- *Timing parameters*. All simulations were run for 50 days with a time step of 1.0 hour. A simple exponential forecasting function was used to predict demand quantity for finished products. The formula was as follows:

Forecasted Demand(t_2) = α * *Actual Demand*(t_1) + *(1 - α)* *Forecasted Demand*(t_1)

Actual Demand —*Actual demand from previous period*

Forecasted Demand —*Forecasted demand from previous period.*

α — *[0,1]; it weights the actual vs forecasted demand.*

The forecast horizon was 10 days. The parameter, α, was set at 0.5 for most of the experiments reported herein. (As illustrated below, there was some significance for $\alpha > 0.5$, especially concerning pooling.)

Independent Simulation Variables

Information precision in conjunction with demand correlation, variability, and pooling were the independent simulation variables. Information precision is a measure of the accuracy of the incoming demand information as it is passed from the broker to the most "upstream" node of the supply chain. The demand variables of correlation, variability, and pooling concern the configuration of orders as they are passed from the broker to the supply chain.

The simulations relied on the following definitions for the independent variables.

- *Demand correlation*. Consider the market demand for quantities of two products, A and B, at time point *t*. The correlation between these demand quantities, DQ_A and DQ_B, is one if $DQ_A = DQ_B$ and less than one if $DQ_A = DQ_B$. Demand correlation $= DQ_A/DQ_B$, where $DQ_A \leq DQ_B$.
- *Demand variability*. The market demand for a quantity of a product A at time point *t* can be represented as normal distribution over a range, [low,high]. At the time each such order enters the simulation, the simulator randomly selects a quantity from the distribution. If low=high, then there is no variability in DQ_A at each time point *t*. Obviously, the larger the value (high - low), the more variability in the demand quantity. Demand variability = (high - low), where for each time point *t*, DQ=Normal Distribution [low,high].

- *demand pooling*. The arrival rate of product orders can vary even while the market demand for a quantity of a product remains constant. For example, a one quantity order may arrive for a product every day, or a ten quantity order may arrive every tenth day. Given a fixed market demand, demand pooling can be measured by the quantity ordered for a product during a time point t. The arrival rate is $DQ/(t_2 - t_1)$, so for a fixed arrival period, (e.g., $k = t_2 - t_1$), the pool size is simply DQ.
- *Information precision*. Generally, for each of the above types of demand information (DI), one can assume that the information received by the supply chain is accurate. That is, $DI_{received} = DI_{actual}$. However, demand information can be inaccurate. Let ρ be the precision of the demand information (DI). Then, we model $DI_{received}$ as follows:

    $DI_{received} = DI_{actual} + (DI_{actual} * \rho)$

    Thus, if ρ is 0, then the demand information is accurate; that is, $DI_{received} = DI_{actual}$. However, if ρ is 1, then the demand received is twice the actual demand. Thus, in this model, imprecise demand information consistently overestimates the actual demand.

    The experiments consisted of simulations with different values of information precision for different configuration of demand information.

Simulation Functions

The simulation begins with the arrival of orders. Each node of the supply chain fulfills orders that arrive from its "upstream" nodes by producing products from parts that arrive from its "downstream" nodes. Two production policies were considered: build-to-stock (BTS) and build-to-forecast (BTF). These basic simulation functions are described below.

- *Order arrival*. Orders arrive for each product after each *arrival interval* elapses. Each order has an associated *quantity* described as a normal distribution. A supply chain node that receives a customer order for a finished product can send orders to its own suppliers for any necessary parts. Thus, a customer order can create a cascade of orders through the supply chain network. In the simulation, a node fulfills its orders by one of two production policies under the constraints of the fixed simulation parameters (see the section Fixed Simulation Parameters).
- *Build to Stock Production*. In a build-to-stock (BTS) production policy, a node produces products as a means to maintain a specific quantity of inventoried products (Mccutcheon, Amitabh & Meredith, 1994). The inventory quantity held is determined using an economic order quantity model.
- *Build to Forecast Production*. In a build-to-forecast (BTF) production policy, a node produces products as a means to fulfill an expected quantity of future

orders, as determined by a forecast (Mccutcheon et al., 1994). As orders arrive at a node, the node can continually update its expectation of future orders. (Section Fixed Simulation Parameters defined the exponential forecasting function used.)

- *Information sharing.* Supply chain nodes can share information. For example, an "upstream" node can share its demand forecast with a "downstream" node. This allows the downstream node to update its demand forecast to be consistent with the upstream node. Figures 2 and 3 illustrate such information sharing.
- *Part arrival.* Part arrival is analogous to order arrival. Parts arrive at supply nodes after each *arrival interval* elapses. Each part shipment has an associated *quantity* described as a normal distribution.

Figure 2: Early differentiation supply chain model.

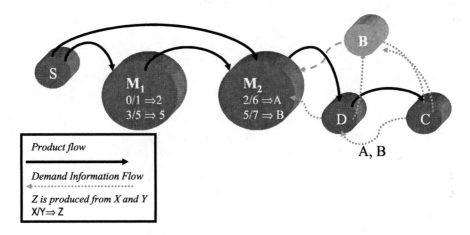

Figure 3: Delayed differentiation supply chain model.

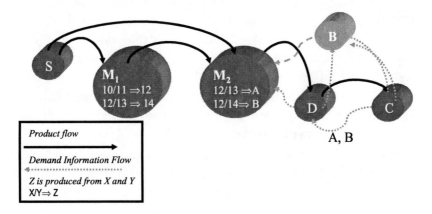

Dependent Simulation Variables

Each simulation run tracks a number of dependent variables, including: cycle time, fulfillment rate, inventory cost, and capital utilization. Inventory cost is the focus on the following experiments and discussion. However, cycle time and capital utilization are referenced as well. Each of these is defined below.

- *Inventory cost.* Inventory costs are computed for each node. It is the holding time multiplied by a fixed cost: $(Part_{exitTime} - Part_{arrivalTime}) * cost$. The graphs of section *Experiments* illustrate the total inventory costs for all nodes of the supply chain excluding the suppliers or customers.
- *Cycle time.* Cycle times are computed for the most upstream node of each supply chain. It is the order fulfillment period: $(Product_{exitTime} - Order_{arrivalTime})$.
- *Capital utilization.* Capital utilization is computed for each node. It is the percentage of time that a node is busy: $(BusyTime / TotalTime)$.

Each of these dependent variables were used to assess the effects of information precision and different configurations of demand information.

Benchmarking the Models

We applied two general methods to benchmark our simulation models. First, we compared the analytic results Anand and Mendelson with our simulation results. Our analysis of inventory costs partially overlaps. Thus, we were able to make a general comparison between our simulated inventory costs and their analytically derived costs. (These results are discussed in the *Experiments* section.) Second, we were able to duplicate the results of the information sharing strategies and manufacturing policies reported in Strader, Lin & Shaw (1999). In fact, our simulation uses the same simulation framework; however, the components are configured to represent the Anand and Mendelson models.

Our simulation models are based on the three-node supply chain described in (Anand and Mendelson, 1999). Their model consists of a supplier, a manufacturer, and a distribution center. The manufacturer produces products using a Build-to-Stock policy. Next, the distribution center uses market demand information to produce a finished product from the intermediate manufactured product. Our simulation models are essentially the same.

Figures 2 and 3 illustrate the two supply chain models. Both models consist of a supplier (S), two manufacturing nodes (M_1, M_2), and a distributor (D). Finally, the common broker (B) is prepended onto the head of the supply chain in those supply chains that included the broker.

While the two models manufacture the same products using the same number of parts, they differ in their means of manufacturing. As illustrated in figure 2, early differentiation produces products through independent streams of manufacturing.

For example, product A is manufactured first by constructing the intermediate product 2 from parts 0 and 1. Finally, A is constructed by combining intermediate product 2 with part 6.

In contrast to the early differentiation model, the delayed differentiation model uses a common intermediate product to produce both final products. For example, as illustrated in Figure 3, product A is manufactured first by constructing the common intermediate product 12 and then combining it with part 13.

In both models, demand information concerning the quantity of each final product is passed on from the distributor to the final manufacturing process (M_2). Such demand information is used to forecast future demand and thereby determine the quantity of products to be manufactured. However, such demand information is not passed onto the initial manufacturing process (M_1). Thus, manufacturing processes M_1 and M_2 use a Build-to-Stock and Build-to-Forecast policies, respectively (Mccutcheon et al., 1994). These are the same policies as those of Anand and Mendelson. They are used to model existing policies as well as the actual information disconnect that occurs from the earlier time of the intermediate manufacturing to the later time of product customization. That is, the intermediate manufacturing node M_1 must begin manufacturing before an accurate forecast of the product mix is known. At a later time, customization can done by manufacturing node M_2, when a better demand forecast is available. Thus, M_1 does Build-to-Stock while M_2 does Build-to-Forecast.

EXPERIMENTS

Here, we report the results of 240 simulations. To provide an understanding of how these simulations were generated, table 1 is provided. It can be used to compare the results between early and delayed differentiation for demand correlation with perfect (CMP broker supplied) demand information.

Table 1 illustrates an empty experiment report table for comparing early and delayed differentiation for demand quantity correlation with perfect information precision ($\rho = 0$). (The dependent variable values for each of the four simulations are not shown.) This table illustrates just one of a number of experiments run. For each of the three demand variables (correlation, variability, and pooling), 20

Table 1: An empty result form for four simulations ($\rho = 0$).

($\rho = 0$)	Early Differentiation	Delayed Differentiation
Low Demand (correlation) High Demand (correlation)		

different input order sequences were considered. For each of those experiments, two different values of information precision were considered. Such experiments were conducted for both ED and DD. Thus, here we report on a total of 240 basic simulations were run (2 * 3 * 20 * 2). In addition to our basic hypothesis testing, we also ran simulations for different values of a; that is, for different degrees of reliance on the demand forecast as opposed to prior demand history. We ran a total of five different α values. So the grand total of experiments reported here is 5 * 240 = 1200.[2] (Most of the graphs in this article show $\alpha = 0.25$ and a = 0.5. Where appropriate, other values of a are shown.)

Information Precision

The broker generates demand information that is passed to the distributor and then to the second manufacturer (M_2). For each final product, the demand information indicates the quantity requested by a customer. Demand information can be accurate; that is, $DI_{received} = DI_{actual}$. However, demand information can be inaccurate. (See the section *Fixed Simulation Parameters*.) Moreover, note that the introduction of misinformation occurs as each node. Thus, the effect is cumulative from node D to node M_2 (where information sharing is provided).

In each of the following experiments, information precision, ρ, was considered at 0 (CMP broker) and 2 (no broker). Additionally, each experiment also shows the results of modifying another variable—specifically, demand quantity correlation, demand quantity variability, and demand quantity pooling.

Demand Correlation

For different values of demand correlation, Figure 4 illustrates the inventory costs for early differentiation (ED), while Figure 5 illustrates the inventory costs for delayed differentiation (DD). The X-axis represents different degrees of demand correlation, from 20 to 1, where 1 is high correlation. (In each of the graphs, an increase in the variable is shown to the right.) The values, 1 to 20, map to orders whose quantities for products A and B increasingly vary in increments of two for each simulation trial, as illustrated below.

(1) A[48,48] B[48,48] *(every 24 hours)*
(2) A[46,46] B[50,50]
(3) A[44,44] B[52,52]
...

(19) A[12,12] B[84,84]
(20) A[10,10] B[86,86]

The range [low,high] indicates the normal distribution from which an order quantity will be drawn. Here, there is no variation for each quantity during each simulation

Figure 4: Inventory costs vs. demand correlation for early differentiation.

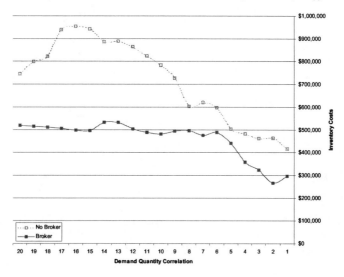

Figure 5: Inventory costs vs. demand correlation for delayed differentiation.

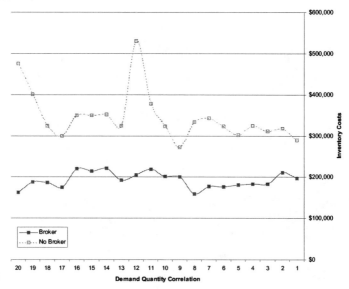

run. Instead, the constant quantity differs for products A and B. For the first simulation, they are the same at 48. However, for the last, 10 of product A is request, while 86 of product B is requested.

Figure 4 illustrates how inventory costs decrease with increasing order quantity correlation for early differentiation (ED).[3] On the other hand, costs remain nearly constant for delayed differentiation (DD) as illustrated in Figure 5.[4]

Figure 6: Value of postponement for demand quantity correlation.

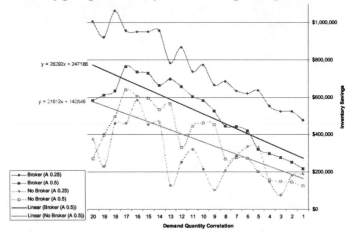

Figure 7: Linear trendlines for different α forecast values; inventory costs vs. demand variability showing VOP from using a Broker.

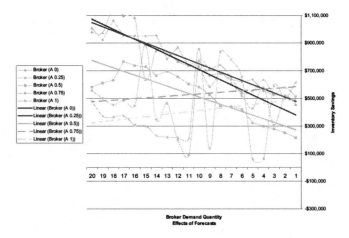

Figure 8: Linear trendlines for different α forecast values; inventory costs vs. demand variability showing VOP without a Broker.

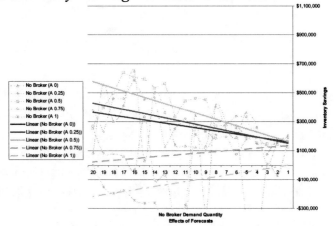

Figure 9: Inventory costs vs. demand variability for early differentiation

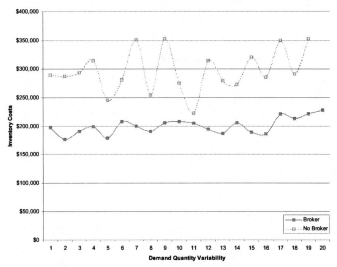

Figure 10: Inventory costs vs. demand variability for delayed differentiation

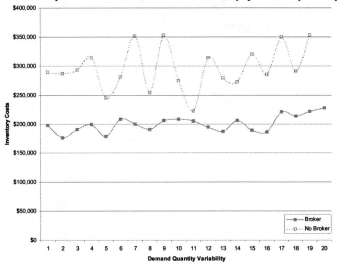

Figure 11: Value of postponement for demand variability

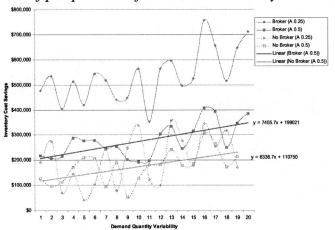

Figure 6 illustrates the savings in inventory costs obtained by delayed differentiation over early differentiation for Broker and No Broker. This can be considered the value of postponement as obtained through inventory cost savings. Notice that the value of postponement decreases in demand correlation. Intuitively, it confirms that, as variability of the product mix decreases, the need to postpone the decision concerning product mix decreases; moreover, a more accurate product mix can be established. Finally, as the order stream nearly narrows to only one product, as perceived by the Non-broker, (e.g., data point 20 where there is 10 of A, and 86 of B), the inventory costs are reduced for early differentiation, thereby reducing VOP.

A two-tailed paired T-test comparison between the Broker and No Broker VOPs indicates a p value of 5.18×10^{-9}, thus supporting the hypotheses that the broker makes a difference. Moreover, note that the Broker configuration has a greater slope than the No Broker configuration. (The Broker VOP slope is 26,292 compared to the No Broker VOP slope of 21,612.) Thus, when information precision is less accurate, delay differentiation is even more important.

Finally, figures 7 and 8 show the effect of forecasting for the Broker and No Broker. Both figures show trend lines for values of $\alpha = 0$ to $\alpha = 1.0$, in 0.25 increments. In general, as reliance on forecast values grows (i.e., smaller α, see §5.2) the VOP also grows. However, where the forecast is given less weight (e.g., $\alpha = 0.75$), VOP decreases with decreasing order quantity correlation. This shows that reliance on a good forecast function enables the increase in VOP as order quantity correlation decreases. This forecast effect also holds for demand variability.

Demand Variability

For different values of demand variability, Figures 9 and 10 illustrate the inventory costs for early and delayed differentiation. The X-axis represents different degrees of demand variability, from 1 to 20. These map to orders whose variation in quantity for products A and B is increasingly more varied (by two) for each simulation trial, as illustrated below.

(1) A[48,48] B[48,48] *(every 24 hours)*
(2) A[46,50] B[46,50]
(3) A[44,52] B[44,52]

...

(19) A[12,84] B[12,84]
(20) A[10,86] B[10,86]

Again, the range [low,high] indicates the normal distribution from which an order quantity will be drawn. Here, there is a variation for each quantity during each simulation run. For each product and for each order, a quantity is drawn from distribution. For the first simulation, the distribution is [48,48], thus every 24 hours there will be an order request for 48 of A and 48 of B. However, for the last simulation, a random quantity, drawn from the distribution [10,86] is request of product A, while random quantity is drawn for product B. Thus, later simulations contain more variability of the order quantity.

Figure 9 illustrates how inventory costs increase with increasing order quantity variability for early differentiation, while Figure 10 illustrates only a moderate increase for delayed differentiation.[5]

Figure 11 illustrates the savings in inventory costs obtained by delayed differentiation over early differentiation for Broker and No Broker. Notice that the value of postponement increases in demand variability.

A two-tailed paired T-test comparison between the Broker and No Broker configurations indicates a p value of 3.07×10^{-8}, thus supporting the hypotheses that the broker makes a difference. Moreover, note that the Broker configuration has a greater slope than the No Broker configuration. (The Broker VOP slope is 7,455, compared to the No Broker VOP slope of 6,336.) Thus, as the broker provides more accurate information, delay differentiation is even more valuable.

Forecasting has a similar effect on demand variability as it does on demand correlation. That is, as reliance on forecast values grows the VOP also grows. However, where the forecast is given less weight, VOP decreases with decreasing order quantity correlation.

Demand Pooling

For different values of demand pooling, figures 12 and 13 illustrate the inventory costs for early and delayed differentiation. The X-axis represents different degrees of demand pooling, from 1 to 20. These map to the following order quantities for products A and B.

(1) A[32,32] B[64,64]; *every 24 hours*

(2) A[38,38] B[70,70]; *every 27 hours*

(3) A[44,44] B[76,76]; *every 30 hours*

...

(19) A[136,136] B[162,162]; *every 78 hours*

(20) A[142,122] B[168,168]; *every 81 hours*

Again, the range [low,high] indicates the normal distribution from which an order quantity will be drawn. An addition variations was added to the pooling experiment. Note that the order arrival period was varied from 24 hour to 81 hours, at three hour intervals. However, note that in each treatment, there is a constant amount of orders requested per hour (i.e., two per hour). Finally, note that there is some variation in ordered quantities between the two products—this allows

Figure 12: Inventory costs vs. demand pooling for early differentiation

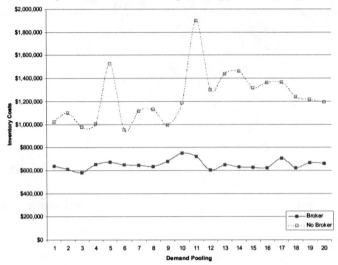

Figure 13: Inventory costs vs. demand pooling for delaying differentiation.

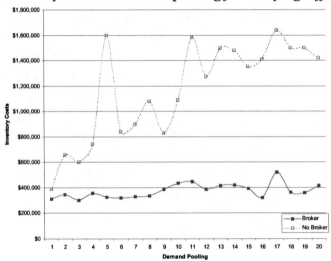

Figure 14: Value of postponement for demand pooling.

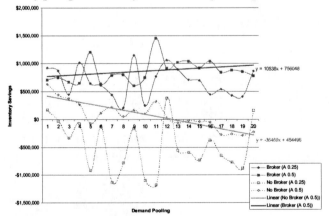

Figure 15: Linear trendlines for different α forecast values; inventory costs vs. demand pooling showing VOP from using a Broker.

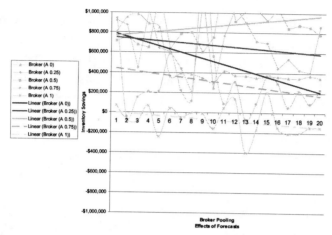

Figure 16: Linear trendlines for different α forecast values; inventory costs vs. demand pooling showing VOP without a Broker.

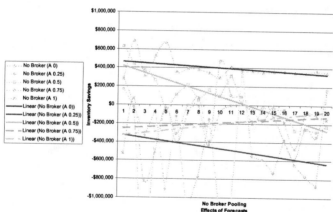

delayed differentiation to be effective. Thus, about 1/2 of product A is requested compared to the quantity of product B that is requested each order period.

Figures 12 and 13 illustrate how inventory costs slowly increase with increasing pooling for early and delayed differentiation.[6]

Figure 14 illustrates the savings in inventory costs obtained by delayed differentiation over early differentiation for Broker and No Broker. Notice that the value of postponement increases in demand pooling for both the broker and no broker configurations.

A two-tailed paired T-test comparison between the Broker and No Broker configurations indicates a p value of 0.037, thus supporting the hypotheses that the broker makes a difference. Moreover, note that the Broker configuration has a positive slope (for increase pool size), while the No Broker configuration has a negative slope. (The Broker VOP slope is 10,538 compared to the No Broker VOP slope of -36,469.)

Figure 14 illustrates an interesting case for the No Broker configuration. The trend line for the No Broker configuration crosses the X-axis at the thirteenth point, indicating that there is no VOP with the No Broker; that is, postponement does not help the No Broker reduce inventory costs. This may be due to the size of the pooled orders. The eleventh simulation has incoming orders arriving every 60 hours. Such a delay allows the supply chain to appropriate allocate inventory. Thus, there is no gain in delaying product finalization.

The forecast function is particularly important if orders are to be pooled while attempting to increase VOP. Note that pooling itself is a means of providing a kind of short-term forecast. That is, knowing the pool size for a large pool over a long time period essentially defines a perfect short-term forecast. Thus, pooling may reduced the need for a forecast function.

Figures 15 and 16 show the effect of forecasting for the Broker and No Broker. Both figures show trend lines for values of $\alpha = 0$ to $\alpha = 1.0$, in 0.25 increments. It is apparent from the graph that increased pooling does not always improve VOP. The Broker graph (figure 15) shows that pooling increase VOP for $\alpha = 0.5$, while the No Broker graph (Figure 16) shows that pooling increase VOP for $\alpha = 0.75$ and $\alpha = 1.0$. The confirms that the No Broker configuration should not rely on its imperfect forecast ($\alpha < 0.5$); rather, it should simply rely on the past order history. This is reasonable given that the experimentally generated orders are an unusually good predictor of future orders. In contrast, the Broker having perfect information, achieves a good forecast when it uses a balanced forecast based on past and forecasted orders. In all cases, the Broker results in improved inventory cost savings over the No Broker configuration.

DISCUSSION

In the section *Impacts of an Electronic Broker*, we posed three hypotheses to test. Here, we discuss how the simulation results illuminate the hypotheses.

H1: Value of Postponement Increases as Demand Variability Increases

Hypothesis H1 states that:

- **H1:** A CMP-broker enabled supply chain will, in the face of increasing demand variability, produce a greater value of postponement than a non-brokered supply chain.

Figure 11 illustrates that the value of postponement increases with increasing demand variability. For both the broker and no broker configurations, VOP

Table 2: Average Costs and the Percentage Improvement (α =0.5).

Average Inventory Costs

		Variability	% Δ
ED	Broker	$345,411	38%
	No Broker	$477,470	
DD	Broker	$200,163	48%
	No Broker	$296,294	

increases substantially with increasing demand variability. Moreover, the broker configuration results in a higher slope. Thus the brokered supply chain benefits more from delayed differentiation than the brokered supply chain. This is because the non-brokered supply chain has less accurate information. Thus, it generally incurs higher inventory costs. Delaying product completion allows the DD supply chain to appropriately allocate its intermediate products. Such a policy is substantially improved with a broker.

Introducing a broker can improve the inventory costs in either a ED or DD supply chain. Table 2 shows the average inventory costs and their decrease with the introduction of a broker for demand variability. Note that both ED and DD benefit in the neighborhood of 38 to 48 percent with the introduction of a broker, indicating the delayed differentiation supply chain benefits more.

H2: Value of Postponement Increases
as Demand Correlation Increases

Hypothesis H2 states that:

- **H2:** A CMP-broker enabled supply chain will, in the face of decreasing demand correlation, produce a greater value of postponement than a non-brokered supply chain.

Prior research indicates that:

While greater correlation increases ED profits, its effect on DD profits is ambiguous. However, the net effect on VOP is unambiguous: it falls with demand correlation.—(Anand & Mendelson, 2000).

Figures 4 and 5 show that inventory costs fall for both ED and DD. Thus, profits increase with demand correlation. Moreover, figure 6 confirms that VOP decreases with demand correlation.

For increasing demand correlation, the value of postponement is greater for a CMP-broker than for non-broker. However, in both cases VOP fall in increase

Table 3: Average Costs and the Percentage Improvement (α =0.5).

		Average Inventory Costs	
		Correlation	% Δ
ED	Broker	$460,276	56%
	No Broker	$715,873	
DD	Broker	$192,621	80%
	No Broker	$346,104	

demand correlation. Said another way, VOP increases as demand becomes less correlated. Moreover, it increases at a greater rate under the CMP-broker.

Table 3 shows the average inventory costs and their decrease with the introduction of a broker for demand correlation. Again, the VOP is higher for a broker than a non-broker, both ED and DD benefit in the neighborhood of 56 to 80 percent with the introduction of a broker.

H3: Value of Postponement Increases as Demand Pooling Increases

Hypothesis H2 states that:

• **H3:** A CMP-broker enabled supply chain will, in the face of increasing demand pooling, produce a greater value of postponement than a non-brokered supply chain.

Prior research (Lee, 1996; Lee & Tang, 1997) indicates that the value of postponement increases with demand pooling. Figures 12 and 13 show that inventory costs increase for both ED and DD. Thus, profits decrease with pooling. (This only considers inventory holding costs—pooling increases inventory. It may be that some production costs are reduced; however, they are not considered here.) Figure 14 confirms that VOP increases with demand pooling under a CMP-broker.

Table 4: Average Costs and the Percentage Improvement (α =0.5).

		Average Inventory Costs	
		Pooling	% Δ
ED	Broker	**$650,280**	**91%**
	No Broker	**$1,240,421**	
DD	Broker	**$373,723**	**213%**
	No Broker	**$1,168,851**	

Table 4 shows the average inventory costs and their decrease with the introduction of a broker for demand pooling. Again, the VOP is higher for a broker than a non-broker. However, here there is a contrast between ED and DD. Early differentiation gains a 91 percent advantage, while delayed differentiation gains a 213 percent advantage.

CONCLUSION

Based on the assumption that a CMP electronic broker increases information precision, we have tested several of its hypothesized effects on the value of postponement in a simple supply chain. Generally, is has been illustrated that a CMP broker in a supply chain increases the value of postponement in both early and delayed product differentiation. Moreover, a CMP broker improves a delayed product differentiation supply chain more than it improves an early product differentiation supply chain. Yet, because there is typically a significant cost associated with redesigning supply chains to take advantage of delayed differentiation, our results may provide an alternative option for redesign that may prove nearly as profitable as delayed differentiation. That alternative is to simply introduce a CMP broker. While the specificity of our simulation does not provide the necessary level of detail to make this calculation a straightforward one, it does suggest that additional research into the sensitivity of parameters and related trade-offs is potentially useful.

Future research may consider the costs of introducing and maintaining a CMP broker. Then, a comparison of the CMP broker costs against the savings obtained by the broker would further specify the circumstances under which a CMP broker will be advantageous. Furthermore, the broker's ability to improve information precision may be explored. Current work only considers the degree of information precision. Future work can consider the specific activities of the broker (e.g., collaborative filtering) and their effects on information precision. Thus, the aggregate function of the broker may be refined to consider how it improves information precision and at what specific costs.

A CMP electronic broker may have compounding beneficial effects. Consider its effects. A CMP electronic broker increases inventory cost savings (compared to a non-broker) and increases the value of postponement in the face of increasing demand variability, increasing demand pooling, and decreasing demand correlation. Now, consider the general properties of a CMP electronic broker (see section Impacts of an Electronic Broker). Through the use of collaborative filtering and negotiation, a CMP electronic broker may, through its own actions, increase demand variability and demand pooling while decreasing demand correlation (Elofson & Robinson, 1998). Thus, it may bring about the very conditions that it depends upon to improve a supply chain. As such, it would appear that further investigation of the properties of a CMP electronic broker is warranted.

APPENDIX

We implemented the two supply chain models using a supply chain simulator developed within the Swarm simulation tool kit.

Swarm is a multi-agent software platform for the simulation of complex adaptive systems. In the Swarm system the basic unit of simulation is the swarm, a collection of agents executing a schedule of actions. Swarm supports hierarchical modeling approaches whereby agents can be composed of swarms of other agents in nested structures (Minar, Burkhart, Langton & Askenazi, 1996).

While a number of researchers have used Swarm to simulate supply chains (e.g., (Fulkerson & Staffend, 1997)), we choose the supply chain simulation framework developed by Strader, Lin and Shaw (1996, 1998, 1999). In their framework, an entity (or node) in supply chain network (SCN) ...

is composed of several agents, such as an order management agent, an inventory management agent, and a SCN management agent. An entity with manufacturing capability includes a production planning agent, a capacity planning agent, a materials planning agent, a shop floor control agent, and manufacturing systems agent. A SCN Entity Swarm holds entity level information such as suppliers, customers, order transfer delay time, and product delivery time, which are accessible by internal agents and other entities. The encapsulated agents perform certain functions in enabling the movement of information and material within the entity and between entities.—(Strader et al., 1999)

In Strader et al. (1999), Strader, Lin and Shaw describe the interactions among these node subprocesses.

... an entity ScnESwarm A receives an order from its customer ScnESwarm C. The order flows to the order management agent (OrdM). According to the customer lead times, the inventory availability information (from InvM), the production plan (from PrdP), and the manufacturing capacity (CapP), the order management agent assigns a due date to the order. If the products are in stock, the order is filled by shipping the products from inventory. If the products are in receiving, the due date is set according to the delivery date of the products.

For an entity with manufacturing capability, the order is forwarded to the production-planning agent (PrdP) where the schedule for making the products is planned. The capacity-planning agent (CapP) and the mate-rial-planning agent (MatP) are partner agents in generating achievable build plans. The material planning obtains build plans from the produc-tion-planning agent to allocate materials for manufacturing. It also contributes information about material availability to production plan-ning for scheduling. The capacity planning agent (CapP) plans capacity by taking the build plan from PrdP and sends capacity usage information to PrdP for scheduling the build plan. The SCN management agent (ScnM) takes the order information to choose suppliers in allocating material sources...

As can be inferred from the above descriptions, the Strader, Lin and Shaw simulation framework provides a rich, detailed, accurate representation of a supply chain network.

Using their framework, we implemented the two supply chain models illustrated in figures 2 and 3. Next, we conducted experiments to uncover the differences between the two models with respect to information precision, demand correlation, and demand variability as affected by an order broker.

REFERENCES

Alderson, W. Factors Governing the Development of Marketing Channels, Marketing Channels for Manufactured Products. Homewood, Ill: Irwin, Inc.

Anand, & Mendelson. (2000). Postponement and Information in a Supply Chain. Management Science, To be published.

Anand, K. S., & Mendelson, H. (1997). Information and Organization for Horizontal Multi-Market Control. Management Science, 43(12), 1609-1627.

Bucklin, L. P. (1965). Postponement, Speculation and Structure of Distribution Channels. Journal of Marketing Research, Summer, 26-31.

Crecine, J. P. (1969). A Computer Simulation Model of Municipal Budgeting. Chicago, Ill: Rand McNally.

Cyert, R. M., & March, J. G. (1963). A Behavioral Theory of the Firm. Englewood Cliffs.

Dixon, D. F., & Wilkinson. (1986). Toward a Theory of Channel Structure. Research in Marketing, 8, 181-223.

Elofson, G. S., & Robinson, W. N. (1998). Creating a Custom Mass-Production Channel on the Internet. Communications of the ACM, March, 56-62.

Feitzinger, E., & Lee, H. (1997). Mass Customization and Hewlett-Packard: The Power of Postponement. Harvard Business Review, January-February, 116-121.

Fisher, M. L., Hammond, J. H., Obermeyer, W. R., & Raman, A. (1994). Making Supply Meet Demand in an Uncertain World,. Harvard Business Review, May-June, 83-93.

Fulkerson, B., & Staffend, G. (1997). Decentralized Control in the Customer Focused Enterprise. Annals of Operations Reserach, 77, 325-333.

Fuller, J. B., & O'Conor, J. (1998). Tailored Logistics: The Next Advantage. Harvard Business Review, May-June(1993), 87-98.

Gaski, J. G. (1984). The Theory of Power and Conflict in Channels of Distribution. Journal of Marketing, Summer, 9-29.

Kotabe, M., Murray, J. Y., & Javalgi, R. G. (1998). Global Sourcing of Services and Market Performance: An Empirical Investigation. Journal of International Marketing.

Lant, T. K., & Mezias, S. J. (1990). Managing Discintinuous Change: A simulation study of Organizational Learning and Entrepeneurship. Strategic Management Journal, 11, 147-179.

Lee, H. L. (1996). Effective Inventory and Service Management through Product and Process Redesign. Operations Research, 44(1), 151-159.

Lee, H. L., & Billington, C. (1992). Managing Supply Chain Inventory: Pitfalls and Opportunities. Sloan Management Review, Spring, 65-73.

Lee, H. L., & Tang, C. S. (1997). Modelling the Costs and Benefits of Delayed Product Differentiation. Management Science, 43(1).

Levinthal, D. A., & March, J. G. (1988). A Model of Adaptive Organizational Search. In J. G. March (Ed.), Decisions and Organizations (pp. 187-218). New York: Basil Blackwell.

Lin, F., Tan, G. W., & Shaw, M. J. (1996). Multi-Agent Enterprise Modeling (Working Paper 96-0134): University of Illinois at Urbana-Champaign, College of Commerce and Business Administration, Office of Research.

Malone, T. W., & Crowston, K. G. (1994). The Interdisciplinary Study of Coordination. ACM Computing Surveys, 26(1), 87-119.

Mccutcheon, D. M., Amitabh, S., & Meredith, J. R. (1994). The Customization-Responsiveness Squeeze. Sloan Management Review, Winter, 89-99.

McGuire, T. W., & Staelin, R. (1986). Channel Efficiency, Incentive Compatibility, Transfer Pricing, and Market Structure. Research in Marketing, 8, 181-223.

Minar, N., Burkhart, R., Langton, C., & Askenazi., M. (1996). The Swarm Simulation System: A Toolkit for Building Multi-Agent Simulations. (Working Paper 96-06-042): Santa Fe Institute.

Mohr, J., & Nevin, J. R. (1990). Communication Strategies in marketing Channels: A Theoretical Perspective. Journal of Marketing, October, 36-51.

Nelson, R. R. a. W., S.G. (1982). An Evolutionary Theory of Economic Change. (Vol. Belknap Press). Boston, MA.

Robinson, W. N. (1997, January 7-10 1997). Electronic Brokering for Assisted Contracting of Software Applets,. Paper presented at the Proceedings of the 30th Annual Hawaii International Conference on Systems Sciences.

Shapiro, R. D., & Heskett, J. L. (1985). Logistics Strategy: Cases and Concepts. St. Paul, MN: West Publishing Co.

Strader, T. J., Lin, F.-R., & Shaw, M. J. (January-March 1999). The Impact of Information Sharing on Order Fulfillment in Divergent Differentiation Supply Chain. Journal of Global Information Management, 7(1).

Strader, T. J., Lin, F.-R., & Shaw., M. J. (1998). Simulation of Order Fulfillment in Divergent Assembly Supply Chains. Journal of Artificial Societies and Social Simulation, 1(2).

vanDoremalen, J., & Flueren, H. (1991). Modern Production Concepts: Theory and Application. In a. Z. Fandel (Ed.), van Doremalen, J., Flueren, H., A quantitative model for the analysis of distribution networks scenarios, Modern Production Concepts: Theory and Application, Eds, Fandel, and Zapfel, Springer-Verlag, Berlin, pp. 660-673, 1991; (pp. 660-673). Berlin: Springer-Verlag,.

Whicker, M. L., & Seligman, L. (1991). Computer Simulation Application: An Introduction. Newberry Park. CA: Sage Press.

Williamson, O. E. (1975). Markets and Hierarchies: Analysis and Antitrust Implications. New York: New York, Free Press.

Zinn, W. (1990). Should you assemble products before an order is received. Business Horizons, 33, 70-73.

Zinn, W., & Bowersox, D. J. (1988). Planning Physical Distribution with the Principle of Postponement. Journal of Business Logistics, 9, 117-136.

NOTES

[1] Relationships (3) and (4) may seem inconsistent. However, note that VOP is defined as the difference of two inventory cost functions. Thus, if the two profits fall at different rates (i.e., each function has a different slope), then the difference between them (VOP) can increase.

[2] As part of our validation process, we actually ran even more experiments than reported here. In this case, we ran (at least) 3000 experiments. Specifically, we ran: 2 configurations (ED, DD), 3 variables (correlation, variability, pooling), 20 different input order sequences, 5 imprecision values, and 5 a values. However, while these other experiments add validity, they add complexity without further clarity to the discussion reported here.

[3] A two-tailed paired T-test comparison between the Broker and No Broker Early Differentiation configurations indicates a p value of 6.92×10^{-9}, thus supporting the hypotheses that the broker makes a difference.

[4] A two-tailed paired T-test comparison between the Broker and No Broker Delayed Differentiation configurations indicates a p value of 5.18×10^{-9}, thus supporting the hypotheses that the broker makes a difference.

[5] A two-tailed paired T-test comparison between the Broker and No Broker configurations indicates a p value of 2.6×10^{-13} for the early differentiation and for $3.07^{\times 10^{-8}}$ delayed differentiation, thus supporting the hypotheses that the broker makes a difference in both cases.

[6] A two-tailed paired T-test comparison between the Broker and No Broker configurations indicates a p value of 0.03 for the early differentiation and for 0.037 delayed differentiation, thus supporting the hypotheses that the broker makes a difference in both cases.

Chapter 10

Internal Audit of Internet-Based Electronic Commerce Transactions: A TQM Approach

Haider H. Madani
King Fahd University of Petroleum and Minerals, Saudi Arabia

The introduction of Internet-based electronic commerce (EC) has brought new risks to internal controls. Increased interdependencies among various parties in an EC transaction shifting organizational focus from an audit-risk to a business-risk exposure. This chapter addresses the nature of EC transactions and control considerations associated with them. The chapter also provides internal auditors with a Total Quality Management (TQM) framework for services performed within EC environment. The framework is developed and based on five principles: activity analysis, control analysis, evaluation analysis, risk assessment, and continuous improvement. This approach provides appropriate continuous monitoring of business practices and internal controls to ensure audit effectiveness and efficiency.

INTRODUCTION

The business world is changing rapidly with the introduction of the Internet. The Internet has allowed businesses to change their processes and implement new services to maintain their competitiveness. The Internet-based EC transactions involve individuals as well as organizations engaging in a variety of electronic busi-

Previously Published in *Managing Information Technology in a Global Economy* edited by Mehdi Khosrow-Pour, Copyright © 2001, Idea Group Publishing.

ness transactions in a virtual setting. EC involves transactions between or among parties, from different parts of a country or the world, engaging in a variety of electronic business transactions without paper documents using the Internet as a viable transport mechanism for business information. Without adequate internal control procedures, EC transactions may be easily changed, lost, duplicated, and incorrectly processed.

The Internet also has implications for the internal audit function. It has changed the environment within which the rules for security, reliability, and allowable margin of error were formed. It is shifting organization focus from an audit-risk to a business-risk exposure because of interconnected business setting. The business internal control framework must fully integrate controls within and outside an organization. Thus, business processes or operational controls must integrate with technical controls so as to assure reliable and recoverable systems and networks. The EC environment requires sophisticated audit techniques and procedures that incorporate more timely operation and response. This shift towards increased reliance on continuous control and monitoring is the trend in many organizations today (Helms and Mancino, 1999). Organizations should have appropriate internal controls for its EC transactions and the internal auditors need to adopt an integrated auditing approach in the evaluation and audit of the new EC risks (Glover and Romney, 1998).

This chapter provides the internal auditor with a TQM framework for the audit of EC transactions. The thesis of this chapter is that the Internet-based EC transactions introduce additional and unfamiliar set of risks to the business setting, which can be minimized through a TQM framework that enhances the internal audit effectiveness and efficiency. First, the paper defines the objectives of internal control and the components of the internal control system. Next, the characteristics of the EC environment are discussed and analyzed as the basis for guidance to the development of internal control procedures. Finally, a TQM framework for EC transactions is presented.

INTERNAL CONTROL OJECTIVES

The Committee of Sponsoring Organizations (COSO) put forth a definition of internal control in its 1992 report (*Internal Control-Integrated Framework*) to represent a consensus viewpoint as (Moeller and Witt, 1999):

A process, effected by an entity's board of directors, management, and other personnel designed to provide reasonable assurance regarding the achievement of objectives in the following categories:

1. Effectiveness and efficiency of operations.
2. Reliability of financial reporting.

3. Compliance with applicable laws and regulations.

The above definition of internal control by COSO emphasizes specific concepts. First, internal control is a process; it is a means to an end and not an end in itself. Second, internal control is implemented by human beings. The COSO report states that management is primarily responsible, but everyone in an organization shares responsibility for internal control. The internal auditor's role is to help management monitor the control system and make them aware of its strengths and weaknesses.   Third, internal control can be expected to provide only reasonable assurance, not absolute assurance, to a firm's management and board of directors. Fourth, internal control is geared to achievement of objectives in one or more separate, but overlapping, categories.

Internal auditors are a form of internal control- a form of internal control that functions by evaluating other forms of internal control (Ratliff et. al, 1996).

COMPONENTS OF INTERNAL CONTROL SYSTEM

In order to meet those control objectives, five inter-related components of internal control identified by the COSO report must be present. These five components are derived from the way management runs a business and are integrated with the management process in an organization. They are:

1. **The Control Environment**: The overall attitude, awareness, and actions of management constitute the control environment. It includes management's philosophy and operating style, organizational structure, methods of assigning authority and responsibility, and integrity, ethical values and competency of employees. It includes regular reviews for compliance with procedures. This component is the foundation for all components of internal control.

2. **Risk Assessment**: Risk assessment involves the identification and analysis of threats or hindrances to the achievement of an organization's objectives. Thus, it is an evaluation of both internal and external factors that may adversely affect the attainment of organizational goals. Because economic, industry, regulatory and operating conditions constantly change, management is challenged with developing mechanisms to identify and deal with risks associated with change. Internal control under one set of conditions will not necessarily be effective under another.

3. **Control Activities**: Control activities are the policies and procedures that help to ensure that management directive are carried out. These procedures are integrated into both the control environment and the accounting systems, and generally include the following:
   - *Authorization*- All transactions and activities should be properly autho rized by management.

- *Recording transactions*- All transactions should be recorded to facilitate the preparation of financial statements and to establish accountability for assets.
- *Pre-numbered documents and records*- To ensure that all transactions are recorded, documents such as invoices and official receipts, should be prenumbered and all numbers should be accounted for.
- *Limited access*- Access to assets should be permitted only with management's authorization. Access to accounting records, including com pany records and computer records, should also be controlled.
- *Periodic independent verification*- The accounting records should be checked against the assets by someone other than the persons respon sible for the records and the assets.
- *Separation/segregation of duties*- The organizational plan should sepa rate functional responsibilities. Within a department, no one person should be in charge of authorizing transactions, handling assets arising from those transactions, and keeping records of those transactions and assets.
- *Sound personnel procedures*- Sound practices should be followed in managing the people who carry out the functions of each department. Among those practices are supervision, rotation of key people among different jobs, insistence that employees take vacations, and bonding of personnel who handle cash and inventories. Prudent personnel proce dures help ensure that employees know their jobs, are honest, and will find it difficult to carry out and conceal embezzlement over time.

4. **Information and Communication**: This component involves the identifica- tion, capture and communication of information that are comprehensive, suffi- ciently detailed and timely, so that people can carry out their responsibilities. There should be effective internal communication system between top manage- ment and personnel in both ways. There must also be an effective system of communicating with outsiders such as customers, suppliers, regulators, and share- holders.

5. **Monitoring**: Monitoring is a process that assesses the quality of an internal control system over a period of time. Monitoring activities are to assure man- agement that the controls are operating as intended and are modified as appro- priate for changes in conditions. There should be a regular monitoring of con- trol policies. Also, there should be an independent internal auditing function to monitor compliance with internal controls on a regular basis.

CHARACTERISTICS OF EC ENVIRONMENT

The assets of an organization are more vulnerable under the Internet than under the traditional electronic or manual systems because the Internet has an open connectivity.   Consequently, the assurance of trusted transactions between participants becomes a major concern. Given the on-line, real time, and dynamic features of the Internet-based EC transactions, the internal control systems must be integrated, designed, and developed within the Internet-based application systems. In addition, the systems must be adaptable and be useful continuously in the monitoring of business practices and internal controls to ensure their continued currency and effectiveness (Bailey et. al, 1998).

There are three main risks associated with Internet-based EC transactions. These are: Business Practices, Transaction Integrity, and Information Protection. Business Practices describes the process of establishing a trust among EC participants. Given the anonymity of EC and the ease with which anyone can establish and abandon electronic identities, the lack of information becomes a major concern for people who want to know the practices of those entities they are doing business with and whether those businesses are following business practices, if any. The lack of such information would expose EC participants to the inconvenience of searching for the practices of doing business and the risk of financial loss and fraud.

Transaction Integrity refers to the stability of EC transactions and the installation of adequate controls that would prevent the loss, duplication, and changes of EC transactions. Without adequate controls, the integrity of EC transactions may be questioned causing disputes in terms of the transactions and related billing.

Information Protection represents the protection of private customer information. The confidentiality of sensitive information transmitted over the Internet can be breached.   If there is a lack of appropriate access control, firewalls, and related security issues, private customer information can intentionally or unintentionally be leaked to third parties not related to the entity's business.   Other security breaches include unauthorized access to corporate networks, Web servers, and the consumer's Internet connection. EC transactions require new sets of control procedures to ensure that transaction integrity and information protection become a part of an internal control system.

A TQM FOR INTERNET-BASED EC TRANSACTIONS AUDIT APPROACH

TQM has gained huge popularity in many organizations as a strategic tool for surviving in global competition. It is a systematic mechanism that guides the process of organizational management with a "customer-oriented" philosophy. It consists of the following processes: planning, doing, checking, and acting (Arter, 1994). To "Plan" is to think about and prepare for an action. To "Do" is to take the planned action. To "Check" is to review the action taken, including detection,

Figure 1: A TQM Framework for Internet-based EC Transactions

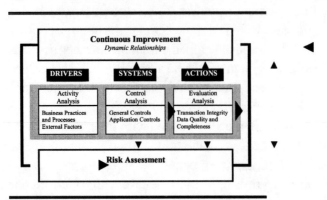

following processes, evaluation and measurement of the output of the action. To "Act" is to correct any problem detected in the "Checking" phase.

A TQM approach to internal audit of EC ensures that horizontal integration across networks and vertical integration through hierarchies are achieved (Flood, 1993). It also has the ability to integrate the internal audit function in dynamic networks of communication and controls (Chou et al., 1998).

Figure 1 depicts the TQM framework for Internet-based EC transactions. The framework is developed and based on the five principles: (1) continuous improvement, (2) activity analysis, (3) control analysis, (4) evaluation analysis, and (5) risk assessment.

THE FRAMEWORK CRITERIA

The Framework has three basic elements:
1. **Drivers**: The internal auditor begins with the analysis of EC activities such as transactions for goods or services. The analysis of activities provides an understanding of each transaction and how the different parties associated with a transaction interrelate with one another. It will identify significant risk factors that threaten the entity's operations.
2. **Systems**: The internal auditor establishes the general and application controls to ensure stability and accuracy of specific application's inputs, programs, and outputs. An EC transaction can be analyzed using a transaction Workflow that can automate sophisticated business processes using graphical builder. A transaction workflow provides visual checks of sub-transactions that constitute the complete transaction. It helps to spot potential risks and gaps in control applications and may point toward the root cause. Workflow extends the business process throughout an organization and beyond to include any Email or Web

user. It also maintains a complete audit trail of each transaction for data processing and analysis. Thus, the necessary controls can be identified, prioritized, and established.

3. **Actions**: The internal auditor takes actions to link and integrate the two preceding elements in order to evaluate the risk implications of EC transactions and the audit approach. This set of actions will provide measurement and data quality to ensure accuracy, consistency, and completeness.

CONCLUSIONS

The Internet has introduced and continues to introduce new risks to the internal audit function. While, the basic control objectives remain the same, the risk assessment mechanisms need to be modified and expanded. A TQM needs to be developed to guide the audit of EC transactions. A TQM offers an integrated approach capable of maintaining continuous monitoring to ensure the effectiveness and efficiency of controls and audit in a rapid changing environment.

ACKNOWLEDGEMENT

The author acknowledges the logistic support provided by King Fahd University of Petroleum and Minerals.

REFERENCES

Arter, D. R. (1994). *Quality Audit for Improved Performance*. ASQC Quality Press.

Bailey, A. D., Barua, A., Wang, W., Whinston, A. B., and Yen, M. Y.-M. (1998). General guidelines of Internal control over Internet-based electronic commerce. *Proceedings of the 1998 Administrative Sciences Conference: New Horizons & Role in Development*, Dhahran, Saudi Arabia.

Chou, D., Yen, D. C., and Chen, J. Q. (1998). Analysis of the total quality management-based software auditing. *Total Quality Management*, 9(7), pp. 611-18.

Committee of Sponsoring Organizations of the Treadway Commision (1992). *Internal Control- Integrated Framework*. Coopers and Lybrand.

Flood, R. L. (1993). *Beyond TQM*. John Wiley and Sons.

Glover, S. M. and Romney, M. B. (1998). The next generation software. *IS Internal Auditor*, 55(4), pp. 47-53.

Helms, G. I. and Mancino, J. M. (1999). Information technology issues for the attest, audit, and assurance services. *CPA Journal*, 69(5), pp. 62-63.

Moeller, R. and Witt, H. N. (1999). *Brink's Modern Internal Auditing* (5th ed.), John Wiley and Sons.

Ratliff, R. L., Wallace, W. A., Sumners, G. E., McFarland, W. G., and Loebbecke, J. K. (1996). *Internal Auditing: Principles and Techniques* (2nd ed.), The Institute of Internal Auditors.

Chapter 11

Electronic Commerce Acceptance: A Study Comparing the United States and the United Kingdom

Donna W. McCloskey
Widener University, USA

David Whiteley
Manchester Metropolitan University, UK

INTRODUCTION

The popularization of the Internet and the rise of Internet electronic commerce (e-commerce) has been one of the major social and business developments of the last few years. Much is made of the rapid development of, for instance, amazon.com and there seems to be an assumption that what has started to happen in the retail book trade will continue and spread with similar effect to all other sectors of the retail market.

Estimates vary as to the size of the business-to-consumer e-commerce market. The International Data Corporation (IDC) estimates that the total purchases made over the web were $10 billion in 1997 and will be more than $220 billion in 2001 (Oliveira, Amorim and Vilao, 1999). These large figures are put in a wider context by KPMG (1999) which reports that, "Direct sales are 5% of retail sales in the UK and 4% in the US. Of this total, 16% of US home sales and 1% of UK home sales are electronic." Forrester Research (Tagliabue, 1999) whose 1999 research showed online shopping accounted for $1.2 billion of Europe's $1.9 trillion in retail sales (0.06%) compared to $8 billion of $2.6 trillion (0.3%) in total sales in the U.S or by Galagher (1999) who writes that "Estimates of the value of

Previously Published in *Managing Information Technology in a Global Economy* edited by Mehdi Khosrow-Pour, Copyright © 2001, Idea Group Publishing.

global internet commerce range from 1.3% to 3.3% of global gross domestic product by 2001. This is equivalent in size to the combined economies of Australia and the Netherlands." These quotes indicate not only the usual story that the volume of electronic commerce is large and is greater in the U.S. than in Europe, and is growing rapidly but also that, as a proportion of overall retail activity, it is still small. (They also illustrate the large disparities between the statistics provided by various organizations). It is suggested that current growth trends can not be just projected into the future without serious examination of the factors that make some people shop online for some goods and services and, conversely, the factors that have to date failed to persuade so many consumers to become active participants in the 'e-commerce revolution.'

The main constraint to the growth of e-Commerce is typically given as the problem of security. Hoffman, Novak and Peralta (1999) found that there is fundamental lack of trust between consumers and web merchants. "Consumers simply do not trust most Web providers enough to engage in 'relationships exchanges' involving money and personal information with them." The underlying suggestion is that with the appropriate technical fixes, all will be right and the boom will continue. This concentration on the issue of e-Commerce security however ignores the many other factors that detract from the convenience of online shopping. These factors include visibility, delivery and after sales (Whiteley, 2000) and the rather old fashion notion that some people might actually like going shopping, selecting their own purchases and taking it home with them - there and then.

This chapter reports on a survey carried out in both the U.S. and the UK aimed at discovering what people bought online, why they did or did not use Internet e-Commerce, any differences in activity and attitude between the U.S. and UK and what might persuade people to take part in online shopping in the future. The results of this survey are reported in the rest of this chapter.

METHODOLOGY

Sample
This study sought to examine whether there were differences in e-commerce usage and attitudes for US and UK consumers. Identical questionnaires were distributed to undergraduate students, in selected classes, at universities in the US and the UK.

Measures
Respondents were asked a number of demographic questions, including gender, age and annual budget for consumer products. Internet access and usage at work and home was addressed with a number of questions. Additionally, respondents were asked to rate eleven statements concerning electronic commerce on a five-point scale from 1=strongly disagree to 5=strongly agree.

Table 1: Demographic Comparison of E-Consumers and Non-E-Consumers from the US and the UK

	US (N = 110)			UK (N = 164)		
	E-Consumers (N=51)	Non E-Consumers (N=59)	**Total**	E-Consumers (N=117)	Non E-Consumers (N=47)	**Total**
Age						
Under 20	23 (45%)	34 (58%)	**57 (52%)**	93 (79%)	35 (74%)	**128 (78%)**
20 - 24	25 (49%)	24 (41%)	**49 (45%)**	21 (18%)	10 (21%)	**31 (19%)**
25 - 29	1 (2%)	0 (0%)	**1 (1%)**	2 (2%)	0 (0%)	**2 (1%)**
30 - 34	0 (0%)	0 (0%)	**0 (0%)**	0 (0%)	1 (2%)	**1 (1%)**
Over 35	2 (4%)	1 (2%)	**3 (3%)**	1 (1%)	0 (0%)	**1 (1%)**
Gender						
Male	29 (57%)	39 (66%)	**68 (62%)**	70 (60%)	32 (68%)	**102 (62%)**
Female	20 (39%)	19 (32%)	**39 (35%)**	28 (24%)	11 (23%)	**39 (24%)**
Annual budget for consumer products ($US)	$2914 (£1994)	$2709 (£1854)	**$2809 (£1922)**	$2158 (£1477)	$2236 (£1530)	**$2179 (£1491)**

Please note that some respondents chose not to answer the demographic questions.
1.00 USD = 0.684400 GBP

Table 2: Internet Access for E-Consumers and Non E-Consumers from the US and UK

	US (N = 110)			UK (N = 164)		
	E-Consumers	Non E-Consumers	**Total**	E-Consumers	Non E-Consumers	**Total**
Internet access from work	Yes = 17 (33%) No = 31 (61%)	Yes = 11 (19%) No = 47 (80%)	**Yes = 28 (25%) No = 78 (71%)**	Yes = 14 (12%) No = 98 (84%)	Yes = 2 (4%) No = 43 (91%)	**Yes = 16 (10%) No = 141 (86%)**
Internet access from home	Yes = 40 (78%) No = 11 (22%)	Yes = 47 (72%) No = 18 (28%)	**Yes = 81 (74%) No = 29 (26%)**	Yes = 76 (65%) No = 41 (35%)	Yes = 17 (36%) No = 29 (62%)	**Yes = 93 (57%) No = 70 (43%)**

DATA ANALYSES

As indicated in Table 1, the respondents from the U.S. and the UK were young (52% under the age of 20 in the U.S. and 78% under the age of 20 in the UK) and predominately male (62% for both the U.S. and UK samples). The U.S. respondents, regardless of electronic commerce participation, reported spending more per year on consumer goods than the UK participants. U.S. e-commerce participants reported spending the most per year ($2,914) and UK e-commerce participants reported spending the least ($2,158).

Table 3: Types of E-Commerce Activities

	US (N=51)	UK (N=117)
Books	26 (51%)	67 (57%)
Entertainment (tickets, music, etc.)	32 (63%)	78 (67%)
Software	13 (25%)	52 (44%)
Hardware or Electronics	11 (22%)	50 (43%)
Clothes	8 (16%)	6 (5%)
Travel	2 (4%)	6 (5%)
Cars	1 (2%)	1 (1%)
Flowers	0 (0%)	1 (1%)

Table 4: E-Commerce Attitudes

		US	UK	t
1	On-line shopping is more convenient than conventional shopping.	3.29	3.35	.461
2	On-line shipping gives better value for money than purchases in a conventional shop.	3.02	2.90	1.109
3	Internet commerce is advantageous for the purchase of books and CDs.	3.47	3.88	3.964***
4	Internet commerce is advantageous for the purchase of clothing.	2.95	2.60	3.198***
5	Internet commerce is advantageous for the purchase of groceries.	2.44	2.39	.395
6	Internet commerce is advantageous for the purchase of travel tickets.	3.48	3.92	4.158***
7	Internet commerce is advantageous for the maintenance of a bank account.	3.05	3.45	3.566***
8	Credit card information sent via the Internet is as secure as any other use of credit cards.	2.42	2.69	1.987*
9	Home delivery of e-commerce purchases is more convenient than collecting goods from a shop.	3.18	3.44	2.498*
10	Any problems with products bought from on-line vendors can be readily rectified.	2.80	2.62	1.890
11	Internet e-commerce is superior to other direct sales channels, such as catalogue mail order.	3.08	3.17	.723

*p ≤ .05   **p ≤ .01   ***p ≤ .001

Of the 110 respondents from the United States, 51 (46%) reported that they had either browsed or purchased from an e-commerce site and 59 (54%) reported they had not. Electronic commerce participation was much higher in the sample of UK respondents, 117 (71%) reported they had browsed or purchased from an e-commerce site and 47 (29%) reported they had not.

As indicated in Table 2, very few of the respondents from both the U.S. (25%) and the UK (10%) had Internet access from work whereas many more had access from home. The majority of U.S. (74%) and UK respondents (57%) reported that they have Internet access from home. Not surprisingly, Internet access is higher for those individuals who have participated in electronic commerce. Of those respondents who reported that they had either browsed or made a pur-

Figure 1: Comparison of E-Commerce Attitudes by Usage and Country

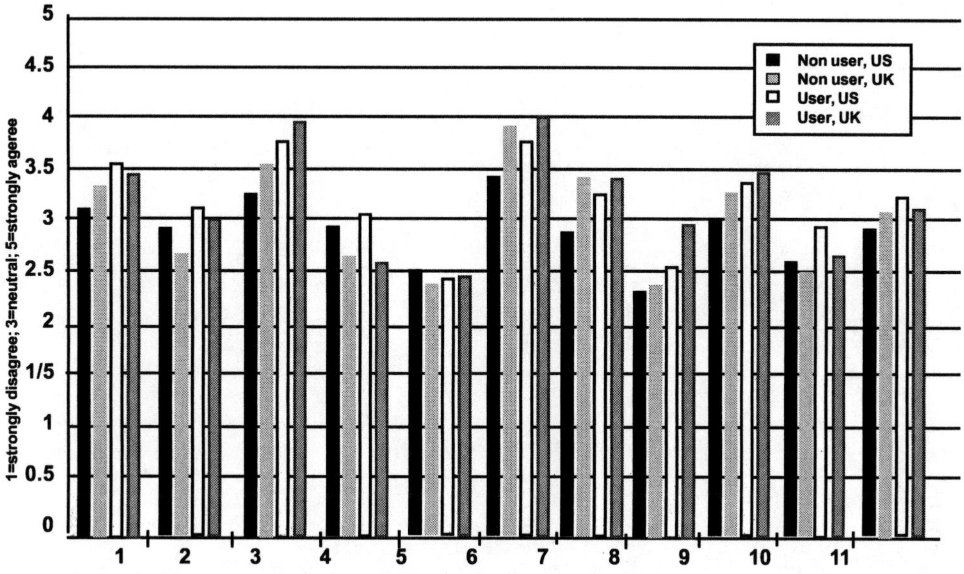

chase from an electronic commerce site, 78% of the U.S. respondents and 65% of the UK respondents have Internet access from home

As indicated in Table 3, the purchase of entertainment goods, such as tickets to events and music, was the most common on-line purchase. Of those who had bought something on-line, 63% of the U.S. respondents and 67% of the UK respondents reported purchasing an entertainment product.

Figure 1 contains a graphical representation of the attitudes U.S. and UK students have towards eleven statements about e-commerce. Perhaps, the most striking outcome is that both groups of students reported agreement with only six statements. Both the U.S. and UK students reported agreeing that electronic commerce is convenient and advantageous for the purchase of CDs and books, travel tickets and maintaining a bank account. Both groups were very near neutral (3.08 for the U.S. and 3.17 for the UK) when asked whether Internet shopping is superior to other direct sales channels, such as catalogue shopping.

Table 4 shows the average response for both groups. There were some statistically significant differences between the US and UK respondents. The UK students were more positive concerning Internet shopping for CDs and books and travel tickets, maintaining a bank account and the convenience of home delivery. Although both groups reported concern with the security of credit card information on the Internet, the UK respondents were less concerned. Both groups expressed that Internet commerce is not very advantageous for the purchase of clothing. The UK respondents were less positive than the U.S. respondents (2.60 vs. 2.95).

Figure 2: Comparison of E-Commerce Attitudes for Non E-Commerce Users

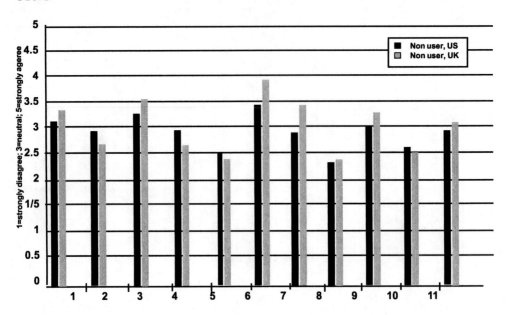

Table 5: E-Commerce Attitudes of Non E-Commerce Users

		US	UK	t
1	On-line shopping is more convenient than conventional shopping.	3.09	3.26	.863
2	On-line shipping gives better value for money than purchases in a conventional shop.	2.90	2.60	2.077*
3	Internet commerce is advantageous for the purchase of books and CDs.	3.24	3.65	2.566*
4	Internet commerce is advantageous for the purchase of clothing.	2.88	2.67	1.082
5	Internet commerce is advantageous for the purchase of groceries.	2.50	2.26	1.391
6	Internet commerce is advantageous for the purchase of travel tickets.	3.33	3.74	2.420*
7	Internet commerce is advantageous for the maintenance of a bank account.	2.84	3.46	3.491***
8	Credit card information sent via the Internet is as secure as any other use of credit cards.	2.29	2.33	.174
9	Home delivery of e-commerce purchases is more convenient than collecting goods from a shop.	2.95	3.33	2.347*
10	Any problems with products bought from on-line vendors can be readily rectified.	2.70	2.50	1.177
11	Internet e-commerce is superior to other direct sales channels, such as catalogue mail order.	2.90	3.09	1.209

*p ≤ .05   **p ≤ .01   ***p ≤ .001

It is reasonable to expect attitudes concerning electronic commerce to differ for those who have participated in this form of shopping and those who have not. For this reason, these attitudes were examined separately for each sub-group,

Figure 3: Comparison of E-Commerce Attitudes for E-Commerce Users

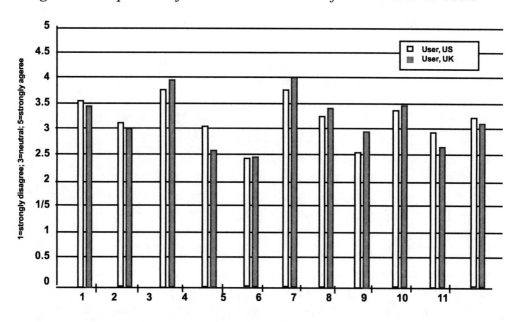

Table 6: E-Commerce Attitudes of E-Commerce Users

		US	UK	t
1	On-line shopping is more convenient than conventional shopping.	3.53	3.39	.839
2	On-line shipping gives better value for money than purchases in a conventional shop.	3.16	3.02	.936
3	Internet commerce is advantageous for the purchase of books and CDs.	3.74	3.97	1.672
4	Internet commerce is advantageous for the purchase of clothing.	3.04	2.57	3.264***
5	Internet commerce is advantageous for the purchase of groceries.	2.36	2.44	.477
6	Internet commerce is advantageous for the purchase of travel tickets.	3.66	3.99	2.368*
7	Internet commerce is advantageous for the maintenance of a bank account.	3.28	3.45	1.115
8	Credit card information sent via the Internet is as secure as any other use of credit cards.	2.57	2.83	1.389
9	Home delivery of e-commerce purchases is more convenient than collecting goods from a shop.	3.43	3.48	.362
10	Any problems with products bought from on-line vendors can be readily rectified.	2.92	2.66	2.053*
11	Internet e-commerce is superior to other direct sales channels, such as catalogue mail order.	3.29	3.20	.577

*p ≤ .05   **p ≤ .01   ***p ≤ .001

electronic commerce users and non-electronic commerce users. As graphically presented in Figure 2, both the U.S. and UK respondents had an average rating that was positive on only three of the eleven statements. Both groups of non-ecommerce users reported agreeing that electronic commerce is convenient and advantageous for the purchase of CDs and books and travel tickets. The UK respondents were more positive on these issues and were positive concerning an additional three statements. The non-ecommerce users from the UK agreed that the Internet is advantageous for the maintenance of a bank account (3.46) and that home delivery of e-commerce items is more convenient than collecting goods from a shop (3.33). Respondents were slightly above neutral (3.09) regarding the superiority of e-commerce compared to other direct sales channels. Both populations reported disagreement with the security of credit card on-line and electronic commerce being advantageous for purchasing groceries.

Table 5 contains the average responses for non-ecommerce users. There were significant differences in the attitudes of the U.S. and UK non-electronic commerce participants concerning five statements. The UK non e-commerce users were significantly more positive concerning the convenience of home delivery of goods, and that e-commerce is advantageous for the purchase of CDs and books and travel tickets. The greatest difference between the U.S. and UK respondents was regarding Internet banking. Students from the U.S. were more likely to be negative or neutral concerning managing a bank account on-line whereas the UK students were more positive (2.84 vs. 3.46).

Those individuals who have purchased items over the internet were more positive about electronic commerce. Figure 3 contains a graphical representation of their attitudes on eleven items. Both U.S. and UK electronic commerce users reported positive attitudes toward seven of the items, compared to only three for non-ecommerce users. In addition to agreeing that electronic commerce is more convenient than traditional shopping and is advantageous for the purchase of books and music and travel tickets, the electronic commerce users were also positive about electronic commerce offering a better value, being beneficial for the maintenance of a bank account and being superior to other direct sales channels.

Table 6 contains the average response on each of the eleven items. U.S. and UK respondents who have participated in an electronic commerce transaction reported significantly different attitudes on three of the items. The UK respondents were more negative concerning the advantages of purchasing clothing online whereas the U.S. respondents were neutral (2.44 vs 3.04). Both groups were concerned with being able to readily rectify problems with products purchased on-line, however the U.S. students were not as concerned as the UK students (2.92 vs. 2.66).

DISCUSSION AND DIRECTIONS FOR FUTURE RESEARCH

Regardless of culture, it appears that security is a concern for on-line shoppers. Both the U.S. and UK respondents, regardless of e-commerce participation, reported that they did not agree that credit card information sent via the Internet is as secure as any other use of credit cards. This concern has been found by other researchers (Hoffman, Novak and Peralta, 1999; Pitkow and Kehoe, 1996) and is of critical importance. Future research should continue to address the security of on-line shopping. Are there true security concerns or is it the perception that e-commerce is not secure?

Not far behind security, there is also some concern with the process of after sales service. Participants in the survey, on average, thought online shopping would be convenient and give reasonable value, and home delivery would be helpful; but, there was less confidence in the process of rectifying any problems with products that were bought online. As discussion has concentrated on the payment issues that arise in e-commerce this area has arguably been neglected. It is inherent in the process of direct selling that goods bought remotely can't be inspected by the customer prior to purchase and can not be returned as easily or securely as is the case with (most) conventional shopping. The issue of returns, "money back guarantees" and the like, is one that the traditional mail order operations have given much attention, and the new, online direct sellers will need to establish similar reputations (in what seems likely to be a much more fragmented market).

A further differentiation is identifiable in the attitude of participants to the five "commodity" groupings sampled in the survey. Books, CDs, travel and banking (despite security concerns) were each seen as areas where online transactions would be advantageous (particularly by the e-commerce users). These ratings were in some contrast with those achieved for clothing and groceries where arguably the ability to inspect the product before purchase is more important (not tested in the survey), and the issues of returning unsatisfactory or unsuitable merchandise would be more likely to arise.

Turning to the issue of cultural differences, it has been reported that although e-commerce acceptance is growing in Europe, it is not as widely accepted as it is in the U.S. Bellman, Lohse and Johnson (1999) reported that among online shoppers, the median number of transactions in a six-month period was 2 for Americans and 1 for Europeans. European adoption of online shopping is expected to continue to grow from 11% in 1998 to 25% by 2002. Usage in Western Europe is expected to grow even faster to 35%, the same level of usage that exists in the U.S. today (McGrath, 1999). Yet the results of this study seem to indicate that e-commerce acceptance and adoption among students in the UK exceeds that of the U.S. This was a very surprising finding. One possible explanation is that while overall acceptance levels of e-commerce are relatively low in the UK, acceptance by computer literate young people (such as the students that were surveyed) is relatively higher.

Finally on the issue of future research, it is intended that the survey will be repeated again, in a similar form, with U.S. and UK students in the 2000-2001 cohorts. The continuation of the survey will facilitate the checking of the results reported in this chapter and provide a basis for identifying trends in e-commerce awareness and e-commerce acceptance.

PRACTICAL IMPLICATIONS

Approximately 70% of the U.S. companies selling on-line do not accept international orders (Stedman, 1999). The complexities of accepting and shipping international orders can be daunting. However, these results should serve as a wake up call to those organizations that are neglecting to develop an international web presence.

Organizations wishing to reach a global market via the web will face a number of challenges. Capturing the global on-line market will require additional considerations, such as calculation engines to correctly calculate tariffs, duties and cross border shipping fees (Stedman, 1999). Additionally, as Internet availability and electronic commerce acceptance continues to grow worldwide, language will become more of an issue. English is the dominant online language, but to truly have a worldwide Internet presence, companies will have to have multi-language sites. Practical issues for multi-language sites include finding in-country translators who have experience with your industry's jargon, buying software that can handle Arabic, Hebrew and Asian languages and listing your site on the 500+ non-English search engines (Betts, Sliwa and DiSabation, 2000).

REFERENCES

Bellman, S., Lohse, G. L., and Johnson, E. J. (1999). Predictors of online Buying Behavior. *Communications of the ACM*, 42(12), pp. 32-38.

Betts, M., Sliwa, C., and DiSabatino, J. (2000, August 21). Global web sites prove challenging, *Computerworld*, 34(34), 17.

Gallagher, P. (1999). E-Commerce Trends. *International Trade Forum*, 2, 16-18.

Hoffman, D. L., Novak, T. P., and Peralta, M. (1999). Building Consumer Trust Online. *Communications of the ACM*, 42(4), 80-85.

Kalin, S. (1997). The Importance of Being Multiculturally Correct. *Computerworld*, 31(40), 16-17.

KPMG (1999). Home Shopping - Retailers urged to experiment whilst matching customer needs, KPMG Home Page. http://www.kpmg.co.uk.

McGrath, D. (1999). When "E" Stands for Europe. *Computerworld*, 33(36), 52-53.

Oliveira, L., Amorim, P., and Vilao, C. (1999). Electronic Commerce. International Financial Law Review, Supplement - Spain and Portugal: A Legal Guide, 37-42.

Pitkow, J. E. and Kehoe, C. M. (1996). Emerging Trends in the WWW User Population. *Communications of the ACM*, 39(6), 106-109.

Radosevich, L. (1999). Going Global Overnight. *InfoWorld*, 21(16), 1, 34.

Stedman, C. (1999). E-Retailers Eye Overseas Dollars. *Computerworld*, 33(29), 1, 101.

Tagliabue, J. (1999). Internet Shopping is (Sort of) Catching on in Europe. *New York Times,* Sec C, Col 2, P. 1,

Tweney, D. (1999). Increasingly Global, the Web Challenges US-Based Companies. *InfoWorld*, 21(29), 52.

Whiteley, D. (2000). *e-Commerce: Strategy, Technology and Applications*, McGraw-Hill, Maidenhead.

Chapter 12

Intelligent Software Agents in Electronic Commerce: A Socio-technical Perspective

Mahesh S. Raisinghani
University of Dallas, USA

Chris Klassen
The Software Construction Company, USA

Lawrence L. Schkade
University of Texas, Arlington, USA

"The future business culture will be one in which innovation is necessary, learning is constant, organizations need to act collaboratively and work is its own reward...It will not be business. It will not be government. It is the social sector that may yet save the society." ——*Peter F. Drucker*

INTRODUCTION

Although there is no firm consensus on what constitutes an intelligent agent (or software agent), *when* a new task is delegated by the user should determine precisely what its goal is, evaluate how the goal can be reached in an effective manner, and perform the necessary actions by learning from past experience and responding to unforeseen situations with its adaptive, self-starting, and temporal continuous reasoning strategies. It needs to be not only cooperative and mobile in order to perform its tasks by interacting with other agents but also reactive and autonomous to sense the status quo and act independently to make progress towards its goal (Baek et al., 1999; Wang, 1999). Software agents are goal-directed and possess abilities such as autonomy, collaborative behavior, and infer-

Previously Published in *Challenges of Information Technology Management in the 21st Century* edited by Mehdi Khosrow-Pour, Copyright © 2000, Idea Group Publishing.

ential capability. Intelligent agents can take different forms, but an intelligent agent can initiate and make decisions without human intervention and have the capability to infer appropriate high-level goals from user actions and requests and take actions to achieve these goals (Huang, 1999; Nardi et al., 1998; Wang, 1999). The intelligent software agent is a computational entity that can adapt to the environment, making it capable of interacting with other agents and transporting itself across different systems in a network. "…The state of the running program is saved, transported to the new host, and restored, allowing the program to continue where it left off" (Kotz and Gray, 1999).

THE CURRENT STATE OF RESEARCH ON SOFTWARE AGENTS

Software agents were first used several years ago to automate repetitive behavior in simple tasks such as filtering and sorting information or making basic price comparisons (Maes et al., 1999; Kirsner, 1999). This first phase of software agents has been superceded by sophisticated software agents that keep a detailed profile of demographics and psychographics. They can track interests and preferences in order to offer customized services in business-to-business, business-to-consumer, and consumer-to-consumer e-commerce based on some embedded mobility metadata (Maes, 1999; Wong et al., 1999). In automated negotiation in retail e-commerce, electricity markets, manufacturing planning and scheduling, distributed vehicle routing among independent dispatch centers, and electronic trading of financial instruments; computational agents find and prepare contracts on behalf of the real world parties they represent (Sandholm, 1999). Gloshko et al. (1999) believe that over time, most merchant web sites will provide agent-searchable catalogs that supply product descriptions and information about price and availability. The stage is set for applications that can benefit from the mobile agent paradigm, such as personal assistance by monitoring and notifying/ information dissemination, secure brokering, distributed information retrieval, telecommunication networks services, and workflow applications, and parallel processing (Lange & Oshima, 1999; Hauk & Chen, 1999).

Much research and many articles have been devoted to this topic, and software products billed as having intelligent agent functionality are being introduced on the market every day. The articles and research, however, do not wholeheartedly endorse this trend. A growing number of computer information professionals recognize that there are certain problems and issues surrounding intelligent agent terminology and technology that must be resolved if agent technology is to continue to develop and mature.

The current research into intelligent agent software technology can be divided into two main areas: technological and social. The latter area is particularly important since, in the excitement of new and emergent technology, people often forget to examine what impact the new technology will have on people's lives. In fact, the social dimension of all technology is the driving force and most important consideration of technology itself. Technology is not created and produced for its own sake, but to improve people's lives. Technology and computers and software are not created simply to see what the human mind can achieve, they are created for the sake of human beings.

TECHNOLOGICAL ISSUES

The first and most fundamental technological aspect that must be considered is what constitutes an intelligent software agent: What is the definition of an intelligent software agent? It is here that the first major problem for intelligent agent technology emerges. "In order for this term [intelligent agent] to have any effectiveness, there must first be a universal definition that can be agreed upon and used consistently."[1] Unfortunately, though, there is in fact no commonly agreed upon definition of an intelligent agent or even an (software) agent. Many proposals for a formal definition of "intelligent agent" have been made, but none has been widely accepted.[2] The following are a few of the more promising definitions:

"An agent is anything that can be viewed as perceiving its environment through sensors and acting upon that environment through effectors."[3]

"Let us define an agent as a persistent software entity dedicated to a specific purpose. 'Persistent' distinguishes agents from subroutines; agents have their own ideas about how to accomplish tasks, their own agendas. 'Special purpose' distinguishes them from other entire multifunction applications; agents are typically much smaller."[4]

"Intelligent agents are software entities that carry out some set of operations on behalf of a user or another program with some degree of independence or autonomy, and in so doing, employ some knowledge or representation of the user's goals or desires."[5]

"An **autonomous agent** is a system situated within and a part of an environment that senses that environment and acts on it, over time, in pursuit of its own agenda and so as to effect what it senses in the future."[6]

Some of the key terms found in the preceding definitions are: sensing, environment, persistent, 'own agendas', autonomy, goals, and knowledge. Ma (1999) defines intelligent/mobile/multi-system/profiling agents as working through actions and characterizes agents as "atomic, software entities that operate through autonomous actions on behalf of the user-machines and humans-without human intervention." Each of these terms seems to appropriately describe characteristics of what an intelligent agent is, yet none of them has gained wide recognition as *the* definition of a software (intelligent) agent. Woolridge and Jennings [1996], give a compelling reason why a definition consensus has not yet been reached. They point out that agent technology is so popular partly because the idea of an agent is extremely intuitive.[7] The intuitive aspect of the term "intelligent agent" leads to many different people having different ideas of what an agent is. As Franklin and Graesser [1996], point out, most of the definitions proposed thus far seem to have originated from particular examples that the people who have proposed of the definitions already had in mind.[8] It is important to note here that the same intuitive aspect of the term "intelligent agent", while making it difficult to establish a broadly accepted formal definition, actually makes marketing a product billed as incorporating intelligent agent software technology much easier.

Another reason that a consensus has not been reached is that much of the agent research is proprietary. Companies that sponsor the research do not want to give away their work for free, since they have made significant monetary contributions to this research. This makes standardization of the new technology difficult. Intelligent agent technology will continue to suffer from this difficulty either until the companies and individuals with the proprietary information recognize that sharing it will benefit everyone, including themselves, or until the companies and individuals with the proprietary information recoup enough of their expenditures to feel justified in making available their research.

A third reason for the difficulty in reaching a generally approved definition of what comprises an intelligent software agent is that so-called intelligent agent software does not seem to be qualitatively different from any other software. "Is it an agent, or just a program?"[9] In their article of the same title as the previous question, Franklin and Graesser note, correctly, that all software agents are programs. They go on to state that not all programs are agents, the implication being that some programs, then, are in fact agents.[10]

This third reason for the difficulty in reaching a generally approved definition of "intelligent agent software" revolves around a key term, "quality". The term "intelligent agent" does not simply mean a more complicated program. If it did, not much controversy would ever have been generated about what actually is an intelligent software agent. If "intelligent agent" only signified a more complicated program, the term "intelligent agent" would mean that a so-called intelligent agent software program was simply more complex and possibly more useful that other typical computer programs. This sense of "intelligent agent" is a *quantitative* sense.

However, those who are doing research into so-called intelligent agent software technology do not mean that an intelligent agent is only more complicated than other computer programs. A true intelligent agent would have to be *qualitatively* different from a mere computer program. An agent is, broadly speaking, someone or something that acts. However, in order to act, the thing that acts must have a purpose or a goal. This is included in the third and fourth proposed definitions set forth earlier. Do any computer programs have their own goals or purposes? Not really. All a computer program does is perform a set of instructions that were programmed into it. An intelligent software agent is no different from any other computer program in this respect. It simply has more possibilities than less complicated computer programs.

Even if we do grant that a computer program may act, it certainly does not act autonomously as the fourth definition asserts. For something to act autonomously it must have independence and freedom. Philosophically, for something to be autonomous, it must have knowledge of what it is doing and it must *will* to do what it is doing. Computer programs do not *will* to do anything. Again, we reiterate that the program may be quite complex and be able to react to many different events, but the key is that the computer simply reacts, it does not act on its own.

The word, "react", further clarifies the inherent limitations of computer programs, and why they cannot truly be called intelligent or autonomous agents. An agent, in the true sense of the word, initiates action. True agents are proactive as well as reactive. They have beliefs, intentions, and desires. It is absurd to speak of computer programs of any sort as having desires. This, then, sums up the problems with calling computer programs "intelligent agents".

This leaves us with a question. What are we to make of the all of the software currently on the market or in production that is billed as having intelligent agent functionality? Certainly we do not wish to demean all of the research that has gone into these products. Products such as email filters, help engines (such as the Microsoft Office Assistant), data warehousing tools, news filters, etc. all have the potential to be highly useful to human beings. But look at how they work. They are all based on the detection of patterns in conjunction with explicit user commands and preferences. At their core, all of these computer programs are based on mathematics and logic. The help engines and data warehousing tools, for example, search for built-in patterns, but the programs do not generate the patterns on their own. They have the patterns pre-built into them.

The news and searching tools (often marketed as intelligent agents), while having great potential given the explosion of information accessible on the Internet, pose an interesting problem. The problem is this: if many users have news searching "intelligent agent" tools constantly searching for information, isn't it likely that the Internet may be clogged up? It is likely that each person would have quite a number of these programs running in order to get a wide variety of information. To further complicate this picture, there is also the possibility that these "intelligent agents" will be programmed with the capability to spawn other agents. Imagine if one of these "intelligent agents" had an error (bug) built in which caused the program to continuously spawn agents. What if each one of these spawned agents also spawned other agents?

Furthermore, it is conceivable that a certain number of the "intelligent agents" searching the Internet for information would get lost, that is, they would not return with the requested information to the entity which spawned them. Thus, one can begin see the technical dangers in having such "intelligent agents". They might create severe bottlenecks on the already crowded Internet.

TRANSITIONING TO THE KNOWLEDGE SOCIETY

The transition from the industrial age to the information age to the knowledge age is a continuum that is evolutionary. A final destination will never be reached since new knowledge and experiences are continually added and refined and outside forces can create a change in corporate strategy. Although there have been several definitions of knowledge management published, the one, which conveys the concept best in the context of this paper is by Malhotra (1999);

"Knowledge Management caters to the critical issues of organizational adoption, survival, and competence in the face of increasingly discontinuous environmental change. Essentially it embodies, organizational process that seeks synergistic combination of data and information processing capacity of information technologies, and the creative and innovative capacity of human beings".

This definition not only recognizes the discontinuous environment but also the importance of both techno-centric and socio-centric approaches. The traditional view of knowledge management mostly relies on the prepackaged or taken for granted interpretation of the knowledge. Such knowledge is generally static and does not encourage the generation of multiple and contradictory viewpoints in a highly dynamic and ever-changing environment. The concept of "best practices" and "efficiency optimization" cannot provide the competitive advantage that companies may be striving for. This is where the concept of intelligent agents acting as catalysts of knowledge management is not only effective but also essential for the organization's survival.

According to Churchman (1971) "To conceive of knowledge as a collection of information seems to rob the concept of all its life…Knowledge resides in the user and not in the collection. It is how the user reacts to a collection of information that matters." Intelligent agents can facilitate the process of filtering and reacting to information. Since they are heterogeneous, robust, fault-tolerant; and able to encapsulate protocols, adapt dynamically and execute asynchronously and autonomously; they can reduce the network load and overcome network latency (Lange and Oshima, 1999). Kotz and Gray (1999), state that the rise in the use of mobile agent technology on the Internet will be due to several factors such as availability of increased bandwidth, need of technology to ease information overload, increasing need for individual customization to meet user expectations, increasing use of mobile devices, dependence of Internet technology by mobile users, and proxy sites which will provide for the specific needs of individual users.

Knowledge Discovery Using Intelligent Agents: A Proposed Framework

The transformation of data into knowledge can be accomplished in several ways. In general, it is a process that starts with data collection from various sources. These data are stored in a database. Then the data can be preprocessed and stored in a data warehouse. To discover knowledge, the processed data may go through a transformation that makes it ready for analysis. The analysis is done with data mining tools, which look for patterns, and intelligent systems, which support data interpretation. The result of all these activities is generated knowledge. Both the data, at various times during the process, and the knowledge, derived at the end of the process, may need to be presented to users. Such a presentation can be accomplished by using presentation tools, and the created knowledge may be stored in a knowledge base (Turban, Mclean and Wetherbe (1999).

Having understood the need for a change in organization theory and managerial style, it is essential to develop a system architecture for implementation of knowledge management systems. Brook Manville, Director of Knowledge Management at the consulting firm McKinsey & Co. in Boston, proposes three architectures needed for implementing a shift from traditional emphasis on transaction processing, integrated logistics, and work flows to systems that support competencies for communication building:

- A new information architecture that includes new languages, categories, and metaphors for identifying and accounting for skills and competencies.
- A new technical architecture that is more social, transparent, open, flexible, and respectful of the individual user.
- A new application architecture oriented towards problem solving and representation, rather than output and transactions.

The application of this framework will facilitate business model innovation necessary for sustainable competitive advantage in the new business environment characterized by dynamic, discontinuous and radical pace of change. This proposed architecture helps integrate the key ideas of this paper, i.e., a socio-technical perspective of intelligent agents facilitating the transition to the knowledge society. The social and ethical implications are discussed in the next section.

SOCIAL AND ETHICAL IMPLICATIONS

The social implications, as might be expected with a relatively new and partially developed technology, include both positive and negative issues. The author recognizes that the current discussion and research into intelligent agent software technology deals quite sparingly on the topic of the social and ethical implications of this new technology. This lack of serious consideration of the impact intelligent agent software technology on people's lives is a problem that this paper hopes to begin to address.

The first area that must be addressed is the philosophical nature of technology itself. Technology is created by human beings for human beings. Technology has always been pursued by mankind in order to improve his quality of life. Sometimes men engage in technological projects to help themselves only, but more often men pursue technological improvements for the good of mankind in general. All new technology must be tested in order to see if it meets the requirements of the person(s) who have invented them, and one of the tests must be: does the new technology provide significantly more benefit to mankind or a portion of mankind, than it causes harm? This is the most general test of any new technology, and it is also the most important test, since if the new technology fails this test, it should not be implemented at all. So let us apply this test to the new intelligent agent software technology.

To begin with, let us consider the positive aspects of intelligent agents. One of the biggest benefits to intelligent agents is that they have the potential to free humans from the tedious work of searching for information on the Internet and in databases. The amount of information and data both on the Internet and in corporate databases is already enormous, and it is continuing to grow exponentially. For any given search by a human being, however, much of the information available on the Internet and in databases is of little value. The intelligent agent is supposed to aid in the searching by filtering out the information and data which is of little or no value with little human intervention. If the intelligent agents are successful in this task they certainly can provide a significant benefit to human beings.

Unfortunately, intelligent agents also have the potential to harm human beings. First, if human beings rely too much on intelligent agents, they (human beings) may possibly lose too much freedom. This is a problem with technology and computers in general. A very good article by Jaron Lanier describes in detail the potentially harmful effects of technology on humans.[11] Lanier objects to the use of the words "intelligent agent" to describe any type of computer program. His argument centers around the concept that computers contribute substantially to the dulling of the human mind and human creativity. Confining oneself to an artificial world created by some human programmer(s) does limit human potential. This argument, though, lends itself more to the development of children's minds rather than human beings in general.

Another objection Lanier raises is that human beings end up degrading and lowering themselves when they accept computer programs as "intelligent agents".[12] This argument is more applicable than the first to human beings in general. While information technology professionals and those more aware of what intelligent agents actually are and how they function realize the limitations and scope of so-called intelligent agents, the general public who are the intended audience and users of intelligent agents are less aware of the inner-workings and limitations of intelligent agents. These are the people who Lanier suggests will be psychologically harmed by "intelligent agent" terminology. When individuals begin to think of computers as actually possessing intelligence and autonomy, they will begin to treat the computers like people rather than the (helpful) tools which they are intended to be. The result of treating computers like people will actually be that people begin to view themselves and others around them as computers. "As a consequence of unavoidable psychological algebra, the person starts to think of himself as being like the computer."[13] This is a serious problem that must be avoided at all costs.

Another more technical problem that Lanier raises is this:

"If info-consumers see the world through agent's eyes, then advertising will transform into the art of controlling agents, through bribing, hacking, whatever. You can imagine an "arms race" between armor-plated agents and hacker-laden ad agencies."[14]

The point here is that if intelligent agents are used to find useful information what will end up happening is that the agents themselves will be manipulated by producers of goods and services. Imagine an agent searching for information on airline flights being manipulated by the various advertising agents sent out by the more clever airline companies. This problem is not insurmountable for those creating "intelligent agents", but it is a significant problem that needs to be addressed.

SUMMARY AND CONCLUSION

In conclusion, while intelligent agent technology has potential to be useful to mankind, many fundamental problems remain to be solved. These problems are both technical and social or ethical in origin, and require careful thought and consideration by those who are developing intelligent agent technology. This paper has been critical of the current state of intelligent agent software technology in the hope of making these developers aware of problems they do not seem to have taken into account. The issues such as lack of standardization in mobile agents may cause lack of identity traceability due to multiple transfers among networks.

Security concerns relate to machine protection without artificially limiting agent access rights. Finally, there are issues surrounding performance and scalability such as the performance effects that high levels of security would have on networks, as well as the effects of having multiple mobile agents in the same system. These issues are fundamental to the well-being of those for whom intelligent agent technology is ultimately intended and need to be carefully considered.

Intelligent agent software technology has made some progress but has much, much further to go before it can and should be accepted as a tool to improve the quality of people's lives. The emergence of intelligent mobile/software agents not only will change the way that we communicate across networks, but also have a profound impact on the way that we accomplish many tasks.

NOTES
[1] Roberto Vinaja and Sumit Sircar (1999), "Agents Delivering Business Intelligence," 478.
[2] Ibid: Stan Franklin and Art Graesser, "Is It an Agent, or Just a Program?: A Taxonomy for Autonomous Agents," Proceedings of the Third International Workshop on Agent Theories, Architectures, and Languages, Springer-Verlag, 1996, 3.
[3] Stuart Russell and Peter Norvig (1995), Artificial Intelligence: A Modern Approach, Engelwood Cliffs, NJ: Prentice Hall, 33.
[4] D. C. Smith, A Cypher, and J. Spohrer (1994), "KidSim: Programming Agents Without a Programming Language," Communications of the ACM, 37, 7, 58.
[5] "The IBM Agent," http://activist.gpl.ibm.com:81/WhitePaper/ptc2.htm.
[6] Franklin and Graesser, "Is It an Agent or Just a Program?" 3.
[7] Michael Woolridge and Nicholas Jennings (1996), "Pitfalls of Agent-Oriented Development," Section 4.2.
[8] Ibid.
[9] Franklin and Graesser, "Is It an Agent or Just a Program?", Title.
[10] Ibid, 4.
[11] Jaron Lanier, "Agents of Alienation," http://www.well.com/user/haron/agentalien.html.
[12] Ibid.
[13] Ibid.
[14] Ibid.

REFERENCES
Baek, S., Liebowitz, J., Prasad, S., and Granger, M. (1999). Intelligent Agents for Knowledge Management—Toward Intelligent Web-Based Collaboration

within Virtual Teams. In *Knowledge Management Handbook*, J. Liebowitz (Ed.), CRC Press LLC, 11-1: 11-23.

Franklin, S. and Graesser, A. (1996). Is It an Agent, or Just a Program?: A Taxonomy for Autonomous Agents, *Proceedings of the Third International Workshop on Agent Theories, Architectures, and Languages*, Springer-Verlag.

Hauk, R. V. and Chen, H. (1999). Coplink: A Case of Intelligent Analysis and Knowledge Management, *Proceedings of the Twentieth Annual International Conference on Information Systems*, Charlotte, North Carolina.

Huang, M.-J. (1999). Intelligent Diagnosing and Learning Agents for Intelligent Tutoring Systems, *Journal of Computer Information Systems*, Fall, 45-50.

Lange, D. B. & Oshima, M. (1999). Dispatch your Agents, Shut off your Machine, *Communications of the ACM*, 42(3), 88-89.

Lanier, J., Agents of Alienation, http://www.well.com/user/jaron/agentalien.html.

Kirsner, S. (1999). The bots are back, *CIO*, 12:14. Section 2, 26-28.

Kotz, D., and Gray, R. (1999). Mobile Agents and the Future of the Internet, ACM Operating Systems Review, August, ftp://ftp.cs.dartmouth.edu/pub/kotz/papers/ papers/kotz:future2.ps.Z

Ma, M. (1999). Agents in E-Commerce, *Communications of the ACM*, 42(3), 78-80.

Maes, P.(1999). Smart Commerce: The Future of Intelligent Agents in Cyberspace, *Journal of Interactive Marketing*, 13:3, 66-76.

Maes, P., Guttman, R. H. and Moukas, A. G. (1999). Agents that Buy and Sell, *Communications of the ACM*, 42:3, 81-87.

Malhotra, Y. Deciphering the Knowledge Management Hype, Available at www.brint.com

Nardi, B.A., Miller, J.R., and Wright, D. J. (1998). Programmable Intelligent Agents, *Communications of the ACM*, 41:3, 96-104.

Russell, S. J. and Norvig, P. (1995). *Artificial Intelligence: A Modern Approach*, Englewood Cliffs, NJ: Prentice Hall.

Sandholm, T. (1999). Automated Negotiation, *Communications of the ACM*, 42:3, 84-85.

Smith, D. C., Cypher, A. and Spohrer, J. (1994). KidSim: Programming Agents Without a Programming Language, *Communications of the ACM*, 37, 7, 55-67.

Turban, Mclean and Wetherbe (1999). *Information Technology for Management, Making Connections for Strategic Advantages* (2nd ed.), John Wiley & Sons, Inc. 2nd edition.

The IBM Agent, http://activist.gpl.ibm.com:81/WhitePaper/ptc2.htm.

Vinaja, R. and Sircar, S. (1999). Agents Delivering Business Intelligence, In *Handbook of IS Management*, Auerbach Publications, 477-490.

Wang, S. (1999). Analyzing Agents for Electronic Commerce, *Information Systems Management*, Winter, 40-46.

Wong, D., Paciorek, N., and Moore, D. (1999). Java-based Mobile Agents, *Communications of the ACM*, 42:3, 92-95.

Woolridge, M. and Jennings, N. R. (1996). Pitfalls of Agent-Oriented Development. In *Intelligent Agents*, Section 4.2, Springer-Verlag, Berlin.

Chapter 13

Impacts of Software Agents in eCommerce Systems on Customer's Loyalty and on Behavior of Potential Customers

Juergen Seitz
Berufsakademie Heidenheim, Germany

Eberhard Stickel and Krzysztof Woda
European University, Germany

Most of the software agents only perform simple product price comparisons; some support the purchase of products or the negotiation over multiple terms of a transaction, such as, e. g., warranties, return policies, delivery times and loan options. Auctions help to find an effective pricing mechanism in electronic commerce. The active technologies enabling customers to purchase efficiently force the merchants to offer high personalized, value-added and complementary services. The techniques such as rule-based matching or collaborative filtering provide contents that are appropriate to the customer's preferences or analyze past purchases of other clients. The one-to-one marketing may be especially useful for sophisticated products demanding explanation or to enable cross-selling of other products. The merchants might achieve additional reduction of transaction costs (especially transport, storage and safety measures) using electronic money systems.

INTRODUCTION

Electronic commerce on the Internet introduces a new marketspace for large numbers of relatively unknown companies often offering substitutive products and

Previously Published in *Challenges of Information Technology Management in the 21st Century* edited by Mehdi Khosrow-Pour, Copyright © 2000, Idea Group Publishing.

services. The merchants profit from reductions in costs, time and unsold stock. Customers browsing and ordering products over the Internet are attracted by increasing convenience and speed of procurement.

Suppliers offering substitutive products in the marketspace need to acquire new customers and sustain ongoing business relationships. Actually, most merchant's sites are passive catalogs of products and prices with mechanisms for receiving orders from buyers (Dasgupta et al., 1998). The pull strategy is also applied in auctions available over the Internet, where the offerer waits passively for bids. The new-push technologies for electronic commerce including software agents enable customers to compare a bewildering array of products efficiently and automatically. Switching costs for customers and, thereby, their loyalty to previous suppliers in the marketspace decline.

Using the Internet the producers profit from reduction of costs through direct sales (non-intermediation) and through staff reduction. The dimension of such cost reductions and consequently the possibility to offer price discounts is the same for all suppliers involved in e-commerce. Therefore, the key elements to successful long-term relationships between merchants and buyers will be the offering of personalized and value-added services, such as one-to-one marketing services, discounts, guarantees and savings coupons. Additional cost reductions, especially for small-value products, may be achieved by using electronic payment systems. This is especially true for merchants.

In this chapter, we will analyze possible consequences of new push and pull technologies in e-commerce for customer's loyalty. The active technologies enabling customers to purchase efficiently and force the merchants to offer high personalized, value-added and complementary products and services. We will provide some examples of such services and of personalization techniques sustaining one-to-one relationships with customers and other actors involved in e-commerce. Finally, we will discuss the additional cost and benefits for suppliers and customers using electronic payment systems.

CHANGE BARRIERS FOR CUSTOMERS IN ELECTRONIC COMMERCE

The Internet-based World Wide Web provides a great opportunity to compare better products and services. Consumers as well as competitors may quickly gain detailed and up-to-date product information. Especially, suppliers of digital products (software, financial products, consulting services) over the Internet are in fear of declining customer's loyalty. Customers compare the catalogs of products of diverse merchants and producers and conduct transactions independently of their geographic localization. There are three crucial basic factors responsible for limited loyalty of consumers in e-commerce: convenience, time, and cost of the procurement process. An e-commerce system should support the ability to embed intelligence to automate decisions (Dasgupta et al., 1998). A customer should not only be able to passively compare products and prices from merchants' catalogs, but also to delegate software agents, which can retrieve information, negotiate and finally purchase products. Nowadays, most e-commerce procurements still involve a substantial human element, which is from the consumer's perspective neither convenient nor timely or cost efficient. Human involvement in the procurement process should be limited to transaction specification at the beginning and to the buying or refusal decision at the end of the process. In the intermediate stages of the e-commerce-based purchase consumers should be involved as seldom as possible. On the one hand, such reduction in interaction time through automation requires close coordination between buyers and suppliers. On the other hand, an appropriate technology is necessary. Mobile software agents emerge as ideal mediators in electronic commerce and thereby as an appropriate technology for an automated procurement process. Consumers may specify constraints on the features of products which enable mobile agents to select products from the merchant's catalog and finally to determine the terms of the transaction. Otherwise, software agents can be used by suppliers as market surveyors to determine the current demand and an appropriate price for the product. Software agent technology also abolishes the problem of diverse technological standards as, e. g., hardware platforms and operating systems of remote computers. Summarizing, geographical or technological barriers for consumers in e-commerce are of no significant importance. The key factors are convenience, time and cost of procurement process. They may be satisfied by new mobile software agent technologies and other e-commerce systems like auctions. These automated push-and-pull technologies will replace the traditional long-term consumer's loyalty to the suppliers with the concept of only limited loyalty. This calls for more active and personalized interaction between consumers and merchants.

One way to save costs and running time in a distribution process and therefore to be more competitive is the concept of non-intermediation. The producers or service suppliers may sell their products directly to the customer avoiding intermediators such as whole-sale, discount or specialized dealers.

ACTIVE E-COMMERCE SYSTEMS

There are several e-commerce systems, that support customers in the buying process. Especially, the push strategies for e-commerce are appropriate for active and automated information retrieval. After registration at a WWW content provider, the customers may get automatically emails or faxes for requested topics. They may also send software agents comparing products from multiple merchants.

The primary goal of customers is to maximize their benefit by reducing costs (or product's prices through comparison), running time and human involvement in the buying process. Otherwise, suppliers may use their active e-commerce systems to acquire new customers and to enhance loyalty of present clients. They may send, for example, supplier mobile agents, which query many WWW sites of possible buyers, analyze the responses and determine the optimum price for the product (Dasgupta et al., 1998). The goal is to maximize the gross returns of the supplier, on the one hand, and to sustain the long-term relationship to the clients, on the other hand.

In the following, we will analyze some strategies for e-commerce supporting both customers and merchants in the procurement process.

Agent-mediated electronic commerce

Software agents are computer programs showing the following characteristics (Joshi & Ramesh, 1998):
- Reactivity (agent senses and reacts to the environmental changes)
- Autonomy (agent has its own program code, data and execution state)
- Proactivity (agent takes initiatives to change the environment)

The ability of an agent to travel enhances it to a mobile agent. Software mobile agents may be classified based on their attributes, such as mobility, type of cooperation and level of interactions (Joshi & Ramesh, 1998). For further possible classification schemes see, e. g., Nwana (1996) or Sycara et al. (1996).

Competitive agents, mostly single-agents, maximize the interests of their owners. Collaborative agents on the contrary share their knowledge and try to maximize benefits of the community as a whole (Joshi & Ramesh, 1998). Mobile agents differ also in terms of the ease of an agent's mobility between two remote computers (Gilbert, 1996). A continuously traveling nomadic agent such as, e. g., the mobile sales agent (containing information of the total quantity of the product to be sold, the initial price of the product and the list of buyers to visit) arrives at a buyer site and communicates with a stationary buyer agent, which determines the quantity to be purchased at a given price (Dasgupta et al., 1998). The buyer agent uses tables containing the market values and demand curves of the product. The sales agent must adjust the price dynamically during the negotiations in order to maximize the gross returns. The price for the product may not be settled too low (an agent sells all of his inventory at a bargain price) or too high (a given quantity of the product may be unsold). Such a supplier-driven e-commerce system enables merchants to maximize their gross return, but also to identify quickly the customers' needs and finally to cultivate the long-term relationship with them. The architecture of the supplier-driven system was presented by Dasgupta et al. (1998).

Figure 1: Non-intermediated distribution in electronic commerce (Schoder, Strauss, 1999)

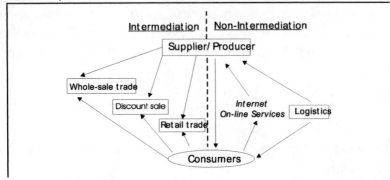

Figure 2: Classification of software agents (Joshi, Ramesh, 1998)

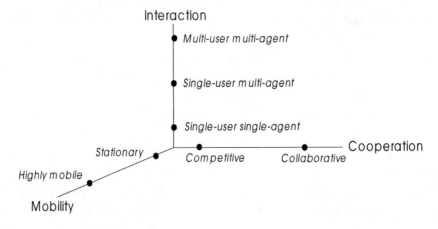

Figure 3: Agent's functions

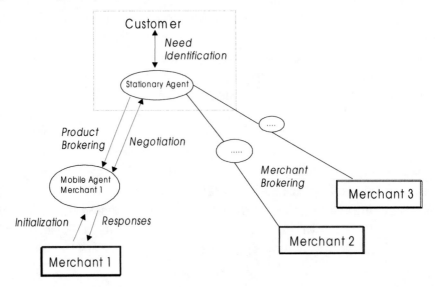

From a consumer's perspective, software agents should be highly personalized, continuously-running and autonomous mediators, that have to delegate some process management tasks (Guttman, 1998). An agent should firstly identify consumer's needs, then retrieve information about the product from the merchants sites, compare the offers and finally determine the terms of the transaction. These requirements result from the Common Consumer Buying Behavior Model (CBB model), which divides the procurement process in six stages: need identification, product brokering, merchant brokering, negotiation, purchase and delivery, and product service. Thesedays, consumer agents are used mostly for product and merchant brokerage and for negotiation. In the product brokering stage of the CBB model, consumers determine the product to be bought. Agents, like e. g. PersonaLogic, help them to select the best product from the merchant's list that satisfies the consumer's constraints (Guttman, 1998).

While PersonaLogic filters out unwanted products, Firefly system recommends products, which are highly rated through other shoppers. In the merchant brokering stage, agents compare merchant offerings, e. g. through an on-line price comparison. Jango and Andersen Consulting's BargainFinder are very appropriate for such price comparisons. BargainFinder collects price information from merchants at a central site. The disadvantage of that method is that some merchants, who do not want to participate in the price competition only, block the requests of the agent (Guttman, 1998). Jango removes such limitations of the suppliers originating requests directly from a consumer's WWW browser. Such agents bring the consumers only a limited benefit, because the comparison is driven only by price, not by service. The agents bypass the value-added and post-purchase services from merchants. Andersen Consulting argues that the BargainFinder's implementation showed, how WWW stores with on-line merchandising (attractive graphics, clips, etc.) could increase on-line traffic, but not necessarily sales.

The price of a product may also be dynamically negotiated instead of being fixed. MIT Media Lab's Kasbah is an on-line multi-agent system allowing negotiations. A user creating a buyer agent provides it with such criteria as price, time constraints, quantity of merchandise and sends it into a centralized agent marketplace. There the agent filters, offers and begins to negotiate with a selling agent, which responds only with either "yes" or "no" (Dasgupta et al., 1998). While agents in Kasbah's system negotiate competitively over price, tête-à-tête agents (also from MIT Media Labs) cooperatively negotiate multiple terms of a transaction, such as, e. g., warranties, return policies, delivery times and loan options (Guttman, 1998). The buyer agent in the tête-à-tête system negotiates towards a pareto-optimal deal with sales agent. Such a system does not maximize gross returns to the suppliers or price discounts for consumers. However, it takes into consideration the important value-added merchant's services.

Summarizing, software agents are helping consumers to compare and to purchase products in the Internet. Most of them are agents for a simple on-line product price comparison (PersonaLogic, Firefly, BargainFinder, Jango) or for competitive negotiation over price (Kasbah), without considering the value-added and post-purchase services from merchants. Such agents decrease customer's loyalty to a merchant towards zero. However, additional transaction's services such as guarantees, return policies, loans, gifts, discounts and insurance are of interest to consumers. Therefore, they should rather use agents comparing or negotiating over multiple terms of a transaction (tête-à-tête). Otherwise, merchants may also send their own sales agents to the potential buyer in order to acquire new consumers and remind the previous clients of new sales offerings (an active supplier-driven agent system).

Auctions

Auctions are an independent instrument in electronic commerce as well as a basic component of software agents. As an independent instrument, a human being acts by itself. As a component of a software agent, the agent acts as a deputy of a human being. The software agent needs a strategy, one or more goals and the dependencies between the goals for acting.

There are several requirements to efficient and effective coordination mechanisms of auctions in electronic commerce. Efficient allocation of resources are a criterion to get global acceptance. To implement auctions in an electronic commerce system, it is necessary that the actors don't need information about concurrent actors. The actors must not act strategic. For a local acceptance, the actors don't need to disclose their information. A minimized mean need for communication leads to low transaction costs (Gomber et al., 1996). We make the assumptions that the actors don't have preferences with regard to the actor, who gets the knocking down and that the human beings or software agents act economically rational and symmetric. Economically rational means that the actor bids with the goal to maximize his utility. Symmetric behavior means that bids are equal if the subjective values are.

In the following, we discuss four types of auctions that are possible in electronic commerce (McAfee & McMillan, 1987):

- The **English auction**: Starting with a low price, the actors make open bids. Each bid has to exceed the known highest bid. The auction is finished if nobody is ready to pay a higher price. The actor who makes the highest bid gets the knocking down and has to pay the price he bids.
- The **Dutch auction**: The auctioneer starts with a high price that will be lowered step by step. The fist actor who stops this gets the knocking down and has to pay this price.

- The **first price sealed bid auction**: Each actor makes exactly one bid that he gives to the auctioneer so that nobody will see it. All bids will be opened at the same time. The actor with the highest bid gets the knocking down to the price of his bid.
- The **second price sealed bid auction (Vickrey auction)**: The difference to the first price sealed bid auction is that the actor with the highest bid gets the knocking down to the price of the actor who makes the second highest bid (Vickrey, 1961).

All of the four types of auctions grant efficient allocation because always the actor with the highest bid gets the knocking down (McAfee, McMillan, 1987). Strategic behavior and the necessity of information about concurrent actors is only avoided by the English and the Vickrey auction. In case of the English auction, the actors know the bids of each other. It is also not useful to act strategically or procure more information in the Vickrey auction, see e. g., Weinhardt and Gomber (1996). In case of the Dutch or first price sealed bid auction, the bidders will act strategically. They make assumptions about the concurrent bidders, and, therefore, they need information. Disclosure of information is only necessary in English auctions. In case of the Dutch auction, the first bid gets the knocking down; the other two types of auctions implement an invisible bidding process. The need of communication is determined by the number of interactions. In the case of sealed bid auctions, each actor makes exactly one bid to the auctioneer. In Dutch auctions, there is only one bid. Under the assumption of linear price cuts in constant time intervals, the bidder needs only information about the starting price, the price cuts and the time interval. This means a low need of communication. The English auction has the highest need of communication because of the bidding process. Figure 4 gives an overview on the suitability of different types of auctions for electronic commerce.

Figure 4 shows that only the Vickrey auction fulfills all criteria. We don't have enough empirical information at the moment to give an overview of which type of auction is preferred for auctions where human beings or software agents bid. We will do this in further research.

Figure 4: Comparison of different types of auctions

	English auction	Dutch auction	first price sealed bid auction	Vickrey auction
efficient allocation	I	I	I	I
no need of Information/ no strategic behavior	I	-	-	I
no disclosure of information	-	I	I	I
small need of communication	-	( )	I	I

INCREASING CUSTOMER'S LOYALTY THROUGH COMPLEMENTARY SERVICES

In general, software agents, auctions and others technologies helping consumers in the buying process may minimize their loyalty to the merchants. Suppliers, who do not want to compete solely on the basis of price, provide their customers with highly personalized and value-added services that will help to sustain the long-term relationship to the clients.

Personalization and privacy

Personalization is defined as the customization of the WWW site to meet the particular needs of individual users (Dean, 1998). The goal of personalization technologies is to encourage repeated visits and to enhance user loyalty. The identification of private users' needs occurs through the observation of consumer behavior or through collection of user's data (filling out a form or following a decision-tree set of questions).

There are some advanced personalization techniques helping to personalize WWW contents, such as rule-based matching or collaborative filtering. Using rule-based matching, users have to answer a set of yes/no or multiple-choice questions to settle a set of user's criteria. Such filtering then provides content that is appropriate to the customer's responses. The collaborative filtering method combines the user's personal preferences with the preferences of like-minded people (Dean, 1998). Such recommendations to each others use, e.g., the already mentioned Firefly system, which is currently helping consumers to find appropriate (recommended) books and music. Amazon.com also involves the recommendation engine to analyze past purchases and post suggestions of the clients. Clients, who want to actively rate books, receive recommendations from Amazon's BookMatcher. The collaborative filtering is also very useful for bidders and offerers at auctions. The TopDeal auction in Germany offers both suppliers and shoppers to rate the partner of the sale/purchase that may help the users, who haven't sold/bought there before, to avoid unfair players.

In regard to personalization techniques, one-to-one-marketing should be noticed. This strategy enables targeting unique offers and products to specific customers (Dean, 1998). Institutions offering such individualized services have to dispose of accurate user profiles before. Examples may be found especially under on-line brokers offering stocks and bonds, such as e. g. Etrade or ConSors (in Germany). At Etrade, the customer may have his own WWW Site ("My Etrade") containing only information desired by the user. When paying with a credit card and after achieving an appropriate turnover, the customer will be informed about the advantages of premium credit cards. If his stocks will attain a previously settled limit, the Etrade customer will be informed by telephone, fax or email. Also at ConSors, customers may create their personal "Watchlist" with information and analysis from stocks, bonds, futures and currency markets. Users trading at ConSors may also get advice from their personal advisor's team that is helping customers in technical as well as in investment affairs. A new quality for one-to-one connections between a client and his advisor offers the TeleWeb-System X-Agent developed by Brokat (Germany). X-Agent combines the services from call centers and Web-sites within an institute using video and chat simultaneously. A client connecting to an advisor is able to see him at the WWW site (the advisor is filmed by a camera) and communicate with him at the same site. The advisor is helping the customer in filling out the forms or finding an appropriate product or service that improves customer's service in the institute. Such one-to-one marketing may be especially useful for sophisticated and tailor-made products demanding explanations or to enable cross-selling of other products.

A critical factor of personalization is the privacy issue. Filtering and customization techniques entail the collection and use of personal data, such as name, email, address, age, gender, income, internet connection, zip code, country, and/or employment status, which must be protected from abuse (Dean, 1998). Furthermore, a lot of suppliers in the Internet deriving revenues mainly from advertising need to identify their users in order to better customize the content to the readers and to attract the advertisers being interested in specific audience. Hence, the user should be informed by suppliers how they use the personal data, how they correct or change it and how they protect it. Nowadays, there are a few initiatives and standardization projects for the privacy of data interchange. P3P (Platform for Privacy Preferences project) developed by WWW Consortium provides an infrastructure for the privacy allowing users to tell automatically trusted sites personal information without typing it for each site. TRUSTe organization is a nonprofit initiative that certificates WWW sites accepting the specific principles of disclosure and user's content. Such initiatives increase user trust and confidence in electronic commerce; however, no organization or institution has the power to enforce it to the wide usage of suppliers.

Value-added services

Suppliers, who do not want to compete solely on then basis on price, often offer their customers value-added or complementary services. Complementary products imply higher benefits for the customer in the case he only buys the product he looks for (Seitz, Stickel and Woda, 1999). Such products or services increase the value of the primary good to the customer. Examples for value-added services in e-commerce are sales discounts, savings coupons, additional insurance and guarantees, gifts, but also free software to test. Often CDNOW offers their customers CD bestsellers with 30 to 50 % discount. New customers at BrandsForLess.com are attracted by 10 % off for the first order. The Internet merchant Buy.com established a BuySurplus.com store, whose inventory consists of brand-name products from liquidations, overages, and discontinuations where sales are made at great discounts. Content providers, e.g., Save-Net, offer saving coupons entitling users to buy cheaper at some merchants. Such sales discounts at Internet stores are possible through the reduction of branch offices and of costs. In contrast to stationary stores, on-line merchants don't pay rental charges for sales areas. They want to sell products as fast as possible to reduce costs for valuable warehouse areas.

The providers of digital products in the marketspace offer their customers software for testing or specific software tools for free. The bank's customers may often calculate their savings, credit and other budget plans at the WWW sites of the financial institute. Other suppliers, e.g., BrandsForLess or ebay, provide special guarantees or insurance covering items bought there. Ebay's insurance (from Lloyd's) covers purchases for up to $200 at no cost for the customer. In general, value-added services enable buyers to trade at favorable terms and with confidence. They increase the attractiveness of the merchant to present customers and attract new customers.

Reduction of transaction costs through electronic payment systems

On-line merchants might achieve additional reduction of transaction costs using electronic money systems. Electronic money is defined as an electronic store of monetary values that may be widely used for making payments without involving bank accounts but acting as a prepaid bearer instrument (BIS, 1996). Current e-money products my be classified as card-based (hardware) or network-based (software). The multipurpose prepaid chip cards have a great potential to be used for small-value retail payments as well as for Internet payments (by embedding a special reader in the keyboard as e. g. for the German GeldKarte) (Deutsche Bundesbank, 1999). The network-based electronic money working with a special software is used for small-value payments to purchase products and services only in the Internet. Both systems reduce cash handling costs for merchants and improve speed and convenience for customers. Currently, there are over a dozen of electronic payment systems, which are being implemented or tested in many countries (inTouch, 1998). In general, such payment systems are particularly implemented in countries, where the telecommunication costs for local calls are very high, as e. g. in Europe. Specifically, the smart card technology that allows off-line authorization is a cost effective way of processing financial transactions.

Figure 5: Status of implementation of the most important electronic money systems

System (Provider)	Service Provider (Issuer)/Status
GeldKarte (ZKA, Debis AG) (Deutsche Bundes-bank, 1999)	The German banking industry, Ca. 40 million chip cards issued in March 1999; share of transaction's turnovers in retail trade less than 1%
Mondex (Mondex Int.) ber1998 (Mondex, 1999)	NatWest Bank, Bank of Scotland (UK) - Pilot test at the University of Edinburgh, Start Octo- Chase Manhattan, Citibank, Morgan Stanley, MasterCard, Michigan National Bank, Wells Fargo (USA) - Pilot test within Wells Fargo Institute, Start September 1998 Hong Kong Bank Bank of Canada
Visa Cash (Visa Int.) (Visa, 1999)	Projects in 15 Countries (Argentina, Australia, Brazil, Canada, Colombia, Germany, Hong Kong, Italy, Japan, Mexico, Norway, Spain, Taiwan, United Kingdom, United States) In USA provided by First Union Bank, NationsBank, Visa International Headquarters, Wachovia Bank – Pilot projects: San Francisco, California; Bronx, New York; Tampa, Florida; Celebration, Florida
eCash (DigiCash) (Deutsche Bank, 1999; eCash, 1999) BA	Deutsche Bank AG (Germany) - Pilot project (Start October 1997), 35 Merchants, 1500 customers), On-line shop since January 1999 Mark Twain Bank (USA) - Pilot project (Oct. 1995 – Sept. 1998), 300 Merchants, 5000 Customers Swiss NetPay AG - Pilot project (Start June 1998), 28 merchants St. George Bank (Australia) – Pilot project (since October 1996), 50 Merchants Bank Austria - Pilot project (Start May 1998), test shop
CyberCoin (CyberCash Inc.) (CyberCash, 1999)	11 Banks (Germany) – Pilot project (since November 1997), 27 Merchants
Minipay (IBM) (Clark, 1998)	Tested by IBM
Millicent (Digital Equipment Corp.) (Digital, 1999)	KCOM (Japan)

The aggregated costs of each payment consist of transformation costs (e.g., the fees for conversion from assets to cash and vice versa), transport and storage costs, costs for safety measures, and search and time costs (Hakenberg, 1996). The charges for withdrawal of paper-based money may be related to the costs of transformation and clearance between electronic money and cash. For software-based electronic payment systems, we may assume that search costs are equal to zero, while for smart card users charges for loading funds exist. There are three types of costs that may be reduced by using electronic payment systems: transport, storage and costs for safety measures. The transport and storage costs are very high for fiat money because of its physical characters. Transport costs for intangible electronic payment systems are generated from charges imposed by local Internet access providers. Safety costs consisting of costs for technical infrastructure and software (cryptography) are currently relatively high. If it is possible to exploit economies of scale, these costs might decrease and eventually be lower than in case of paper money. Nowadays, the main problem of electronic money lies in missing acceptance by a large number of merchants and institutions. The willingness of merchants to accept electronic money depends on fees imposed by the issuer and operators, hardware costs and the reduction of costs of handling money in comparison to traditional paper-based money.

CONCLUSION

This work discussed consequences of electronic commerce on customer's loyalty. Electronic commerce is analyzed especially in the environment of the World Wide Web. The World Wide Web offers the possibility to create a perfect marketspace. The intermediation in distribution will be reduced. This means lower costs for both suppliers and customers.

We analyzed and classified different types of existing software agents with regard to their use on supporting electronic commerce. Most of the software agents only perform simple product price comparisons; some support the purchase of products. These agents reduce customer's loyalty because the price is the only variable. Quality and added values are not considered. Therefore, the on-line multi-agent systems allowing negotiation might be useful from a consumer's perspective. MIT Media Lab's agent systems is able to negotiate competitively over price (Kasbah) or cooperatively over multiple terms of a transaction, such as, e.g., warranties, return policies, delivery times and loan options (tête-à-tête). Merchants may also send their own sales agents to the potential buyer in order to remind the previous clients of new sales offerings or to suppliers in order to maximize their gross return. Auctions help to get an efficient and effective pricing mechanism in electronic commerce.

As instruments for increasing customer loyalty we discussed the personalization and customization of World Wide Web sites, value-added services and the reduction of transaction cost through electronic payment systems. The personalization techniques such as rule-based matching or collaborative filtering provide WWW contents that are appropriate to the customer's preferences or analyze past purchases and prior suggestions of other clients. An other personalization techniques like one-to-one marketing may be especially useful for sophisticated products demanding explanations or to enable cross-selling of other products. The registration of customers allows the merchant to build user profiles and therefore to make customer-oriented offers or build special offers including additional services. The value-added services attract the clients to trade at favorable terms. The usage of electronic money systems may result in additional reduction of transaction costs for merchants. This is especially true in Europe where telecommunication costs are high.

REFERENCES

Bank for International Settlements (BIS) (1996). Implications for Central banks of the Development of Electronic Money, Basle, October.

Clark, T. (1998). DigiCash loses U. S. toehold. CNET News.com, http://news.cnet.com/ news/0-1003-200-332852.html (09/29/1999).

CyberCoin (1999). http://www.cybercash.de/ccservices/cybercoin.html (29/09/1999), http:// www.cybercash.com/cybercash/services/cybercoin.html (09/29/1999).

Dasgupta, P., Narasimhan, N., Moser, L. E., and Melliar-Smith, P. M. (1998). A supplier-driven electronic marketplace using mobile agents. *Proceedings of the First International Conference on Telecommunications and E-Commerce*, Nov., Nashville.

Dean, R. (1998). Personalizing your Web site. CNET Builder.com, http://builder.cnet.com/ Business/Personal (09/29/1999).

Deutsche Bank (1999). Zahlungssysteme & Standards, http://public.deutsche-bank.de/deuba/ ui/ec/navb_ec.nsf/Frameset/DMEL-45NS9L?OpenDocument (09/29/1999) (in German).

Deutsche Bundesbank (1999). Neuere Entwicklungen beim elektronischen Geld, In *Monatsbericht* (6), http://www.bundesbank.de/de/monatsbericht/bericht06/99/elektrogeld.htm (09/29/1999) (in German).

Digital (1999). http://www.millicent.digital.com/spotlight/1999_06.html (09/29/1999).

eCash (1999). eCash (TM) - CurrenteCashIssuers, http://www.ecashtechnologies.com/ecash/issuers/index.html (09/29/1999).

Gilbert, D. (1996). IBM Intelligent Agents. White Paper, http://www.raleigh.ibm.com/iag/ iaghome.html (09/29/1999).

Gomber, P., Schmidt, C., and Weinhardt, C. (1996). Synergie und Koordination in dezentral planenden Organisationen. In *Wirtschaftsinformatik* 38(3), pp. 299 - 307 (in German).

Guttman, R. H., Moukas, A. G., and Maes, P. (1998). Agents as mediators in electronic commerce. In *EM-Electronic Markets* 8(1), pp. 22 - 27.

Hakenberg, T. (1996). Elektronische Zahlungssysteme im Wettstreit mit dem Bargeld. In *Sparkasse* (6), pp. 271 - 274 (in German).

inTouch (1998). *inTouch Newsletter* online Payment (9), http://www.intouch.de/ archiv/ oc_9_98.html (09/29/1999).

Joshi, N. and Ramesh, V. C. (1998). On mobile agent architectures. In *Tech Report*, http://vcr.iit.edu/papers/mobileagents/mobileagents.html (09/29/1999).

McAfee, R. P. and McMillan, J. (1987). Auctions and Bidding. In *Journal of Economic Literature* 25(6), pp. 699 - 738.

Mondex (1999). Mondex Electronic Cash, http://www.mondex.com (09/29/1999).

Nwana, H. S. (1996). Software Agents: An Overview. In *Knowledge Engineering Review* 11(3), pp. 205 - 244.

Schoder, D. and Strauss, R. E. (1999). Electronic Commerce – Herausforderungen aus Sicht der Unternehmen. In *Industrie Management,* 15, pp. 55 - 60, (in German).

Seitz, J., Stickel, E., and Woda, K. (1999). Electronic payment systems: A game-theoretic analysis. In Khosrowpour, M. (Ed.), *Managing Information Technology Resources in Organizations in the Next Millennium. Proceedings of the 1999 Information Resources Management Association International Conference*, Hershey, PA, USA, May 16 - 19, 1999, pp. 564-568.

Sycara, K., Decker, K., Pannu, A., Williamson, M., and Zeng, D. (1996). Distributed Intelligent Agents. In *IEEE Expert*, http://www.cs.cmu.edu/~softagents/ (09/29/1999).

Vickrey, W. (1961). Counterspeculation, Auctions and Competitive Sealed Tender. In *Journal of Finance* 16(1), pp. 8 - 37.

Visa (1999). Visa-Visa Cash-Where To Find, http://www.visa.com/pd/cash/ where.html (09/29/1999).

Weinhardt, C., and Gomber, P. (1996). Domänenunabhängige Koordinationsmechanismen für die dezentrale betriebliche Planung. In *IM Information Management* 11(1), pp. 6 - 16 (in German).

WEBSITES

Amazon.com's BookMatcher: http://www.amazon.com/exec/obidos/ bookmatcher/enter/ (09/29/1999).

BargainFinder: http://bf.cstar.ac.com (09/29/1999).

BrandsForLess.com: http://www.brandsforless.com (09/29/1999).

Broadvision, Inc.: http://www.broadvision.com (09/29/1999).

BROKAT: http://www.brokat.de (09/29/1999).

Buysurplus.com:- http://www.buy.com/surplus/about.asp (09/29/1999).

CDNOW: http://www.cdnow.com (09/29/1999).

CSTaR: http://bf.cstar.ac.com (09/29/1999).

eBay Inc.: http://pages.ebay.com/aw/safeharbor-insurance.html (09/29/1999).

ConSors: http://www.consors.de (09/29/1999).

Etrade: http://www.etrade.com (09/29/1999).

Save-Net: http://www.save-net.com (09/29/1999).

TopDeal Auktionen: http://www.topdeal.de (09/29/1999).

TRUSTe: http://www.truste.org (09/29/1999).

Chapter 14

Internet Payment Mechanisms: Acceptance and Control Issues

Ulric J. Gelinas, Jr. and Janis L. Gogan
Bentley College, USA

Internet online sales totaled $7.8 billion for 1998, with the average online shopper spending $629 (Fasig, 1999). During the 1999 holiday season, online sales were reportedly double that of 1998 at many "e-tailers" (although final statistics had not been published as this chapter went to press). As Web-based consumer sales grow, so does interest in new online payment mechanisms. This paper reviews several mechanisms that were in use in fall 1999. We assess control issues associated with each and use Diffusion of Innovations theory to assess perceived payment mechanism benefits and risks. We do not pretend to offer the "latest word" on any particular forms of payment, since by the time of publication, new or improved mechanisms will have emerged.[1]

DIFFERENT CONVENTIONAL PAYMENTS FOR DIFFERENT TRANSACTIONS

To understand the likely paths of acceptance for new forms of payment, it is helpful to recognize that different payment mechanisms, be they conventional or online forms of money, serve different consumer needs. In the "dirt world," when Americans pick up the lunch tab for friends, they are likely to be reimbursed (individual to individual) via cash or personal check. The payment to the restaurant (individual to business) is usually via credit card, whereas the subsequent payment to the card issuer (also individual to business) will usually be via personal check. A purchase at a local retail store (individual to business) is paid in cash,

Previously Published in *Challenges of Information Technology Management in the 21st Century* edited by Mehdi Khosrow-Pour, Copyright © 2000, Idea Group Publishing.

check, credit card or debit card. The consumer's choice of payment is based on a combination of perceived convenience and security. For small amounts, most consumers still prefer cash because of the convenience of a speedy conclusion of the transaction. For larger amounts, Americans prefer credit cards. If the consumer is purchasing an item that is at risk of breakage, they might use the American Express card because of the Buyer Protection plan. Should the buyer subsequently return merchandise, the merchant might reimburse them (business to individual) via cash, check, or credit card refund. The merchants tend to have different payment preferences. For example, the restaurant owner prefers cash payment, since each credit-card transaction costs the restaurant about $1.50 in processing fees.

INTERNET PAYMENT MECHANISMS FOR ELECTRONIC COMMERCE

Internet payment mechanisms can entail the issuing of software that is stored on the client side and/or on a merchant's or payment intermediary's server. A card (conventional credit card, smart card, or other physical storage "token") may also be issued. Many payment mechanisms use existing infrastructures (e.g., checks, banks, credit cards). Merchants receive payment at different times for different categories of payment mechanisms (either at the time of the sale or after the sale).

Four basic categories of Internet payment mechanisms are currently in use, as described below.

- *Direct Online Credit/Debit Payments*: A consumer provides a conventional credit card number online, either directly or via an intermediary. The transmitted number is usually secured either by SSL (Secure Sockets Layer, an encryption protocol that is included in browser software such as Netscape Navigator) or SET (Secure Encryption Technology, a security standard that is promoted by MasterCard, Visa and others). SSL provides for secure transmission of data, while SET adds a digital certificate that authenticates the consumer, merchant, and bank. Either way, the merchant receives payment following conventional clearing. Examples: Visa, MasterCard

- *Mediated Credit/Debit Payments*: Consumers may also provide account numbers via an intermediary. In February 1999, CyberCash introduced the InstaBuy service; consumers register credit or debit card numbers with InstaBuy (for free), and thereafter do "one-click" shopping with participating online merchants[2]. The merchant software, upon recognizing a registered consumer, sends a digitally-signed message to the InstaBuy server. This server examines the digital signature to determine merchant validity, then returns a message containing the consumer's shipping and billing addresses, shipping method, order ID, credit card number and expiration date. The merchant receives payment following conventional credit-card clearing. Trivnet's Wisp customers sign up through their Internet Service Provider (ISP). Software installed on the ISP's server allows for a Wisp participant's purchases to accumulate and be invoiced via their monthly TSP bill (Trivnet customers may also choose to have their online purchases be billed via their credit-card statements). Examples: CyberCash InstaBuy, Trivnet Wisp.

- *Stored-Value Money*: Consumers transfer money from a conventional (cash, checking, credit card) account to a stored-value account, with this data stored on the consumer computer or an intermediary's server, or on a microprocessor-based "smart card." In Great Britain, the Mondex wallet card supports specially equipped telephones, cash dispensers, and merchant card readers (for Internet purchases, the consumer needs a PCMIA slot). The Mondex merchant receives payment immediately at the point of sale. In 1999, Visa (and other credit card companies) developed a "hybrid" smart card that works as both a stored-value card (for small payments) and a credit card (for higher-value payments). Another stored-value payment mechanism, MilliCent, was designed for "micropayments" (as small as 1/10 of one cent). However, as of fall 1999 MilliCent was not yet in commercial use. Examples of Stored Value Cards: Mondex, VisaCash.

- *Electronic Bill Payment*: Upon receiving an invoice (be it on paper or via an electronic bill presentment service, such as CheckFree Web E-Bill or CyberCash Biller Direct) a consumer contacts a merchant Web site (e.g., PayNow) or intermediary Web site (e.g., Web BillPay), to authorize payment. Payments may be transferred via the Web and the existing banking infrastructure, from a checking account, to the merchant via their bank or intermediary (e.g., PayNow and Web BillPay). Some intermediaries (e.g., Web BillPay) will also write a traditional check to the merchant, where an online relationship has not yet been established. Examples: CheckFree Web BillPay, CyberCash PayNow[3]

E-Check (Gelinas & Gogan, 1997), designed by the Financial Services Technology Consortium (FSTC, a group comprised of banks, hardware and software companies, and others), is not yet in use for business-to-consumer transactions. E-Check is currently being tested in an extensive business-to-business pilot test involving the United States Treasury Department and key suppliers. Since E-Check is not yet available to consumers, we have excluded this important new technology from our discussions in this paper.

USING ROGERS' DIFFUSION MODEL TO ASSESS PERCEIVED FUNCTIONALITY

Diffusion of Innovations studies support the existence of five innovation characteristics, as perceived by target adopters (Rogers, 1995, pages 15-16):

1. *Relative Advantage*: degree to which an innovation is perceived as better than the idea it supersedes...
2. *Compatibility*: degree to which an innovation is perceived as being consistent with the existing values, past experiences, and needs of potential adopters...
3. *Complexity*: degree to which an innovation is perceived as difficult to understand and use... requiring the adopter to develop new skills and understandings..
4. *Trialability*: degree to which an innovation may be experimented with on a limited basis.
5. *Observability*: degree to which the use or results of an innovation are visible to others...

Each characteristic helps to reduce a potential adopter's uncertainty about an innovation. Relative Advantage, Complexity, Observability and Trialability reduce uncertainty regarding perceived benefits of adoption, while Compatibility, Observability and Trialability reduce uncertainty regarding anticipated behavior changes necessary to adopt the innovation. Figure 1 (below) proposes how different Internet payment mechanisms would compare along the five innovation characteristics. An explanation follows.

- *Relative Advantage*: Online credit card payments — whether directly secured via SSL, SET or via an intermediary — offer one "plus" in the United States; due to buyer protection features that most credit-card companies offer (whether for Web-based or conventional transactions), a consumer is only liable for the

Figure 1: Consumer's View: Comparison of Perceived Characteristics

Payment Mechanism	Perceived characteristics				
	Relative Advantage	Compatibility	Complexity	Trialability	Observability
Credit/debit card					
SSL	+	+	+	-	-
SET	+/-	-	-	-	-
Mediated credit/debit:					
InstaBuy	+/-	+	-	-	-
Wisp	+/-	+	+	+	-
Stored-value money:					
Mondex (in card)	+/-	?	-	+	-/+
Bill payment:					
PayNow	+/-	?	-	-	-
Web BillPay	+/-	?	-	-	-

Key: + likely to be considered a positive aspect
    - likely to be an undesirable aspect
    ? uncertain to predict how the innovation might be viewed by potential adopters on this aspect

first $50 of charges if a card is lost or stolen). SET requires a lengthier consumer registration process than is necessary for other payment mechanisms (in order for a consumer to acquire a digital certificate). This up-front step may deter some consumers. Mediated credit payments such as Wisp enable consumers to download copyrighted articles, songs, video-clips, and other very low-value items, thanks to the economies gained through integration with Internet Services Providers' billing systems. Electronic bill payment offers a relative advantage over other methods for invoiced transactions, in that the consumer avoids having to manually prepare checks or re-key data into their computer at tax time (however, for the many transactions where an invoice is not involved, this payment mechanism is not a solution). Stored-Value mechanisms eliminate the necessity of carrying cash, which can be an advantage; however, the requirement that funds must be transferred in advance into a stored-value account means that the consumer foregoes receiving interest on that money. When used for micropayments (e.g., if MilliCent is commercialized) stored value systems could offer a compelling advantage for the new pay-per-page types of transactions that they enable. For micropayments, where small amounts of money are involved, presumably the consumer will not see a disadvantage in lost interest income.

Note that Figure 1 summarizes only consumers' views. Different payment mechanisms will entail different costs, which will affect banks' and merchants' views on the relative advantage of different mechanisms. Micropayment mechanisms will entail the lowest merchant transaction costs.

- *Compatibility*: Online credit card payments ratik highly here; consumers engage in a familiar practice when they provide numbers to merchants (however, in Europe, where credit cards are less ubiquitous adoption is lower). SET's extensive registration processes may be seen as incompatible with existing practice, whereas SSL is unobtrusive. Stored-value debit cards (such as Mondex) have achieved greater consumers acceptance in Europe as of 1999. In the U.S., smart-card use has grown in certain vertical markets, such as university campuses. One would expect that a U.S. college student, who is already comfortable using their college's fast-funds card, would view a Mondex card as compatible with their existing practice (provided that lie already has a PCMCIA slot on his computer). Use of an electronic bill payment service may be viewed favorably by a consumers who already uses personal financial software such as Quicken. A consumer who currently pays bills manually might view online bill payment as incompatible. So, we put a question mark by this innovation. Again, Figure 1 takes a consumer's view. Since online credit card payments clear through standard channels, banks should view these as "more compatible" than mechanisms which bypass banks.

- *Complexity*: Given how fast payment mechanisms have changed, we propose that consumers view most Internet payments as "complex," especially from the standpoint of security, since most consumers do not understand how the underlying technologies of encryption and digital signatures work. The use of SSL to secure online credit card payments is probably viewed as involving less complexity, since from a consumer's point of view, SSL is almost transparent in the transaction. Payment mechanisms which are mediated by a familiar third party (such as one's ISP) may be viewed as the least complex.

- *Trialability*: Since making a credit payment via SSL requires 110 set-up cost to the consumer, it would seem to rank highly on this dimension. Yet, a Harris poll (Masterson, 1999) reported: "73% of Americans are not comfortable giving their credit card information to online businesses." Perhaps out of fear that, if one's card number is illegally intercepted, it cannot be reined back in (a breach of security would necessitate canceling that account and acquiring a new account and card). Most bill payment services require a fairly extensive registration and set-up, which can deter both consumer and merchant. Stored-value cards offer a low-risk consumer trial, since many allow the consumer to place as little as $10 at risk. Anonymous payment mechanisms reduce the consumer's risk, since they do not put one's privacy in jeopardy.

- *Observability*: Most Internet transactions take place in one's office or home, which limits the opportunities for potential adopters to observe early adopters' usage. In locales where merchant trials are taking place, stored-value cards, such as Mondex, could have an observability advantage, since people can observe retail transactions taking place with these cards. The lukewarm results of a Mondex trial in New York, however (concluded in fall 1998), suggests that observability may be very much in the eye of (and subject to the attention of) the beholder.

What about the relative weight of each diffusion characteristic? We propose that, since it is likely that consumers view most online payment mechanisms as similarly complex, perceived complexity is unlikely to differentiate one from another (except, perhaps, use of SSL). Observability is also unlikely to be a strong predictor, since as noted above, much Internet shopping occurs in private. For these reasons, we believe that relative advantage, compatibility, and trialability should "trump" complexity and absorbability in the view of consumers, bankers and merchants. This would be a useful question for empirical study.

PRELIMINARY EVIDENCE OF ADOPTION

As of fall 1999, banks, online merchants, credit card companies, and others had not achieved a broad consensus as to which of the above-noted emerging online payment mechanism is "best." In 1999 most U.S. consumers paid for online purchases using credit cards. Some provided their credit card number offline, via a telephone call. Others provided numbers online, secured by SSL. The stronger SET standard, released in May 1997 and backed by all major credit-card issuers, has met a lukewarm reception by U.S. consumers, merchants, and banks. Gartner Group predicts that "by year-end 2003, the Far East, South America and Europe will see 40 percent of Internet-based payments secured by SET ... (while) in the United States the penetration rate will be ... less than 15 percent ... by year-end 2003" (Source: Gartner Advisory Service Research Note). Although most consumers did not yet use the "one-click" InstaBuy service for credit card payments, the InstaBuy program listed about 300 merchants, including Amazon.com, ebay, and other major sites by Fall 1999. Meanwhile, the Trivnet Wisp program, introduced in 1999, was rapidly building up its base of ISP partners. Interest in online bill payment services also increased markedly in 1999. PSI Global observed that approximately 1% of bill payments were made electronically in 1999, and they estimated that by 2005, 20% of all bill payments would be made online, accounting for $5 billion in payments (Rohde, 1999).

We expect that different online payment mechanisms will be optimized to suit different consumer and merchant needs, just as choices of conventional payment mechanisms today vary according to different types of transactions. Having concluded that multiple payment mechanisms are likely to prevail, we next compare transaction security and merchant control issues (which presumably affect perceived "relative advantage") for different payment forms.

SECURITY AND CONTROL ISSUES

Consumers do not want to receive or be charged for goods that they did not order, and many do not want personal data revealed to others without their consent. Merchants do not want to send goods to those who should not receive them or who will not pay for them. These concerns may be expressed as a set of questions (see Figure 2) in three categories: authentication, authorization, and transaction integrity.

1. *Authentication*: Are you who you say you are? This is primarily of interest to consumers, who want to know that they are transacting business with real merchants.

2. *Authorization*: Are you authorized to place and pay for this order? Will this payment be repudiated? The merchant wants to know if, for example, this is a minor attempting to purchase alcohol. Both merchant and consumer also want to know that a payment has not been duplicated, either inadvertently or fraudulently. And, the merchant needs to know: will I receive the funds? Failure to receive payment could result from fraud or from a buyer's lack of sufficient funds.

Figure 2: Security and Control Questions

Payment mechanism	Authentication: 1. Are you who you say you are?	Authorization: 2. Are you authorized to make this payment?	Authorization: 3. Has this payment been duplicated?	Authorization: 4. Is this transaction fraudulent?	Authorization: 5. Are there sufficient funds to pay for this order?
Credit card					
-- SSL	-	-	-	+	-
-- SET	+	+	-	+	-
-- InstaBuy	+	+	-	+	-
Eectronic bill payment:					
-- Web BillPay	+	+	NA	+	+
-- PayNow	+	-	NA	+	-
Stored-value money					
-- in cards (Mondex)	-	+	-	+	+
-- in software (AOL wallet)	+	+	+	+	+

Key: +   Provides this protection

   -   Does not provide this protection

   NA Mechanism does not apply to this question

   ?   Depends on options chosen

3. *Transaction Integrity*: Both the merchant and customer want to know: are the payment data complete, unchanged, and confidential? Did the merchant receive all of the order and for correct amounts? Both consumer and merchant want to know that sensitive customer data, such as credit card number, PIN and telephone number are protected.

Payment mechanisms directly affect Authentication and Authorization, but other e-commerce software (e.g., order entry, order fulfillment, and customer elationship management software) are primarily responsible for protecting Transaction integrity. Hence, we describe how each type of payment mechanisms addresses key control issues of Authentication and Authorization. This discussion is summarized in Figure 2.

Authentication:
Question 1: Are you (the merchant) who you say you are?

Digital certificates, used with the SET protocol, verify merchant and customer identities. Digital certificates are issued by trusted certificate authorities. When transaction software encounters a certificate, it "knows" that at one point in time the certificate-holder proved their identity to the authority.

Public key cryptography, which is used in SSL, offers a lower level of assurance of identity than a digital certificate. When merchant software opens an encrypted message (using the consumer's public key) it "knows" that the message has not been tampered with during transmission, but without a digital certificate, the merchant software only knows that someone claims to be this customer.

The InstaBuy icon on a merchant's web site assures customers that the merchant has established a relationship with InstaBuy. When customers see their own shipping address, preferred payment method, etc., on the merchant's order form, they can feel confident that the data was just provided by InstaBuy.

When using CheckFree's Web BillPay, a consumer provides (or selects) such information as the merchant name. The consumer already has a history of dealing with that merchant. The CheckFree payments, using EFT or paper check, provide no more assurance than these mechanisms would traditionally provide.

When paying bills using CyberCash's PayNow service, consumers connect to each merchant's web site to receive their bill and initiate payment. The consumer's review of the bill determines its validity and, indirectly, the validity of the merchant's site. Similarly, the Trivnet Wisp customer will review the bill from their lSP to determine transaction validity.

Authorization:
Question 2: Are you authorized to make this payment? Will this payment subsequently be repudiated?

For most payment mechanisms, the consumer must provide a user name and password (which are usually protected during transmission by SSL) to initiate a payment, which helps to prevent unauthorized payments. Payments signed with a digital signature (e.g., SET) are difficult to repudiate (since the signature includes a certificate provided by a third part), and the software also verifies that the message was not altered during transmission.

The CyberCash PayNow CashRegister sends a consumer's payment as an ACH Pre-authorized payment Debit (PPD) to the merchant's bank. The merchant's and consumer's banks receive the ACH debit without transaction authorization (this is a standard process for ACH debits).

Merchants receiving a payment via Mondex or Visa Cash cannot determine the payer's identity, and therefore cannot determine if the order is authorized. However, values are encrypted and stored in the Mondex card, which can only be accessed with a PIN, thus reducing the possibility of unauthorized orders. Similar controls prevent unauthorized access to stored value on Visa Cash and other stored-value cards, as well as mediated services such as InstaBuy and Wisp. Thus both of these types of transactions are difficult to repudiate, assuming that passwords are properly used to initiate transactions. If a consumer later objects to a micropayment, the merchant will not lose much by providing a refund, and presumably merchants will track "chronic complainers."

Web BillPay transactions will be processed as checks. A consumer's bank may be liable for a bad check unless they return it within a specified amount of time. If the transaction were processed as an ACH debit, such as with PayNow, the merchant and their bank might be liable for the debit. ACH transactions can be reversed if a consumer's bank or consumer claims that payment was not authorized, or if there are insufficient funds in the consumer's account. Consumer ACH debits are subject to return for 60+ days.

Question 3: Has this order been duplicated?

Most forms of payment apparently do not include duplicate-detection mechanisms; it is assumed that the customer will take note of the extra money coming out of their available funds. Micropayment mechanisms, such as those proposed by Millicent, will prevent duplicate use of payment tokens.

Question 4: Is this transaction fraudulent?

All of the payment mechanisms described herein provide a reasonable level of protection against fraud.

In the U.S., a consumer's loss for fraudulent credit card transactions is limited to $50. A merchant assumes the balance of loss from a fraud, unless a third party is involved, such as when a certificate authority is used with the SET protocol (then the authority assumes the loss). The digital signature thus reduces the likelihood of fraud considerably.

User names and/or passwords help prevent unauthorized payments in most other payment mechanisms. Furthermore, those payment mechanisms that involve an ongoing relationship between customer and merchant (such as bill paying services) are protected by that longstanding relationship.

Question 5: Are there sufficient funds to pay far this order?

With SSL, SET, InstaBuy and Wisp a merchant receives the same point-of-sale approval as in any retail setting. A credit card companies' ability to collect from cardholders should not change with electronic commerce. Similarly, bill payment mechanisms have no better guarantee that funds are available for EFTs, checks or ACH debits (unless the bill payment host is the customer's bank). If payment is made with a check, the consumer's balk is liable for insufficient funds unless the check is returned in a specified amount of time.

Since consumers prepay their stored-value cards, Mondex and VisaCash involve immediate transfer of funds from consumer to merchant, and are thus superior on this dimension.

CONCLUSIONS

As with conventional payments, different payment mechanisms will likely serve different parties to different types of online transactions. We propose that acceptance is most affected by perceived relative advantage, compatibility, and trialability and that these perceived characteristics are in turn affected by consumers', merchants', bankers' and regulators' understanding of the security and control issues surrounding them. We expect further technical and strategic change in the years ahead, creating high demand for systems professionals who understand how new payment mechanisms can affect their clients' strategy, operations, and internal controls.

REFERENCES

Fasig, L. B. (1999, January 16). Expectations fulfilled for online shopping. *The Cincinnati Enquirer.*

Gelinas, U. J. and Gogan, J. L. (1997, January). The FSTC electronic check project. Case no. 96-10, *American Institute of Certified Public Accountants Academic and Career Development Division Case Development Program.*

Masterson, M. (1999, May 20). Study: six million victimized by e-commerce fraud. Internet *Internet News.*

Rogers, E. M. (1995). *Diffusion of Innovations* (4th ed.). New York: The Free Press.

ENDNOTES

[1] This field has been extremely turbulent. For example, several payment mechanisms that were in use in 1997 — including First Virtual, Cybercash's CyberCoin, and DigiCash's eCash — were 110 longer offered in 1999.

[2] CyberCash previously offered CyberCoin, a mechanism for payments in the 25 cent to $10 range. This was discontinued in April 1999.

[3] Cybercash refers to PayNow as an "electronic check; this should not be confused with the FSTC "Electronic Check," below.

Chapter 15

Approaches to a Decentralized Architecture for an Electronic Market - A Study for the Air Cargo Business

Freimut Bodendorf and Stefan Reinheimer
University of Erlangen-Nuremberg, Germany

This chapter proposes a decision support model for electronic markets using software agents. The model is based on the value chain concept applying to interorganizational information technology (IT), and the consideration of new coordination mechanisms to increase the efficiency of business processes. The proposed framework is used to design an electronic air cargo market. Companies involved in air cargo have lagged in recent years to adapt to the needs of their customers. Our framework suggests the decentralized implementation of software agents to support the transaction process. These autonomous software agents will support users to accomplish the various phases involved in a business transaction from information gathering to negotiation.

INTRODUCTION

The development of electronic markets (EM) has gained enormous interest among both, academics and practitioners. EM mechanisms are expected to increase market transparency, transaction speed and allocation efficiency while reducing biased decisions and time intensive routines. However, current EM can at

Previously Published in *Challenges of Information Technology Management in the 21st Century*
edited by Mehdi Khosrow-Pour, Copyright © 2000, Idea Group Publishing.

best be described as an automated version of non-Internet-based market trans-actions with focus on information delivery (e.g., WEB homepages as information centers) and on data transactions (e.g., WEB browser-based ordering, sales auctions, and customer support). As such, current EM implementations fail to take advantage of the well-proven potential of decision support technology. Furthermore, existing EM are typically designed following a centralized clearinghouse approach with all transactions being performed at the server site with traders accessing the EM via remote clients. In this chapter, we describe a different type of EM that fundamentally departs from the microeconomic model of market competition (with perfect atomicity among buyers and sellers) and which requires a well-defined mode of business processes. To address this particular type of EM, we propose the use of software agents.

To facilitate the discussion of the use of software agents in the design of EM, we report a case study pertaining to the air cargo business. The next section presents an overview of the air cargo business, its market characteristics, and the specific requirements for an effective electronic air cargo market. The following section presents a taxonomy of software agents and presents an agent-based approach to design EM. Then the next section highlights the key implementation aspects of the electronic air cargo market and is followed by a short illustration. Lessons learned and directions for future research are presented in the last section.

SPECIFITIES OF AIR CARGO BUSINESS

For most of the major airlines, cargo business has been insignificant compared to that of passenger transportation. The volume of goods to be shipped by air is, however, predicted to double by the year 2000 compared to 1995 (Alt & Cathomen, 1995). Airline companies have started to adapt their strategic goals accordingly, i.e., to find new computer-supported market mechanisms to competitively respond to their forwarders.

The business process itself will be affected by the introduction of computer support. Potential benefits of such an effort would be even greater for the forwarders. So far, transactions in the cargo business have relied mainly on informal relationships between officers-in-charge on either side of the market. Long term agreements have dictated general conditions including prices. As communication by telephone and fax still dominate the coordination process between a forwarder and its airlines, only a very small choice of airlines are considered for a shipment. Consequently, forwarders tend to stick to airlines they know and have success-fully done business with before. As such, preferences of officers-in-charge of the requesting forwarder dominate the choice of an airline transporter instead of the goal to find an efficient fit between supply and demand. Thus, the reduced number of interaction relationships a forwarder can handle during one transaction is very small, resulting in potential loss of business.

A very special demand of the cargo business is tracking and tracing of a shipment, so that the forwarder always knows where the shipments are located at that moment. So far this is achieved by telephone and fax calls which need to be performed and received by officers-in-charge.

The idea of a virtual corporation (see for example, Davidow & Malone, 1992; Gamble, 1992; Goldman, 1992; Klein, 1994), connecting partners, whose combined core competencies guarantee the best possible result for a transaction, has not been picked up in air cargo business, yet. It is this type of organization that can improve service quality and–combined with modern IT–can minimize ineffective communication and coordination. Time lags caused by call-backs, misunderstandings and double-checking can be avoided. In addition, integrated computerized support will prevent business partners from repeated data inputs which often cause errors.

When comparing the needs of an electronic air cargo market to those of other electronic coordination mechanisms, e.g., like electronic stock markets or computerized reservation systems (CRS), a number of major differences can be observed.

The stock markets as well as the computerized reservation systems in the passenger transportation sector are characterized by a great number of potential buyers and sellers germane to the concept of *many-to-many relationship* in database design. In the air cargo market, however, the uniqueness of each single shipment requires a special treatment so that it is usually the sender who will call for offers for the shipment in question. As this is done with all the shipments of a particular sender as well as the shipments of all the other senders on the market, we can portray this situation as a *multiple one-to-many relationship*. In other words, the relationship between airlines and forwarders will not be a perfect market in the neoclassical sense. We, therefore, contend that existing coordination mechanisms as applied in common competitive markets are not appropriate for the specific needs of air cargo business.

In a centralized market, information, negotiation, and settlement procedures are controlled by a centralized system. A CRS, for example, consists of a core system where all requests and actions are executed.

Common competitive markets are centrally structured as well. All data are typically stored in a central database. Access and retrieval mechanisms are provided by the system owner or administrator, resulting in enormous investments for system installation. A centralized market structure limits flexibility of negotiation considerably since no direct, personalized communication is possible.

Figure 1: Centralized market structure

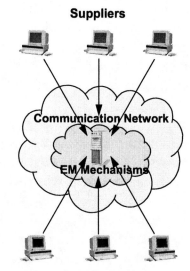

Figure 2: Decentralized Market Structure

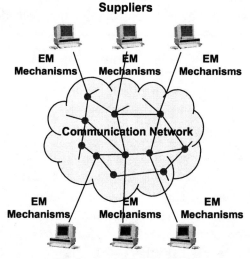

A decentralized market system coordinates market transactions by locally driven procedures, for example by systems implemented on the supplier's side and on the customer's side.

Data are stored in the decentralized systems. Communication and coordination take place in a one-to-many way, as opposed to a many-to-many communication in a centralized competitive market. This leads to smaller investments and greater flexibility.

As the air cargo market is not a perfect competitive market, the structure of a support system has to adapt to the special needs. Due to the fact that the air cargo business is a customer driven market dealing with customized services, the initiative has to come from the forwarders, addressing not all potential suppliers but only those that can meet the demand. Additionally, the special needs in the settlement phase call for a market structure where bilateral relations can easily be realized as well.

In order to communicate with market partners other than via telephone or fax, the Internet can be applied without major infrastructure investments. With this as a working assumption, we argue that smart and autonomous software agents can accomplish numerous routine tasks and, when needed, provide "intelligent" decision support as well.

As mentioned earlier, the needs of an air cargo market resemble the concepts of virtual organizations, since both forwarders and airlines enjoy a great degree of autonomy. Their interaction can very well be described as highly temporal business relationships. Decentralized structures provide a high degree of flexibility for the market partners and enable more personalized communication for bilateral business relationships. Decentralized coordination procedures can be supported easily by software agents guaranteeing the high flexibility desired.

ELECTRONIC MARKET ARCHITECTURE APPLYING SOFTWARE AGENTS

Software Agents

A (human) agent is defined as an individual who is authorized by the principal to perform tasks and interact with third parties in the name of the principal (Hess, 1983). By analogy, a software agent mimics the role of an intelligent, dedicated and competent personal assistant (e.g., assistant of an engaged forwarder). Software agents are one result of a paradigm shift in developing application software. Software is no longer regarded as a tool. Rather, it is considered as an autonomous assistant to the users. In other words, the traditional approach to software development is a reactive one where the computer is programmed to perform functions according to the user's instruction. Instead, the software agent approach is a proactive one, in that the user specifies what he/she wants the computer to accomplish, and the latter performs tasks the way it does best (Demazeau & Muller, 1990).

An "intelligent" software agent should be able to perform the following tasks:
- search and retrieve information,
- manage information overload,
- perform routine office activity,

- assist in mundane personal activity, and
- refer to domain expert.

To accomplish these tasks, it should possess the following general characteristics (Kalakota, Stallaert & Whinston, 1996):

- independence,
- learning,
- cooperation,
- reasoning, and
- intelligence.

Software Agents and Transaction Flow

Air Cargo Transaction Flow: A Software Agent Perspective

Transactions in the air cargo business involve several business partners. The most important are airlines and forwarders. Other stakeholders implicated in the process are banks, custom agencies, and airport companies. In the following, we will concentrate on the supplier - customer-relationship between airlines and forwarders. An architecture of cooperating software agents is introduced (see Figure 3).

In a networked organization, software agents can be regarded as teleworkers as they are assigned specific tasks and sent to the field to interact with other software or human agents. In an electronic air cargo market, two clusters of agents can be distinguished according to the ownership. Forwarders as initiators of a coordination process own user agents providing the interface between the system

Figure 3: Software agents supporting transactions between airlines and forwarders

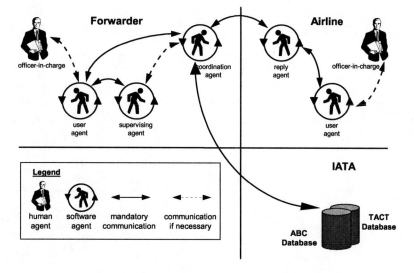

and the officers-in-charge at the front end. At the back end there are supervising agents which control the processes and intervene when necessary. Also, as back end support coordination agents perform the interorganizational transaction tasks.

The airlines' officers-in-charge access the system through user agents as well. Inquiries are handled by the airlines' reply agents.

Software Agent Activities

Market transactions are classically divided into three main phases: information, negotiation and settlement phase (compare Schmid; Schmid & Zbornik, 1991; Williamson, 1985). In the following, these phases are subdivided (see Table 1). In the table, *data input*, *market overview* and *offer collection* can be assigned to the information phase. *Offer evaluation* and *auction* can be assigned to the negotiation phase. *Document dispatch* and *tracking and tracing* can be assigned to the settlement phase.

Marks in brackets denote agent support not necessarily but optionally involved in the process.

An entire transaction with software agent support can be detailed into several steps, refining the activities (represented by columns in Table 1).

Table 1: Processes and their agents

	Data Input	Market Overview	Offer Collection	Offer Evaluation	Auction	Document Dispatch	Tracking & Tracing
FORWARDER							
Human agent	X				(X)	(X)	(X)
User agent	X				(X)	(X)	(X)
Supervising agent		X	X		X	X	X
Coordination agent		X	X	X	X	X	X
AIRLINE							
Reply agent			X		X	X	X
User agent					(X)	(X)	(X)
Human agent					(X)	(X)	(X)

Data Input

1. After the forwarder received an order to send a shipment he calls the user agent, thus initializing a transaction.
2. The user agent receives fundamental specifications of the shipment from the officer-in-charge (e.g., weight, destination, time window of arrival, documents to be included, additional attributes like "poisonous goods") using a standardized form.
3. The user agent asks for the human agent's preferences to be considered. Preferences could be the exclusion of certain airlines, airports, routings, etc. In addition, qualitative requirements can be specified by weighting the needs for punctuality, reliability, minimization of reloads, etc. The officer-in-charge specifies the deadline for offer collection.
4. The user agent initializes the supervising agent giving information concerning this deadline.

Market Overview

5. The user agent instructs the coordination agent to retrieve information about possible routings and corresponding airlines meeting the constraints of steps 2 and 3.
6. The coordination agent contacts the public ABC database to select appropriate routings.

Offer Collection

7. The coordination agent sends the calls for offers to the reply agents of the selected airlines.
8. The reply agents automatically provide offers for standard shipments. In more complicated cases they return their offers after checking with the human officer-in-charge.
9. The supervising agent keeps an eye on the given deadline. In case of no reactions it causes the coordination agent to send reminders to the reply agents concerned.
10. The coordination agent sends reminders to the reply agents trying to get the required information.
11. The supervising agent collects the results from the coordination agent. As soon as all airlines answered the call for offers the information phase is terminated. If this goal cannot be achieved, the deadline introduced in Step 3 terminates this phase. The supervising agent informs the user agent about the offer collection results.
12. The user agent forwards the information to the officer-in-charge. Details included are the number of airlines asked for an offer and the number of airlines

that answered the call for offers. In the same step, the human agent (i.e., the officer-in-charge) is requested to fix the deadline for the following auction.

13. The user agent forwards the deadline to the supervising agent.

Offer Evaluation

14. The user agent triggers the coordination agent to calculate net value prices for each offer considering quantitative and qualitative factors.

15. The coordination agent calculates net value prices and produces a ranking of the offers including information about the relative differences between the offers.

Auction

16. The coordination agent distributes this ranking to all of the airlines involved.

17. The airlines' reply agents receive the rankings and contact the user agent handing over this information. In case the agent's competence is sufficient it can react to the state of the auction without contacting the user agent and the officer-in-charge (step 18 can be skipped).

18. The airline's user agent asks the officer-in-charge whether or how to adapt the offer to the market situation. The result is given back to the reply agent.

19. The coordination agent collects new offers from the reply agents and recalculates net value prices.

20. The supervising agent terminates the negotiation process and instructs subsequently the coordination agent not to accept any further offers.

21. The coordination agent hands over the final ranking to the user agent.

22. The user agent displays the results to the officer-in-charge and leaves the decision about the market partner for this transaction to the human agent. This closing of a contract terminates the negotiation phase.

Document Dispatch

23. In the settlement phase the forwarder's user agent collects data for the necessary documents from the officer-in-charge and hands them over to the coordination agent.

24. The coordination agent transfers the documents to the recipients, e.g., airlines involved, custom agencies, or handling companies.

25. The documents are accepted by the partner's reply agent.

26. The whole process including the order of the documents is controlled by the supervising agent.

Tracking and Tracing

27. At the beginning of the actual transport process the user agent hands over milestones of the shipment to the supervising agent. These data are fed into the system in step 22 when the decision of the routing is made.

28. According to these milestones the supervising agent triggers the coordination agent to request a status report from the airline.

29. The coordination agent demands this status report from the airline's reply agent and delivers it to the supervising agent.

30. If expected and actual status differ the supervising agent sends this information to the user agent, which reports this exception to the officer-in-charge and saves the information in the local quality database.

31. Once the last milestone is verified by the coordination agent, the user agent informs the human agent about the closing of the transaction.

AN EXAMPLE

When a forwarder receives an order to send a shipment, he needs to feed the relevant data into the access system of the electronic air cargo market with the screens designed like paper forms (see Figure 4).

Here the most important facts can be seen at a glance. Buttons provide access to more detailed, specialized information. The button *On Market* allows this order be offered to other forwarders on a market with horizontal coordination structures. This can be necessary when the forwarder has no resources left to settle the order himself due to a lack of manpower or competence.

In the next step, the officer-in-charge defines the requirements of a shipment

Figure 4: Data input - order

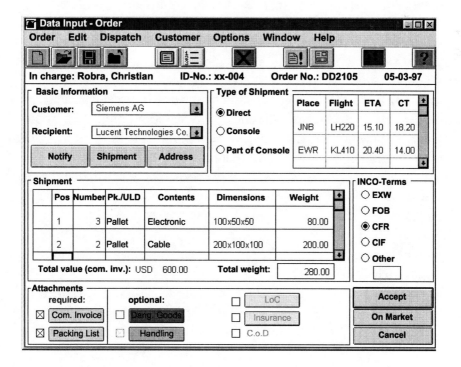

Figure 5: Offer request specification

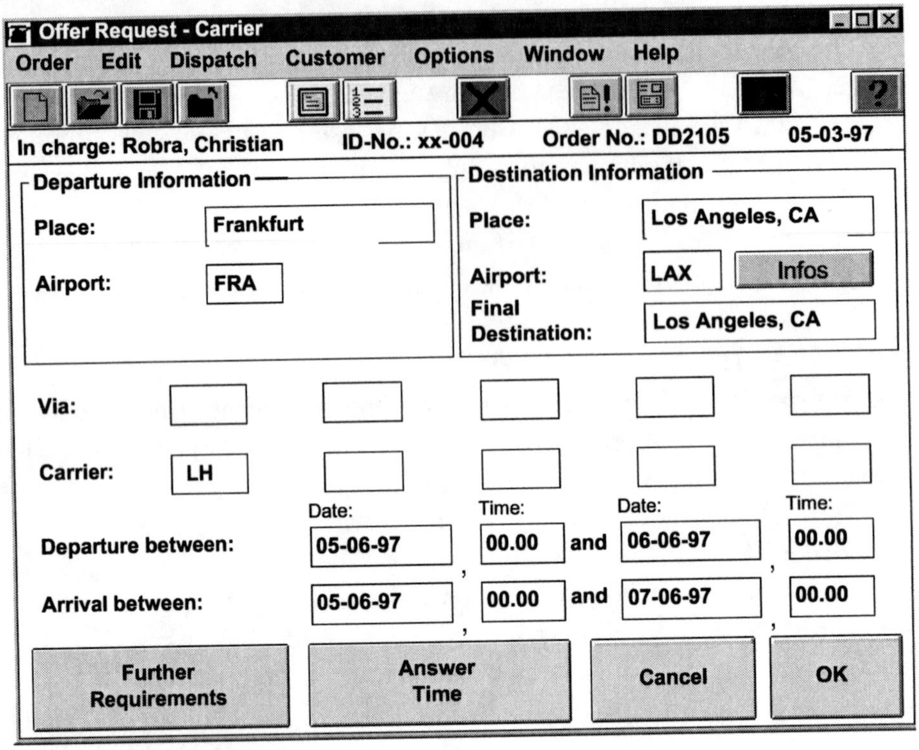

concerning information on departure, destination and arrival (see Figure 5).

The screen also offers access to more detailed specifications considering qualitative issues (*Further Requirements*) and time restrictions for the coordination process (*Answer Time*) instructing the supervising agent to close offer acceptance at a certain time.

According to the special needs of a shipment, the forwarder can indicate his preferences for qualitative factors like punctuality, duration or reliability. Mandatory criteria about which countries, cities and airports to avoid, as well as which airlines not to consider can also be fixed here.

Additionally, the number of reloads might be of importance for the choice of a market partner for a certain shipment. The system's supervisor can integrate additional quality criteria (last scroll bar in Figure 6) as he sees fit.

When the user agent received all necessary data from the officer-in-charge, he inquires basic routing information. The coordination agent forwards this information demand to the ABC database.

The coordination agent then contacts the airlines that could possibly handle the shipment and asks their reply agents for offers, thus initializing the auction during the negotiation process. After a number of iterations, final offers from the

Figure 6: Further requirements

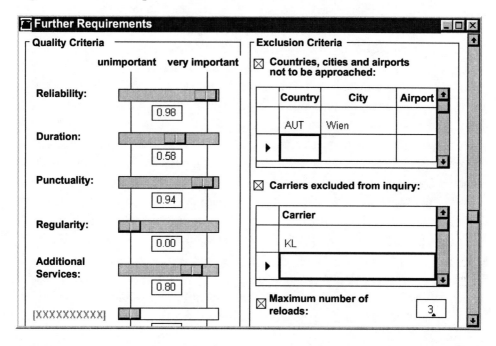

airlines are accepted and recalculated into the net value price. This leads to a final ranking which is delivered to the user agent and processed for the officer-in-charge. He is the one to finally decide which offer to pick.

According to the milestones determined by the routing, supervising and co-ordination agents dispatch the documents to the places where and when they are needed. Only in special situation interference of the officer-in-charge is necessary. Tracking and tracing are performed autonomously as well, handing over exception reports to the officer-in-charge when necessary. All relevant data are stored in the quality database without any time expenditures on the side of the officer-in-charge.

LESSONS LEARNED

The idea of an electronic market for the air cargo business was adopted quickly. The decentralized concept is an attractive one for both the forwarders and the airlines. Of particular interest for all market agents is the integration of tracking and tracing, which today is a very time consuming aspect in the communication between forwarders and airlines.

Impacts on Forwarders

The most apparent advantage for the forwarders is the reduction of telephone and fax calls. Transaction costs can be reduced as time can be saved for routine communication on information collection, negotiation and status requests. Additionally, cycle times for transactions are cut back through integration of the whole process and the ability of software agents to communicate with other agents much more efficiently compared to personal communication. Data, once put into the system, can be made available for all market partners avoiding multiple data input. The fact that communication can be simplified through the implementation of software agents allows expansion of much more market partners than before. The increase of market transparency enlarges the choice for the forwarders, resulting in better fitting of problem solutions and better prices due to more competition.

The approach to electronically support negotiation about prices and services is looked at reluctantly. Forwarders fear that the computer system might take over their jobs and doubt that their knowledge about the influencing factors on the decision about the market partner can be properly represented. On the other hand, the forwarders gladly accept a decision support component which does not deprive them from free decisions but structures influencing patterns on a certain shipment and helps finding an appropriate market partner.

Impacts on Airlines

On the airline's side transaction costs can be reduced as well since repeated data input can be avoided. This saves time and reduces the risk of wrong inputs. Since most of the communication with forwarders takes place in the information phase (offer inquiries) and in the settlement phase (tracking and tracing) the implementation of software agents that take over these tasks increases efficiency on the supplier side.

After a hesitant first reaction on the fact that an electronic market increases transparency and competition, the airlines realized that an electronic market can also be a valuable tool for them. Market transparency enables airlines to better advertise their core competencies since qualitative issues like reliability or punctuality gain in importance compared to the status quo. In addition new markets can be developed and the presence in an electronic air cargo market will lead to competitive advantages when the added services are useful for the forwarders.

CONCLUSIONS

Considering the airlines-forwarder-relationship and neglecting the presence of other market partners (banks, customs, etc.) of an electronic air cargo market advantages for both sides, namely suppliers (airlines) as well as customers (forwarders) seem to be obvious. An enhanced market transparency will increase efficiency from the customers' points of view and give the airlines a better chance to acquire new customers in and outside their home countries where they have traditionally been strong. Instead of regional preferences the forwarders' choice will move towards the more suited supplier for their current requirements. The airlines' success will more and more depend on their service qualities and less on market intransparencies.

The introduction of inter-organizational computer support will decrease transaction costs while increasing transaction speed. Time consuming tasks can be moved from human to software agents, saving time on the one hand and decreasing biased decisions on the other hand. Due to the distributed architecture high investments can be avoided.

The implementation of an electronic market in the air cargo business completely changes existing structures, creating new opportunities for both market sides without changing processes significantly.

REFERENCES

Alt, R., and Cathomen, I. (1995). *Handbuch Interorganisationssysteme*, Braunschweig.

Davidow, W.H., and Malone, M.S. (1992). *The Virtual Corporation: Structuring and Revitalizing the Corporation for the 21st Century*, New York.

Demazeau, Y., and Müller, J.-P. (1990). Decentralized Artificial Intelligence. In Demazeau, Y. and Müller, J.-P. (Eds.), *Decentralized A.I.*, Amsterdam, pp. 3-16.

Gamble, P.R. (1992). The Virtual Corporation: An IT Challenge. In *Logistics Information Management* 5(4), pp. 34-37.

Goldman, S.L. (1992). Co-operating to Compete: from Alliances to Virtual Companies. In *CMA - The Management Accounting Magazine* 68(2), pp.13-16.

Hess, J.D. (1983). *The Economics of Organizations,* Amsterdam.

Kalakota, R., Stallaert, J. and Whinston, A.B. (1996). Mobile Agents and Mobile Workers. In Nunamaker, J.F., and Sprague, R.H. (Eds.), *Proceedings of the 29th HICSS*, Washington, Vol. 3, pp. 354-365.

Klein, S. (1994). Virtuelle Organisation. In *WiSt* 23(6), pp. 309-311.

Martial, F.V. (1992). *Coordinating Plans of Autonomous Agents*, Berlin.

Robra, C. (1996). Prototypische Entwicklung eines Zugangssystems für Speditionsbetriebe als Teil eines Elektronischen Markets im Luftfrachtbereich. Master Thesis, University Erlangen-Nuremberg.

Schmid, B. Elektronische Märkte. In *Wirtschaftsinformatik* 35 (5), pp. 465-480.

Schmid, M., and Zbornik, S. (1991). Kommunikationsmodelle und Architekturkonzepte für Elektronische Märkte. *Arbeitsbericht IM2000/CCEM/* 12, Hochschule St. Gallen.

Wiesner, T. (1996). Integration von Geschäftsprozessen einer Luftfrachtgesellschaft in einen unternehmensübergreifenden Elektronischen Markt und Modellierung zwischenbetrieblicher Koordinationsmechanismen. Master Thesis, University Erlangen-Nuremberg.

Williamson, O.E. (1985). *The Economic Institutions of Capitalism: Firms, Markets, Relational Contracting*, New York.

Chapter 16

A Web Usability Assessment Model and Automated Toolset

Shirley A. Becker, Anthony H. Berkemeyer & Natalie A. Roberts
Florida Institute of Technology, USA

Many organizations are taking advantage of World Wide Web market opportunities through the development of electronic commerce (E-Commerce) web sites. The implementation of an E-Commerce web site, however, doesn't guarantee marketing and financial success. In fact, it could adversely impact the organization when the site is viewed as consumer "unfriendly" or "unusable." An E-Commerce site will be most successful when consumer usability attributes (e.g., performance, design layout, navigation) drive its development. This chapter describes a web usability assessment tool that is being developed to provide usability feedback on a particular web site. The tool incorporates a set of usability attributes with user profile data and organizational goals for ongoing assessment of the effectiveness of a web site.

INTRODUCTION

Many organizations are exploring the potential for increasing their customer base and market share by taking advantage of electronic commerce (E-Commerce) capabilities via the web[1]. The success of companies such as eBay and Amazon, online customer-based web sites, has shown that the Internet provides a viable medium for reaching customers. With the expected growth of E-Commerce exploding to over $300 billion in the next five years, it is almost imperative that companies expand their traditional means of reaching consumers to include internet options (Makmuri, 1998).

Previously Published in *Challenges of Information Technology Management in the 21st Century* edited by Mehdi Khosrow-Pour, Copyright © 2000, Idea Group Publishing.

What is required is an effective business strategy that encompasses the consumers wants and needs when developing an E-Commerce site. It is not sufficient to have a strategic plan that focuses on the technological aspects without taking into consideration a consumer profile of web use. E-Commerce sites will be most successful when technology and consumer usability attributes (e.g., understandability, ease-of-use) drive the development of a web site. For example, eBay's business goals of creating and rapidly expanding its on-line auction services has been supported by the usability aspects of its system including simple page layout and easy navigation. As a result, a broad range of consumers from novices to experienced web users have not only reached but have become repeat users (Spool, 1999).

Though there are tools and templates for supporting the creation of usable designs, there is still a significant amount of work that needs to be done to determine what usability means for a particular E-Commerce site. What may seem an inconsequential design decision (e.g., animated logo on the top of each page), may have dire consequences in keeping old and attracting new consumers to the site. Unless these usability issues are addressed, we face an explosion of unusable sites resulting in a "usability meltdown of the Web" (Nielson, 1999, p.66).

This chapter proposes a web usability assessment tool for providing insight into the potential success of an E-Commerce site. This tool gathers information about target users and the web site under study and produces a set of metrics based on usability selection criteria. Our initial development efforts are summarized in the following sections. The next section briefly explains a usability assessment model that is the basis for tool development. The following section presents an overview of the web usability assessment tool and its components. The next section describes the tool and an assessment process that is associated with the good use of our tool. The section following presents a simple example, and the last section concludes the chapter with future research opportunities.

A USABILITY ASSESSMENT MODEL

A usability assessment model has been developed in order to identify a comprehensive set of usability components needed to evaluate various aspects of an E-Commerce web site. The model, as shown in Figure 1, is comprised of aggregated usability factors including *page layout, design consistency, information content, design standards, performance,* and *navigation.* Each of these factors is comprised of a set of usability attributes, which is further decomposed into a set of usability elements. A usability attribute and its element set take into account behavioral, visual, and information content associated with consumer use of the web site.

Figure 1: The Components of the Web Usability Model

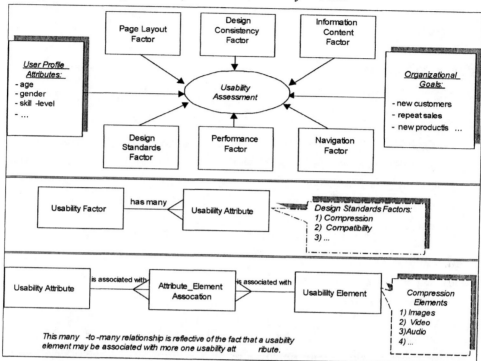

The usability model takes into consideration the user profile of the organization's target market (or other user group under study) in order to draw associations between consumer and usability data. User profile data may include such factors as age, gender, typing speed, web skill level, and others.

This model incorporates the goals of web usability that may be inclusive of market, financial, and internal improvement, among others. These goals drive the data collection and analysis process inclusive of baseline and improvement perspectives.

The usability factors and their attributes have been extracted from usability issues identified by Schneiderman (1987), Nielson (1999), and Lynch and Horton (1999) as well as from the authors' research in evaluating E-Commerce sites. Each usability factor is briefly defined as:

- *Page Layout* - The overall visual presentation of the web site is taken into consideration. Usability elements include color, white space, scrolling, separators, text, frames, links, and data entry labels.
- *Design Consistency* - Design components are consistent within and across web pages that compose the E-Commerce site. Usability elements include location consistency of objects, text consistency for labels, prompts, and other information, link color consistency, and consistency of color scheme throughout the site, among others.

- *Information Content* – The information content of each page is consistent, timely, correct, and complete. Usability elements include prompts and messages, default values, edit checks on data entry, timeliness, help, and data lookup and updates.
- *Design Standards* – The design is standardized to support understandability and easy maintenance. Usability elements include compression, compatibility, accessibility, scripting, common location, naming conventions, site sectioning, page organization, and scripts.
- *Performance* – Performance is maximized in terms of consumer wait time and system response times. Usability elements include download time and data lookup and retrieval times.
- *Navigation* – The navigational aspects of the system are intuitive and flexible. Usability elements include links, buttons, and browser capabilities.

For our web usability tool, eighty-five usability components (factors, attributes and elements) have been identified for use in the assessment of a web site. The complete set of usability components is not presented in this paper due to size limitations.

Not all of the components in the usability model need to be part of a web usability assessment. The tool that is described in this paper allows the organization to determine which components and level of granularity is needed to provide feedback on its usability goals.

THE WEB USABILITY ASSESSMENT TOOL

The web usability assessment tool executes in a web-based environment such that the assessment may be performed in a real-time environment. The user enters data in the web application while gaining access to one or more web pages of the targeted site. Figure 2 shows the overall architecture of the tool and each of its components is briefly described below.

- *User Profile* – The user enters personal data upon logging into the web usability assessment tool. User profile data, such as age, gender, color-blindness, typing speed, skill level, and others, is captured by the tool in order to make it available during the data analysis phase. Information about the monitor size, modem speed, and browser, among others is stored.
- *Usability Assessment* – The tool has the capability of capturing data regarding the eighty-five usability components identified in our model. The data gathering is done by:
  - *Software applications* – Automated support is being developed to capture as much information from a web page as possible to minimize the amount of data entered by the assessor. The number of gif/jpg files and links,and or-

phan links are examples of data that can be gathered when applications in the toolset are selected.

- *Usability forms* - Other data, such as, the effective use of white space, appropriate font size, and others, is entered by the assessor to reflect personal preferences.
- *Relational Database* – A relational database stores information about user profiles, data generated from the automated toolset, and data entered by the user during a usability assessment session.
- *Report Generation* – Various reports may be generated via the tool including:
  - *Assessment Score Sheet* - Report that is generated to show the assessor's raw scores per page and page averages associated with usability elements for a particular assessment activity. Figure 3, for example, shows part of the scores for the Design Standards factor provided by an assessor.
  - *Summary Profiles* – A summary of user profile data as specified by a selection criteria (e.g., individual, by web site, by web site category, for all web sites that have been assessed).
  - *Data Analysis & Metrics Reports* – Report generation capabilities primarily based on SQL queries embedded in ST-HTML files.

THE USABILITY ASSESSMENT PROCESS

The good use of the web usability assessment tool is ensured by having an assessment process in place. We briefly define each process step.

1) Set Usability Assessment Goals – Goals need to be identified in order to ensure alignment of assessment activities, data gathering, and metrics generation. The goal of a particular usability assessment activity might be to reach new

Figure 2: Web Usability Assessment Tool Architecture

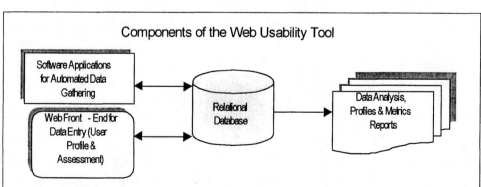

Figure 3: Compilation of Score Sheet Data

Sample scoring sheet	Page 1	Page 2	Page 3	Page 4	Average	Weighted
Design Standards	2.90	2.70	2.90	2.90	2.85	2.23
Compression	**3.80**	**3.40**	**3.80**	**3.80**	**3.70**	**2.47**
Images	3.00	2.00	3.00	3.00	2.75	1.83
Video	5.00	5.00	5.00	5.00	5.00	3.33
Audio	5.00	5.00	5.00	5.00	5.00	3.33
Animations	2.00	2.00	3.00	2.00	2.25	1.50
Consistency	4.00	3.00	3.00	4.00	3.50	2.33
Compatibility	**2.00**	**2.00**	**2.00**	**2.00**	**2.00**	**2.00**
NN only	0.00	0.00	0.00	0.00	0.00	0.00
IE only	5.00	5.00	5.00	5.00	5.00	5.00
NN & IE 3.0 or higher	0.00	0.00	0.00	0.00	0.00	0.00
NN & IE 4.0 or higher	0.00	0.00	0.00	0.00	0.00	0.00
						5.00

consumers, expand on repeat visits by existing consumers, improve performance of the site, or lengthen each visit (increase the number of shopping links traversed by the consumer) among others.

2) *Select the web site and page(s) to be assessed* – The web site and page for which data is gathered is selected via the web usability tool. The assessment may include all of the pages for a particular site or it may focus on one page (e.g., main page) in order to evaluate main page effectiveness across sites. This selection criteria is based on the goals of the assessment.

3) *Identify individuals that match the target market* - The targeted consumer group is identified in order to gather meaningful data about the effectiveness of the web site.

4) *Gather consumer profile data* – Information about gender, age, typing speed, color blindness, computer experience, and web skill level is entered into the tool by the individual assessor. Later, this information may be used to identify usability assessment variations by user profile type.

5) *Execute automated toolset* – The usability elements for which data gathering has been automated are identified and the applications executed. For example, the number of orphan links, download time for graphics, and number of and type of colors, may be automatically calculated for inclusion in the metrics report.

6) *Gather user assessment data* – The assessor enters a response to a particular element as he/she uses the web site. Depending on the element being assessed, the data entered may be a numeric value, Likert scale value, or yes/no response.

7) *Perform data analysis* – The score sheets are stored in an online database in order to provide the flexibility needed to calculate the usability weights and comparative indexes. The objective is to have data manipulation capabilities that would allow for sophisticated data analysis of consumer behavior in terms

of mistakes, link traversals, length of a visit, and the impact of information content, among others.

8) *Perform Data validation* – The data generated is only as good as the web usability assessment tool and its supporting process. What is needed is ongoing validation of the appropriateness of the usability goals, user profile data, data usability components, measurement associated with each usability component, and data analysis capabilities. (Though the tool does not support data validation at this time, it is an essential component of our future research.)

9) *Gather Lessons Learned* – An exit survey is provided to each assessor in order to obtain feedback on his or her perspective of the functionality of the web usability assessment tool and the data gathering process. This information would be used as a basis for making modifications and enhancements to the tool.

AN EXAMPLE

Several business-to-consumer E-Commerce sites for ordering computer products were manually evaluated in order to illustrate the web usability assessment capabilities. The goal of the assessment was to understand potential "usability impediments" that would impact a new consumer's use of each site for placing an order. This usability goal would provide a baseline for future assessments (hence, "understand" is used instead of "improve" or "enhance" the existing site).

Table 1 presents several major and minor usability issues discovered during the user's assessment of this site. Data inconsistency in terms of pricing information and a system error during the update and review of the shopping cart are of critical concern because of the immediate, negative impact on consumer use of this site. Neither of these problems occurred during the competitor's site assessment. The other usability issues may impact repeat purchases because the user perceived the competitor's site as more favorable in terms of readability, design layout, and navigation capabilities. Both sites required the use of the browser buttons to navigate backwards; however, this is not the case with other E-Commerce sites that have been financially successful. Though this example is for demonstration purposes, it clearly points out the need for a web usability assessment tool to support the data analysis process.

FUTURE RESEARCH

The web usability assessment model provides an opportunity to evaluate the effectiveness of an E-Commerce site based on a consumer profile and the organization's goals. However, more work is needed to make it a viable approach for real-world assessments in terms of its data analysis capabilities. We are cur-

Table 1: User Profile and Assessment Data

User Profile: Male, 40-50 age range, experience web user, low typing speed, no color impairment, and 20/20 vision (no eyeglasses).	
Usability Issues:	Explanation:
Use of Color	Dark background colors with white colored text and white background with gray colored text impacted reading ability, resulted in a high "noise" level, and overall was not pleasing to look at.
Font size	Small size in addition to font color impacted reading ability
Design layout	Many screens appear cluttered and user experiences information overload. Lack of white space among components, display layout is disorganized (doesn't always read top/bottom, left to right), and redundant buttons/selections clutter the page.
Navigation	Deep traversal path to place an order. Competitor's page required fewer link traversals to show pricing information and to place an order.
Orphan Links	Forced use of browser BACK button for reverse navigation means that each page is an orphan link.
Number of system errors	One major system error occurred when updating the shopping cart. The status of the shopping cart became unknown and the user was not returned to the same page from which the error occurred.
Data Quality	Pricing data was inconsistent across pages causing confusion as to the "correct" price associated with the product.
Legend	A legend was provided on a parent page to identify components. None of the linking children pages used the legend but instead relied on textual descriptions to relay this information.

Figure 4: The Web Usability Assessment Tool Architecture and Process

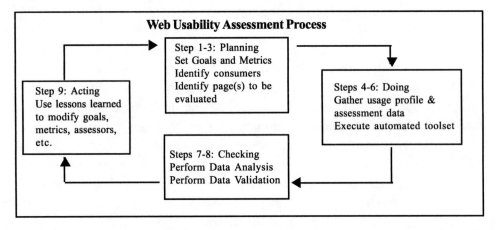

rently in the development phase of more sophisticated report generation capabilities inclusive of data analysis across pages and sites.

We are also studying the use of a web usability index that would provide comparison capabilities within and across web sites. The index is presented in Figure 5 with an example of its application. Though the index may provide some quick insight into usability issues associated with a site, there are limitations to its use especially as data is aggregated to a web-site level. It may prove that the index is more useful for providing feedback at more granular levels of data analysis.

Figure 5: An Example of a Web Usability Index for Data Analysis

Index:
ua$_i$ = usability attribute weight calculated as a weighted average of its elements' weights (6 attributes).
ui = weighte d average of usability attribute weigthts that is then normalized to produce a usability
index

$$\text{usability index (ui)} = \frac{\sqrt{\sum_{i=1}^{6} ua_i^2}}{\sqrt{6}}$$

Example:
Given : Usability Attribute Weights

- *Page Layout - .70*
- *Design C onsistency - .80*
- *Information Content - .80*
- *Design Standards - .75*
- *Performance - .70*
- *Navigation - .85*

$$\text{usability index} = \frac{\sqrt{1.8728}}{\sqrt{6}}$$

$$= .75$$

To illustrate the use of this index, we use an example. Let's say that we have assigned weights to all six attributes resultin g in an index of .75. This in itself seems rather meaningless. But when compared to a previous version of our web site with an   index of .55, where we had problems with orphan links and cluttered space, we find that the consumer's assessment (weights) sho   w an improvement in usability. We may want to run our assessment techinque against popular sites (e.g., Amazon.com) or competit   or's sites for comparison purposes. We may also want to focus on a particular aspect of usability such as maximizing the numbe   r of links traversed to ensure consumers are not leaving the site prematurely before exploring all of our product lines.

All si x usability attributes contribute equally in calculating the index value of .75 though this doesn't have to be the case. For exa mple, we could weigh performance more heavily than the other usability attributes if it has a greater impact on consumer behavio   r (e.g., repeat visits).

We could also use the index at more granular levels of data analysis. For example, we could calcula   te the index for a particular attribute (design layout) in terms of weights associated to each page in our web site. In this fa shion, we are comparing design layout indexes in order to evaluate consistency across pages.

REFERENCES

Deming, E. (1986). *Out of the Crisis MIT Center for Advanced Engineering Study*, Cambridge, MA: MIT Press.

Donaldson S. & Siegel S. (1997). *Cultivating Successful Software Development: A Practitioner's View*, Englewood Cliffs, NJ: Prentice Hall.

Lynch, P. & Horton, S. (1999). *Web Style Guide: Basic Principles for Creating Web Sites*, New Haven, NJ: Yale Press University.

Makmuri, S. (1998). Best Practices for Internet Commerce. *Intelligent Enterprise,* 1(3), pp. 29-41.

Mayhew, D. (1999). *The Usability Engineering Lifecycle.* San Francisco, CA: Morgan Kaufmann.

Nielsen, J. (1999). User interface directions for the Web. *Communications of the ACM* 42(1) (January), 65-72.

Schneiderman, B. (1987). *Designing the User Interface,* Reading, MA: Addison-Wesley.

Spool, J. (1999). "Branding and Usability," *User Interface Engineering,* http://www.world.std.com/~uieweb/.

ENDNOTE

[1] We limit our discussion to business-to-consumer electronic commerce.

Chapter 17

Categorizing the Supplier Content of Public Web Sites

Dale Young
Miami University-Ohio, USA

Web-based supplier communication and supplier diversity efforts have received little research attention to date. This study identifies the supplier communication and supplier diversity content on the public Web sites of the firms on the 2000 Fortune 500 list and creates a categorization scheme for that content. Just over a quarter (27.1%) of these large firms' public Web sites mention majority (i.e., primary) supplier issues or supplier diversity. Only 28.4% of Fortune 500 firms with supplier content actually describe a formal supplier diversity program on their public Web site. Therefore, public Web sites are largely underutilized as a means of interacting with potential suppliers from a diverse population. The most common supplier diversity content for prospective suppliers on Fortune 500 public Web sites is: certification requirements, on-line applications, and a contact name/title for the diversity manager.

INTRODUCTION

Public Web sites are actively used for both business-to-consumer and business-to-business commerce. Organizations are finding the Web to be an effective way to attract, communicate, and carry out transactions with trading partners such as customers and suppliers. For supplier interactions, the Web is beginning to

Previously Published in *Managing Information Technology in a Global Economy* edited by Mehdi Khosrow-Pour, Copyright © 2001, Idea Group Publishing.

replace earlier technologies, such as EDI, as a fast and efficient means of paperless interaction.

Suppliers can have an existing relationship with a buying firm and link to that firm using either the buyer's public Web site, or a private Web-based extranet. The Web may also serve as a means of communicating with potential suppliers. A public Web site is a convenient means of "telling" prospective suppliers about the buyer's price and quality expectations, and for publishing application forms. Many firms are interested in attracting a diverse base of suppliers, so the public Web sites of buying firms can also be an outlet for publicizing supplier diversity efforts.

This study examines Web-based supplier communications. The public Web sites of each of the firms on the 2000 Fortune 500 list were examined for majority, or primary, supplier communication and supplier diversity content. The objectives of the study are to describe and then categorize Web-based supplier communication and supplier diversity content on the public Web sites of these large corporations. The following sections review related studies, describe this study, discuss the findings, and suggest directions for future research.

SUPPLY CHAIN AND DIVERSITY RESEARCH

Two areas in the research literature support this present study: electronic, business-to-business (B2B) supply chain linkages, and diversity programs, including supplier diversity efforts. Electronic B2B supply chain linking is by far the most actively researched of these two areas.

Web-based B2B commerce has many benefits, such as enabling firms to create "end-to-end supply grids containing real time business process facilities" (Fingar, 2000). Some industries have not aggressively sought Web-based supplier links. A recent survey of large retailers found that these firms have been slow to use the Web to link with suppliers; "only seven percent of respondents with Web sites ...use them to collaborate with trading partners" (CSC, 2000). The CSC study notes that Web links can improve inventory management in the areas of shipment tracking and merchandise allocation. Conversely, other firms actively use the Web for supplier interactions. For example, IBM does business with 95% of its suppliers over the Internet (Carbone, 2000). Many of IBM's suppliers are transitioning from EDI to Web links.

B2B procurement is assisted by Web-based catalogs that link buyers and sellers (Baron, Shaw and Bailey, 2000). These Web interactions eliminate many manual and paper-based procurement activities. Baron et al. note that the Web is replacing EDI for some B2B transactions because of the need for high volumes of transactions to justify the cost of EDI. They categorize information exchanges between buyers and sellers, and each category focuses on ordering and payment processes. Suppliers in their study saw benefit for participating in these electronic interactions and were willing to "trade information to become a member of a restricted set of suppliers."

Lancioni, Smith, and Oliva (2000) identify benefits the Web has brought to supply chains (e.g., cost reduction and service improvement). They observe that the Web is useful for supply chain management in the areas of procurement, transportation scheduling, and customer service. However, the use of the Internet for managing supply chains is relatively new and "there have been few, if any, studies done on the use of the Internet in supply chain management." They studied how firms are using the Web in the operation and management of supply chains. Most of the respondents use the Web for some aspect of supply chain management. Many of the firms in the study use the Web for supplier interactions (e.g., purchasing, negotiating, checking price quotes, and order processing). None of these previous supply chain studies mention prospective suppliers or supplier diversity programs.

Workplace diversity has been studied, but the issue of supplier diversity receives little mention in the literature. Fine (1996) takes a negative view of diversity as a "tool" for organizational success, and focuses on multi-cultural organizations for a multi-cultural world. Her study does not discuss supply chain or trading partner issues. Wentling and Palma-Rivas (2000) interviewed diversity managers at eight Fortune 500 firms. Their study describes the content of diversity programs and very briefly notes the usage by one firm of "minority vendors and suppliers." However, they do not mention the Web as a communication outlet for supplier diversity efforts, and the study does not directly address supplier diversity as an element of corporate diversity programs. *Purchasing* magazine (1998) ran a special section on supplier diversity, which discussed the business case for these types of programs. They note that it is good for business when the supplier base matches the customer base. The special section provides practitioner insights but does not discuss the role of the Web in supplier diversity efforts or describe the content of these programs.

A few studies have examined the role of the Web in supply chain interactions, and a few have looked at diversity programs. Almost no research to date has carefully examined how the Web can be an element of a supplier diversity program. In addition, Web-based supplier diversity efforts have not been described or categorized. This exploratory study is an initial effort to describe the content of Web-based supplier communication and supplier diversity efforts and to develop a categorization scheme for Web sites with this content.

THE STUDY

To gather the data for this study, the researcher visited the public Web sites of each of the firms on the 2000 Fortune 500 list in June of 2000. The list, and the accompanying URLs, is on the Fortune magazine Web site (fortune.com). The researcher developed, tested, and modified a form to inventory the most common Web site content related to both majority supplier communication and supplier diversity by visits to the first 50 sites on the list. The form's content was influenced by these Web site visits, by previous supply chain and diversity studies, and by the researcher's experience studying electronic commerce and electronic supply chain links. The form went through several rounds of modifications during its development. The supplier communication and diversity grid was developed in a similar, iterative fashion, by discovering common patterns of majority supplier communication and supplier diversity content on these Web sites.

The data collection form and the classification grid were used in visits to each Web site of the Fortune 500. The home page and site index of each Web site was scanned for references to suppliers and supplier diversity. When available, the site search engine was used to search for key terms related to the study topics. The search terms used were: "diversity," "supplier or vendor," "minority or women-owned or small business," and "procurement." The most common abbreviation used on these sites for supplier diversity programs was "MWBE" meaning minority and women-owned business enterprises. Most firms in the study included disabled veterans and small or disadvantaged businesses in this general category.

The Web site supplier content identified during the site visits enabled the researcher to categorize each firm onto the supplier communication and diversity grid. The grid has two variables, "supplier diversity" and "communication to suppliers." Supplier diversity may be one aspect of majority supplier communications, but MWBE programs are often presented independently of other supplier issues on a Web site. Other topics that may appear under majority supplier communications include: price and quality expectations, procedures for submitting samples, labor compliance requirements, and instructions for interacting with buying personnel (e.g., gift giving). Web-based supplier diversity efforts were placed into three categories:

- the site describes a formal MWBE program,
- the site notes the importance of supplier diversity, lists a phone number and says "call us," or
- the site provides no mention, or brief mention (e.g., "a diverse supplier base is important"), about supplier diversity but does not give any contact information.

Likewise, majority supplier communications were placed into three categories:

- there are multiple site pages that deal with a variety of supplier issues,
- the supplier content deals with a single topic such as labor compliance or EDI standards, or
- the site provides no public access to supplier information (i.e., there is a secured extranet), or makes no mention of supplier issues.

Table 1: Supplier Communication and Diversity Grid

Supplier Diversity

	No/brief mention; no public access to supplier info.	Single Topic (e.g., labor compliance)	Site segments covering multiple supplier issues
Describe Formal MWBE Program *Row Total:* N = 38 (28.4%)	**1.** N = 24 (17.9%)	**2.** N = 8 (6.0%)	**3.** N = 6 (4.5%)
"Call Us" Notice *Row Total:* N = 24 (17.9%)	**4.** N = 10 (7.5%)	**5.** N = 7 (5.2%)	**6.** N = 7 (5.2%)
No/brief mention but no contact information *Row Total:* N = 72 (53.7%)	**7.** N = 18 (13.4%)	**8.** N = 48 (35.8%)	**9.** N = 6 (4.5%)
134/495 = 27.1% Sum N = 134	*Column Total:* N = 52 (38.8%)	*Column Total:* N = 63 (47.0%)	*Column Total:* N = 19 (14.2%)

Communication to Suppliers

10. No mention of suppliers or supplier diversity (n= 361, 72.9%)
No Web Site 5/500 = 1%

Table 1 shows the resulting three-by-three supplier communication and diversity grid.

FINDINGS

Public Web sites are common for these large firms; all but five firms on the 2000 Fortune 500 have a Web site. Although many firms may interact with majority suppliers using extranets or other private networks, the number of firms that use their public Web sites for communicating with suppliers is surprisingly low given the importance of electronic supply chain interactions. Just 134/495 Fortune 500 firms (27.1%) have some form of majority supplier communication or supplier diversity content on their public Web site.

Only 82/495 firms (16.6%) provide technical or other majority supplier content, and only 38/495 firms (7.7%) describe a formal supplier diversity program on their public Web site. Most of the Fortune 500 public Web sites (361/495 - 72.9%) mention neither supplier issues in general, nor supplier diversity specifically. Of the 134 firms that were classified on the supplier communication and diversity grid, 38 (28.4%) describe a formal MWBE program and 19 (14.2%)

have site segments that address multiple, majority supplier issues. The number and percentage of firms in each quadrant of the supplier communication and diversity grid are listed in Table 1. A Chi-square test shows that the values across the cells are significantly different (p<.001) than the expected values.

The 38 firms with formal MWBE programs on their public Web sites are in 19 different industries. The 24 firms with "call us" pages in their supplier diversity segment are in 14 industries. There is no clear pattern of interest across industries in using the Web for supplier diversity given the mixture and number of different industries in each category of the grid.

Majority Supplier Content

Communication to majority suppliers on Fortune 500 public Web sites falls into five categories: procurement, compliance, quality, supplier evaluation, and technology. Procurement issues include on-line bidding, order status, and logistics. Compliance covers labor laws, workplace safety, and environmental issues. Under quality firms mention ISO certification and continuous improvement. Existing suppliers are evaluated by a variety of performance metrics, such as on-time delivery. Technology covers topics such as EDI and electronic payments. Most sites (63/134) mention a single operational topic while a few cover multiple issues (19/134) in the Web site segment dedicated to majority suppliers.

Supplier Diversity Content

Several different content items make up the supplier diversity sections of the Fortune 500 public Web sites that have either "call us" pages or descriptions of formal MWBE programs. The most frequently appearing supplier diversity content items follow (see Table 2).

Table 2: Supplier Diversity Content on Fortune 500 Web Sites (N=134)

Supplier Diversity Content Item	# Sites	% Sites
Certification by outside agency required	50	37.3
On-line application form, or form to print and mail	40	29.9
Contact information: name, address, phone, e-mail	35	26.1
Financial information required (e.g., annual sales)	34	25.4
Definitions for MWBE categories	33	24.6
Technical requirements (e.g., EDI, bar coding)	26	19.4
Contact information *without* a contact name	25	18.7
Links provided to certifying agencies (e.g., SBA)	22	16.4
Letter from officer about diversity program	21	15.7
List MWBE awards or case studies	18	13.4
Second-tier supplier diversity mentioned	16	11.9

- Contact information (e.g., name, e-mail link, phone number, address) is provided on 35/134 sites (26.1%). Another 25 sites (18.7%) provide contact information without giving a person's name.
- A few sites (21/134 - 15.7%) display a letter from an officer such as the chairman or CEO, which discusses the importance of the firm's supplier diversity efforts.
- Approximately a quarter of the sites (33/134 - 24.6%) give definitions for each category of MWBE business (e.g., small, minority, or women-owned). A commonly used MWBE definition is: "A MWBE is a minority and/or women-owned business enterprise that is at least 51% owned, controlled, and operated by men and women who are African-Americans, Hispanic-Americans, Asian-Americans, Native Americans, or Non-minority women."
- Over a third (50/134 - 37.3%) require the business to be certified by an outside agency (e.g., the National Minority Supplier Development Council) that it is really a minority or women-owned business. A few sites (22/134 - 16.4%) provide links to certifying agencies such as the Small Business Administration.
- Only 40/134 firms (29.9%) provide an on-line application form or a printable form for mailing.
- A number of the firms use the supplier diversity section to mention technical requirements such as bar coding or EDI (26/134 - 19.4%). Others mention financial requirements such as a D&B number and past year's sales (34/134 - 25.4%).
- A few firms list MWBE awards they have received or case studies of their successful MWBE vendors (18/134 - 13.4%).
- Mention of second tier supplier programs is rare (16/134 - 11.9%).

Reasons for Supplier Diversity Initiatives

Several firms (39/134 - 29.1%) stated explicit reasons for their interest in supplier diversity. In general, firms cite both business and humanitarian issues when explaining the development of supplier diversity programs. Their reasons for these programs fall into four broad categories: customers, competitive advantage, communities, and common good. Examples of statements, and the number of firms making each type of statement, are listed below.

- *Customers* (16 firms) – MWBEs are potential customers, enable the firm to be a more compelling place to shop and invest, diverse suppliers help the firm understand/attract diverse customers.
- *Competitive Advantage* (11 firms) – provides competitive advantage; makes good business sense; required for government contractors; supports continuous improvement of products and processes.
- *Communities* (19 firms) – way to invest in/help grow the communities served or operating in; way to insure community growth.

- **Common Good** (7 firms) - way to express concern for the public good; it's the right thing to do; a healthy company and society depend on enabling all to share in the national economic growth; shows a high-performance, value-driven culture.

DISCUSSION

Most Fortune 500 firms (72.9%) are not actively using their public Web sites to interact with existing, majority suppliers, or as a means of attracting a more diverse supplier base. A few firms are actively moving supplier interactions to the Web, but many are not. The single most common usage of Fortune 500 public Web sites regarding supplier communications (63/134 sites, 47.0%) is for explaining specific requirements such as labor law compliance or for publishing technical specifications (e.g., for EDI). *Publishing* technical or operational information (63 sites) outweighs *promoting* supplier diversity with a formal MWBE program (38 sites). Therefore, concerning supplier information, the public Web sites of large corporations are primarily used as a publishing outlet describing how to transact business with the buying firm.

Firms with descriptions of formal MWBE programs or "call us" segments on their public Web sites are more likely to have no public, majority supplier communication than they are to have single-topic or extensive supplier communication. Specifically, over half (34/62, 54.8%) of the formal or "call us" MWBE programs are on Web sites that have no mention, or no public access, to majority supplier information. Firms that publish supplier diversity material on their public Web site (62 firms) are slightly more inclined to discuss supplier diversity alone (34 firms) than to mention both supplier diversity and suppliers in general (28 firms). However, for the entire group of 134 firms on the supplier communication and diversity grid, more firms publish majority supplier information only on their Web site (54 firms) than publish supplier diversity information alone (34 firms).

Although many of these firms may have active supplier diversity programs, only 7.7% of the Fortune 500 are using their public Web site to describe their MWBE programs. A few more (4.8%) of the Fortune 500 tell prospective diverse suppliers to "call us." Given the growing access to the Web across the United States the Web seems to be an underutilized resource for growing a diverse base of suppliers. There is no indication in the data that any single industry is actively leading in the development of Web-based supplier diversity programs.

Even for firms with formal, Web-based MWBE programs, there are some glaring omissions in the content of their Web sites. Just over a quarter of the sites (26.1%) list a contact name; another 18.7% have contact information without a name. The lack of contact information presents an "unfriendly" face to prospects. Listing awards and case examples help improve the visitor friendliness of the Web site, but again, these items appear infrequently (13.4%). Something as simple as an on-line application appears less than 30% of the time. Links to certifying agencies could be helpful for non-certified supplier firms, but only 16.4% of the sites with supplier diversity content offer this feature. The percentages of Web sites with each type of supplier diversity content are generally low (see Table 2) suggesting that no consensus has emerged about what should, and should not, be included when discussing supplier diversity on a public Web site. Firms with established processes for dealing with diverse suppliers are just beginning to move those processes to their public Web sites.

A negative view of public, Web-based supplier diversity efforts is that they represent an open invitation for special treatment. The number of firms that specify price, quality, geographic coverage, and financial or technical requirements (e.g., EDI is required) argues against special treatment. Although the percentages of firms that publicize specific requirements are generally low (e.g., 25.4% ask for sales and other financial data), other statements about price, quality and on-time delivery on these Web sites suggest that prospects must compete against other suppliers with established relationships. Web-based supplier diversity programs place the responsibility on the prospect for certification, for follow-up contacts with the buying firm, and for meeting the buyer's requirements for electronic linkages and financial stability.

The stated purposes for developing supplier diversity programs (e.g., new customers, gain competitive advantage) argue against altruistic motives alone. Firms see sound business reasons (e.g., lower operating costs, better understanding their customer's needs) for developing a diverse supplier base. Supplier diversity is one way firms are able to understand and sell to a very diverse set of customers in an increasingly diverse marketplace. However, the low occurrence of Web-based supplier diversity programs contrasts sharply with this imperative for understanding and selling to diverse markets.

CONTRIBUTION

The primary contribution of this study is to identify the content of Web-based majority supplier communication and supplier diversity efforts and then create a categorization scheme for that content. Although firms may actively use private extranets for majority supplier interactions, their public Web sites are generally underutilized for this purpose.

Fortune 500 firms appear to be in the early stages of interacting with majority or MWBE suppliers through public Web sites. Publishing technical or operational specifications on the Web is a relatively safe way to use this medium. A few firms are publishing supplier diversity program materials; fewer still are "transacting" with prospective diverse suppliers by taking on-line applications or accepting email questions. The number of Web-based supplier diversity efforts should increase as firms gain confidence in the Web as a means of communication. Corporate diversity efforts relating to suppliers are a given, but the role of the Web in these efforts is still emerging.

This study faces the same limitations as other Web-based surveys. The content of public Web sites changes frequently and so presents a "moving target" to researchers. The public Web sites of the Fortune 500 are not representative of every firm's Web site, but certainly represent how huge firms, with very large supplier bases, interact with those suppliers using the Web. This study looks from "the outside in" by visiting public Web sites. Follow-up studies should survey and interview supplier diversity managers at these firms to better understand the firm's business objectives regarding the role of the Web in supplier diversity programs.

ACKNOWLEDGMENT

The author acknowledges the research support of the R.T. Farmer School of Business Administration, Miami University, Oxford, Ohio.

REFERENCES

Baron, J., Shaw, M. and Bailey, A. (2000). Web-based E-catalog Systems in B2B Procurement. *Communications of the ACM* (43, 5), 93-100, May.

Carbone, J. (2000). E-procurement at IBM: POs are just the beginning. *Purchasing*, S50-S55, March 23.

CSC – Computer Science Corporation (2000). The E-merging Future in Retail. 10th Annual Retail Technology Study, http://www.csc.com.

Fine, M. (1996). Cultural diversity in the workplace: The state of the field. *The Journal of Business Communication*, (33, 4), October.

Fingar, P. (2000). E-commerce: Transforming the supply chain. *Logistics Management and Distribution Report*, E7-E10, April.

Lancioni, R., Smith, M. and Oliva, T. (2000). The Role of the Internet in Supply Chain Management. *Industrial Marketing Management* (29), 45-56.

Purchasing (1998). Obstacles on the road to supplier diversity. *Purchasing*, (125, 2), 64S14-64S19, August 13.

Wentling, R. and Palma-Rivas, N. (2000). Current status of diversity initiatives in selected multinational corporations. *Human Resource Development Quarterly*, (11, 1), 35-60 spring.

Chapter 18

Multi-Dimensional B2B Auctions for Electronic Commerce[1]

Marilyn T. Griffin and France Belanger
Virginia Polytechnic Institute and State University, USA

Craig Van Slyke
University of Central Florida, USA

INTRODUCTION

Since the early days of Electronic Data Interchange (EDI), many business-to-business (B2B) models of electronic commerce have been developed. Currently, the fastest growing segment of e-commerce is the B2B Web-based marketplace (Wilder, 2000). The dynamic nature of this business environment is driving major changes in business strategies and models, marketing, and information systems development. In order for new companies to compete in this extremely competitive environment, they must understand the nature of the market, and the vast commitment of resources necessary to establish a presence in that market.

Early online auction models were based on price alone. Today, businesses must consider the total cost of the transaction, including transportation, storage, financing, and insurance. Businesses must also consider whether an offering matches qualitative and quantitative specifications besides price (delivery date and conditions, quantity range, product quality, service, etc.) (Lenz, Andren & Hope-Ross, 2000). These multiple variables have increased the complexity of B2B auctions and led to the implementation of multidimensional B2B auctions (Teich, Wallenius & Wallenius, 1999).

Previously Published in *Managing Information Technology in a Global Economy* edited by Mehdi Khosrow-Pour, Copyright © 2001, Idea Group Publishing.

LITERATURE REVIEW

The e-marketplace is an Internet location where buyers and sellers can come together to transact business. B2B auctions started in the basic commodity markets, but are rapidly moving into more complex industries. The major driving force behind the growth of online auctions is the fundamental concept of market efficiency, which exists when all buyers and sellers have complete information and supply is in balance with demand. Perfectly efficient markets do not exist, but the Internet has the potential to move markets in that direction by its instant communications capability. Where once negotiations were conducted by human, Internet-based negotiations can be performed at a fraction of the cost (Quan, 2000).

Auction Models

Auction models take different forms in a continuum from one buyer and one seller to many buyers and sellers. The classification of B2B auctions is based on whether the price is ascending or descending, who initiates the bidding process, and the interactivity format (which is presented in Figure 1).

The simplest auction model is negotiation. In traditional or *forward auctions* the only factor determining the winning bid is usually the highest price. *Reverse auctions* are used primarily for procurement. *Exchanges* are generally very fast and efficient and work best for commodities with well-defined attributes (Messmer, 2000).

Direction of Bidding. *English auctions,* typically used in forward auctions, start the bidding at the lowest acceptable price and solicit higher bids until the auction closes. The highest bid wins. In *Dutch auctions*, the bidding starts at a high price and decreases by successive bids until the auction closes. It can be used in reverse or procurement auctions. A *Vickrey auction* is like an English auction except that the second highest sealed bid wins. In *Japanese auctions* the bidding begins at a low price and increases in fixed amounts. As the amount increases, bidders drop out until there is only one bidder remaining.

Figure 1: B2B Auction Market Framework (Teich et al., 1999; van Heck & Vervest, 1998)

BUYERS

		One	Many
SELLERS	One	Negotiations	Forward Auctions
	Many	Reverse Auctions	Markets/ Exchanges

Markets. B2B auctions are also categorized based on the market served. A *horizontal marketplace* specializes on limited products/services for many industries. A *vertical marketplace* serves only one industry with a broad range of products/services (Butler, 2000).

Technology

Technology infrastructures are mission-critical to B2B auctions. Establishing such an infrastructure is an extremely complex project. Since the B2B marketplace can give a "winner take all" advantage to the first in an industry, having the shortest possible time to market is a necessity (Herman, 2000; Intira). Currently, most B2B marketplaces support only rudimentary online transaction processes that do not truly automate supply-chain processes. However, e-marketplaces now require additional auction models, more advanced catalog management, collaboration, integration, and direct materials procurement capabilities as well as other third party e-commerce services (global payment, escrow, insurance, shipping, logistics, inspection). In addition, these B2B auction environments also require fast implementation (short time to market), flexibility to integrate many platforms, support for real time auctions, 24x7x365 availability, and customer service/relationship management support. These disparate business applications require integration to execute a B2B exchange, and fuel the rapid evolution of technology developments to support e-marketplaces.

SURVEY

A survey was conducted to better understand the perceived critical success factors, technology requirements, and the extent to which current technologies meet those requirements, for the B2B auction industry. The survey also collected information about the usage patterns of current B2B auction sites. Invitations to participate were sent to 133 e-marketplaces by email, with a reminder two weeks after the original message. Fifteen companies returned completed surveys (11.3%).

Auction Models, Services, and Revenue Sources

Respondents' firms utilized twelve different auction models and offered fourteen types of intermediary services. Many firms used multiple auction models. Twenty-nine percent said their auction models were very complex to implement, 43% said complex and 29% said average complexity. The number of transactions supported by the B2B sites ranged from one per week to 200 per day. All respondents, with one exception, defined their markets as B2B. Table 1 summarizes revenue sources for the companies surveyed.

Table 1: Revenue Sources

Revenue Source	Companies
Provide information at no charge to participants	9
Sell advertisements/affiliates links	4
Brokerage fees paid by sellers	12
Brokerage fees paid by buyers	7
Commissions from affiliates	3
Sell subscriptions to buyers	3
Sell subscriptions to sellers	3
Revenue for other types of lead generation	2
Provide workflow tracking/collaborative services for projects	1
Refurbish/ configure equipment	1
Revenue from:	
credit checks	1
logistics	4
fulfillment	3
insurance	2
other components of transaction process	4

Privacy and Security

Eighty percent of respondents used factors like customer service records, third party ratings, warranty, and performance to prescreened sellers. All respondents prescreened buyers using creditworthiness (73%), identity verification (60%), third-party ratings (27%), or performance (33%) as criteria.

For 86% of respondents, their marketplace provided support for anonymous bidding, and 57% for anonymous negotiations. Participants were primarily notified by e-mail regarding bids and changes. Other notification methods included regular mail, Web site, telephone and mobile telephone messaging. Third parties (transportation, financing, insurance, appraisals, logistics, etc.) were able to participate simultaneously with buyers and sellers in 73% of e-marketplaces.

All companies tracked failed transactions to maintain the quality of participants and enable continuous process improvement. Audit data about the company was provided by 36% of them.

Success Factors

Respondents equally ranked "security and privacy of the bidding process" and "creditability of company's specific marketplace" as the most important e-marketplace success factors, with "software support" as a close second. Other success factors ranked as "very important" by more than half the respondents included "participant trust in auction process," "ability to protect participant anonymity/privacy," and, "critical mass of buyers and sellers." Previously Published in *Managing Information Technology in a Global Economy* edited by Mehdi Khosrow-Pour, Copyright © 2001, Idea Group Publishing. Respondents overwhelmingly rated the factor "insufficient number of buyers and sellers" as contributing most to the failures of B2B marketplaces.

Table 2: Technological Functions

Function	Currently supported (%)	Desired additional functionality (%)
Access control management	64	8
Automated approval mechanism	50	15
Business intelligence reporting capabilities	36	23
Buyer accounts supporting multi-item RFQ's	57	15
Consulting resources	29	31
Content management	79	23
Customizable	64	15
Demand chain	21	15
Document exchange, including images	43	38
Fulfillment expertise	36	8
Fully automated bidding	71	15
Indicative bidding rules (non-binding bidding)	21	23
Integration of internal & external systems	64	8
Multiple currencies	36	38
Multiple languages	14	46
Multi-variant product/ bid criteria	64	23
Network platform	50	0
Online community connecting buyers/ sellers	71	8
Participant education/scenario simulation	21	31
Post-bid negotiation (one-to-one)	21	38
Rapid application development	43	8
Real time bid/ask	57	46
Real time wireless communication capabilities	21	23
RFQ filtering	36	31
Scalability	86	15
Secure bidding via encryption	64	15
Secure membership registration	86	15
Seller catalogs	36	38
Supply chain management	36	15
Trading models:		
Procurement/RFP/RFQ	57	15
Auctions	93	15
Exchange	79	23
Reverse auction	57	15
Catalog sales	43	23
Work flow management for projects	29	15

Technology

Respondents were asked what functions their auction/exchange software supported, and which additional functions would be desirable. The results are presented in Table 2.

DISCUSSION AND IMPLICATIONS

This study explored the general state-of-the-art in the B2B auction community, in particular multidimensional B2B auctions, in hopes of identifying issues to consider when making a decision about infrastructure components to include in an e-commerce B2B auction platform. There are some important considerations highlighted by the study:

- **Critical Success Factors**: With the high ratings among survey participants for the importance of credibility of auctioneer and trust in the auction process, preventive policies and controls should be implemented, and it should be clearly communicated to participants that the company adheres to its confidentiality and privacy policies.

- **Technology Solutions**: With the rapid evolution of new technologies, companies should stay abreast of new **standards** for the IT infrastructure, and anticipate future trends and evolving standards in the industry. Companies should especially consider incorporation of new standards like XML and wireless standards as they will be necessary to further develop the exchange of information.
- **Third Party Services**: It is noteworthy that nearly all respondents to the survey enabled simultaneous third party participation in the auction/negotiation process between buyers and sellers. Many experts believe that these added services are becoming a necessity for business survival.

CONCLUSION AND FUTURE RESEARCH

It is predicted that B2B online business will become increasingly more saturated with auction mechanisms in the near future. B2B marketplaces will succeed by offering additional value-added services (Yankee Group, 2000). To develop the potential for value-added services, auctions must integrate software systems, as well as add more comprehensive commerce service capabilities such as global payment systems, and financial, logistics, insurance, inspection, and shipping services.

Investment models will change, replacing "return on investment" with "return on relationship," which will be measured in terms of market expansion, revenue per customer, and customer satisfaction metrics (Caruso, 2000). A business must identify what is important to customers to enable its differentiation from the other online marketplaces.

To ensure a good "return on relationship," it will be necessary for online B2B auctions and exchanges to meet their customers' increasing expectations in the areas of privacy, trust, and security. Some of the authors' future research efforts will focus on identification of specific trust, privacy and security issues from both buyers' and sellers' perspectives, and the challenges to online B2B auctions and exchanges in meeting those customer demands.

END NOTE

[1]   This research was partially funded by a grant from Virginia's Center for Innovative Technology, in collaboration with the Virginia Tech Information Center.

REFERENCES

Butler, S. (2000). Redefining B2B Exchanges. *E-Marketer*, June 19, http://www.emarketer.com/enews/20000619_b2b.html.

Caruso, D. (2000). Business Demands Continual Business Model Reevaluation. http://www.amrresearch.com/EXV/default.asp?i=33 , Retrieved July 27.

Copeland, L. (2000). B-to-B Auctions from A to Z. *ComputerWorld*, Framingham, April 17.

Herman, J. (2000). Shared Business Services on the 'Net'. *Business Communications Review*, June 20.

Intira. http://www.intira.com.

Lenz, C, Andren, E. & Hope-Ross, D. (2000). Muldimensional Bidding Increases E-Marketplace Liquidity. Gartner Group, http://jin.dis.vt.edu/GartnerGroup/research/ras/88700/88732/88732.html, January 4.

Messmer, E. (2000). Online B2B Exchanges Still Have a Long Way to Go. *Network World*, May 8.

Quan, M. (2000). Online Exchanges Face Uncertain Road to Web Heaven. *Electronic Engineering Times*, May 8.

Teich, J., Wallenius, H., & Wallenius, J. (1999). Multiple-Issue Auction and Market Algorithms for the World Wide Web. *Decision Support Systems*, February 11.

van Heck, E. & Vervest, P. (1998). How Should CIO's Deal with Web-Based Auctions? *Communications of the ACM*, July.

Wilder, C. (2000). Business Booms for Specialized Web Marketplaces. *InformationWeek*, February 7.

Yankee Group (2000). B2B MarketView: E-Commerce Execution, Recent Analysis, and Online Exchange, FTC on BtoB E-Marketplaces.http://www.yankeegroup.com/webfolder/yg21a.nsf/7e7c1b5f396afbd380256800004c7b65/4bd6a3495309741485256913004l3dec?OpenDocument, July 21.

Chapter 19

Mobile Agents, Mobile Computing and Mobile Users in Global E-Commerce

Roberto Vinaja
University of Texas Pan American, USA

Mobile agents may reside in a host or client computer, and can also roam other computers, networks or the Internet to execute their tasks. In this chapter, we will examine the implications of mobility in three aspects: mobile code, mobile hardware and mobile users. The impact of mobility on electronic commerce in the areas of security issues; export controls, legal jurisdiction, taxation and international issues is also analyzed. Mobile agent technologies and mobile computers will play an important role in the new cyberspace economy, however many issues need to be addressed before the technology can be fully implemented.

INTRODUCTION

The Internet is now the main communication platform in the new digital society. Internet communications are efficient and low cost. The Internet and electronic commerce activities involve multinational sourcing of information, and both have helped stimulate the flow of information across international borders in recent years. The architecture of the Internet is based on the principle of geographic indeterminacy. The mobile agent model seems to provide one of the most suitable technologies for distributed systems in order to integrate the Internet in a synergetic way (Corradi et al., 1998). Mobile agents may reside in a host or client computer, and can also roam other computers, networks or the Internet to execute their tasks. In this chapter, we will examine the implications of mobility in three aspects: mobile code, mobile hardware and mobile users. The impact of mobility on electronic commerce in the areas of security issues; export controls, legal jurisdiction, taxation and international issues is also analyzed.

THE MOBILITY CONCEPT

Tolksdorf (1999) applies the notion of mobility to different classes of entities in information systems. He distinguishes passive versus mobile information, active versus mobile agents, and the concept of mobile human users. We can distinguish between three categories of mobility: hardware mobility, software mobility and user mobility.

Mobile hardware: Mobile computing provides the ability to connect to the Internet and have access to a variety of resources while away from the home base. Examples of computers that are often disconnected from the network are: mobile computers, laptops, personal digital assistants, and modem-connected computers.

Mobile users: In this highly computerized era, users are highly mobile and relatively more transient. Hence, there is a need to manage the infrastructure so that remote users can access needed resources in order to accomplish their jobs (Murch and Johnson 1999).

Telecommuting is becoming more widespread as a growing percentage of employees are working from home. This convenience is made possible by using dial-up lines and telecommunication links. Both mobile networking and mobile agents facilitate another work modality that can be called "mobile working." Mobile working has grown significantly thanks to the widespread adoption of laptop computers and mobile phones, especially among salespeople (Australia 2000).

Mobile software: Mobile agent technology introduces the notion of moving

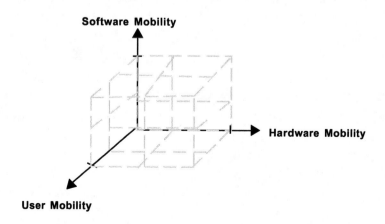

Hardware	Software	User	Sample Scenario
Static	Static	Static	A PC user at home
Static	Static	Mobile	A user at the ocmputer center
Static	Mobile (Agents)	Static	A user launching mobile agents at the computer center
Static	Mobile (Agents)	Mobile	A user launching agents from several static computers
Mobile	Static	Mobile	A salesperson using a laptop with office software
Mobile	Mobile (Agent)	Mobile	The optimum configuration

an active entity over spatially different places. Systems may combine static agents with mobile agents (Kearney, 1998). Mobile computing has been already very successful, and mobile agents are now revealing that software can also be mobile.

We can use the three dimensions of mobile/static computers, mobile/static software and mobile/static users to plot a three-dimensional matrix. Different applications can be differentiated in this basic classification matrix based on the criteria of computers, software and users.

Personal computers, mainframes and computing centers are examples of static computing environments. The table above describes sample scenarios combining the three dimensions.

MOBILE AGENTS

The mobile agents metaphor is analogous to how most people conduct business in daily activities: visit a place, use a service, perform a task, and finally move on (Johansen et al., 1998). In addition, mobile agents are applications that can move through a network carrying out a given task on behalf of the user. According to Nwana and Ndumu (1998), a mobile agent can roam wide area networks (WANs) such as the World Wide Web. Mobile agents interact with foreign hosts, performing tasks on behalf of their users and subsequently return to the original computer after achieving the goals.

According to Chen (2000), mobile agents can provide ubiquitous access to information, data, and applications. Ubiquitous access refers to the ability of users to access these computing resources from almost any terminal. This ubiquitous access is made possible by the latest Internet developments and the development of cross-platform languages, such as Java. Java can be used for the deployment of applications that can be executed across multiple platforms and networks.

MOBILE AGENT APPLICATIONS

Some examples of mobile agents are Telescript (White 1997), developed by General Magic, D'Agents (Brewington et al., 1999) designed at Dartmouth, IBM's Aglets, Grasshopper and Mobiware.

Gehmeyr et al. (1998) propose the combination of the use of mobile agent techniques for information retrieval. Mobile agents are also useful for the implementation of information gathering systems exploring the World Wide Web (Hanachi et al., 1999). A serious problem with search services is the amount of network traffic they generate. Mobile agents can be used to reduce network load when searching information in the Web. Mobile agents can encapsulate the filtering function and perform the filter process at the respective data server locally (Theilmann and Rothermel, 1999). Mobile agents could be used to enforce copyright protection laws. An agent could roam servers and sweep through the server files to find copies of copyrighted material (Murch and Johnson, 1999).

MOBILE AGENTS IN E-COMMERCE

Mobile agents can be the best medium to conduct e-commerce transactions in a mobile computing scenario. In a mobile computing scenario, browsing an on-line catalog can be extremely expensive, given the high-priced wireless channels. However, the consumer can send a mobile agent out as both a broker and negotiator, and subsequently disconnect, and later reconnect to obtain the results.

Wang, Lam and Yi (1998) have proposed the use of mobile agents for e-commerce brokering, negotiation and payment. Current payment mechanisms like SET require the user to be connected to the Internet during the purchase transaction. This requirement might be costly when using cellular connections and mobile computers. The high cost of connection charges can also become an obstacle for electronic commerce purchases. Romao and Mira da Silva (1998) have proposed the alternate SET/A payment mechanism based on mobile agents, in which the cardholder can send a request, disconnect and later reconnect to receive the response from the merchant. The user can save his or her mobile computer battery, and costly network connection costs. Instead of using the user's computing resources, a mobile agent can consume service providers' resources (Plu 1998). After the user's mobile computer or PDA is turned off, the agent should move to a host that it is on-line (Huhns and Singh, 1998).

A mobile agent could be sent out on behalf of its owner to find information. However, the information may not be freely available, and a payment may be required. The solution would be a mobile agent equipped with electronic commerce capabilities (Vogler et al., 1998). The agent would be an autonomous entity in the electronic marketplace, with the ability to search for a product or service, compare prices, negotiate and deal with payment mechanisms.

MOBILE COMPUTING AND WIRELESS NETWORKS

Nowadays, it is vital to be able to be active regardless of the geographic location, and this need has been fulfilled by wireless and cellular technology. In recent years, PDAs, laptop computers and communicator devices are providing a convenient platform for e-commerce transactions. Communicators are the next generation of cellular phones which include functionality of PDAs and palmtop computers such as e-mail, web browsing, and scheduling (Singh et al., 1999).

Mobile agents are particularly useful in mobile-computing environments that need to deal with low-bandwidth, high latency, and unreliable network links. An agent can continue interaction with a resource or user even if the network connections go down temporarily (Brewington et al., 1999). A mobile agent can travel in the Internet and retrieve information on behalf of a consumer. Later on, the mobile agent can return to the user's laptop and report the results when the laptop is reconnected to the network (Zhang, 1999).

Mobile devices have low-bandwidth, high latency and high cost connections (Wang, Lam and Yi, 1998). In addition, mobile computers have limited storage and processing capacity. A mobile agent can perform information retrieval, filtering and processing activities at a server, and return only the relevant (and reduced) information (Chess et al., 1995) This approach can significantly decrease the volume of data handled by the mobile computer connection. Gray et al. (2000) define mobile agents as programs that can move through a network under their own control, migrating from host to host and interacting with both other agents and resources on each host.

MOBILITY AND SECURITY ISSUES

Agent mobility might create security concerns. Unreliable agents may visit or request information from a system. Some server administrators will want to prevent agents to visit their web sites and use special software to block their entry (Murch and Johnson, 1999). A malicious mobile agent could attack a server, and on the other hand, a malicious server can delete a mobile agent, or modify it so it produces abnormal results (Huhns and Singh, 1998). The first security problem is easier to overcome; however, in the second case, in order to be executed, the agent has to open both its code and data to the server and be exposed to alteration.

MOBILITY AND LEGAL JURISDICTION

Jurisdiction is a legal term for the restriction on the ability of a court to resolve disputes. According to this definition, companies (or individuals) from foreign countries can be sued in a U.S. court if the organization has had some minimum contacts with the U.S. electronic actions through the Internet such as sending an e-mail, downloading data, or executing a mobile agent might satisfy the minimum contact requirement. The reverse situation might also be true: U.S. citizens may be sued in foreign courts with a similar minimum contact requirement for on-line activities (Perritt, 1996).

Typically, states' jurisdictional limits are related to geography. However, geography is a virtually meaningless construct on the new e-commerce marketplace. Distance and geographic location are irrelevant for the capabilities of the electronic marketplace (Reidenberg, 1998). Data input, data processing, and data storage may take place at very different locations.

In mobile code systems, programs may come from unknown or unreliable sources. Current cyberlaw treats a program as an extension of the user or programmer; however, this assumption may not be true for mobile agent systems. Determining responsibility for data protection is very complex given the open nature of the distributed architecture of the Internet.

A mobile agent could be used to collect private information located in multiple sources and consolidate it. A single sequential operation might involve cross-border data flows. Notice that in a mobile code scenario, the owner of the hardware, the user of a program, and the author of the software can be all distinct entities, possibly at different nations under distinct security regulations (Tschudin, 1999). The activity of a mobile agent with access, collection and processing in several countries simultaneously offer many nations prescriptive jurisdiction in order to define the terms and conditions of fair information practices (Fordham, 2000)

It is likely that companies and individuals might try to evade the jurisdiction of one nation by using mobile agents and mobile computers to relocate information and services to another nation. The Internet network architecture certainly blurs the meaning of the concept of "border." Jurisdiction may be an anachronism in a borderless world where time and distance have little meaning (Katsh, 1995).

Kitamura et al. (1999) have proposed that one way to deal with this dilemma is to create virtual "places" for electronic communication on the Internet. In this place-oriented communication model, an agent is authenticated before it is allowed to enter a virtual meeting place. This approach provides a meaningful model for agent authentication and the creation of virtual communities.

MOBILITY AND DATA EXPORT CONTROLS

The objective of export control implementations is to protect national security and avoid the unregulated dissemination of certain sophisticated encryption technologies. Given the existing barriers on the export of intangibles, people may try to circumvent controls by using mobile technology or mobile agents. One may try to embed encryption technology inside an intelligent agent, or in the case of equipment, as part of a mobile computing device. Because mobile software and equipment traverse from one location to another, this equipment might be used for transferring controlled technologies (Bohm, Brown and Gladman, 2000).

A mobile agent can be used to overcome limitations on cross-border data transfers. By moving to the location of an information resource, a mobile agent can search the resource locally, eliminating the network transfer of data (Brewington et al., 1999). Hence, instead of bringing data into an application, one can send the application (the mobile agent) to process data at the resource, and subsequently return with consolidated results that are not the same as the primary data. As a result, we are not exporting private primary data (which is not allowed), but the results obtained by running the mobile agent (which is considered, conglomerated or derived data). We are moving the computation (agent) to the data, rather than the data to the computation. The agent will filter the data it reads. Hence there is almost no need to transmit raw data from one site to another, and therefore cross-border data flows can be kept to a minimum (Johansen, 1998). Using a mobile agent is very useful when moving the data is often not feasible or difficult, moving the computation to the data with a mobile agent is a convenient and efficient alternative (Rus et al., 1997).

Just as mobile agents can be used to circumvent security controls they can also be used to help implement data export controls. Tschudin (1999) describes how a database owner can offer a flexible interface without losing control over the amount and type of data that is exported. Mobile agents can be allowed to freely browse the full database content, but they would be prevented to leave the server, and would be terminated after the agent had obtained its results. These results could be transformed by the host into a query result and sent back to the client.

MOBILITY AND TAXATION

The application of current tax regulation to e-commerce is very difficult. In the United States, a state can assess sales taxes on a company when the company establishes "nexus" in the state. Nexus is a concept of physical location; therefore a company must have a branch in the state in order to pass the nexus test. Nexus is the most important issue of taxation relating to e-commerce (Castellucio, 1996).

Hellerstein (1997) states, "To ask about the 'location' of e-commerce is to ask a question that is not worth answering," whereas Posch (1997) asserts that, "Electronic commerce has dissolved the linkage between an income producing activity and geographic boundaries."

Mobile agents could be used to evade taxes. Both Weiner (1997) and Fox and Murray (1997) point out that e-commerce capital is much more mobile than other forms and is highly sensitive to tax differentials. Taxpayer compliance in electronic commerce transaction may be really difficult. Tax rates vary by state, and some companies or consumers may utilize mobile agents to evade taxes. A mobile agent may be sent to a host computer at another location where tax rates are lower or even avoid paying state sales taxes altogether.

The U.S. Department of Treasury is specifically concerned about the following e-commerce mechanisms: electronic money, identity verification, record keeping and integrity, and disintermediation (Levey, O'Donnell & Powers, 1997). Esser (1997) raises the concern that inappropriate Internet tax regulations might reduce the volume of collected taxes, and subsequently reduce the available state resources for safety, health and education services.

MOBILITY AND INTERNATIONAL ISSUES

Individual consumers are now able to buy across national borders without even leaving their own country. If a dispute arises, there are not many applicable laws for international arbitration of a consumer's dispute with a merchant. Kido (1999) describes several potential cross-cultural issues in the cooperation of agents and humans in a global network. These issues include language differences, differences in human-computer interaction, negotiation strategies depending on the culture, the importance of culture-adaptive web sites. Because mobile agents may interact with users or users' agents in diverse cultures, they should be customized to deal with different negotiation strategies or languages depending on the culture.

CONCLUSIONS

Mobile agents have several characteristics, which can be applied, in mobile wide area network architectures and in several aspects of electronic commerce. Mobile agent technologies and mobile computers will play an important role in the new cyberspace economy, however many issues need to be addressed before the technology can be fully implemented.

REFERENCES

Brewington, B., Gray, R., Moizumi, K., Kotz, D., Cybenko, G. and Rus, D. (1999). Mobile Agents for Distributed Information Retrieval. In Klusch, M. (Ed.), *Intelligent Information Agents*, Germany: Springer-Verlag, 354-395.

Castelluccio, M. (1996). Who will collect the taxes on the new silk road? *Management Accounting*, 78(5), 58.

Chen, L. T. AgentOS: The Agent-based Distributed Operating System for Mobile Networks.

Chess, D., Grosof, B., Harrison, C., Levine, D., Parris, C. and Tsudik, G. (1995). Itinerant agents for mobile computing. *IEEE Personal Communications*, 2(5), 34-49.

Corradi, A., Cremonini, M., and Stefanelli, C. (1998). Melding Abstractions with Mobile Agents. In Klusch, M. and Weib, G., *Cooperative Information Agents II*. Germany: Springer-Verlag, 278-289.

Esser, J. L. (1997). Internet commerce and state/local sales taxes. *Government Finance Review*, Dec., 13(6): p5(1).

Fox, W.F. and Murray, M.N. (1997). The sales tax and electronic commerce: so what's new? *National Tax Journal*, 50(3), 573-575.

Gehmeyr, A., Muller, J. and Schappert, A. (1998). Mobile Information Agents on the Web. In Klusch, M. and Weib, G., *Cooperative Information Agents II*. Germany: Springer-Verlag, 262-277.

Gray, R.S., Kotz, D., Nog, S., Rus, D., and Cybenko, G. (1999). Mobile agents for mobile computing. Dartmouth PCS-TR96-285.

Hanachi, C., Hameurlain, N., and Sibertin-Blanc, C. (1999). Mobile Agents Behaviours: From Declarative Specifications to Implementation. In *Cooperative Information Agents III*. Germany: Springer-Verlag, 196-207.

Hellerstein, W. (1997). Transaction taxes and electronic commerce: designing state taxes that work in an interstate environment. *National Tax Journal*. 50(3), 593-606.

Huhns, M.N. and Singh, M. (1998). *Readings in Agents*. San Francisco, CA: Morgan Kaufmann, 11-12.

Johansen, D., van Renesse, R. , and Schneider, F.B. (1998). Operating System Support for Mobile Agents. In Huhns, M.N. and Singh, M. (Eds.), *Readings in Agents*. San Francisco, CA: Morgan Kaufmann, 263-266.

Katsh, E. M. (1995). Cybertime, cyberspace and cyberlaw. *Journal of Online Law*.

Kearney, P. (1998). Personal Agents: A Walk on the Client Side. In Jennings, N.R. and Wooldridge, M.J. (Eds.), *Agent Technology*, Germany: Springer-Verlag, 125-136.

Kido, T. (1998). Grand Challenge Problems on Cross Cultural Communication - Toward Socially Intelligent Agents. In Klusch, M. and Weib, G. (Eds.), *Cooperative Information Agents II*. Germany: Springer-Verlag.

Kitamura, Y., Mawarimichi, Y. and Tatsumi, S. (1999). Mobile-Agent Mediated Place Oriented Communication. In Klusch, M. and Weib, G. (Eds.), *Cooperative Information Agents III*. Germany: Springer-Verlag, 232-242.

Kovacs, E., and Röhrle,K. (1998). Integrating Mobile Agents to the Mobile Middleware. In Kurt R. and Fritz H. (Eds.), *Mobile Agents*, Lecture Note in Computer Science (LNCS). 1477. Germany:Springer-Verlag.

Küpper, A., and Park, S.B.. (1988). Stationary vs. Mobile User Agents in Future Mobile Telecommunication Networks. In Kurt R. and Fritz H. (Eds.), *Mobile Agents*, Lecture Note in Computer Science (LNCS). 1477. Germany:Springer-Verlag.

Levey, M.M., O'Donnell, T.A. and Powers, J. P. (1997). Cyberspace transactions present interesting international, state and local tax issues. *Tax Executive*, 49(6), 476-486.

Nwana, H.S., and Ndumu, D.T. (1998). A Brief Introduction to Software Agent Technology. In Jennings, N.R. and Wooldridge, M.J. (Eds.), *Agent Technology*, Germany: Springer-Verlag, 29-47.

Perritt, H. (1993). Metaphors for understanding rights and responsibilities in network communities: Print shops, barons, sheriffs and bureaucracies. *Villanova Information Law Chronicle*, Available on-line at http://www.law.vil l.edu/chron/articles/metafin.htm.

Plu, M. (1998). Software Technologies for Building Agent Based Systems in Telecommunication Networks. In Jennings, N.R. and Wooldridge, M.J. (Eds.), *Agent Technology*, Germany: Springer-Verlag, 241-266.

Posch, R.J. (1997). Transactional and attributable nexus in cyberspace. *Direct Marketing*, 59(10) 62.

Reidenberg, J.R. (1998). International Data Transfers and Methods to Strengthen International Co-Operation. *20th International Conference of Data Protection Authorities*. Santiago de Compostela, Spain.

Romao, A. and Da Silva, M. M. (1998). An Agent-Based Secure Internet Payment System for Mobile Computing. *Proceeding of Trends in Distributed Systems* 1998: Germany: Springer-Verlag.

Rus, D., Gray R., and Kotz D. (1997). Transportable Information Agents. *Proceedings of the International Conference on Autonomous Agents*, ACM, 228-236.

Singh, M., Jain, A.K. and Singh, M. (1999). E-Commerce over Communicators: Challenges and Solutions for User Interfaces. *Proceedings of the ACM Conference on Electronic Commerce*, EC'99, Denver, Colorado.

Theilmann, W. and Rothermel, K. (1999). Maintaining Specialized Search Engines through Mobile Filter Agents. In Klusch, M. and Weib, G. (Eds.), *Cooperative Information Agents III*. Germany: Springer-Verlag, 208-219.

Tolksdorf, R. (1998). Coordination Patterns of Mobile Information Agents. In Klusch, M. and Weib, G. (Eds.), Cooperative Information Agents II. Germany: Springer-Verlag, 246-261.

Tolksdorf, R. (1999). On Coordinating Information Agents and Mobility. In Klusch, M. (Ed.), *Intelligent Information Agents*, Germany: Springer-Verlag. 396-411.

Tschudin, C.F. (1999). Mobile Agent Security. In Klusch, M. (Ed.): *Intelligent Information Agents*, Germany: Springer-Verlag. 431-445.

Vogler, H., Moschgath, M.-L. and Kunkelman, T. (1998). Enhancing Mobile Agents with Electronic Commerce Capabilities. In Klusch, M. and Weib, G. (Eds.), *Cooperative Information Agents II*. Germany: Springer-Verlag, 148-159.

Wang, X.F., Lam, K.Y. and Yi, X. (1998). Secure Agent-Mediated Mobile Payment. In Ishida, T. (Ed.) *Multiagent Platforms,* PRIMA 98, Singapore, November 1998, LNCS 1599, Germany: Springer-Verlag, 162-173.

Weiner, J.M. (1997). Discussion of papers on telecommunications taxation. *National Tax Journal*, 50(3), 623-630.

Zhang, M. and Li, W. (1999). Persisting Autonomous Workflow for Mobile Agents using a Mobile Thread Programming Model. *Proceedings of the Second Pacific Rim International Workshop on Multi-Agents*, PRIMA'99, Kyoto, Japan, Germany: Springer-Verlag, 84-95.

Chapter 20

Evaluation of Electronic Commerce Adoption within SMEs

Marco Tagliavini, Aurelio Ravarini, and Alessandro Antonelli
Università Cattaneo, Italy

The exponential growth that has recently characterized the diffusion of electronic commerce (EC) applications could lead companies of any size to plan new investments, in order to compete in an increasingly dynamic market. The first business experiences show that EC should be considered a competitive instrument not simply affecting economic transactions, but significantly influencing the business organizational structure and strategic objectives. Although this issue has recently been object of considerable attention, the research on the evaluation of EC adoption for Small and Medium Enterprises (SMEs) is still relatively new. This chapter aims at supporting SMEs in choosing the most suitable EC approach according to their peculiarities and strategic goals. First, it identifies five EC approaches supporting different business activities. Then, it describes the business variables involved in any EC project and identifies four SME profiles characterized by different values of these variables. Finally, a cross analysis between EC approaches and SME profiles allows developing a framework suggesting the most suitable EC solution for each business profile.

INTRODUCTION

"Every business today competes in two worlds: a physical world of resources that managers can see and touch, and a virtual world made of information" (Rayport & Sviokla, 1996). In such a virtual world, Electronic Commerce (EC) is becom-

Previously Published in *Challenges of Information Technology Management in the 21st Century* edited by Mehdi Khosrow-Pour, Copyright © 2000, Idea Group Publishing.

ing increasingly imperative for companies of any size aiming at improving their competitiveness in a constantly changing market (Chaumont, de Charentenay, Esnault, Fay, Iglesias & Silvestre, 1998; OECD, 1998), since its impact is not limited to economic transactions but can significantly influence both organizational and strategic issues (COM, 1997). In this chapter, we will refer to *Internet-based EC*, i.e., any commercial activity carried out through the Internet.

Although some research has been carried out to analyze the relationships between Small and Medium Enterprises (SMEs[1]) and EC, the real opportunity of EC adoption for SMEs is still unclear. A lot of research (Davies, 1997; Ford & Baum, 1997; Loeb, 1998) shows that most SMEs are not making use of EC because of information security problems (a serious concern for SMEs, traditionally jealous of their privacy) and the legislative uncertainty (Baker, 1998; Mitrakas, 1997; OECD, 1998).

Nevertheless, the main obstacle to the adoption of EC and modern Information and Communication Technologies (ICT) among SMEs seems to be the lack of knowledge about the real advantages these technologies could add to their business (Buonanno, Ravarini, Sciuto & Tagliavini, 1998; OECD, 1998) and, more generally, the culture and resistance to change that characterizes small entrepreneurs (Bedeian, 1980; Huczynsky & Buchanan, 1991; Julien, 1998; King & Teo, 1994; Palvia, Means & Jackson, 1994; Vidal, 1991).

This chapter aims at supporting the entrepreneur in choosing the most suitable EC approach for his/her organization and its strategic goals. In order to be suitable for SMEs, the reference schema must be simple, easy to use and clear enough to be understood by people without specific technical and economic skills.

Next sections will outline five EC approaches, characterized by different requirements as well as objectives achievable through their implementation. Then, the expected results of the EC implementation, together with the analysis of existing literature, will support the identification of the business variables possibly involved in EC projects. In particular, we will describe:
- the key-variables for implementing the project (i.e. the variables determining which is the most suitable EC approach to every kind of business); and
- the key-variables related to strategic changes achievable through EC (i.e. variables that are expected to change their values as a consequence of EC adoption).

The description of the involved business variables together with the results of a survey on a sample of 55 SMEs will lead to the identification of four SME profiles (characterized by different values of these variables). Finally, a cross analysis between these profiles and the EC approaches will support the detection of the EC approaches that best fit these profiles (Figure 1).

Figure 1: Steps toward the identification of the most suitable EC approach

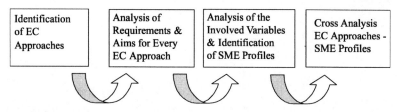

Contribution to the identification and analysis of EC approaches

Companies already exploiting EC applications offer multiple services: a recent research on the Internet adoption within European SMEs (Chaumont et al., 1998) describes six different "levels" of Internet applications, from the simple data transfer (e.g., through e-mail) to the complete integration of the business core processes.

One of the more widespread EC approach is the digital storefront, i.e., the use of web browser interface for advertising, display and purchase of goods and service on the Web (Bayne, 1997; Janal, 1998; Schwartz, 1997). Moreover, recent research (Wigand, Picot & Reichwald, 1997) underlines the differences between "traditional" and "electronic" commerce: while the first is characterized by a clear distinction between business functions, the latter enables a complete integration of the following activities: on receipt of the order, the EC system could automatically check the product availability, notify it to the accounting and logistic offices, request a new supply from the purchase office.

Contribution to the analysis of the involved variables

The implementation of an EC system could turn out to be so pervasive as to involve many important business variables; previous research considers the business impact of EC systems from many different points of view. Some authors focus on *technical skills* needed by the project leader (as well as his/her assistants) to internally manage the implementation of an EC system (Chaumont et al., 1998); since SMEs are often characterized by lack of specialized staff and strategic management of ICT (Buonanno et al., 1998), they often choose to outsource these activities, possibly even the complete EC project, to reduce the internal costs and improve the business performance (Di Romualdo & Gurbaxani, 1998).

Another important issue is the *resistance to change* (Clark, 1995): a high value of such a business variable could put at risk the results of the EC project. Some authors refer to the "champion of innovation," a new business role aimed at ensuring the alignment between the strategic objectives and their implementation, by supporting the culture of change (Kanter, 1983; McLoughlin & Clark, 1994).

Table 1: Relationships between the company size and the Internet adoption

Company size (number of employees)	Internet connected
50-99	41%
10-49	30%
1-9	16%

Many studies prove a connection between the adoption of Internet and the *company size*: a recent survey (OECD, 1998) on a set of 2,881 European SMEs shows how the percentage of Internet connected SMEs is directly proportional to the company size (Table 1).

As cited above, the use of ICT could significantly change the way people work: a lot of research focuses on the *organizational impact* and the need of structural changes due to the adoption of ICT (Bock & Senne, 1997; Chaumont et al., 1998; Gramignoli, Ravarini & Tagliavini, 1999; Hills, 1997), considering the new competencies, roles, and skills required by innovation.

A business variable considered very important when evaluating the EC adoption is the *product characteristics*. An "intangible" product made of bits (such as software packages) is surely easier to be sold because it can be supplied directly on the Internet (Negroponte, 1995). Moreover, most researchers agree in considering more suitable to be sold electronically those products with low asset specificity, ease of description, and a consumer market willing to buy without recourse to visiting retail stores (Benjamin & Yates, 1991; Wigand et al., 1997; Wigand, 1996).

The literature shows how ICT can influence any *competitive strategy*, based on cost or differentiation. A correct adoption of EC could lead to a reduction of transaction costs (Chaumont et al., 1998) and coordination costs (Wigand et al., 1997). On the other hand, today it is widely accepted the influence of ICT not only on operating activities but on the redefinition and pursue of the business strategy (Boynton & Zmud, 1994; Drucker, 1988; Piore & Sabel, 1984).

Another EC-enabled change described by the literature is the transformation of the *relationships with intermediaries*. Many authors refer to EC as the cause of important changes in the company value chain (Chaumont et al., 1998; Wigand et al., 1997). Reynolds (1997) asserts that relationships with customers will become increasingly remote and impersonal and that suppliers will have to fight against retailers in a changing market. Other authors (Wigand, 1996) uphold the theory that the complete disintermediation is unfeasible, because it would jeopardize the existence of the market itself.

Finally, EC has an important influence on SMEs' *range of activity*, providing increased competition on a global scale and allowing them to access wider markets (Chaumont et al., 1998; Krause, Doblies & Raupach, 1998; Wigand et al., 1997).

Contribution to the identification of SME profiles

A major contribution to the identification of SME profiles comes from previous research on SMEs' internationalization (Depperu, 1993), which is strictly related to EC and market globalization (Wigand et al., 1997). Another important contribution is related to the business opportunities related to the ICT adoption within SMEs (Chaumont et al., 1998). The authors identified three kinds of enterprises according to the values of important business variables: the business impact on the market, the management inclination to innovation, and the competitive strategy.

ELECTRONIC COMMERCE APPROACHES

EC can be approached in many different ways: many companies have been publishing a web site describing their activities and possibly the products or services offered (Bayne, 1997; Chaumont et al., 1998; Janal, 1998; Schwartz, 1997). However, the experiences of larger companies showed that often it is worth realizing more complex systems, significantly affecting various activities of the value chain, therefore influencing organizational and strategic practices (Andrews & Hahn, 1998; KPMG, 1998).

Since modern organizations have been progressively defining their activities according to business processes instead of functional areas, every EC approach is supposed to support a specific business process that could be carried out through the Internet:

- **public relations**: the diffusion of information related to the company activities, products and services to a selected target of customers can be effectively carried out by means of electronic mail (e-mail);
- **company promotion**: the development of a web site sponsoring the company activities, products, and services through a virtual catalogue. The output of this approach ranges from a simple promotional web site with a few static pages to a professional site providing information through dynamic pages directly linked to the company databases;
- **pre/post sales support**: pre/post sales support (which in this context also includes all the activities related to helpdesk systems) can exploit Internet technologies to provide a cheaper, more effective, and user friendly interface between the company and its customers. This activity may simply be based on the e-mail service or it could be accomplished through the development of an Internet site. The most effective support service should combine these approaches to offer multiple services to real and potential customers;
- **order processing**: on line order processing systems aim at allowing customers to order products through the Internet. Such a solution is an integration of the

simple product catalogue on the web, although the economic transaction is still performed in a traditional way, such as through a bank transfer or by communicating the credit card number by phone; and

- **payment management**: an on line payment system is an integration of the order processing activity allowing to conclude the economic transaction through the Internet. This is the most complete EC application: customers can analyze the company products on a virtual catalogue on the web, send an order for one or more products, and terminate the economic transaction by charging it to a credit card.

PLANNING EC AMONG SMES: IMPORTANT BUSINESS VARIABLES

The described analysis could represent a starting point for those companies planning to adopt EC. In fact, as in any IS development plan, the feasibility study is a crucial phase and includes the explication of the project constraints and opportunities. By examining the requirements and expected results for each EC approach, as well as the described results of previous studies (Chaumont et al., 1998; Depperu, 1993), it is possible to identify few items that could represent critical variables for the EC project planning.

Table 2 shows the relationship between requirements and aims of an EC project and the related business variables, together with the range of values they can assume. The business variables have been separated into two main groups. The first refers to economic, organizational and technical requirements related to the

Table 2: Critical variables for an EC project and their possible values

		EC project planning variables	Value range
EC project requirements	Economic	Company size	Small (0-50 employees) Medium (51-250 employees)
		Degree of diversification	Low-high
	Organizational	Characteristics of the product	Tangible-Intangible Unique-Standard
		Marketing abilities	Low-high
		Resistance to change	Low-high
	Technical	Technical skills	Low-high
EC project expected results	Increase company market share	Range of activity	National-International
	Increase decision making autonomy	Degree of third party dependence	Low-high
	Decrease costs/increase service quality	Competitive strategy	Cost leadership-Differentiation
	Shorten/automate distribution channel	Relationship with intermediaries	Traditional(internpersonal)-Automated

EC project implementation. The second refers to the strategic changes (and the related business variables) achievable through this implementation.

- The *company size* is fundamental since it usually influences the maximum absolute value of any investment (OECD, 1998). Besides, size should be taken into account in order to avoid waste of resources due to investments over exceeding actual company needs.
- The EC solution choice should also be adequate to the *degree of diversification*: assuming that this variable is positively related to the organizational complexity, any increase of its value causes the need of more coordination and automation between company divisions and functional areas.
- *Characteristics of the product*: the success of an EC project seems to be related to the product *tangibility* and *availability*. Selling an intangible product through the Internet means very low constraints and costs due to its logistic management. Besides, EC could turn out to be a powerful promotion channel for unique products (such as handicrafts of specific regions), not subject to constraints deriving from customers' geographical distance. On the other hand, the incidence of shipping costs (mostly for cheap products), the need of seeing and touching an item rather than simply viewing an on-line image, as well as the possible difference between the characteristics of the product target and the typical profile of Internet users are all good reasons that should make companies carefully evaluate the opportunity of implementing an EC system.
- *Marketing abilities* represent an important leverage for the exploitation of the EC opportunities. Since the adoption of EC could affect all the variables of the marketing mix (product, price, promotion, and presence), companies should make a specific online marketing plan. Examples of typical marketing problems that companies could have to face are price versus non price competition, disintermediation, push versus pull communication strategies. Besides, the intrinsic characteristics of Internet could make it the natural application field of direct marketing techniques.
- *Resistance to change*: assuming that the EC adoption could imply organizational transformations in terms of task changes, introduction of new roles, and rearrangement of the organization as a whole, innovative organizations should face less resistance to change while implementing any of the EC activities. Resistance to change is typical of family companies often characterized by stable job relationships and by the transmission of knowledge from parents to children.
- *Technical skills* heavily influence the degree at which the EC system could be actually exploited, therefore determining its global effectiveness for the company.

A second set of variables should be useful to assess the **aims**, in terms of opportunities coming from the EC adoption within SMEs.

- The *range of activity* denotes the geographical extension of the market area. This variable can positively be influenced by the adoption of EC applications and can be assessed through the proportion of turnover per geographical area.
- The *degree of third party dependence* refers to companies belonging to the same value system, which choices can be more or less constrained by commercial partners. The company negotiating power is often proportional to its size: EC systems have the potentiality to break, or at least reduce, the typical SME dependence, by allowing them to increase the number of partners without increasing the cost of the distribution channel.
- The company *competitive strategy* has a strong leverage in EC applications, both when it aims at fulfilling a leadership in costs and when it is based on the differentiation of products and services.
- EC applications could make more effective the *relationships with commercial intermediaries*, could allow companies to change their traditional intermediaries with more innovative ones (i.e., virtual malls) or to directly sell their products to consumers.

SME PROFILES

The described business variables have been evaluated through a survey on a set of 55 SMEs. A cross analysis on the values of these variables enabled the identification of four SME profiles, each of which could achieve different benefits through the implementation of an EC system:

1. the Hand Crafted Enterprise;
2. the SubContractor Enterprise;
3. the Traditional Independent Enterprise;
4. the Innovative Diversified Enterprise.

Next subsections will outline the profiles of such enterprises, by specifying the typical values the identified business variables assume for each profile. Every profile is characterized by one or more "required variables" (highlighted in tables 3, 4, 5 and 6) which have to be considered a necessary (but not sufficient) condition to belong to a certain profile. For example, a company can be defined a SubContractor Enterprise only if the value of "third party dependence" is high.

Hand Crafted Enterprise

The *Hand Crafted Enterprise* (HCE) provides its customers with commodities peculiar for their unique properties, therefore hardly available anywhere else. It is usually a small or very small company basing its competitive advantage on close relationships within the local market and environment. It is typically charac-

Table 3: Typical values of the business variables for Hand Crafted Enterprises

Requirement variables		Expected result variables	
Company size	Micro/Small	Range of activity	Local
Degree of diversification	Low	Third party dependence	Low
Characteristics of the product	Tangible and Unique	Competitive strategy	Differentiation
Marketing abilities	Low	Relationships with intermediaries	Traditional
Resistance to change	High (rarely low)		
Technical skills	Low		

Table 4: Typical values of the business variables for SubContractor Enterprises

Requirement variables		Expected result variables	
Company size	Small	Range of activity	Regional
Degree of diversification	Low	Third party dependence	High
Characteristics of the product	Tangible and Unique	Competitive strategy	Cost leadership
Marketing abilities	Low	Relationships with intermediaries	Traditional (rarely automated)
Resistance to change	High		
Technical skills	Low (rarely high)		

Table 5: Typical values of the business variables for Traditional Independent Enterprises

Requirement variables		Expected result variables	
Company size	Medium	Range of activity	Naitonal
Degree of diversification	Low	Third party dependence	Low
Characteristics of the product	Tangible and Standard	Competitive strategy	Differentiation
Marketing abilities	High	Relationships with intermediaries	Traditional
Resistance to change	High		
Technical skills	Low		

Table 6: Typical values of the business variables for Innovative Diversified Enterprises

Requirement variables		Expected result variables	
Company size	Medium	Range of activity	International
Degree of diversification	High	Third party dependence	Low
Characteristics of the product	Tangible or Intangible and Standard	Competitive strategy	Cost - Differentiation
Marketing abilities	High	Relationships with intermediaries	Automated
Resistance to change	Low		
Technical skills	High		

terized by a highly centered decision-making power; it is independent and seldom innovative. Usually it does not develop a marketing strategy neither does its staff have the technical skills required to manage an in-house EC application.

SubContractor Enterprise

The *SubContractor Enterprise* (SCE) is often an industrial company focused on the production of a small set of items. It sells its products to distributors or, more often, to a limited number of large enterprises with which it has established strong relationships. As a consequence, it bases its competitive advantage on efficiency and low prices. This kind of company is typical of industrial districts and it rarely adopts innovative technologies unless enforced by a powerful partner.

Traditional Independent Enterprise

The *Traditional Independent Enterprise* (TIE) typically competes through a differentiation strategy aiming at satisfying a limited number of market niches. Its size often allows it to hold high bargaining power with commercial partners and to limit their influence on strategic choices. Moreover, its organizational structure is rather complex, whereas the national extension of the market requires attention to customer assistance and the coordination between strategic and operative activities. These activities are rarely supported by the company IS, because of the usual resistance to change of its managers.

Innovative Diversified Enterprise

The *Innovative Diversified Enterprise* (IDE) competes within the international (or at least national) market, and aims at reaching and maintaining its leadership within specific market niches, thanks to its constant product innovation. Differentiation is reachable only by means of a complex but efficient organizational structure and meaningful financial efforts: therefore, this company has to be able to efficiently manage both horizontal and vertical information flows. As a consequence, ICT is perceived as a strategic resource and actually represents the organizational backbone: the IDE context is thus clearly favorable to the EC adoption and use.

It is worth underlining that these profiles should be interpreted purely as points of reference, i.e., *sample business solutions within the highly differentiated environments of SMEs*. Nevertheless, this intrinsic simplification should help SMEs recognizing the EC opportunities that best fit their peculiarities: the entrepreneur (or at least a high level manager) should depict its own profile by evaluating the ten variables. The resulting profile should then be compared with the four just outlined (Figure 2) in order to find out the most similar, and then step to the next phase of the model.

Figure 2: A framework for identifying SME profiles

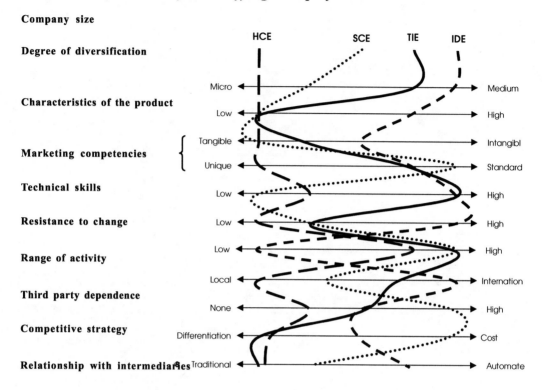

EC SOLUTIONS FOR SPECIFIC SME PROFILES

Once the company has identified the profile best representing its peculiarities, the last step is the choice of the most appropriate EC system. The final framework, depicted in Table 7, aims at supporting this task:

- for each SME profile, it specifies which business variables (consequently which expected results) could benefit from the EC adoption; and
- for each SME profile, it identifies the most suitable EC solution, i.e., how to implement each EC activity.

Hand Crafted Enterprise

The *HCE* could benefit from EC by gaining access to a wider market and/or empowering its position in the market niche by providing its customers with differentiating services. However, because of the economic and organizational constraints, e-mail is a fundamental service for any EC activity chosen. Due to its low costs, the *public relations* activity represents a preferential choice to improve external communications. Moreover, if the company plans to *promote* itself, it could publish a simple web catalogue. If the number of products and their charac-

Table 7: EC solutions for different SME profiles

Expected results	SME profiles			
	Hand Crafted Enterprise	SubContractor Enterprise	Traditional Independent Enterprise	Innovative Diversified Enterprise
Increase company market share	X	X X	X	
Increase decision making independence	X	X		
Decrease costs/increase service quality	X	X	X	X
Shorten/automate distribution channel		X	X	X

EC activity	Hand Crafted Enterprise	SubContractor Enterprise	Independent Enterprise	Diversified Enterprise
Public relations	External communication	External communication	Internal/External communication	Internal/External communication
Company promotion	Product catalogue	Basic company information	Customized catalogues	Differentiated catalogues
Pre/post sales support	E-mail based	E-mail based	Depending on product features	Customized system
Order processing	Simple	Partial logistics management	Partial/Complete logistics management	Complete logistics management
Payment management	Simple	Not Recommended	Business to consumer	Business to consumer

teristics raise the strategic importance of *on line pre/post sales support*, HCEs should consider implementing an e-mail based support system. Since HCEs typically deal with consumers, it should be easier to implement a low-cost *on line order processing system* (possibly together with an *on line payment system*).

SubContractor Enterprise

With regard to *SCEs*, the EC adoption could improve all the variables related to expected results. In fact, EC could enable vertical integration towards customers and the development of an international network amongst SCEs sharing the same market. Consequently, it could radically modify the relationships of strength within the industry and promote the creation of industrial districts no longer limited within a specific geographical area. The first step toward a networking strategy could be the implementation of the *public relations* activity .

On the other hand, the *company promotion* represents a strong leverage for SCEs. This solution increases the company visibility at an international level and empowers its marketing abilities, thus reducing its dependence on main and geographically close contractors.

Since the SCE usually deals with a limited number of partners and provides few products, its customers should not need particular on line *pre/post sales support*: the customer care could simply be based on the e-mail service. On the other hand, because of this kind of relationships, an SCE could benefit from an *on line order processing system*, possibly integrated with the existing IS.

Finally, considering the described problems regarding *on line payments* together with the intrinsic business to business nature of SCE commercial relationships, this activity currently does not seem to fit SCE requirements and aims.

Traditional Independent Enterprise

The higher organizational complexity and the differentiation strategy characterizing the *TIE* make it benefit from EC adoption, even though it could imply significant investments.

A simple *public relations* activity, besides improving relationships with external partners (as well as for HCE), could help the improvement of internal efficiency, by reducing the amount of paper used.

The *company promotion* could support the expansion of the market area, one of the main aims of this kind of independent firm. Moreover, to be an effective differentiation leverage, a TIE web site should be carefully developed and managed both on its graphics and its structure, and customized on specific clients' peculiarities. An indirect benefit coming from the adoption of this activity is the development of marketing abilities, which are fundamental for a company basing its strategy on differentiation.

On line pre/post sales support could be, depending on the product characteristics, a strong differentiation leverage for TIEs. Hence, this activity could be considerably empowered by exploiting the potentialities of the related EC solutions.

On the other hand, adopting an *on line order processing* and an *on line payment system* should be thoughtfully assessed because of the probable sustained financial efforts due to the high organization complexity. Moreover, these activities could extensively change the relationships with the company intermediaries. According to the company inclination to innovation and its financial constraints, a TIE could opt for a more or less complete management of logistics based on the integration between EC and the existing IS. According to previous remarks, on line payment systems seem to be particularly suitable for business to consumer relationships.

Innovative Diversified Enterprise

Most relevant impacts of EC adoption within an *IDE* concern the increase of business process automation by forwarding efficient exchange of information within the organization as well towards intermediaries, leading to cost performance improvement. IDE high inclination to innovation, together with its less strict financial constraints, could promote EC as the solution for lack of coordination between functions and/or divisions, which is one of the most important weak points of this kind of enterprises.

According to these remarks, *public relations* could represent the basic activity for a strategy aimed at increasing company integration. Likewise, the *company promotion* could be usefully integrated with a private intranet. Whereas, even when fulfilling purely marketing purposes, it would involve significant investments: IDE will need to promote its innovative image also through the web medium and should differentiate the structure of its web site, according to both its multiple clients and products.

The complexity of the product/client mix should also drive the adoption of an *on line pre/post sales support*: the development of customized solution, although initially requiring a strong financial effort, could provide high level customer service, supporting a differentiation strategy.

Finally, the financial availability and degree of innovation should push IDE, whenever considering *on line order processing*, to a solution integrating the logistic support, possibly completed by an *on line payment system* (as for the TIE, devoted to support business to consumer transactions).

CONCLUSIONS

The increasing diffusion of Internet applications and especially EC are making companies of any size consider their adoption. This work aimed at supporting the entrepreneur in evaluating the most suitable EC solution for his/her organization and strategic goals. This goal has been pursued through the classification of five main EC activities, characterized by different requirements and possible results: before planning an EC investment, companies should assess the strategic importance of their value chain activities, to determine which EC approach could turn out to be more profitable.

The identification of the main business variables involved in an EC project and the resulting classification of SME profiles should help the entrepreneur in becoming aware of his/her organization. Finally, the cross analysis between EC activities and SME profiles should drive the choice of the most suitable EC solution for each profile.

The developed framework provides SMEs with a simple and easy to use tool to perform a *qualitative* evaluation of the EC opportunity. If in the next future the expected growth of Internet connections will take place, those SMEs who will have invested in EC could have the chance to exploit precious competitive and know-how benefits, avoiding the risk to lose those customers who decided to make EC the key channel for their commercial activities.

ENDNOTE

[1] This paper will refer to the current definition of SMEs provided by the European Community (1996), which identifies those companies with less than 250 employees, a turnover lower than 40 million ECU, and which are owned for less than 25% by non-SMEs, except banks or venture capital companies.

REFERENCES

Andrews, P., and Hahn, J. (1998). Transforming value chains into value webs. *Strategy & Leadership*, July/August.

Baker, S. A. (1998). *The Limits of Trust: Cryptography, Governments, and Electronic Commerce*. Ed. Kluwer Law International.

Bayne, K. M. (1997). *The Internet Marketing Plan: a Practical Handbook for Creating, Implementing and Assessing Your On line Presence*, Ed. John Wiley & Sons.

Bedeian, A. G. (1980). *Organization Theory and Analysis*. Hinsdale, IL: Dryden Press.

Benjamin, R. and Yates, J. (1991). The Past and Present as a Window on the Future. In Scott Morton, M.S. (Ed.), *The Corporation of the 1990s*, Oxford University Press, New York, pp.61-92.

Bock, W., and Senné, J. (1997). *Net Income*, New York, Ed. ITP.

Bolton, J.E. (1978). The financial need of the small firm, The banks and small business, The Institute of Bankers, London.

Boynton, A.C. and Zmud, R. W. (1994). The Influence of IT Management practiceon IT Use in Large Organizations. *MIS Quarterly,* Sep94, 18(3), p299, 20p, 4 charts, 3 diagrams.

Buonanno, G., Ravarini, A., Sciuto, D., and Tagliavini, M. (1998). How Internet Connected SMEs Exploit the Potential of the Net. In *Proceedings of International Conference on Information Resources Management Association* (May 1998), Boston, Massachusetts, USA.

Chaumont, C., de Charentenay, T., Esnault, L., Fay, E., Iglesias, N., and Silvestre, H. (1998). SMEs and Multimedia, Final Report, E.M. Lyon.

Clark, J. (1995). *Managing Innovation and Change*, London, Sage Publications.

COM (1997). A European Initiative in Electronic Commerce: Communication to the European Parliament, the Council, the Economic and Social Committee and the Committee of the Regions. http://www.cordis.lu/esprit/src/ecomcom1.htm (October 7th, 1999).

Davies C. (1997). An assessment of accounting information security, *CPA Journal*, 67(3).

Depperu, D. (1993). L'internazionalizzazione delle piccole e medie imprese, (In Italian: SME internationalization), Ed. EGEA, Milano, Italy.

DG XII at the European Commition (1996). A new common definition for SMEs, Press Releases, http://europa.eu.int/comm/dg12/press/1996/pr13-2bi.html (October 7th, 1999).

Di Romualdo, A. and Gurbaxani, V. (1998). Strategic Intent for IT Outsourcing, *Sloan Management Review*, Summer98, 39(4), p67, 14p, 1 chart, 3 digrams, 1bw.

Drucker, P.F. (1988). The Coming of the New Organization. *Harvard Business Review* (66:1), 1988, pp. 45-53.

Ford, W., and Baum, M. S. (1997). *Secure Electronic Commerce: Building the Infrastructure for Digital Signatures and Encryption*, Prentice Hall Press.

Gramignoli, S., Ravarini, A., and Tagliavini, M. (1999). A Profile for the IT Manager within SMEs. In *Proceedings of ACM International Conference SIGCPR 1999: Managing Organizational Knowledge for Strategic Advantage: The Key Role of Information Technology and Personnel* (April, 1999), New Orleans, Louisiana, USA.

Hills, M. (1997). *Intranet business strategies*, New York, Ed. John Wiley & Sons.

Huczynsky, A. and Buchanan, D. (1991). *Organizational Behaviour* (2nd ed.), Hemel Hempstead: Prentice Hall.

Janal, D.S. (1998). *Online marketing handbook, how to promote, advertise, and sell your products and services on the Internet*, New York, Ed. ITP.

Julien, P.A. (1998). *The state of the art in small business and entrepreneurship*, Ashgate, Aldershot.

Kanter, R.M. (1983). *The Change Masters*, New York: Simon and Shuster.

King, W.R., and Teo, T.S.H. (1994). Facilitators and inhibitors for the strategic use of information technology, *Information and Management*, 27, 71-87.

KPMG (1998). Electronic Commerce Research Report 1998, http://www.kpmg.co.uk/kpmg/uk/services/manage/research/ec/ecom98.html (October 7th, 1999)

Krause, F.L., Doblies, M., and Raupach, C. (1998). Simulation-based Analysis and Internet-based Realisation of Collaborative Product Development Processes, In *Proceedings of Prolamat '98*, (September 1998), Trento (Italy).

Loeb L. (1998). Secure Electronic Transactions: Introduction and technical Reference, Artech House.

McLoughlin, I. and Clark, J. (1994). *Technological Change at Work* (2nd ed.), Milton Keynes: Open University Press.

Mitrakas, A. (1997). *Open EDI and Law in Europe: A Regulatory Framework*, Kluwer Law International.

Negroponte, N. (1995). *Being digital*, Ed. Knopf.

OECD (1998). SMEs and Electronic Commerce, Working Party on SMEs to the OECD Ministerial Conference on Electronic Commerce, (October 1998), Ottawa http://www.oecd.org/dsti/sti/it/ec/prod/sme18e.pdf (October 7th, 1999).

Palvia, P., Means, D.B., and Jackson, W.M. (1994). Determinants of computing in very small businesses. *Information and Management*, 27, 161-174.

Piore, M.J. and Sabel, C.F. (1984). *The Second Industrial Divide*, Basic Books, New York, NY.

Rayport, J.F. and Sviokla, J.J. Exploiting the virtual Value Chain, *McKinsey Quarterly*, 1996 Issue 1, p20, 17p, 3 diagrams, 1c

Reynolds, J. (1997). The Internet as a Strategic Resource: Evidence from the European Retail Sector. In *Managing IT as a Strategic Resource*, McGraw Hill, 1997.

Schwartz, E. I. (1997). *Webonomics, nine essential principles for growing your business on the World Wide Web*, Ed. Broadway books, New York.

Vidal, F. (1991). *Il management all'italiana: creatività, pragmatismo, flessibilità,* (In Italian: Italian management: creativity, pragmatism, flexibility), Ed. Il Sole 24 Ore, Milano, Italy.

Westland, J.C. and Clark, T.H.K. (1998). *Global Electronic Commerce Theory and Case Studies*.

Wigand, R., Picot, A., and Reichwald, R. (1997). *Information, Organization and Management*, John Wiley and Sons Ltd, New York.

Wigand, R.T. (1996). An Overview of Electronic Commerce and Markets. Paper Presented to the *Annual Conference of the International Communication Association*, Chicago, IL, 23-27 May.

Chapter 21

The Cost of Email within Organizations

Thomas W. Jackson and Ray Dawson
Loughborough University, UK

Darren Wilson
The Danwood Group, UK

A pilot exercise on the cost-benefit analysis of the use of internal email was performed at the Danwood Group. This forms part of a larger exercise to evaluate computer communication to help enhance performance throughout the organisation. The chapter has resulted in the creation of an internal email costing process showing when it starts to become a more efficient means of communication.

In this study, the times taken to read, write and perform other functions with email were measured for a sample of employees. The email content was also monitored to determine which emails were business related. It was found that nearly two thirds of all emails were non-business related at the start of the research, but this decreased to a consistent 43% towards the end.

INTRODUCTION

Through communicating, we exchange our thoughts, ideas, opinions, feelings with other people, at work, and in all aspects of life. The communication process is so commonplace that it becomes second nature, though analysis shows it is much more complex and much less efficient than is normally assumed.

As companies struggle to shed excess costs and to respond more nimbly to customers and competitors, they are being urged to adopt new organisational forms, tightened inter-organisational linkages, and improved management practices (Miles &

Previously Published in *Challenges in Information Technology Management in the 21st Century*, edited by Mehdi Khosrow-Pour, Copyright © 2000, Idea Group Publishing.

Snow). To support these "network" forms of organisation, more and more firms, especially those that are geographically dispersed, are turning to electronic networks – advanced communication media, such as electronic mail (White, 1996). By understanding the communication process we can optimise networks to increase communication efficiency with benefit to our productivity. As communication pervades nearly everything we do, even small improvements in the effectiveness and cost of our communication processes can have significant benefits. The chapter builds on published work, by Solingen, Berghout and Latum (1998) and Jackson, Dawson and Wilson (1999), identifying email productivity and efficiency costs and generating questions on how to enhance performance throughout an organisation using electronic networks.

As new communication methods are introduced into organisations it is important to understand how and why managers use the new media (Markus, 1994), as it is not the media per se that determines communication patterns, but rather the social processes surrounding media use (DeSanctis & Poole, 1994). By understanding communication methods, the mediums can be optimised to enhance performance within organisations. We still have much to learn about interactions among computer-mediated communication technologies, new organisational forms, and changes in work and communication (Daft & Lewin, 1993), but the ability to monitor email now provides organisations with the opportunity to improve communication practices.

SOFTWARE TO RECORD EMAIL METRICS

The Danwood Group had no email usage policies that would restrict and bias monitoring, which was performed in two phases. The users were aware that email metrics were being recorded for research purposes in stage one, but not in stage two.

Stage one involved developing a special, client based email application, 'The Danwood Mail', to analyse the users activities whilst using email for internal communication. The program records the message word length, how long it takes the user to read or compose the email, the subject, the recipient, the author, the time and the date the email was sent. The deletions of emails were logged but were not timed, as the time taken was insignificant.

Stage two involved replacing the Danwood Mail application with Microsoft Outlook and using a new server based email recording application.

EMAIL COMMUNICATION ANALYSIS

The following results have been given in terms of business email (contains business related information) and non-business email (not business related, such as jokes or messages regarding social activities). It is assumed in this paper that non-business email implies it is non-productive, however, this is the subject of ongoing research.

At the start of stage one, 69% of email was non-business related and during stage two that figure decreased to at a consistent level around 43% for several months (see

Figure 3). The authors believe that this level of non-business email will not change unless an email policy or a different email application is introduced. The high non-business usage of email shown could perhaps be explained by the privacy that email offers compared to other communication mediums.

A level of 69% non-business email shows that employees spend an average of 54 hours in a working year on non-business communication (Figure 2), or 14 minutes a day, even before any recovery time for each interrupt is added. It takes 15 minutes to recover from a phone call interrupt, according to DeMarco's research (DeMarco & Lister, 1987), so it is clearly going to take some time to recover from an email interrupt. The extent of the recovery time will vary from person to person; many employees appear to react to an incoming email immediately, implying the recovery time is likely to be similar to that of a phone call for these employees. Other employees wait until a more convenient moment and then deal with several emails together resulting in a much shorter recovery time.

Figure 1: A breakdown of email messages at the beginning of stage one(Solingen et al., 1998).

Email Communication

Business Email   Non-Business Email

Figure 2: The time the average employee spends on email communication

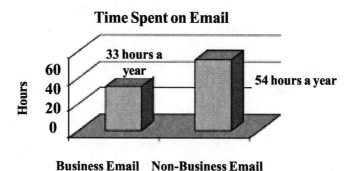

Time Spent on Email

Business Email   Non-Business Email

Figure 3: A breakdown of email messages at the end of stage two

Email Communication - Stage 2

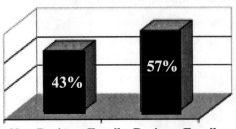

There are currently no figures for how long it takes an employee to recover from each email interrupt but an estimate based on an informal survey of user opinion is just over 1 minute, a saving of just over 13 minutes compared to the phone (Jackson et al., 1999).

MEDIA SELECTION AND EDUCATION

A multi-method investigation by Markus (1994) assessed the power of information richness theory, relative to alternative social theories, to explain and predict managers' use of email. Managers were found to perceive various media in ways that were relatively consistent with information richness theory, but to use email more and differently than the theory predicted. In particular, effective senior managers were found to use email heavily and even for equivocal communications tasks. The effectiveness of the manager could be related to the interrupt recovery time associated with the media, as email has a relatively low recovery time compared to the phone and face-to-face meetings. By educating employees on information richness and interrupts as shown by Solingen et al. (1998) in his research, an organisation can become more efficient in the way it communicates.

INTERNAL EMAIL COSTING FORMULAE

Table 1 shows that in the early days of implementation more time is spent on non-business email, though this decreases exponentially. The analysis has provided the Danwood Group with a baseline to work from in trying to increase employee productivity.

Cost of Internal Email

The current cost of non-business email can be calculated by using Table 2 in conjunction with formula 1 below. To illustrate the costs, formula 1 is applied to a medium size company with 120 employees with the average wage at £320 per week and an assumed overhead of a further £320 per week, where the email system was installed more than 85 days beforehand.

Cost = Total Minutes * Email users * Average Employee Wage per minute

Formula 1 – Current Cost of Non-Business Email

The daily cost to the company for 120 employees to use the internal email system for non-business purposes is £524 making the cost for the year over £25,000.

The cost of business email can be calculated in the same way using formula 2:

Cost = Business Email minutes * Email users * Average Wage per Minute

Formula 2 – Current Cost of Business Email

The daily cost to the same 120-employee company to use the internal email system for business purposes is £968 making the cost for the year more than £46,000.

Formula 3 below can be used to calculate the joint cost of using the internal email system for both business and non-business activities.

Cost = (Total Non-Business + Business Minutes) * Email Users * Average Wage per Minute

Formula 3 – Current Cost of Running Email for a Day

The daily cost to the company for 120 employees to use the internal email system is nearly £1,500 with the cost for the year being over £71,000.

Table 1: Breakdown of time spent by an average employee on Email a day without Recovery Time

Days Since Implementation	Non-Business Email	Business Email	Total
1 – 39 days	13.53 minutes	8.34 minutes	21.87
40 – 84 days	10.98 minutes	11.84 minutes	22.82
85+ days	8.43 minutes	15.33 minutes	23.76

Table 2: A breakdown of time spent by an average employee on Non-Business Email and Recovery Time a day

Days Since Implementation	Non-Business Email	Estimated Recovery Time	Total Minutes a Day
1 – 39 days	13.53 minutes	14 minutes	27.53
40 – 84 days	10.98 minutes	11 minutes	21.98
85+ days	8.43 minutes	8 minutes	16.43

Table 3: A breakdown of time spent by an average employee on Business Email and Recovery Time a day

Days Since Implementation	Business Email	Estimated Recovery Time	Total Minutes
1 – 39 days	8.34 minutes	8 minutes	16.43
40 – 84 days	11.84 minutes	12 minutes	23.84
85+ days	15.33 minutes	15 minutes	30.33

Cost of External Email

Little research has been carried out into the costs of using external email. Initial research carried out so far by the Danwood Group shows that 73% of the emails are non-business related, though further research is required to confirm this.

FUTURE WORK

If it is assumed that non-business email is unproductive, then the results highlight employee productivity could be significantly higher but further research is required to achieve this. In particular, the following points need investigating:

1. The recovery time after reading email needs to be more accurately quantified as opinion could prove to be unreliable for this type of measure. This could reveal issues of how and when people react to incoming messages, which may establish a need to educate employees in the best practices for handling incoming messages.
2. Informal observation by the authors shows that 50% of email could be handled in a one-line message. The authors are researching whether an add-on to Microsoft Outlook prioritising one line emails could reduce pleasantries at the beginning and at the end of traditional email messages and potentially reduce the time employees spend on communication.

CONCLUSIONS

While the results are not yet complete the study has already increased the understanding of use of IT within the organisation and has shown both the value of obtaining metrics on their activities and the difficulties involved. The company has also learned that the IT cannot simply be evaluated in isolation, but as an integrated part of the company processes it must be studied in conjunction with the effects on the surrounding people and environment.

This pilot exercise has successfully shown the value of carrying out a cost-benefit exercise on the company's IT infrastructure. The results obtained can provide the basis for communication usage policies and education, which could then reduce wasted time and improve employee productivity.

REFERENCES

Daft, R.L., and Lewin, A.Y. (1993). Where Are the Theories for the 'New' Organizational Forms? *Organizational Science*, 4(4), pp.I – IV.

DeMarco, T., and Lister, T. (1987). *Peopleware: Productive Projects and Teams*, New York: Dorset House.

DeSanctis, G., and Poole, M.S. (1994). Capturing the Complexity in Advanced Technology Use: Adaptive Structuration Theory, *Organizational Science*, 5(2), pp.121 – 147.

Jackson, T.W., Dawson, R., and Wilson, D. (1999). Improving the Communications Process: The costs and effectiveness of email compared with traditional media, *INSPIRE – Training and Teaching for the understanding of Software Quality*, No.4, pp.167 – 178, September.

Markus, L.M. (1994). Electronic Mail as the Medium of Managerial Choice, *Organizational Science*, 5(4), pp.502 – 525, November.

Miles, R.E., and Snow, C.C. Organizations: New Concepts for New Forms, *California Management Review*, No.28, pp.62-73, 3 (Spring).

Solingen, R., Berghout, E., and Latum, F. (1998). Interrupts: Just a Minute Never Is, *IEEE Software*, 15(5), pp.97 – 103, September/October.

White, K.B. (1986). Current Technology Practices: Perspectives from information Systems Managers, *SIM Spectrum*, No.2, pp.1-5, December.

Chapter 22

Electronic Commerce: Determining B2C Web site Functions

Bijan Fazlollahi
Georgia State University, USA

The web site is a central component of B2C Electronic Commerce. However, there are few guidelines on how to design and develop an effective web site. Most discussions address technical issues of building WebPages. The requirement stage of web site design is poorly understood. This chapter discusses requirements for web site functions from the point of view of both the firm and the customer. Firm's business strategies and customer decision support needs are mapped into web site functionalities. Two existing web sites of firms in the building industry are analyzed for illustrative purposes.

INTRODUCTION

E-Commerce has become one of the major factors essential to the future survival and success in the market place. A survey, sponsored by AOL found that making purchases was the fastest growing on-line activity and more than half the respondents had engaged in the activity (IW, 11/6/2000). The volume of on-line purchases is predicted to increase from $20B in 1999 to $50B in 2002 (IW, July 1, 2000 page 27).

Electronic commerce is at an early stage of development with few established rules on how to organize and implement E-commerce. The source of e-commerce knowledge is generally unreliable and often comes from venture capitalists, investment bankers, and technically oriented entrepreneurs who do not

Previously Published in *Managing Information Technology in a Global Economy*, edited by Mehdi Khosrow-Pour, Copyright © 2001, Idea Group Publishing.

have a good track record of building B2C organizations that endure the test of time. The majority of B2C business models are innovative and unproven. Many underlying assumptions for B2C business models such as "more disintermediation is better" are suspect.

B2C is uniquely customer centric. Major automotive manufacturers have launched web-based initiative to build vehicles to individual customers' specifications and deliver them in one to two weeks (EW-July 24,2000, page 63). Many firms have learned to compile customer information from a range of sources and build a comprehensive view of the customers. They have developed capabilities to anticipate and meet customer needs in real time by delivering customized services superior to their competitors leading to higher revenues and customer retention.

Consumers exhibit different behavior and express varied concerns. For example, a recent survey study showed that 25% browse on-line and buy from brick and mortar stores, 19% are brand loyalists and buy from merchants they know, and 17% are interested in saving time and maximizing convenience (IW, July 15, 2000 page 25). According to another survey, consumers concerns on late delivery has increased from the 1999 level to 59% in the 2000 holiday season. However, concerns over the security of credit cards and personal information have reduced from 50% in 1999 to 33% in the year 2000.

B2C customers demand superior shopping experience spanning the entire process from articulating to fulfillment of their needs. They expect not only on-time delivery but also instant access to their order histories, shipping information and up to the second product availability information. Many of these functions require deep integration between front-end on-line ordering systems and back-end supply chain and logistic applications. Both FedEx and UPS offer systems that can integrate delivery status and other information from the shippers directly into the e-commerce systems. They can also provide on-line capability for customers to initiate return of packages on the web and link them to drop-off locations. They also provide the customer with the ability to track returns and ensure his/her account is appropriately credited (EW- November 20, 2000). Each phase of e-commerce impacts customer satisfaction differently. For example, the fulfillment impacts satisfaction 55% and selling only 5%. Fulfillment problems such as lost orders, incomplete or inaccurate product availability information, and late shipments were common customer experience in 1999.

The web site is where the consumer and the firm conduct their business. The web site must have the functionalities that enable the firm to acquire, sell to, and retain customers. E-commerce sites are eminently easier to leave than physical store as the customer has less time invested than shopping in a physical store. Consumers are frequently disappointed at how little depth exists beneath the user interface for providing customer support (IW- December 15, 2000, page 114). Customer support was claimed as the main reasons for the demise of Priceline.com [Computer World, Oct 6, 2000]. Naveen Donthu and Boonghee Yoo (December, 2000) have developed a scale to measure the perceived quality of web sites called SITEQUAL. The scale measures nine unique dimensions: Aesthetic design, competitive value, clarity of ordering, corporate and brand equity, security, processing speed, product uniqueness, product quality assurance. They found that the sites from which the goods were purchased were about 30% more attractive on the scale than competing sites.

The web site should support the implementation of business strategy and help customers in their decision making process. In the past, discussions of web site design have over emphasized the technical aspects, such as web page graphic design, or static or active web pages using HTML, ASP, or JavaScript. These discussions do not adequately address how to determine web site functions that drive web site design. This chapter will examine web site functions from both the organization's and the customers' viewpoints. It will also present two cases to illustrate how web sites should achieve the dual objectives of carrying out organizational strategies and supporting customers in making decisions.

WEBSITE FUNCTIONS, FROM ELECTRONIC COMMERCE PERSPECTIVES

Holsapple and Singh (2000) identified five perspectives on electronic commerce: the trading view, the information exchange view, the activity view, the effects view and finally the value chain view. They further expanded the notion of information exchange to knowledge management, and integrated these five views to represent the enhanced knowledge-based organizations in a knowledge-driven economy.

The web site functions for the trading view would support electronic buying and selling of products and services. For the information exchange view, it would support multi-channel communication to forge closer ties with customers, suppliers and other business partners. For the effects view, it would streamline business transactions and improve customer service, reduce costs, and increase dollar sales per customer. The web site will also facilitates other activities such as pre-sale and post-sale efforts, and inter-corporation collaboration. Finally, from the value chain view, the web site functions would support activities that reduce cost and add value on the value chain, thereby contributing to competitive advantages.

The web site is the primary means for customers to interact with the firm for satisfaction of their needs. From the trading view, the web site enables electronic access to products and service anytime and anywhere. From the information exchange view, the web site provides relevant information to customers and receives information that benefits the organization. The information received may be used to improve such activities as customer service and new product design. From the effects view, the web site helps customers to fill their needs by making good decision in a hassle-free environment through electronic billing, order tracking, account maintenance. The web site also facilitates other activities such as information update and after-sale feedback. From value chain perspective, the web site delivers value to the customer through better service and reduces tangible and intangible costs of doing business.

The central component of the electronic business processes is the web site where the interactions take place. Website functionalities operationalize these interactions. However, identification of specific website functionalities requires examination of business strategies as well as customer decision support requirements.

WEB SITE FUNCTIONS, FROM FIRM'S VIEW

A reasonable way for determining the web site functions is to examine the strategies employed to strengthen a firm's competitive position. For example, if the firm is pursuing a strategy of customer relationship marketing (CRM), then the site must have the corresponding functionality to support this strategy. If the firm is pursuing a strategy of mass customization, then it must have functionalities to collect data for mass customization.

CRM is a business strategy and directs the business to think from the point of view of the customers to figure out how to add more value to its services. It refers to applications that manage all aspects of customer encounters. CRM cuts across many corporate functions including sales, administration, marketing, fulfillment, distribution and post-sale service. The three main areas of focus are on sales, customer and marketing automation (Robinson, 2000).

Figure 1: Main Areas and Channels for CRM

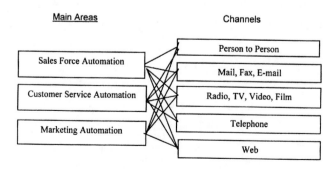

The web site, therefore, should include the following four functions:

1. Sales Force Automation: **Web Based Selling** – This function assists the on-line buyer make satisfying purchase decisions. The design of this function emphasizes the web page as purchase decision support systems with special attention to decisional guidance.
2. Customer Service Automation: **Web Based Self-Service** – This function provides services to on-line users. The emphasis is on providing personalized services.
3. Marketing: **Data Collection and Analysis** – This function concentrates on direct or indirect collection of customer information. This data and the data collected through other channels provide the basis for making marketing and other strategic decisions.
4. **Support to Other Channels** – The web channel is not the only business communication channel and other channels are used as well to exchange information. This function is frequently ignored.

Mass customization is where "the company provides personalized, custom-designed products at prices close to those traditionally offered only for mass-produced merchandise" (Duray and Milligan,1999). Similar to CRM, mass customization emphasizes adding value to the customers' services. Different from CRM, mass customization concentrates more on product manufacturing where unique products are made for each customers. By adopting mass customization, customized goods are produced at the same or lower cost than mass-produced products through reduction in inventory and working capital (Alexander, 1999).

Web site is the interface for **order penetration,** where a production unit is tied to a given customer order. Internet as a two-way communication channel allows for the exchange of information between the customer and the firm in a reasonable time frame. However, the process of customized order is complex and special attention needs to be paid to the order penetration functionality of the web interface. The challenge to the web designer is to make the customers feel com-

Figure 2: Web Site as Point of Order Penetration

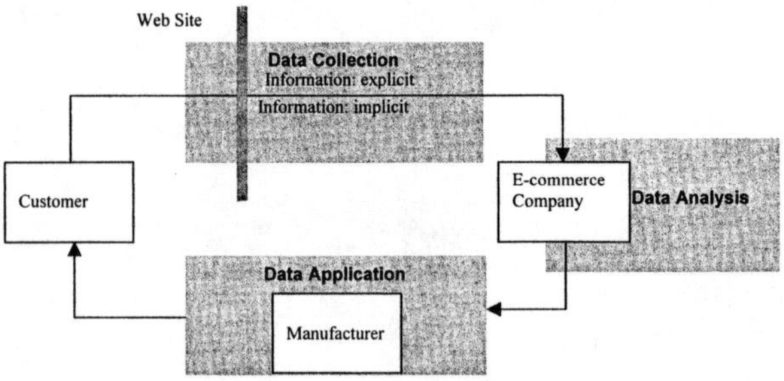

fortable through their on-line ordering experience by providing good decisional guidance.

In reality bad web site design has contributed to the ineffectiveness of business strategies. Sites generally collect marketing data, site usability data, and customer support data such as frequeently used response templates, problematic areas, and problem resolution time (IW, December 15, 2000, page 49). The analyses are often done after the fact and not in real-time. Several tools analyze data collected from visits to web sites and provide information on the level of stickiness of the site, level of interest of visitors, and repeat traffic (IW, July 15, 2000, page 42). However, most e-commerce applications would benefit from real-time analysis. For example, BTO automotive initiative requires real-time visibility into most aspects of the supply chain, fulfillment process, and demand trends (EW- July 24, 2000, page 63). Some tools provide real-time data. Informatica Corporation and BuyStream software perform market analysis and provide supply side analytic to sellers and demand side analytic to buyers. They analyze which pages are clicked-on and assign value to these clicks and report where the customer came from.

WEB SITE FUNCTIONS, FROM CUSTOMER'S VIEW

Currently the web site functionalities for the consumer side are very limited. Consumers favor features such as online order tracking, comparison shopping, on-line product review, product search tool, photos/ virtual graphics, and clearance/ sale page or selection (IW, December 15, 2000, page 23). Some e-commerce portals provide support for transactions, and allow the user to access information on products, and permit participation in group discussion with sellers and buyers. In general portals provide functions such as voluntary and in-voluntary personalization, search, push technology, collaborative support, and information retrieval and integration.

The web site should support customers for making purchasing decisions. The classical concepts of decision support advocates support for all stages of the decision process as well as tailoring the support to fit the user, task, and the decision context. (Keen and Scott Morton, 1978). The classical buyer decision-making process consists of five stages: problem recognition, information search, evaluation of alternatives, purchase decision, and post-purchase behavior [Engel, Kollat, and Blackwell, 1973; Howard and Sheth, 1972; Nicosia, 1982]. Problem recognition occurs when a consumer senses a disparity between his or her actual state and his or her desired state (Bruner, 1987). Problem recognition can be activated when a consumer is exposed to external stimuli, such as the smell of food. This causes the consumer to become aware of an unmet need such as hunger.

Aware of an unmet need, the consumer is motivated to gather information on finding a way to satisfy the need. Information gathering helps consumers become aware of competing brands or products and their features. If the consumer has low involvement with the products that can satisfy the perceived need, little effort will be exerted in the information search. For example, the consumer may process information through peripheral routes, relying more heavily on cues as opposed to detailed and elaborate product specific information (Cacioppo, Petty, and Kao, 1986).

The information search results in the identification of a set of alternative products that will reduce or eliminate a felt need (Howard and Shelth, 1972). The consumer will then identify product features/characteristics to determine the likely consequences of purchasing from the considered set of alternative products (Phillips, Olson, and Baumgartner, 1995). Using available internal, form memory, and external information, the consumer may process information by attributes or by products to develop a set of beliefs, or "product image", about a product with regard to its ability to deliver the desired benefits (Bettman, 1979; Jacoby, 1975).

After evaluating alternatives, consumers typically form product preferences and perhaps the intention to purchase what they perceive as the most desirable. Several sub-decisions may be involved including brand choice, vendor selection, quantity to purchase, timing of purchase, payment method, etc.

In the final post-purchase behavior stage the consumer experiences some level of satisfaction or dissatisfaction. Marketers strive to satisfy consumers in order to enhance their relationship with the consumers (Spreng, MacKenzie, and Olshavsky, 1996).

Functionalities of an efficient and effective web site that may provide relevant information at all phases of consumer decision-making include:

- *Problem recognition*: The web selling design of Amanzon.com is a good example. When a user searches for a book, he/she gets access to the links similar customers used for other books. Users are considered similar if they searched for the same book. Customers are provided with these links because he or she may potentially needs those books.
- *Information search*: To help the users make informed decisions, the web site may provide more information on the different features of a series of products and the appropriate situations in which to use or apply those various products. During this phase of decision making, more information is helpful.
- *Evaluation of alternatives*: During this phase of the decision making process, the web site may provide decisional guidace on forming the criteria for making a choice.
- *Purchase decision*: Here the problem is how to help the consumer process a large amount of information that can potentially overwhelm the consumer.

Figure 3: Using Decisional Guidance to Guide the Design of Web Selling and Ordering

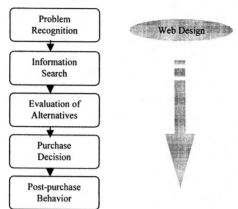

- *Post purchase behavior*: From a customer's point of view, the web site should inform the decision making process.

    The concepts of decision support were presented almost thirty (30) years ago advocating specific support, where support is specific to the three elements-user, context and task. However, the decision support provided to B2C customer is often general. A web site that can deliver focused support must be adaptable to the three elements. Adaptable decision support is technologically possible through the use of intelligent technologies.

    The popular concept of personalization is an attempt for providing user specific decision support. Web personalization involves tailoring web content directly to a specific user [Tim Ouellette, 1999]. Personalization is voluntary where the customer provides information directly, or involuntary when the customer behavior information is captured on the site. Amazon generates 500 giga bytes of click stream data a week. Even if 10% was useful, it could update the profile and business rules for the customer (eCRM, september 2000, page e4). The web site software can use the customer profile information to modify the decision support content to match the customer needs. For example, the web site can provide information about classic music to people who like classic music.

    Personalization has been the focal point of software development. Yahoo lets users set-up their own fairly primitive personalization. Supergo.com, an on-line bike shop, uses BSelect to make suggestions and recommendations based on collaborative filtering which uses tastes of similar customers to make recommendations. They scan their site with and without personalization and found that personalization results in tangible benefits in terms of increased sales (EW, July 3, 2000, page 22). However, personalization at its best may archive results as good or better than the best salesperson. Dell is using sophisticated analysis tools to predict customer preferences and behaviors by dynamically combining data from numerous sources. Currently customers make an average of 5 visits to the site before they buy. Dell's objective is to get the customer to buy with fewer visits to the site. The biggest challenge for any firm is to determine the content of personalization (EW, October 2, 2000, page 61).

Personalized information is high value commodity for customers and Marketers. For customers the usefulness of the site is increased. For marketers the value of each customer is increased. Personalizing customer interactions may help recruit and retain customers. This requires integrated functionalities of data store analytics, psychographic profiling, demographic profiling, histograms, archives, audits, etc. Single customer views in real-time may help to empower customer relationship as well as broader strategic decision making. Value added comes in terms of knowledge or information which helps the customer make faster decisions and improve their decision making process. Real-time information is more effective because it helps apply business rules intelligently. Applying a rule such as "anyone who buys shoes needs socks" may miss the point that the individual buyer may not ware socks at all.

Personalization is useful to all the phases of the decision making process. The current practice of personalization concentrates only on the problem recognition phase. For example, the customer's interests in alternative products are discovered through collateral analysis of the interest of similar sample group. Application of personalization may be extended to information search, evaluation of alternatives, purchase decision, and post-purchase behavior. For example, in purchase decision phase, the web site may alert the customer of potential problems or decisions to make in accordance with their risk tolerance.

Privacy has also been an important concern. A survey of Harris interactive showed that Americans are more concerned about loss of privacy (56%) than health care, crime, and taxes. In a matter of time selling, renting, sharing of private information may become illegal. The most valuable customers are long time loyal customers. Trust and loyalty go hand in hand and trust is built by protecting privacy, which may convince them to share more data with the firm. The firm may want to give the customers control over their data and solicit their inputs to update and revise the data (e-CRM, May 2000, page e5). Some companies such as expedia.com have clarified their privacy policies and made it stricter, giving the customers the ability to control their private information.

Tools that allow personalizing without relying on private data may prove more useful in the future. Collaborative filtering technology allows anonymity while still personalizing product recommendations. Some tools anonymously analyze customer on-line behavior in real time and find commonalities with millions of other visitors' product purchases and make recommendations (EW, October 16, 2000, page 73).

There are additional possibilities for making enhancements to decision support through the analysis of context and tasks. For example, in purchasing an airline ticket, it is important to consider the context. When the customer is taking a vacation, the passenger may prefer to find the most inexpensive ticket. On the other hand, if the purpose is a time-sensitive business trip, a flight that best fits the schedule is more relevant.

An example of the expansion of personalization to tasks and context analysis is the concept developed at DataSage (Morgan, 1999). DataSage collects data on Web visitors' behaviors and mines the resulting huge database for information on buying patterns. DataSage marries an already huge database of a customer's click streams, shopping-cart holdings and queries with other non-web data sources, such as off-line purchases and queries, customer service records and product registrations. The result is a Web site that not only knows what you're buying online but also your entire company relationship. It might, for example, notice that you purchase home improvement books every time your address changes and offer you special discounts next time.

There is some limited activity in building software that provides decision support for e-commerce customers. SopTok Inc. markets a software to personalize recommendations based on context. Tokboards is community managed boards. Tok Clubs are on-line affinity clubs. The Suggestive seller analyses the data on these systems and builds user and product profile to make highly tailored product recommendations.

ANALYSIS OF EXAMPLE WEB SITES

Based on the previous discussion, we analyze the web site designs of Homes.com and Homebuilders.com from two viewpoints. First, how is the web site designed to help the company achieve its business strategies? Second, how is the web site designed to assist a consumer to make a home buying decision?

Homes.com is an end to end online source for home buying, selling and renting and a valuable tool for real-estate professionals. HomeBuilder.com provides builder information on new homes, subdivisions and developments. It has developed a customized, nationwide listing of builders' models, newly built homes and housing plans. Users may search for new homes, builders, custom builders and real estate agents.

Support for the five phase purchasing decision-making process:
Problem recognition stage- deciding to buy a home
Homes.com provides no support. Homebuilders.com provides a buyer guide index covering most topics ranging from the advantages of home buying to the moving process. These topics inform a potential homebuyer in fulfilling their needs.

Improvements may include additional information such as advantages of buying vs. renting, to inform problem recognition phase. Also chat rooms may be useful to potential home buyers to learn and define objectives before embarking on a search for a specific home.

Information search – information on target homes

Both sites require similar inputs from the customer such as location and specification of the home. However, the output of Homes.com includes additional information on the community. Both sites can improve information content for example, by providing driving path from the potential homes to the customer's workplace.

Evaluation of alternatives – comparisons of homes

Homes.com does not provide support while homebuilders.com provides a service for ranking the alternatives based on criteria such as price, location, etc.

Purchase decision – commit and implement

Both Homes.com and homebuilders.com do not support this activity. They may provide more decision-making assistance by developing a home purchasing decision-making model. Such a model can process the characteristics of the homes and suggest the top few homes that fit the requirement of the buyer. Once the buyer commits, then another system can take over to complete the deal.

Post-purchase behavior – home decoration, etc.

Homes.com does not provide any support, however homebuilders.com provides specialized information on home decoration, etc. Both sites can expand their support by including free advice from commercial services as well as links to other sites.

Decision support – users, context and tasks

User specific support

Homes.com collects personal information such as name and e-mail address and provide the user with personal archive to store his/her queries. Homebuilders.com does not collect user personal information. Both sites could collect more user information through explicit specific user queries as well as click streams. The data can be mined to infer user objectives and preferences to help make purchase decisions.

Context specific support

Homes.com collects information on the location of the user while homebuilders.com gets no user specific information. By comparing the location of the user with the locations of homes queried, it is possible to predict the user intentions for moving across cities or states. Specific information on services may be provided to long-distance movers. Also context specific information may be provided to first time or second time, or third time buyers.

Task specific support

Support must be tailored to the type of task such as buying existing new home, ranch, townhouse, etc. Support at both sites is not task specific. Homes.com uses the data provided by the user and infers whether the user prefers new homes or existing homes, condos, or townhouses. Both Homes.com and Homebuilders.com may provide information on decoration and furniture to buyers of new homes and home improvement information to buyers of existing homes.

Customer Relationship Management

Sales force automation – web based selling

Homes.com does not support this activity. However, Homebuilders.com provides links to other web sites such as stacks and stacks.com and Mercata.com where customers can shop for appliances, lawn and garden etc.

Customer service automation – web based self-service

Both sites provide automated customer service in conducting searches and making various financial calculations. However, these services are not tailored to specific users who may be novice or experts in performing the automated tasks.

Marketing data collection and analysis

Both sites may have some degree of data collection which is not readily recognizable. Generally data flows are in one direction from builders and sellers to the customer. It can be inferred that the data collection at the site is inadequate for CRM.

Support for other channels

The support in both web sites is limited to providing phone numbers of contact persons, realtors and other e-commerce companies. Additional support maybe provided by sharing information with partners in home-related industries subject to privacy concerns.

Mass Customization

Mass customization is applicable to most products and services. It is natural for clothing because everybody has a different body shape and different tastes. Clothes manufacturers need electronic order-acquisition systems that capture people's measurements over the web or in retail stores. Similarly, mass customization is applicable to homes. Homebuilders normally provide several home models and allow buyers to select alternative shapes for the windows, colors for the interior walls, and type of carpets. Normally, homebuilders assign agents to capture such information. However, the person-to-person discussion is expensive and time and location specific. The web site is a good channel to communicate without time or location constraints. For example, the HomeBuilder.com may want to provide samples for all the alternatives of home models, shapes of the window, colors of the wall, types of carpet on line. Customers may participate in home customization by entering information or make changes to the information on electronic order-acquisition forms.

CONCLUSIONS

Currently the prevailing practice in web site design is to what new technology to employ. This skips a very critical step, which is to link web site design to business strategy and customer decision support requirements.

In this chapter, the support for customer relationship management and mass customization strategies and decision support for purchase decision making process were mapped to web site functions. A three step web site design process is shown in Figure 4.

The analysis of the web site of two building industry companies shows that web sites functions are inadequate in supporting business strategy and customer decision support requirements. General recommendations for determining the objectives of B2C web sites functions may include:

- Operationalize business strategy
- Establish long lasting, high value, individualized relationship with the customer based on serving customer needs and earning customer trust.

Figure 4: B2C Web Interface Design Framework

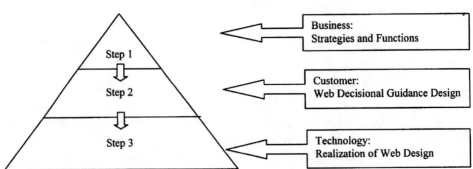

- Establish two-way communications with the customer where both sides provide and seek information and learn from each other.
- Facilitate formation of small communities of customers and exchange information among them to learn from each other.

This study has not addressed the environmental influence on required web site functions. The international nature of e-commerce requires the web site to conform to various cultures and government regulations. For example: The French law requires the use of French language and forbids sale of certain items such as Nazi memorabilia on the site. Furthermore, some countries require the identification of individuals for reporting purposes. Future research in this area may address how the user, task and context influences web site functions. For example: risk averse vs. risk takers, buying a home vs. buying groceries and the international context.

REFERENCES

Alexander, S. (1999). Business QuickStudy: Mass Customization. *Computer World*. 9/06/99

Bettman, J. R. (1979). *An Information Processing Theory of Consumer Choice*. Reading, MA: Addision-Wesley.

Bruner, G. C. (1987). The Effect of Problem Recognition Style on Information Seeking. *Journal of the Academy of Marketing Science*, 15(Winter), 3341.

Cacioppo, J., Petty, R., & Kao, C. (1986). Central and Peripheral Routes to Persuasion: An Individual Difference Perspective. *Journal of Personality and Social Psychology*, 51, 1032-43.

Duray, R. & Milligan, G. W. (1999). Improving customer satisfaction through mass customization. *Quality Progress*. V32n8, p60-66.

Engel, J. F., Kollat, D. T. & Blackwell, R.L.D. (1973). *Consumer Behavior* (21 Edition). New York: Holt, Rinehart & Winston.

Eweek. July 24, 2000. *Revving up BTO*, pp 63.

Eweek. November 20, 2000. *Time to Deliver the Goods*, pp 57.

Eweek. July 3, 2000. *Portals Getting Personal*, pp 22.

Eweek. October 2, 2000. *Getting Personal*, pp 61.

Eweek. October 16, 2000. *Customer Privacy Lockdown*, pp 73.

Hogan, S. B. (March 1999). To Net of Not to Net: Singapore's Regulation of the Internet, *Federal Communications Law Journal*, 51(2), pp 429-447.

Holsapple, C. W., and Singh, M. (2000). Electronic Commerce: From a Definitional Taxonomy Toward a Knowledge-Management View, *Journal of Organizational Computing and Electronic Commerce*, 10(3), pp 149-170.

Howard, J. & Sheth, J. (1972). *The Theory of Buyer Behavior*. New York: Free Press.

http://legalnews.findlaw.co...s/20000811/techyahoofrance interview.html – "IN-TERVIEW – Internet future in French hands – Yahoo France, " Reuters, Aug 11, 2000

InfoWorld. November 6, 2000. *E-commerce activities on the rise*, pp 16.

Internet World. July 1, 2000. *A Steady Climb*, pp 27.

Internet World. July 15, 2000. *The Six Faces of Online Shoppers*, pp 25.

Internet World. December 15, 2000. *Another Pretty Face*, pp 114.

Internet World. December 15, 2000. *Putting Customer Data to Work*, pp 49.

Internet World. December 15, 2000. *Knowing the Target*, pp 42.

Internet World. December 15, 2000. *Features that Shoppers Favor*, pp 23.

Knowledge Management, e-CRM. September 2000. *E-Business Intelligence*, pp e4.

Knowledge Mangement, e-CRM. May 2000. *Three Steps to Building e-Trust*, pp e5.

Morgan, C. (1999). A new dimension in personalization tools. *Computer World*. 09/06/99.

Nicosia, F.N. (1982). Consumer Decision Processes: A Futuristic View. *Advances in Consumer Research*, 9, 17-19.

O'Keete, R.M. and McEachern, T. (March 1998). Web-based Customer Decision Support Systems, Association of Computing Machinery. *Communications of the ACM*, New York, 41(3), pp 71-78.

Robinson, R. (2000). Customer Relationship Management. *Computer World*. 02/28/2000

Spreng R., MacKenzie, S. & Olshavsky, H. R. (1996). A Reexamination of the Determinants of Consumer Satisfaction. *Journal of Marketing*, 60, 1532

About the Editor

Bijan Fazlollahi is an educator and a consultant. He teaches and conducts research at Robinson College of Business, Georgia State University. His area of research is MIS, Decision Support Systems, and Electronic Business. He has published in the *Journal of Decision Support Systems*, *Journal of Management Information Systems*, *Interfaces*, *Information Systems Research*, *Fuzzy Sets and Systems*, *International Journal of Intelligent Systems*, *Journal of Intelligent and Fuzzy Systems*, and *Information and Management*. His teaching area is Computer Information Systems, Decision Support Systems, Database Management Systems, and International Business. He is the project director for several federal grants for establishing institutions for business education in the Newly Independent States. He also teaches internationally in NIS and Eastern Europe. He was a Fulbright Lecturer in the Former USSR and received two honorary doctorate degrees from major universities there. He has consulted for large organizations such as Atlanta Airport and Atlanta Police Departments in the area of computer information systems. Prior to his career in education, he worked in the field of engineering here and abroad. He is a member of the Editorial Board of the *Journal of Database Management Systems*.

Index

NEW from Idea Group Publishing